The
Publications
of
The Harleian Society

ESTABLISHED A.D. MDCCCLXIX

New Series
Volume 9

FOR THE YEAR MCMXC

The Bigland Pedigree Index

AN INDEX TO THE PEDIGREES
IN THE GENEALOGICAL MANUSCRIPTS OF

SIR RALPH BIGLAND

Garter King of Arms

FROM A MANUSCRIPT INDEX IN THE COLLEGE OF ARMS

PREPARED FOR PUBLICATION BY

P.Ll. GWYNN-JONES, M.A.

Lancaster Herald

AND

SUSANNA TOVEY

LONDON

1990

ISBN 0 9513335 1 8

Produced by Alan Sutton Publishing Ltd., Gloucester
Printed and bound in Great Britain

Contents

Introduction

BY PETER GWYNN-JONES, LANCASTER HERALD OF ARMS
HONORARY SECRETARY, THE HARLEIAN SOCIETY

In 1839 the Chapter of the College of Arms acquired from the executors of Sir Ralph Bigland, Garter King of Arms, 49 volumes of considerable genealogical importance.

Sir Ralph Bigland was born 1 May 1757, being the son of Joseph Owen of Salford, Lancashire, by the latter's wife, Elizabeth Maria, the daughter of Richard Bigland of Gray's Inn and Stepney. His uncle and namesake was Ralph Bigland, Bluemantle Pursuivant 1757–1759, Somerset Herald 1759–1773, Clarenceux King of Arms 1774–1780, Garter King of Arms 1780–1784. This elder Ralph Bigland played one of the major roles in the revival of genealogical interest at the College of Arms following the long decline which had set in after the termination of the Visitations at the end of the 17th century. Although the elder Ralph Bigland acquired the reputation of a good and sound genealogist, he is best remembered for his work on Gloucestershire, his Historical, Monumental and Genealogical Collections of Gloucester being published by his son in 1792. His own manuscript collection contains volumes of church notes, book plates, will extracts and parish register entries; these are numbered among the 49 volumes in the 1839 acquisition. Unfortunately, this reputation has been allowed to overshadow that of his nephew who was a man of considerable stature in his own right and whose genealogical production stands today as being of far greater importance than the activities of his better known namesake. Indeed, much of the younger Bigland's work has frequently and erroneously been attributed to his uncle.

The younger Ralph Bigland took the surname of Bigland, at the request of his uncle, by Royal Licence 21 October 1774. He was appointed Bluemantle Pursuivant in 1774 and was subsequently Richmond Herald 1780–1803, Norroy King of Arms 1803–1822, Clarenceux King of Arms 1822–1831, Garter King of Arms 1831–1838. He was knighted 7 December 1831 and died 14 July 1838.

The 49 volumes of the Bigland Collection contain the manuscripts of the elder Ralph Bigland; but of these only four specifically relate to pedigrees. Volumes XIX and XX relate to Gloucestershire families. Volume XIV is a comparatively slim volume consisting of pedigrees and some general papers dating from the 1760s; it is inscribed as belonging to Ralph Bigland the elder with the date 31 June (sic) 1763. The fourth volume is the errant volume XVIII, which is principally concerned with pedigrees compiled by Sir Isaac Heard, 1750–1822. Heard's vast genealogical activity is incorporated in a separate collection at the College of Arms; and it is therefore intriguing to find this volume, largely compiled by Heard in the 1760s, straying into the collection of the elder Ralph Bigland and thence into that of the latter's nephew. These four volumes are all incorporated in The Bigland Index. The remaining volumes fall into two categories.

Volumes I to VIII contain approximately 4000 pages of well scrivened pedigrees compiled by Sir Ralph Bigland from the time of his appointment as Bluemantle Pursuivant in 1774 until about 1810. These pedigrees are richer in dates and places than those found in the Visitations. Wills and other records are frequently cited. As they form a private collection, this genea-logical material was never subject to the system of examination which came to replace that prevailing at the time of the Visitations. Bigland's material therefore remains a collection and does not form part of the official records of the College. Nonetheless, anyone who has worked with it has found Bigland genealogy generally sound and reliable. None can doubt its importance at a time of great social and economic changes and population mobility. The late 18th century is well known as a difficult genealogical period, being prior to Census Returns and National Registration and the proliferation of written family histories. It accounts for a great number of families whose fortunes had risen during the 18th century and whose origins have remained obscure and are so often far removed geographically from the place of residence of the first known forbear.

It should be emphasised that a high proportion of these Bigland pedigrees relate to non-armigerous families. Many of his clients belonged to families striving to find armigerous roots. They proved unsuccessful in the attempt; but their more humble origins were revealed in the process.

The second category comprises Volumes IX to XIII and Volumes XV to XVII. These volumes contain assorted pedigrees in a variety of hands, submitted by clients of Sir Ralph Bigland and bound together with collated letters and evidences. Some of this material runs back into the 1760s and clearly relates to the work of his uncle, the elder Ralph Bigland; others run forward to 1810 and thus comprehend genealogical work undertaken by Sir

Ralph Bigland when Norroy King of Arms. Similar material bound in seven additional volumes covers his subsequent years as Clarenceux and Garter King of Arms. The Bigland Index does not comprehend these later volumes.

The Bigland Index was compiled in 1911. It superseded the inadequate original Index in which Volumes XLIII–XLIX are noted separately. These are now given as an Appendix to this publication.

It is to be hoped that this volume will serve to redress the balance of reputation between uncle and nephew in the latter's favour, and it is also to be hoped that it will provide welcome material for genealogists confronted with the particular problems of upper and middle class families of the late 18th century.

Personal and place names have been left as found in the manuscript index and have not been standardised.

A

Abarle connected with Blount	XIX 60
Abarrow of North Charford co. Southampton	XIX 54
Abell of Sandon near Chelmsford, Much Badow co. Essex	XIII 87
Abercorne, Earl of, connected with Huddlestone and Mackworth	III 341
Abergavenny, Earl of, precedence of,	IX 6
———— Lord	II 493
	VI 52
———————————— connected with Pooley	VI 204
Abrahall of Newhouse near Ross connected with Bonner and Brain	XV 78
Abraham als Poole of London co. Middlesex, Kingston in Jamaica, and of Poole	XVII 26
Abrahams of London co. Middlesex and of Barbadoes, connected with Willet and Hill	III 58
Aburhall connected with Adeane and Gryndom	XIII 100
Abyngton als Habington	XIX 169
Acton of Aldenham co. Salop connected with Moseley	VIII 13
———— of Bentworth co. Hants, connected with Sheppard	II 484
———— of Sutton, Burton co. Worcester, Longhope and Upton St Leonards co. Gloucester	XIX 6
Adams connected with Collingwood	X 156
———— Jorden	V 78
	XVIII 36
———— of Lechlade co. Gloucester connected with Higgins	IV 355
———— of London co. Middlesex	VII 509
———— of Patterchurch, M.I. at Brecon Ash Church co. Norfolk	VI 118
———— of Shrewsbury connected with Hunt	V 72
	XVIII 35, 36
Adderley of Innishannon co. Cork	II 90
———————————— & of Gloucester	IV 166
Adderton of Carlisle co. Cumberland and of Harrington, connected with Culwen or Curwen	II 461
Addington connected with Lysons	XIX 139
Addison of Dunkirk, Milston near Ambrosbury co. Wilts, Lichfield, Coventry and of Fort St George	I 457
———— of Preston	XV 10
———— of Ravenglas co. Cumberland	XVII 1
———— of Workington co. Cumberland connected with Curwen or Culwen	II 461

Adeane of Chalgrave co. Oxon connected with Tipping   III 471
———— of Deane co. Gloucester connected with Aburhall   XIII 100
a Deane see Deane   XX 104
Adelmare als Caesar connected with Angell   I 79
Adey of Wooton under Edge and of Oxford connected with Capel   XX 81
Adye of Dodington, Barham co. Kent, and of the Middle Temple
    co. Middlesex   XXI 211
Adye of St Christopher's and of London co. Middlesex   I 187
———— of Island of St Christopher and of Merley in the psh of
    Great Canford co. Dorset, afterwards Willett   VII 485
Affleck of Dalham co. Suffolk   VIII 396
Agar or Hager of Bourne co. Cambridge connected with Hewitt   VII 3
Agnew connected with Blennerhasset   II 149
———— of Bishop Auckland co. Durham and of America   IX 140
Alslabie of Studley Park co. York connected with Rawlinson   XIII 11
Ake connected with Athall   XVIII 84
Akerman of co. Wilts, London co. Middlesex and of Battersea Rise
    co. Surrey   IX 135
Albany of Kings Holm co. Gloucester connected with Arthur   XIX 158
Alcock connected with Fuller   XV 69
———— of Loughborough near Stow Gloucester   VIII 432
Aldburgh of Aldburgh co. York connected with Sykes and
    Lodge   VII 473
Alderford of Salford co. Warwick connected with Sheldon   VII 42
Alderman of Bath and of co. Surrey   II 484
———— of Harowden Wellingborough co. Northampton   XVII 31
Alderney M.J. St Peters Church Chester   XIV 9
Alderson of High Enbank in Stainmore co. Westmorland, Tickhill
    co. York, and of Addington co. Gloucester   III 210
———— William and Christopher   II 242
Aldington connected with Lysons   XIII 97
———— of Evesham co. Worcester, Bristol co. Gloucester and
    of London co. Middlesex   I 46
Aldred Earl of Northumberland   VIII 254
Aldridge of Stroud co. Gloucester   XVII 56
Aldus connected with Spaw and Golding   II 317
Alen of Scraptoft co. Leicester connected with Wigley   XV 25
Alexander connected with Stebbing   VII 320
———————— Willett   VII 491
Alford connected with Strickland   VIII 345
                                                                       XIV 10
Alfreton Lord of Alfreton co. Derby, Baron of Norton connected
    with Lathom   XXI 296
Allanson of Bramham Biggin co. York   III 501
Allard connected with Tate   III 201–2
Allen ———— Tetlow   X 81–96
———— of Cromhall connected with Raymond   XVI 88
———— of Darlington co. Durham connected with Pemberton
    and Killinghall   VII 277
———— of Finchley and Hornsey co. Middlesex   I 517
———— of Lez Ayre Isle of Man connected with Heywood   II 128

Allen of Notts, Rector of Clough co. Wexford, and of
    Southwark co. Surrey; Master of Dulwich College   XVII 31
———— of Ramsbury co. Wilts   XXI 210
———— of the Hoggins in the psh of St Briavells and of Bristol
    co. Gloucester   XX 16ᵃ
———— of Thrunscoe near Doncaster co. York   III 45
———— of Warrington co. Lancaster connected with Birch   X 77
Alleyn of Abbots Hall and of Winnington co. Chester   XXI 127
———— of Hatfield Peverell   XXI 157
Allgood M.I.   XXI 171
———— Sir Lancelot   XXI 143–5
Allison connected with Jepson   I 96
———— of Richmond co. York   XXI 210
Allot of Bentley co. York   IX 53
Allyson of Pardsey Hall co. Cumberland and of London co.
    Middlesex   XXI 26
Alsager of Alsager Hall co. Chester and of Staun co. Stafford   VII 34
———— of the Brook in Alsager and of Namptwich   VII 32
———— of Radwell Green in the psh of Barthomley in the
    County of Chester, Newington co. Surrey, Holmerend in
    psh of Audley, Trentham co. Stafford and of London co.
    Middlesex   VII 36
Alsopp connected with Glen   XVII 67
Alt ———— Bowles Thomas & Lisle   I 141
Alured of Charles Houle near Hull   I 498
Alvarez see Alvez   III 317
Alven of Walbrook, London co. Middlesex, and of Battersea co.
    Surrey   XVII 38
Alvez or Alvarez of — in Algarve Portugal and of London co.
    Middlesex   III 317
Alye of Hereford connected with Thompson and Andrews   XX 39ᵃ
Anderson M.I. St Nicholas Church Newcastle upon Tyne   VII 378
———— of Boughton co. Lincoln and Eyworth co. Bedford
    connected with Bendish   I 114
———— of Newcastle upon Tyne co. Northumberland   III 136
———— Wallsend Panns and of Howdon Panns co. Northum-
    berland   X 140
Anderson of Whitechapel co. Middlesex and of Lincoln   III 102
Andrew connected with Pitman   I 320
———— or Andrews of Denton near Eltham in Kent and of
    London co. Middlesex   III 242
———— of Kennert near Wellington connected
    with Wolrich   V 204
Andrewes afterwards Uthwatt of Baylam co. Suffolk, Ryborough
    co. Norfolk, Hitchin St Albans, Libury co. Hertford,
    Lathbury Great Linford co. Bucks and of London co.
    Middlesex, see also Andrews   VIII 267
———— of Bristol   IX 35
Andrews connected with Alye   XX 39ᵃ
———— Bickerton   XIV 24
———— Windsor   XIII 1

Andrews of Alham co. Somerset and of London co. Middlesex — XX 225

——— of Barn Elms co. Dorset, Meer co. Wilts — IV 412

——— of Charwelton co. Northampton connected with Arden — XI 16

——— of Cheltenham co. Gloucester and of Stanmore co. Middlesex — XIII 70

——— of Frefoulke co. Southampton connected with Walshe — XVIII 12

——— of Lathbury co. Bucks London co. Middlesex and of Blakesley co. Northampton, see also Andrewes — VII 92

——— of London co. Middlesex and of Shaw Hall Newbury co. Berks — II 227

——— of Old Sodbury co. Gloucester — XX 36[a]

——— of Osgodby and Alford co. Lincoln connected with Booth — VIII 216

Andrews see Andrew

Angell and connections of Peakirke co. Northampton Enfield co. Middlesex Little Wittenham co. Berks Marsh Balden and Benson co. Oxon — VI 267

——— of Peakirke co. Northampton London co. Middlesex Seaton co. Rutland, Crowhurst and Stockwell co. Surrey and of Binfield co. Berks — XI 55–6

——— of Wighton, Downham co. Norfolk, Cobham co. Kent, Marsh Balden co. Oxon, Deeping co. Lincoln, Peakirke co. Northampton, Seaton co. Rutland, Crowhurst co. Sussex, Stockwell co. Surrey, London, Enfield co. Middlesex, Binfield co. Berks, and of Worboy and Paxton co. Huntingdon — I 75

Anglesey Earl of, connected with Phipps and James II — II 146

Angus Douglas Earls of, a genealogical tree of the family — VII 449–52

Anjou Arch. Douglas Earl of, — XVI 9

Annesley connected with Cotton — X 124

——— of St Briavels co. Gloucester connected with Webley — XX 237

Annlee see Ennlee

Anstruther afterwards Leslie of Great Driffield co. York — VII 130

——— of that Ilk of Great Driffield co. York, Welles co. Somerset and of London co. Middlesex — VII 129

Aplin of Banbury co. Oxon from the County of Southampton connected with D'Oyley — VII 63

Appelby of St Briavells co. Gloucester connected with Bond — XX 51–2

Appleby of co. York and of Kirklington co. Cumberland — VII 175

Appleby of Kirklington co. Cumberland and of co. York — XIV 25

——— afterwards Dacre — X 140

Applegarth of Pottern co. Wilts connected with Clare — I 340

Archard of Littleton North Nibley co. Gloucester — XIX 247

Archdeacon of Moncton near Cork, Rotterdam and of Newcastle upon Tyne — XXI 147 / I 307 / XVI 69

Archer als Eyre of co. Berks see Eyre — V 137

——— connected with Babington — XVI 91

——— Evans — VIII 522

——— Lambert — III 223

Archer connected with Newton   XX 175
————— formerly Eyre   II 392
Arden of Parkhall connected with Andrews, Conway, and
    Throckmorton   XI 16
Ardesoif connected with Akerman   IX 135
Ardglasse Earl of, see Cromwell   XV 18, 19, 22
————————————————————————— XXI 242–3
————— Essex, Earl of   XIII 68
Argyle Campbell, Earl of   II 155
Arkwright of Preston; Willersley co. Hereford and of Wirksworth
    and Bakewell co. Derby   I 411
Armiger of London co. Middlesex and of Chelmsford   I 123
Armroid of London co. Middlesex   I 412
Armstrong M.I.   XIV 8
Arnet of Buckingham connected with Ford   XI 39
Arnold connected with Knipe   IV 121
————————— Porter   X 69
————— of Ashby Lodge Northampton, Wolvey co. Warwick
    and of Hilsdon park co. Bucks   III 52
————— of Beckles co. Suffolk and of Portsmouth co. Hants   III 291
————— of Benson co. Oxon connected with Angell   I 79
Arnold of Cornwall, Exeter Plymouth, Borrough Hatherley co.
    Devon connected with Sargent   I 456
————— of Higham connected with Porter and Dennis   XIX 158
————— of Laycock and Corsham co. Wilts   III 269
————— of London co. Middlesex connected with Huntingdon   III 153
Arris of Steple Clayton co. Bucks and of London co. Middlesex
    connected with Hodgkin   IV 359
Arrowsmith connected with Rigby   IX 83
Arthur connected with Hyet and Porter   X 69
————— of Bristol co. Gloucester   XX 196
————— of Clopton   XVIII 62
————————— connected with Porter and Hyet   XIX 158
————— of Wadworth, Doncaster, Howden Place co. York –
    took surname and arms of Worsop   V 301
Arundel, Baron, of Trerise co. Cornwall connected with Beau   IV 100
————— Fitzalan Earl of, connected with Lovell   VIII 248
————— Fitz Allen Earl of, connected with Holland and with
    Hookes   XVIII 105
————— Fitzallen Earl of, connected with Spencer   VI 52
————— Howard ————————— Daubigny   VIII 469
————— of Kenvelhelvas, Lord of Kenelhooke, Baron Arundel
    of Trerise co. Cornwall; of Allerton Maulevorer co. York   III 338
————— of the Field near Stroud   II 99
————— of Thrithehall in the psh of Cornwall   III 70
————— of Wardour Castle co. Wilts   XXI 15
Arundell of London co. Middlesex and of Saltash   I 211
————————————————————————— III 352
————————————————————————— IV 95
Ascough of Lacra co. Cumberland afterwards Askew   XVI 82
Ash connected with Stansall   I 125

Ash of Paston near Peterborough connected with Ashby IV 458
————— Ashe of Freshford co. Somerset and of Fifield co. Wilts III 348
————— of Freshford, Westcombe co. Somerset, Fifield Challotts, Teffont, Langley co. Wilts London co. Middlesex and of Clanwilliam co. Tipperary II 350
————— of Freshford Bartrombe, Westcombe co. Somerset, Halsted co. Kent, London Twickenham co. Middlesex, Heytesbury Challotts, Ilford, Langley Burrell near Chippenham, Tefont Enias, Heywood, co. Wilts, Clanwilliam co. Tipperary in Ireland VI 197
————— of Freshford Westcombe co. Somerset Long Street Challotts co. Wilts, and of Clanwilliam co. Tipperary IV 93
————— of Freshford and Westcombe co. Somerset, Langley Hatchbury co. Wilts London and Twickenham co. Middlesex V 40
————— of Freshford and Westcombe co. Somerset, Twickenham co. Middlesex and of Langley co. Wilts XVIII 22
————— Ayshe of Freshford co. Somerset extracts from Registers VII 442
Ashburnham of Bromham in the psh of Gestling co. Sussex and of Tunbridge co. Kent VI 87
Ashby de Quenby, Blaby, Hungerton, Stone Pit Close in the psh of Newton co. Leicester Lynches, Shrewsbury co. Salop, and of Clerkenwell co. Middlesex IV 456
Ashe connected with Jol XVI 30
Ashe see Ash
Asheton or Ashton of Crofton co. Lancs connected with Hesketh XXI 266
Ashfield connected with Rogers XIII 103
Ashmead of Gloucester connected with Jones XX 160[a]
Ashmole of Litchfield connected with Manwaring III 133
Ashton of Liverpool and of Woolton Hall in the psh of Childwall co. Lancaster IX 99
————— of Middleton co. Westmorland XXI 84
————— or Asheton of Crofton co. Lancs, connected with Hesketh XXI 266
Ashurst of London co. Middlesex, Hedingham Castle co. Essex – descended from Ashurst of Ashurst co. Lincoln I 345
Askaugh of Abbots Holme co. Cumberland and of Bliborough co. Lincoln XXI 35
Askell of Gaydon in the psh of Bishops Hilchington co. Warwick connected with Bucknall II 138
Askew connected with Burrell and Blunt II 194
————————————————————————— II 27
————— extract from wills XXI 189
————— formerly Ascough of Lacra and Graymains co. Cumberland and of Newcastle upon Tyne co. Northumberland XVI 82
————— M.I. XIV 8
————— of Kendal M.I. XIV 7
————— of Pallinbourne co. Durham connected with Watson II 143

Askew of Standingstone in the psh of Millom M.I.   XIV 29[b]

Askwith connected with Bigland   XVI 100

Aspeley ——————— Flewelling and Perkins   IV 422

Aspinwell ——————— Stanhope   II 205

Astell connected with St Lo   XVIII 11

——————— of Everton co. Bedford and of Huntingdon connected with Thornton   IV 349

Astley ——————— Leech of Manchester   III 456

——————— Lord; of Wolvey co. Warwick   XIII 98

——————— of Escott Hall co. Warwick   III 513

Aston Lord Aston of Forfar connected with Norfolk and Blount   XVI 64

——————— of Leuer co. Lancaster M.I.   XIV 4

——————— of Newton in the psh of Stotesden co. Staff. connected with Wheeler and Peech   IX 87

Astry ——————— Dormer   XIII 101

——————— lord of Westerleigh co. Gloucester   XIII 103

———————————————————————————   VIII 430

——————— of London co. Middlesex, Hitchin co. Herts and of Haslington co. Bedford, see also Austry   XIII 101

Astyn or Austen of Herenden in Tenterden, Hall Place Bexley, Shafford and Medgrove in Kent and of Stagenho co. Herts   V 385

Atchison connected with Strickland and Bowles   I 145

Athall als Hotham   XVIII 84

Atherton connected with Conyers   VIII 468

——————— of Atherton co. Lancaster and of Beausey connected with Cholmondeley   III 280

——————— of Preston and of Liverpool co. Palatine Lancaster   VII 322

——————— of Walton near Liverpool   IV 195

Athill of Brandiston Norwich and of Sparham co. Norfolk   IV 50

Atholl Duke of, connected with Frederick   IX 69

Atkins connected with Curtis   I 169

Atkins of Clapham in Surrey   XX 241

——————— of Gloucester and of Lincoln's Inn co. Middlesex   XX 213

——————— of London co. Middlesex   X 44

——————————————— Wickham co. Hants Rector of Arreton Isle of Wight   XVII 51

Atkinson of Kelleth in Westmorland   XXI 121

——————— of London co. Middlesex   II 43

——————— of Newcastle upon Tyne co. Northumberland connected with Beaumont   IV 383

——————— of Overcark M.I.   XIV 9

——————— of Ripon co. York, Wapping co. Middlesex and of Rotterdam in Holland   XVI 22

——————— of Rokecliffe co. York, Charles Town South Carolina, London co. Middlesex and of Manchester co. Lancaster   IV 202

——————— of Windermere, Bexhill co. Sussex Bulmer co. York, Hill Top Kendal co. Westmorland   II 40

Atkyns notes from a family pocket book   XX 35

Attenson M.I. St Peter's Church Chester   XIV 9

Attewood — in the Church of Deynton and of Beach co. Gloucester   XIX 213

Attorney and Solicitor General, order as to place and Audience of   XVII 28

Atwell of Somersetshire or Devonshire, of Dublin, Mullingar co.
    Westmeath and of Bridgwater   VX 34
————— of Thornbury connected with Belchier and Crowther   X 60
Atwood connected with James   XXI 225
————————— Warre   II 5
————— of Wyvolverly co. Worcester, Stoke Bishop and of
    Shirehampton co. Gloucester   XIX 213
Aubrey formerly Gough   XIX 186
————— of Abercunrig & Uniskedwin co. Brecon and of
    Slough co. Bucks, of the Royal Blood of France   XX 1
————— of Aberkynurige connected with Jones and James XX 160
————— of Borstall co. Bucks and of Llantuthed co.
    Glamorgan   I 122
————— of Meere co. Wilts connected with Brigham   XIII 29
————— of Uniskedwin M.I.   XX 6
Audeleigh als Stanleigh see Stanley   XXI 289–95
Audley Lord, connected with Davys   I 149
——————————— Hache   VII 75
——————————— Brooke   X 77
——————————— Hookes & with Holland   XVIII 105
Austen connected with Leigh   XX 162
————— see Astyn   V 385
Austin of the City of Oxford, Kidlington co. Oxon and of
    Cirencester co. Gloucester   XV 59
Austry Austrye als Ostrich of Hitchen co. Hertford Harlington co.
    Bedford Stoke co. Bucks and of Somersham co.
    Huntingdon, see also Astry   XX 34
Austrye als Ostrich see Austry   XX 34
Auther of Bethnal Green co. Middlesex   XXI 12
————— of Beverley co. York connected with Darvall   XXI 11
Avery connected with Knipe   IV 119
Axtell connected with Painsett   IX 107
————— formerly Thornton   IV 349
Ayerigg of Twyning co. Gloucester   XX 37[a]
Aylberton of Elton in the psh of Westbury upon Severn and of the
    Moat in the psh of Newent co. Gloucester   XX 38[a]
Aylberton of Westbury on Severn connected with Chinn   I 111
                                                     XX 77[a]
Ayleway connected with Cocks   II 427
————— of the Forest of Dean co. Gloucester and of Teynton XIX 223
Ayleworth of Ayleworth co. Gloucester   XIX 172
Ayliff M.I. at Dean   X 28
Ayliffe afterwards Ilive   IX 42
————— of Hall Place in the psh of Dean Pamber co.
    Southampton   I 543
————— of Skeeres in the psh of Lawrence Wooton, Hall Place
    in the psh of Dean, and of Pamber co. Hants   X 31–41
Ayney connected with Wittey and Bell   III 265
Aynsworth of Long Whatton   II 325
Ayre or Ayres of Abingdon co. Berks London co. Middlesex
    Stratford in the psh of Westham and of Leyton co. Essex IV 11

Ayres of Frome and of London co. Middlesex V 407
———————— see Ayre IV 11
Ayscough connected with Newton I 147
———————— of Louth co. Lincoln connected with Floyer I 117
Ayshcombe of Broughton and Bedford Grange co. Warwick
    connected with Rutter XIX 68
Ayshe Ashe see Ash VII 442
Ayton of West Herrington in the County of Durham connected
    with Blake III 257

B

Baber connected with Keck XVII 15
———————— of Ragilbury Chew Magna, Wraxhall Sutton co.
Somerset Plymouth co. Devon and of London co.
Middlesex XIX 59
———————— of Sunning Hill co. Berks, Great Chesterfield co.
Essex, Newton co. Cambridge, and of London co.
Middlesex I 27
———————— of Twyverton and of Newton St Loe co. Somerset XIX 58
———————— went into France with James II; of Sunning Hill co.
Berks and of London co. Middlesex XX 65ª
Babington Bishop of Worcester – arms XIII 73
———————— connected with Bigland XVI 26
———————————————————————— and Errington XVI 37
———————————————————— Nevil XVI 95
———————————————————— Rudgley I 445
———————— extract from Register XVI 80
———————— of Bridgeford and of Kingston also of Rampton co.
Nottingham and Dethick in the Peake of Derbyshire V 140
———————— of Bridgford upon the Hill co. Nottingham XVI 91
———————— of Cossington X 125
———————————————————— and Rothby co. Leicester XVI 79
———————— of Kiddington co. Oxford, Frampton Cotterel
Yate co. Gloucester and of Newcastle upon Tyne co.
Northumberland VIII 322
———————— of Kiddington co. Oxford & Newcastle upon Tyne
co. Northumberland, connected with Errington IV 520
Babington of Kiddington co. Oxford connected with Errington
and Clavering X 152
———————— of Packington Hall, and of Curborrow in the psh of
Stow, both co. Stafford IV 389
———————— of Ramston connected with Eyre V 136
Babyngton M.I. at Morley co. Derby VI 107

Bach of Leominster and of London co. Middlesex, Vicar of Kington co. Hereford, connected with Wall	VIII 29
Bache of Stanton co. Derby connected with Stanier	IV 16
Bacon afterwards Forster of Newton Cap co. Durham	II 62
—————————————— of Durham	XXI 202
—————————— connected with Forster of Etherstan	X 6
—————————— formerly Williams	VIII 160
—————————— of Erlham, the City of Norwich, London co. Middlesex and of Shrubland co. Suffolk, connected with Waller	XVIII 99
—————————— of Moor Hall als Moor Park als Compton Hall, in the psh of Farnham in Surrey	VIII 160
Badeley of the City of Dublin connected with Mukins	I 417
—————————————— Reeves	II 128
Badger see Bagehott	XIX 202
Badminton co. Gloucester, extracts from the Register of,	VII 198
Bagehott als Badger of Hall Place Presbury co. Glos. and of Leicester	XIX 202
Baghot of Hewletts co. Gloucester	XIII 120
—————————— of Kings Stanley co. Gloucester connected with Wathen and Small	II 93
—————————— of Prestbury, afterwards Delabere	XIII 120
Bagnall see Bagnell connected with Beauchamp and Harvey	XII 66, 70
Bagnell Bagnall connected with Beauchamp & Harvey	XII 66, 70
Bagshawe of Abney Tideswell Castleton co. Derby and of Manchester co. Lancaster	III 33
Bagster of the Isle of Wight and of Abergavenny	I 212
—————————————— connected with Walker	I 436
—————————————— Dover co. Kent and of Abergavenny co. Monmouth	IV 96
—————————————— connected with Walker	III 351
Baguley connected with Barnes	II 232
Bailes of Newcastle connected with Burdon	X 130
Bailey connected with Belcher and Champneys	V 159
—————————————— Hartwell	III 465
—————————————— Potts	III 125
—————————————— Wilbie	II 449
—————————— of Coaley connected with Cam	XX 94ª
—————————— of Drayton co. Salop, the Island of St Martin and of London co. Middlesex	II 19
—————————— of Newcastle upon Tyne connected with Reed	X 137
—————————— of Thatcham Newbury co. Berks London co. Middlesex and of Constantinople	VIII 193
Baily connected with Russell and Stonestreet	VIII 530
Bain Baine Baynes see Bayn	VIII 70–3
Bainbridge of Backston Gell near Kendall co. York, Whitton, St Helen, Auckland co. Durham	III 6
Bainbrigg of London connected with Dyott	II 141
Baine Bain Baynes see Bayn	VIII 70–3
—————————— formerly and afterwards McGregor of the Shire of Perth and of Twickenham co. Middlesex	I 341
Baines Bayne of Leeds Hull Rotherham	VIII 78–9

Baines of co. Suffolk and of Penzance co. Cornwall .... VII 508
Bainton M.I. Shireborne Church co. Gloucester .... VI 114
Baker als Elton .... I 109
———————————— .... XIX 18
———————————— .... XX 116
———————— connected with Ekins and Dawson .... VIII 299
———————————————— Montagu .... VIII 528
———————————————— Walker and Brumall .... III 350
———————— of Sisinghurst connected with Newton .... VI 23
———————— of Swindon co. Gloucester .... XX 206
———————— of Uxbridge connected with Harvey .... I 570
———————— of Warsley Green in the psh of Hartlebury and of
  Redland Court .... X 48
———————— of Windsor Three Mill Cross near Swallowfield co.
  Berks .... IV 104
Balch of Bridgewater, St Andrews, and of Nether Stowey co.
  Somerset .... VIII 24
Baldwin connected with Allgood .... XXI 143
———————— Higgons and Powell .... XVIII 120
———————— M.I. .... XIV 9
Baley connected with Trenchard .... VIII 180
Balfour connected with Wedderburn .... VII 161
Ball of Milton co. Huntingdon connected with Fuller .... I 288
Ballantine formerly Dykes of Warthole, Gilcruse Shadwell and of
  Crookdale Hall co. Cumberland .... II 406
———————— see Dykes Ballantine of Wardhole Crookdale Hall in
  the psh of Bromfield co. Cumberland .... V 303
Ballard connected with Oatridge .... II 310
Ballard of Syleham co. Suffolk connected with Calver .... V 26
———————————————— Carver .... VIII 40
———————————————————————— .... VIII 42
Baltimore, Calvert, Lord .... XXI 181
———————— connected with Wyndham .... I 544
Bamfield Bampfyld of Poltimore co. Devon .... XIX 96–8
Bampfield connected with Drake .... XVIII 43
Bampfielde ———————————— .... IV 416
Bampfyld see Bamfield .... XIX 96–8
Bampfylde of co. Devon .... IX 27
Bampton of Lechlade co. Gloucester and of London co. Middlesex
  connected with Bathurst .... XX 41[a]
Bamvile connected with the Earl of Chester and with Stanley .... XXI 289
Banaster connected with Dynham and Lewis .... I 122
———————— of Apperley co. Gloucester connected with
  Hungerford .... XXI 214
Banbury, Knollis, Earl of, ... III 236
———————— Knollys ———————— .... II 247
Bandihell connected with Dumaresq .... III 463
Banister connected with Randolph .... X 109, 112
Bankes formerly Holmes .... XV 14
———————— of Winstanley co. Palatine Lancaster .... XV 14
———————————————— M.I. .... XIV 9

Banks connected with Waller   XVIII 97
Barbaroux of Hackney connected with Hopkins   VIII 350
———————————————————————————————   VIII 409
Barber of Otley connected with Turner and Robinson   III 415
————— of Tickenham co. Somerset   XX 68
Barclay connected with Vernon and Nicoll   III 137
————— of Peirstoun, Baronet's patent   XVIII 148
————— of Scotland and of Hendon co. Middlesex   II 465
Barford of Nun Eaton co. Oxon   IX 28
Bargus of Fareham co. Hants connected with Eyre   I 185
Baring a native of Holland, of Mount Rodford co. Devon, and of
    London co. Middlesex   III 359
Barker als Coverall of Coverall Castle Coulshurst Hopton Castle
    Haghmond co. Salop and of Fairford co. Gloucester   XIX 197
————— connected with Baber and Keck   XVII 15
————— M.I. St Nicholas Church Newcastle upon Tyne   VII 376
————— of Caversham co. Oxon connected with Brigham   XIII 29
————— of Culworth connected with Danvers   VIII 242
————— of London co. Middlesex and of Haghmond co. Salop
    connected with Kynaston   XVIII 116
————— of Sisinghurst co. Kent connected with Newton   VI 30
————— of Sunning co. Berks connected with Reade   II 189
Barling of Homestall in the psh of Doddington Edgerton in the
    Hundred of Colehill, Norton, Linsted, Faversham co. Kent,
    and of London co. Middlesex   IV 76
Barlow of Bristol connected with Shellard   XX 207[a]
Barlow of Slebege co. Pembroke   VI 88
Barnard of Abingdon co. Northampton and of the City of Gloucester   XVI 39
————— of Waterton in the County of Middlesex New
    England, connected with Nutting   III 376
Barne of Wilsdon co. Middlesex   II 382
Barnes Barnet connected with Beauchamp   XII 66 & 70
————— of Broughton co. Lancaster   II 232
————— of Carshalton and of Ewell co. Surrey   XIII 67
————— of Cockermouth connected with Johnston   III 112
Barnesley lived at Ombersley Court in the Sandys family; of
    London co. Middlesex   XXI 204
Barnesley of Bilbrooke in the psh of Codsall co. Stafford Billington
    in the psh of Bradeley; Omberley co. Worcester London co.
    Middlesex and of Ursley Park   XIX 22
————— of Charingworth and of Broadway co. Gloucester   IX 145
Barnet Barnes connected with Beauchamp   XII 66, 70
————— Barnett notes as to search for the arms of   XVII 46
————— connected with Burrough   IV 174
Barnett Barnet notes as to search for the arms of   XVII 46
Barnewall of Trimlestoun connected with Brinckhurst   III 181
Barnham connected with Woolstone   III 368
Baron connected with Lawrence and Barrow   X 74
————— of Colford co. Gloucester connected with James   XX 158
Barre, de la, of Mons in Hainault in Flanders   I 20
Barré, Earl of, connected with Edward 1st and with Hookes   XVIII 105

Barrett connected with Ford	V 293
———————— Harvey	II 200
Barrington connected with Cromwell	XV 21
———————— Shales	II 44
————— formerly Berrington	VII 58
————— Harris	VII 58
————— see Pope	IX 73
————— Viscount of Ardglasse in the Kingdom of Ireland, M.I.	XVI 41
————— of Barrington Hall	I 227
————— co. Essex	V 175
————— and of Caborne Isle of Wight	IX 73
Barron connected with Greenfield	IV 209
Barron connected with Thompson	XIII 112
Barrow ————— Cox	XIX 246
————— M.I.	XIV 8
————— of Breem and Wollaston Grange co. Gloucester	X 74
————— of Daynham co. Chester, Peckham co. Surrey, London co. Middlesex, and of Bilboa in Spain	III 318
————— of Shankfoot; Newcastle co. Northumberland and of London co. Middlesex	II 201
Bartle of Willarton co. Lincoln connected with Hannah	XIII 74
Bartlet of Castle Norton co. Worcester and of Saintbury co. Gloucester	XIII 100
Bartlett connected with Hird of Ottley	III 303
————— of Bradford connected with Green and Newton	III 282
————— of Castle Morton co. Worcester and of Saintbury co. Gloucester	XIX 20
Barton connected with Lloyd	III 230
————— M.I. in Kirkby Ravensworth Church	VI 122
————— of Brigstock connected with Ayscough and Lisle	I 147
————— of Broad Clist co. Devon and of London co. Middlesex, Rector of Stourton co. Wilts connected with Salter	VIII 445
————— of Cowton co. York and of London co. Middlesex	III 299
————— of Scaresbrick co. Lancaster connected with Wilson	II 75
Baruh Lousada see Lousada	XXI 287
Barwell of Dursley co. Gloucester, Ackworth co. York, and of London co. Middlesex	IX 38
————— of Garradon co. Leicester connected with Bigland	VIII 324
Barwell of Northamptonshire connected with Lowdham and Stratford	XIX 261
Barwick M.I. at Shireborne Church co. Gloucester	VI 114
————— of Salton Hall M.I.	XIV 8
Baseley of the City of Norwich connected with Harwood	VIII 226
Basford connected with Stebbing	VII 318
Baskervile of Eardesley co. Hereford, Longhope co. Gloucester and of Shrewsbury co. Salop	XIX 46
————— of Rickeston co. Wilts	XIX 155
Baskerville connected with Owen and Kynaston	XVIII 115
————————— Scudamore	XVIII 61

Baskerville of Hereford and of Shrewsbury co. Salop connected
with Boughy and Kynaston — XVIII 121
———— of Hereford and of Shrewbury co. Salop connected
with Powell — V 65
———— of Withington M.I. St Peters Church Chester — XIV 9
Basset Lord of Coleston Basset co. Nottingham, Sapcote, co.
Leicester, of Weldon and of Wittering — VIII 51
———— of Tehiddy co. Cornwall connected with Cox — II 421
Bassett — XX 60
———— connected with Pendarves — XVIII 7
———— and Trelawney — III 255
———— of Lan e lay co. Glamorgan connected with Roberts — II 11
Bastian of Salhamsted co. Berks connected with Wickens — III 49
Bate connected with Barker and Baber — XVII 15
———— of Ashford in Kent Colchester co. Essex London co.
Middlesex, Rectors of Wareham and Deptford, Vicar of
Chilham co. Kent — XVI 55
Bateman connected with Dashwood — II 77
———— Denny — II 312
———— Thorold — X 76
Bateman M.I. in Bracon Ash Church co. Norfolk — VI 121
———— of Blease M.I. — XIV 8
———— of Haesbroke in Flanders and of London co. Middlesex
afterwards Viscount and Baron Culmore connected with
de la Barre — I 19
———— of Hartington co. Derby, Baptisms etc. — VI 294
———— of Whitechapel co. Middlesex connected with Berry — VIII 14
———— Viscount, connected with Hedges and Nicoll — III 138
Bates connected with Jackson — VIII 59
———— of Beaconsfield, and of London co. Middlesex — I 326
Bath, of Drogheda, Nights Town, Cashel and of Ladyrath — I 65
Batherst connected with Randolph — X 109, 112
Bathurst ———— Lawrence — VIII 111
———— extracts from Registers — XX 40
———— Lord — XIII 112
———— of Horsmunden in Kent, Finchcocks and of Wilmington — XIII 31
———— of Lechlade co. Gloucester London co. Middlesex,
Canterbury Cranbroke Horsmonden co. Kent and of Phi-
ladelphia in Pensilvania — XX 41a–43
———— of Lechlade co. Gloucester connected with Cutler — XIX 118
———— of London Battlesdon co. Bedford, Clarendon Park co.
Wilts and of Lidney co. Gloucester — II 243
———— sided with Hen. VI forfeiting his Estate in Sussex; of
Canterbury, Cranbrook, Staplehurst, Horsemonden
Horton Kirby co. Kent, Howthorp in Northampton,
Clarendon Park co. Wilts, Battledon co. Bedford, Baron
Bathurst — XIX 1, 2
Batley of Masham co. York and of London co. Middlesex — XVII 50
Batson of Hannington near Highworth, Driffield co. Wilts Milton
co. Oxon Cambden co. Gloucester London co. Middlesex — XIX 252
Battell of Combe Grove Somerset connected with Davies — XVI 57

Battey of Portsmouth co. Hants, and of Knightsbridge co.
  Middlesex   I 550
Battisford of Hottesford co. Worcester connected with Woodward   XX 77ᵃ
Batts connected with Cooke   IV 262
Baugh of Twining co. Gloucester; Pershore co. Worcester Mil-
  comb co. Oxon and of Romford co. Essex   XIX 73
————— of Twyning co. Gloucester connected with Hancock   XIII 97
Bawdrip of Huntspill co. Somerset connected with Morgan   VIII 181
Bawtry of Foston co. York connected with West and Thompson   IV 530
Baxter connected with Huxley   XV 9
————— of Newcastle upon Tyne   IX 64
Bayes of Long Itchington co. Warwick connected with Seale and
  Salmon   III 66
Bayley connected with Hynde and Mansergh   XXI 47
————— Pleydell   XIX 112
————————————— Stuteville   I 82
————— of Chesterton co. Huntingdon connected with Bigland   XIII 12
———   XVI 84

————— of Lidyard and Tregoose co. Wilts connected with
  Dore   VII 467
————— of Peterborough   IV 247
————— of Willow Hall in the psh of Whittlesey in the Isle
  of Ely co. Cambridge, Peterborough Oxney co.
  Northampton, Chesterton co. Huntingdon, Market Harbo-
  rough co. Leicester, and of Uppingham co. Rutland   IX 137
Baylie connected with Packwood and Hanson   VIII 536
Baylis of Gloucester Rector of Ludgershall and of Kingswood co.   XX 69a–
  Wilts   70ᵃ–1
————— of the Rudge and Shepscombe in Painswick New Mills
  in Stroud co. Gloucester, and of Maryport in Cumberland   VIII 393
Baylor of Carolina County in Virginia connected with Tucker   IV 220
————— of King William County, Newmarket in the psh of
  Drysdale in Carolina County in Virignia   IV 372
Bayly lord of the Manor of Wheatenhurst Frethorn co. Gloucester
  and of Rotherhithe co. Surrey   XVI 42
Bayn Baynes Bain Baine of Horbury P. Wakefield City of York,
  Nateley Bridge; wills etc.   VIII 70–3
Baynard connected with de Grey   VI 255
————— of Rochester co. Kent connected with Hodsoll   XVII 42
Bayne Baines of Leeds Hull and of Rotherham co. York   VIII 78–9
Baynes Bain Baine see Bayn   VIII 70–3
————— of Embsay Kirk, Skipton, Richmond, and Middleham
  co. York   III 171
————— of London co. Middlesex settled in the County of York
  but originally from Scotland – arms of   VIII 354
Baynham connected with Throckmorton and Porter   XIX 159
————— de, afterwards Serjeaunt   XIX 44
————— of Cleerwell   XIII 100
Baynham of Clerewell and Westbury in the Forest of Deane   XIX 45
————— of Cleerwell connected with Throckmorton   XX 219b
————— of co. Gloucester   XXI 5

Baynton of Brompton and Bainton co. Wilts   IV 338
Baynton of Bromham, Spy Park, Little Chatfield co. Wilts Grays
    Inn co. Middlesex Bath co. Somerset and of Chadlington
    co. Oxon   VIII 31
Beacon of London co. Middlesex Norwich co. Norfolk Calborne
    Isle of Wight and of Wattesfield co. Suffolk   III 368
Beale connected with Chinn   XX 77ᵃ
——————————————— Hunt   IV 477
——   XVIII 36
————————————————— Spence   IX 69
————————— Trelawny   II 293
————————— extract from Registers and seals   XX 45–6
————————— M.I. Maidstone Church co. Kent   VII 412
————————— of Biddenden co. Kent and of Barking co. Essex   III 103
————————— of London co. Middlesex connected with Draper   XX 107ᵃ
————————— of Newent and English Bicknor co. Gloucester   XX 66ᵃ
————————— see Beel connected with Trelawney
Beames of East Blagrove in the psh of Wroughton co. Wilts
    connected with Dore   VII 462
Bearcroft of Hanbury and Broughton Master of the Charterhouse   II 480–1
Beard of Aldermanbury connected with Halliday   XX 136
————————— of Meret's Mill and of London co. Middlesex   II 181
Beatniff of Lacey co. Lincoln connected with Bentley   IV 301
—— and with
    Saunderson   II 157
Beau of Landaff co. Glamorgan connected with Arundel and Lister   IV 101
Beauchamp Baron of Bedford   VIII 252
————————— Earl of Warwick connected with Spencer   VI 53
————————————————— Hookes and with Lord Ferrar of Groby   XVIII 105
————————— formerly Donnellan connected with Boughton   VIII 410
————————— lords of Elmley Earls of Warwick   VIII 253
————————— of Ballyloughane co. Carlow connected with Harvey   XII 66–70
————————— of Chiseley near Tewksbury co. Gloucester, Langley,
    and of co. Norfolk   II 337
————————— of Powyke   XVI 82
————————— of Powick connected with Read   XIX 254
————————— of the family of Hoch co. Somerset connected with
    Blount   XVI 64
————————— of Trefinse Pengrith in the psh of Gwynhop co.
    Cornwall   VII 436
Beaufoe of Beresford, St John co. Oxon, Edmondscot co. War-
    wick connected with Higford   XIX 210
Beaufort Duke of Somerset   XXI 229
——   VIII 249
————————————————— connected with Stafford   XVI 50
————————— Earl connected with and Marquess of Dorset connected
    with Hookes   XVIII 105
Beaumont connected with Pink   I 498
————————— of Sloughton co. Leicester, Dunmow co. Essex the
    City of Norwich and of Buckland in Surrey   XIII 18–19

Beaumont of the City of Norwich and of West Denton co.
    Northumberland   IV 382
Beauvoir see Beaver   IX 81
Beaver Rector of Wykeham co. Hants   IX 81
———————— said to descend from the Guernsey Beauvoir of Lewker
    co. Oxon, Rectors of Wickham co. Hants, Plymtree co.
    Devon and of Childsey co. Berks   XV 46
                                                XVII 16
Beazley connected with Russell   VIII 348
———————————— and Hopkins   VIII 407
Bech de la connected with Walker   VII 328
Becher of Howbury   VIII 338
Beck of Bombay Anstey Hall co. Warwick, Glasgow and of the
    Island of Maco   VII 460
———————— of Farrig M.I.   XIV 8
———————— of Newcastle upon Tyne and of Grove in the psh of
    Hawshead co. Lancaster   XVII 26
Becket Beckett of Tatham near Hornby co. Lancaster London co.
    Middlesex and of the City of York   II 272
                                               III 487
Beckett see Becket
Beckford of Barking co. Essex   XVIII 114
———————————— & of London co. Middlesex IV 511
———————— of London, Ealing co. Middlesex and of Jamaica I 191
———————— of Ealing co. Middlesex, Ashsted co. Surrey and of
    Jamaica   XII 91–100
Beckington connected with Stanley and Bamvile   XXI 289
Beckman of Frankfort upon the Oder in the Elect. of Bran-
    denbergh and of London co. Middlesex   VII 116
—————————————————————— see Beekman VII 364
Beconshaw of Beconshaw co. Palatine Lancaster, Ringwood co.
    Southampton connected with Wilmot   IX 113[b]
Beddome connected with Brandon   XV 79
Beddow of Kinnerley Hanmer near Whitchurch co. Salop, Penley
    co. Flint and of London co. Middlesex   IV 356
Bedell of London co. Middlesex connected with Hardy II 245
———————— of Wallaston co. Northampton Catworth and Hamer-
    ton co. Hunts   V 455
Bedford, Beauchamp Baron of,   VIII 252
———————— of Monkland co. Hereford connected with Lewis IV 114
———————— of Old Samford co. Essex connected with Atkinson IV 204
Bedingfield M.I. in Bracon Ash Church co. Norfolk VI 119
———————— of Oxborough co. Norfolk connected with de Grey VI 255
———————— of Oxborough and of Wickmere co. Norfolk VI 26
———————— of Redlingfield Knotshall, Thornden co. Suffolk, Ers-
    well, Oxborough Hall, Quidenham, Wigton Canham
    Grange co. Norfolk, and of Co. York   V 312–322
———————— of Wigton co. Norfolk connected with Clarke and
    Paston   III 331
                                             I 322

Beekman of Frankfurt upon the Oder and of London co. Middlesex	XXI 215[a]
———— see also Beckman	
Beel Beale of Barn connected with Trelawney	XVIII 7
	III 255
Beeston of Jamaica Oxford and of Winchester	III 200
Begbie and Foote note as to marriage	XVII 40
Begny connected with La Serre	VIII 400
Behenna of Penrhyn co. Cornwall connected with Reed	I 370
Balasyse of Morton Owton Ludworth and of Branspeth Castle co. Durham	XV 49
———— of Winchester co. Hants and of Pontoise	IX 50
Belch of London co. Middlesex & Coalston co. Surrey connected with Owen	III 310
Belcher connected with Brown of Newbury	V 144
———— of Ulcombe co. Kent connected with Champneys	V 159
Belchier of Yate co. Gloucester	X 60
Beldam afterwards Johns	VIII 422
Bell connected with Clutterbuck	XX 67
———————— Harbin	IV 402
———— of Beaupre Hall, Wallington Hall, Holme co. Norfolk	II 212
———— of Gloucester and Sainthurst co. Gloucester connected with Winchcombe	I 30
———— of Hundath Hill near Cockermouth in the psh of Embledon co. Cumberland, Stamford Hill London Tottenham co. Middlesex, Hertford, Dorking co. Surrey and of Yeovil co. Somerset	III 264
———— of London co. Middlesex connected with Wragg and Oxley	III 314
———— of Newcastle connected with Moore	VII 122
———— Eden	XXI 124
———————— of Scaresbrick and Ormskirk co. Lancaster and of London co. Middlesex	II 38
———— of Tortworth co. Gloucester connected with Mathew	XX 165[a]
Bellairs of Uffington co. Lincoln, Stamford Baron co. Northampton and of the Town of Derby	XIII 20–1
Bellamy afterwards Crayle	I 158
———————————— connected with Gardner	I 564
Bellaque connected with Brose	XXI 113
Bellew of Launceston co. Cornwall	IX 96
Bellingham of Bellingham Greyrig Helsington Oustry co. Westmorland, Finchamsted co. Berks Orston St George co. Wilts, Limister Erringham Houghton co. Sussex Maunton and Groomby Wade co. Lincoln	XXI 84–90
———— of Gemons Town co. Louth now called Castle Bellingham, Dublin and of Weald co. Essex	I 127
———— of co. Hereford connected with Whitcombe	XV 57
———— of Norwich connected with Furs	III 63
Bellinghame M.I.	XIV 29[b]
Bellomont Earl of Leicester connected with Grantesmenil and Gwadir	VIII 250

Bellomont Earl of Mellent and Earl of Leicester connected with
    Poulton   XVI 18
Belshire connected with Rosse   XX 194
Belt of Overton Bossall co. York and of the East Indies   III 306
Bendery of Wroughton co. Wilts connected with Dore   VII 463
Bendish of Great Wishingham and of Bylaugh co. Norfolk   I 116
——————— of Steple Bumsted co. Essex   I 113
————————————— connected with Batson   XIX 253
——————— of Tempsford co. Bedford and of Grays Inn co.
    Middlesex   I 115
Bendysh of London co. Middlesex and South Town Suffolk
    descended from the ancient family of Sir Thos. Bendysh of
    Essex Bart. of Colskirk Norfolk and of Chingford co. Essex
    connected with Ireton   XV 19,22
Benet Bennet of Clapcot near Wallingford co. Berks London co.
    Middlesex, Kew co. Surrey, Shaldon co. Hants and of
    Badburgham   VI 9
Benett of Farham co. Southampton   XXI 199
Benjafield of Blandford and of Horton co. Dorset   IV 342
Benjamin of Clapham co. Surrey – afterwards assumed the name of
    Benson   XVII 21
Benlowes connected with Gage   XIX 65
Bennet als Skeirne connected with Hotham   XVIII 83
——————— came from Fotherby or Thoresby to Keddington co.
    Lincoln of Stouton, Louth, Barton-upon-Humber, Oursby,
    Touse, co. Lincoln, Stratford co. Essex and of London co.
    Middlesex   II 157
——————— connected with Aubrey and Portrey   XX 1
——————— of London co. Middlesex and of High Ongar co. Essex   XIII 23
——————— Serjeant at Law, Master in Chancery connected with
    Brand and Morden   XVII 44
——————— see Benet
Bennett connected with Dethick   VIII 453
————————————— Porter   XVII 34
——————— M.I. St Peter's Church Chester   XIV 9
——————— of Chesters in Scotland connected with Collingwood   X 155
——————— of Iron Acton co. Gloucester connected with Gregory   XX 127[a]
——————— of Onan co. Kilkenny, Dunmain co. Wexford in the
    Kingdom of Ireland, and of North Yarmouth co. Norfolk   VIII 121
——————— of Penzance co. Cornwall connected with Davies   II 72
————————————————————————————   II 443
——————— of Welby Castle co. Leicester   XV 10
Benolt Clarenceux King of Arms, connected with Fermour   V 6
————————————————————————————   VIII 497
Benson afterwards Earle   XXI 116
——————— came from York, of Stockport in Cheshire and of
    Olerton co. Nottingham   I 245
——————— connected with Huxley   XV 9
——————— formerly Benjamin   XVII 21
——————— Lord of Ryssupp, of Halton on the Hill near Skipton in

Craven co. York, and of Bromley co. Middlesex – Lord Bingley	XXI 113–7
Benson M.I.	XIV 4
———— of Bromley co. Middlesex	XXI 257
———— of Charwelton and Towcaster co. Northampton	VIII 375
———— of Croydon co. Surrey connected with Holmes and Lambe	IV 106ª–7
———— of Haverfordwest co. Pembroke, Bishop of Gloucester, connected with Belchier	X 60
———— of Hugell co. Westmorland	XXI 78
Bentham of Bentham co. York, St John's Lee co. Northumberland, and of Chester le Street co. Durham	I 17
Bentley connected with Bernard and Cromwell	XV 21
———— of Shoreditch co. Middlesex connected with Buckee and Gibbons	IV 61
———— of Wielsby co. Lincoln connected with Bennett	II 157
——————————————————— Saunderson	IV 300
Benton of King's Norton co. Worcester and of Birmingham co. Warwick	IV 250
Benwell of Eton near Windsor connected with Franklin	VIII 228ª
Benyon of Giddyea Hall co. Essex and of Englefield House co. Berks	XV 58
Beresford connected with Render	XXI 168
Beresford connected with Thorold	X 76
———— of Newton and Bentley, Cutthorp co. Derby, Bradlow Ash in the psh of Thorp; Long Ledenham, Rowston, Fulbeck co. Lincoln, Scapwick, and of Barbadoes	IX 77–9
———— of Newton and Bentley co. Derby, London co. Middlesex, Hertford Rickmansworth co. Herts and of Long Ledenham co. Lincoln	IV 461
———— of Newton als Newton Grange and of Bentley Chesterfield and Wirksworth co. Derby and of Lichfield co. Stafford	II 207
Bereton, Lord, connected with Willoughby of Parham	XIII 7
Berewe of Awre and of Fieldcourt co. Gloucester	XIX 7
———— Field Court and of Newland co. Gloucester	XIX 102
Berkeley connected with Killigrew	VI 152
———————— Try	XX 138ª
———— Lord	XVIII 62
————————————————————————	XX 260
———— connected with de Lisle, and Beauchamp Earl of Warwick	VIII 255
———— connected with Throckmorton of Coughton co. Warwick	VIII 322
————————————————————————	XI 16
———— connected with Trye	XIII 97
———— of Stoke, Eyecotts in the psh of Randcombe co. Gloucester and of Bruton co. Somerset	XIX 86
———— of Stoke Gifford co. Gloucester	XIII 104
———— connected with Symes	XIX 251
Bernard came from Dauphiny in France, of Kimbleton	IV 112

Bernard connected with St John — XV 21

———— of Nidd and Harrogate co. Yorks connected with Towneley — XIV 22

Berners of Finchfield co. Essex London co. Middlesex and of Wiggenhall St Mary co. Norfolk connected with Davis and Plestow — III 228

———— of Holverston Park and South Town co. Suffolk connected with Bendysh — XV 19, 22

Berney of Dalebank and of Northlies — I 85

———— of Kirby co. Norfolk connected with Woolball — XX 49ᶜ

Berridge connected with Stodart — IV 520

Berrie of Berrie Nerbert co. Devon connected with Turvile — V 95

Berriman connected with Stanhope — II 119

Berrington afterwards Barrington — VII 58

———— of Brick House in the psh of Cannon Pyon co. Hereford connected with Stephens and Harris — VII 58

Berry connected with Whalley — IX 104

———— Windsor — XIII 5

———— of London and Staines co. Middlesex — VIII 15

———— of Ludlow co. Salop and of co. Hereford — II 91

Berrye connected with Paston — IX 113ᵇ

Bertie ———— Heywood — I 52

———— Lord Willoughby of Eresby and Earl of Lindsay connected with Widdrington — XIV 21

———— Sir Peregrine, entry of burial — XIV 12

Berwis connected with Briscoe — XXI 13

Best of Allington connected with Randolph — X 109

Bethell Rector of St Peter Hereford — IX 21

Betsworth of Iping co. Sussex connected with Nalldrett — III 222

Bettesworth of Street Portsea co. Hants — II 120

———— of Petworth and Green co. Sussex, and of co. Hants — II 415

Bettine of East Mardon co. Sussex, came from Havant in Hants, and of London co. Middlesex — II 217

Bevan of Carmarthen in South Wales — XXI 179

———— of Cheriton co. Glamorgan — III 522

———— of London co. Middlesex connected with Gurney — IV 83

Beverley of Tealby and Castor co. Lincoln, Dunnington co. York and of London co. Middlesex — III 139

Bevil of Chesterton connected with Lawrence — XVII 47

Bevis connected with Bridges — XVIII 92

———— and Trapps — V 46

Bewick of Northumberland and Newcastle of that County — I 103

———— of Close House, High Sheriff of Northumberland in 1760 — XXI 2

Bibbee of Clerkenwell and Whitechapel co. Middlesex connected with Coombs and Parry — IV 62

Bick M.I. at Tredington co. Gloucester — IX 48

Bickerton Lord of Cashe in Scotland connected with Stannow — XIV 24

Bickley clerk of the Chapel at Newbrough — IV 2

Biddick connected with Rumsey — II 298

Biddulph ————— Jol   XVI 30
————— of Marchington and of Uttoxeter co. Stafford   III 459
Bidulph of Bidulph M.I.   XIV 4
Bidgood connected with Davye   X 68
Bidlake notes as to will etc   XV 51
————— of Bidlake, Woodford Mead, Bradistow, Bowden,
    Crediton and of Germanswick co. Devon   XIII 54–8
————— of Darlington co. Durham and of Jermans Weeke co.
    Devon   V 231
————— of Totnes co. Devon   XXI 150
Bierley of Hardwick connected with Clarke   VIII 45
Bigge of Benton House Brinkley and of Byker co. Northum-
    berland   VIII 467
————— of Benton co. Northumberland connected with
    Rundall   I 41
Biggen of Lambeth co. Surrey   I 258
Biggs connected with Smyth   XX 48
————— of London co. Middlesex   X 136
Bigland connected with Errington   X 152
                                                              XVI 36
——————————————— Sells   I 540
————— deed concerning   XVI 90
————— extracts from the Register of Cartmel Church in co.
    Lancaster, deeds etc.   XVI 44–7
————— M.I.   XIV6, 29^{b}–^{c}
————— of Bigland, Mungeon in Cartmel co. Palatine Lancas-
    ter, Bigland Hall in Paston near Kendal co. Westmorland;
    Greys Inn, Stepney co. Middlesex, Kegworth, Long What-
    ton Frolesworth co. Leicester, Peterborough co.
    Northampton and of the Island of Bermuda Garter Principal
    King of Arms   VIII 318
————— of Chelmsford co. Essex   IX 151
———————————————   XVI 10
————— of Frocaster co. Gloucester   XVI 26
——————————————— connected with Wilkins   XX 243–5
——————————————————————— Raymond   XVI 88
——————————————— Garter Principal King of Arms   XVI 37
————— of Hartbarrow and of the Height in the psh of Cartmell
    co. Lancaster   VIII 315
————— of Lambrigg and Cartmel, extracts from Registers   XVI 80
————— of Long Whatton, Frolesworth co. Leicester and of the
    City of Peterborough   XIII 12
Bigland of Long Whatton co. Leicester, Peterborough and of Leek
    co. Nottingham   XVI 84
————— of Scarborough co. York and of London co. Middlesex   XVI 100
————— of Weltenhow   XIV 8
————— Release by Stevens   XVI 81–5
Biglands of Wighton co. Cumberland and of London co.
    Middlesex   XV 48
Bignall of Wilton, Salisbury and of East Harnham co. Wilts   XXI 126
Billers of Scraptoft co. Leicester   XV 25

Billingsley of Ashwick co. Somerset   XX 55
——————— of Chatham co. Kent, London co. Middlesex Vicar of
   St Mary in Chesterfield co. Derby, Rector Newinth,
   Newington and Swincombe co. Oxon   VII 343
——————— of Chesterfield co. Derby   X 73
Billop of Staten Island connected with Willett   VII 490
Bindlosse of Barwick Hall co. Lancaster connected with Holt and
   Entwistle see also Byndlosse   XI 27
——————— connected with Delawar and Perry   XIV 23

      Hunter als Perry   XIX 13
Binfield connected with Smith   X 97
——————— of Ivor co. Bucks and of London co. Middlesex   II 209

      connected with Smyth   XVI 66
Bingle M.I. St Peter's Church Chester   XIV 9
Bingley Fox Lane, Lord,   XVII 59
——————— of Yorkshire London co. Middlesex, Rotterdam in
   Holland and of Newcastle upon Tyne co. Northumberland   III 114
Birch descended according to tradition from the family of Birch of
   Birch in the County Palatine of Lancaster; of Yarum co.
   York, Montego Bay Jamaica, London co. Middlesex
   Whitehaven co. Cumberland, Liverpool co. Palatine
   Lancaster, and of Middleborough Holland   VIII 120
——————— of Ardwick near Manchester   III 305
——————— of Birch in the psh of Manchester connected with
   Audley and Brooke   X 77
——————————— connected with Tetlow and Brooke   X 81–96
Birchenshaw of Plaseisa in Llansanan co. Denbigh   IV 350
Bird of Hereford   VI 385
——————— of London co. Middlesex and of Reigate co. Surrey   II 51
——————— of Westminster connected with Webbe   I 50
Birt of Newland co. Gloucester connected with Bond   XX 52
Bisco of Crofton co. Cumberland connected with Dine   IV 379
Biscoe connected with Seymour   XV 54
Bishop ——————— Hedges and Nicoll   III 138
——————— of Dedington co. Oxon and of London co. Middlesex   XXI 156[a]
——————— of Parham co. Sussex connected with Hedges and Tate   I 204
——————— of Yanworth connected with Webelin   VIII 387
Bishopp late of Westburton in the County of Sussex widow –
   extract from will of –   XIII 22
Blackborow descended from the Blackburns of Lancashire, of
   London co. Middlesex and of Shenley Hill co. Herts   I 566
Blackburn connected with Thornton   XV 24
——————— of Dewsbury near Leeds connected with Ward   IX 146
Blackburn of London co. Middlesex connected with Arris and
   Hodgkin   IV 358
Blackburne of Newton co. Lancaster   VIII 21
——————— of St Nicholas near Richmond and of Cateric co. York   III 304
Blackerby of Worlington in Suffolk, Britwell co. Oxon and of
   London co. Middlesex   XXI 10

Blacket Blackett of Newcastle upon Tyne co. Northumberland,
    Wyllymonswick and of Newby   VII 216
——————— formerly Calverley of Calverley   VII 217
——————— of Ripon co. Gloucester and of Matfen co. Northum-
    berland   XXI 196
——————— of William Newcastle and of Stockholm   X 135
——————— of Wylam and West Denton see Blackett   XXI 2
Blackett of Newby co. York, Plymouth co. Devon and of Bowden
    co. Durham   II 54
——————— of Wylam co. Northumberland connected with
    Burnell   II 202
——————— see also Blacket
Blackleeck of Gloucester and of London co. Middlesex connected
    with Dennis   XIX 160
Blackman of Barbadoes from Norfolk – Chatham Place, and of
    London co. Middlesex   II 482
——————— of Marlborough and of Ramsbury co. Wilts   VII 406
Blackstone of Salisbury and of London co. Middlesex   IX 58
Bladen of Hemsworth co. York and of London co. Middlesex   III 354
——————— of London co. Middlesex   I 67
                                  XVII 55
Blagden of Kingswood co. Wilts connected with Hickes   XIX 239
Blagdon of Nind co. Wilts, Bristol and Uley co. Gloucester
    connected with Hale   I 222
Blagrove of Elton, Buckland, Lamborne, Jamaica, London, and of
    Newbery co. Berks   I 533
Blair of Giffordland in the psh of Dabry in the Shire of Ayr, and of
    London co. Middlesex   VII 188
Blake connected with Merwin   IV 244
——————— of Drum near Galway and of Germany   II 476
——————— of Exeter co. Devon   II 113
——————— of Galway and of London co. Middlesex   IX 2
——————————— Montserrat   III 365
——————— of Jamaica West Indies and of Westmorland connected
    with Williams   III 378
——————— of Stowey Hilton Lower Aisholt co. Somerset   IX 36
——————— of Turzle Castle co. Northumberland, Cogges co.
    Oxford, and of Grays Inn co. Middlesex came from Ireland   XXI 148^a–9
——————— supposed to be of Galway, of Tursell, Turisel Castle
    co. Northumberland Mullockmore Fowtrey Tower co.
    Westmorland, Ardfrey and Monlogh Menlow or Menlogh   III 256–60
Blakeney from Halloran – suggested change of name   XIII 16
Blakett connected with Reed Roddam and Collingwood   X 156
Blakeway of Chadsley Corbet co. Worcester   IX 86
——————— Rector of Filton co. Gloucester and of Neind Savage
    co. Worcester connected with Brickdale   VII 396
Blakey of Blakey Hall in the psh of Colne co. Lancs connected with
    Callis   XXI 284
Blakiston of Stapleton co. Ebor and of London co. Middlesex   II 187
Blamire connected with Christian and Curwen or Culwen   II 462

Blamire connected with Curwen   VIII 35
Blanchard of Marshfield co. Gloucester and of Katherine's Court
    co. Somerset   XIX 85
Bland connected with Fleming   X 47
Blandford M.I. Worcester Cathedral   XIV 9
———————— of Pool co. Wilts connected with Holbrow   I 172
Blastock of Ashby de la Zouche Packington co. Leicester
    Nottingham Town and of Marylebone co. Middlesex   IV 28
Blatchford of Little Ash in the psh of St Budeaux co. Cornwall
    connected with Lawrence   I 217
Blathwayt connected with Winter   XX 200
Blaythwayt descends from Cumberland, Secretary of War and
    Secretary of State to King William   XX 49[b]
Blencow of Blencow, of Penrith co. Cumberland; Ulverstone co.
    Lancaster Toobey Priory near Brentwood or Ingatestone co.
    Essex, and of London co. Middlesex   II 64–5
Blenkinsopp M.I. St Nicholas Church Newcastle upon Tyne   VII 380
———————— of Dryburnhaugh M.I.   XVI 54
Blennerhasset of Killorgland Trelee co. Kerry and of Dublin   II 148
Blethyne ap Maynarth Lord of Brecknock   XIV 19
Blicke of Lambeth co. Surrey and of Old Surnford co. Worcester   XV 36
Blisse connected with Steyt   XX 209
Blofeld connected with Grose   IX 57
———————— of Blofield, Cromer, Gymingham, Alby, Trimingham
    Napton, Southrepps, Sustead Hall Beeston Priory, Nor-
    wich, Westwich, Thorp co. Norfolk; Abingdon co. Berks,
    and of London co. Middlesex   XVII 4
Blofield connected with Calthorpe   XVII 3, 4
Blomberg of Courland and of Kirkby over Car co. York   XIII 81
Blomer of Hatherop co. Gloucester connected with Webbe   XIII 118
———————— connected with Viscount Montagu and with Draycote   IX 120
Blomfield of Ardleigh, Brightlingsea, Colchester, co. Essex, con-
    nected with Sansom   VII 104
Blood Royal   XVI 9
Bloomberg connected with Laying and Francland   XIII 115
Bloss connected with Coel   X 67
Blount connected with Guise   XIX 226
———————————— Tyrell   VIII 101
———————— Le Blond, Le Blund lord of Guines in Normandy
    founder of the Priory Ykesworth co. Suffolk, lord of Belton
    co. Rutland, Sodington co. Worcester, Rock co. Northum-
    berland Maple Durham co. Oxford and of Thornbury co.
    Gloucester – Lord Montjoy   XVI 64
———————— Le Blond lord of Guines in Normandy, of the Rock
    and of Sodington co. Worcester, lord of Belton in Rutland,
    Grendon co. Hereford Maple Durham co. Oxon, Dicham in
    Sussex, Clyton Elbersfield, and of Calais, Lord Montjoy   XIX 218–9
———————— of Mangerfield co. Gloucester, Wotton co. Wilts,
    Inkpen co. Berks, London co. Middlesex, and of West
    Deeping co. Lincoln   XIX 60

Blount of Pembridge co. Hereford   VIII 19
————————————————————— and of Cleobury, Forge co.
    Salop   V 37
———————— of the City of Warwick connected with Windsor   XIII 1
Bloxam of Aston sub Edge co. Gloucester, Offenham co. Wor-
    cester, and of London co. Middlesex   XIX 148
———————— of Hinckley co. Leicester, Alcester, Rugby co. War-
    wick, and of Hanwell co. Middlesex   VII 180
———————— of Severn Stoke co. Worcester, Aston sub Edge co.
    Gloucester, Blythfield co. Stafford, and of Hinckley co.
    Leicester   VIII 374
———————— of Severn Stoke co. Worcester, Aston sub Edge co.
    Gloucester, Hinckley co. Leicester and of London co.
    Middlesex   XX 63
Bludworth connected with Brett and Bertie   III 177
————————————————— and Dacre   VI 104
Blunt als Mills   VI 254
———————————————— of Highhampe co. Hants   XV 61
———————— connected with Bournford   XVI 33
———————————————— Burnford and Feake   XVI 93
———————————————— Hoskins   XX 237
———————— of Eye co. Hereford   II 193
———————— of Freshford near Bath co. Somerset, Wallop and
    Odiham co. Hants   II 190
———————— of Lewes connected with Short   II 194
———————— of London co. Middlesex, Walthamstow co. Essex,
    Croydon co. Surrey, Lewes and Ringmore co. Sussex, and
    of Freshford near Bradford, co. Somerset   II 26
Blurton connected with Sommers and Cooksey   II 425
Blyth of Howden near Hull co. York   XVII 2
Blythe of the psh of Burchit co. Derby connected with Simpson   III 361
Boak of Yanwath Hall in the psh of Barton, Kirkby Kendall co.
    Westmorland, Eamont Bridge co. Cumberland, and of
    London co. Middlesex   VIII 351
Boardman als Cotes afterwards Bowman   VI 222
Bocking connected with Palmer   XIX 14
Boddington see Bodington
Bodenham co. Wilts, connected with Bourchier   I 561
Bodham connected with Sclater   II 151
Bodicoate of Hackney co. Middlesex connected with Tyssen   VII 21
Bodington, Boddington of London and Enfield co. Middlesex   III 78
Boehm of Dunton Hall co. Lincoln took the surname and arms of
    Trafford   II 106
Bogg of Dunnington co. York connected with Beverley   III 141
Boggett of Swillington connected with Burnell   III 40
Bohemia, Prince Frederick, Elector Palatine, and King of   XVI 9
Bohun Boun of Bakewell and Hulme co. Derby; Coventry and
    Coundon co. Warwick, connected with Clarke of Somersall   VIII 47
———————— connected with Clarke   I 6
———————— Earl of Hereford connected with Stafford and
    Plantagenet   XVI 50

Bokilton of Bokilton co. Worcester connected with Fawkes XIX 6
Bold connected with Wigley and Topp XV 25
Bolland of Boston in New England connected with Shirley and
    Westerne XXI 284
Bolton connected with Pudsey II 430
————— or Boulton of Litchfield, Soho in the psh of Hands-
    worth co. Stafford, Birmingham co. Warwick, connected
    with Robinson IV 388
Bond connected with Corbet IV 514
————————————— Hopkins IX 112
Bond of Hendon co. Middlesex connected with Rundall I 41
————— Baptisms etc VI 278
————— of Limerick Carrickdowning Castle and of Ballinhallisk
    co. Cork VIII 4
————— of London co. Middlesex connected with Whitmore VII 195
————— of Newnham, Newland, Bristol, Redbrook, Huels-
    field co. Gloucester, and of Ailesmore XX 51–3
————— of Peckham co. Surrey IX 95
————— of St Briavels, Redbrook, Wye, Seal in the psh of
    Newland, Bristol, Aylesmore co. Gloucester, and of Walford
    co. Hereford XIX 188
Bonington of Barward Cote VIII 483
Bonner connected with Brayne XV 78
————————————— Morton VIII 421
————— see Bonnor VIII 431
Bonnor of Linton near Ross co. Hereford XX 62
————— of Waller connected with Vaughan VIII 431
Bonsy connected with Sudgrove and Gage XIX 12
Bonytham of Grampound and of Redruth co. Cornwall III 83
Boodle of Ongar co. Essex and of London co. Middlesex
    connected with Mitford I 205
Boot ————— Beard II 181
Booth Lord Delamere connected with Clinton IX 114
————— of Barbadoes, Jamaica West Indies III 116
————— of Killingholme, Market Raisin, Harpeswell, East
    Halton, Thorp Hall, Louth, Spilsby, and of Boston co.
    Lincoln VIII 215
————— of London co. Middlesex connected with Willett VII 491
————— of Market Raisin, Thorpe Hall, Boston co. Lincoln, and
    of Hull co. York VII 106
Booth of Wainflete and Spilsby co. Lincoln II 49
————— of St Mark's Raisin, Thorpe Hall and of Boston co.
    Lincoln VIII 158
Boothby of Friday Hill, Chinkford co. Essex connected with
    Onslowe VI 5
Boquet of London connected with Elwes II 486
Borlace of Great Marlow co. Bucks and of Bockmere V 403
Borrill connected with Miles XIII 17
Borwick ————— Barton III 299
Boscawen of Tregothnen connected with Clinton IX 114
Bostock connected with Short VI 367

Bostock of Churchton co. Chester connected with Draper	IV 22
—————— of Moulton co. Chester connected with Weston	V 82
——————————————————————————————	XVIII 38
—————— of Wicksal co. Salop connected with Huddlestone	XXI 283
Bosvill of Arnsford co. Kent connected with Persall	XVI 19
Boteler of Teston, Saltwood, Tunbridge co. Kent and of Oeston	IV 219
—————— of Watton Woodhall co. Herts	XXI 248
Boteller Baron of Wem and Ousley	XIX 90
Bothe M.I. at Morley co. Derby	VI 106
Botiler of Teston Easton co. Kent, connected with Astyn or Austen	V 388
Botreaux, lord of, connected with Hungerford	XIX 204
—————— of Castle Botreaux co. Cornwall connected with Hungerford and Beaumont	V 50
——————————————— connected with Hungerford	V 243
Boucher of Milcombe co. Oxon connected with Bridoake and Halsted	VIII 162
Bouchier connected with Harris	XXI 186
Boughton of Cawston co. Warwick connected with Berewe	XIX 102
—————— of Little Lawford in the psh of Newbold, Bilton Grange, Rugby co. Warwick and of Poston Court co. Hereford	VIII 410
Boughy connected with Baskerville, Powell, and Kynaston	XVIII 123
Bouldler als Ridge of Hope Bouldler, Brampton, the Hall of Ridge co. Salop, see also Bowdler	VIII 477, 485
Boulton of Almondsbury connected with Rosse	XX 194
—————— see Bolton	IV 388
Boun see Bohun	
Bourchier connected with de Lovanio	XIII 1
—————— of Benningborough connected with Blakiston	II 187
—————— of Berdesley als Barnesley Hatherop co. Gloucester, Stanmore, and of London co. Middlesex	I 558
———————————— co. Gloucester, London and Stanmore co. Middlesex	XIX 48
—————— of Fort St George	IV 408
—————— of Newport Pagnell co. Bucks connected with Cleeve	IV 406
Bourk note as to Barony of Russell	VIII 200
Bourke of Knockny co. Limerick – to take surname and arms of Parker or Grimes	XIII 15
Bourne connected with Wilkins and Hall	XX 235ᵃ
—————— of Cold Bath Fields supposed to be born in Hertfordshire	V 17
—————— of Sutton St Clre co. Somerset connected with Kempe	XIX 56
—————— of Windlebury co. Oxon connected with Hall	II 341
Bournford connected with Feake	XVI 33
Bovey of Flaxley Abbey co. Gloucester see Crawley	XX 93ᵃ
Bowdler afterwards Ridge	VIII 201
—————— of Hope Bowdler co. Salop	VIII 202
———————————— Shrewsbury Arlescot Oswestry Wyke co. Salop, London co. Middlesex Marclegott in the Isle of Kerry in the Kingdom of Ireland and of Worceston; see also Boulder	VIII 205

Bowdler of Ludlow co. Salop, London co. Middlesex, and of
    Sevenoaks co. Kent   VIII 211
——————————— and of the City of Bristol   VIII 209
————— of Woolzaston, Shrewsbury and of Cudercot co. Salop   VIII 203
Bowen of Glandead co. Pembroke, and of London co. Middlesex
    connected with Harris   IV 192
————— of Lllyngwaire   XXI 151
————— of Pembroke connected with Innys   X 48
————— of Southwark connected with Drage   I 92
Bower from co. York, of Ashover, and of Darley Hall co. Derby   IV 40
————— of Hawkwell in the psh of Stamford Ham co. Northum-
    berland connected with Dunford and Stodart   IV 518
Bowerbanke of Culgaith co. Cumberland connected with Dent   VII 480
Bowers connected with de Talbot   XVIII 39
Bowes M.I. St Nicholas Church Newcastle upon Tyne   VII 380
————— of Much Bromley, Upton and Tendring co. Essex   I 276
————— of Newcastle, from Cockermouth co. Cumberland,
    connected with Appleby   X 140
————— of Streatlam Castle co. Palatine Durham, and of Gibside
    co. Northumberland   X 131
Bowett connected with Newdigate and Dormer   XVI 95
Bowle of Chesham co. Bucks, and of Idmiston co. Wilts   VIII 428
Bowles connected with Mills   VI 253
————— Modyford and Norton   VIII 536
————— Powell   I 563
Bowles of London co. Middlesex, Governor of Pendennis Castle co.
    Cornwall, Wanstead co. Essex, East Sheen co. Surrey
    Burford co. Salop, and of Sydmouth co. Devon   VII 392
————— of London co. Middlesex   I 448
———————————————————— and of Southwark co. Surrey   VII 90
————— of London and of Spital Fields co. Middlesex   VIII 173
————— of Shaftesbury, Poole co. Dorset, Brackley co.
    Northampton, Woodford co. Wilts, Rector of Uphill and
    Bream co. Somerset   XXI 187
————— of Shaston, Donhead St Andrew, Fontmill co. Dorset,
    Town Malling co. Kent, Brackley co. Northampton, Bristol
    co. Gloucester, and of Hulhouse and Burcomb co. Wilts,
    connected with Lisle   I 143
Bowman came from Scotland and settled near Newcastle   IV 242
————— connected with Master   II 112
————— formerly Cotes als Broadman   VI 222
————— of Kirk Oswald   X 9
————— Carlisle, Stanton in the psh of Stanwix and
    of Egremont   XXI 12
————— of Mains co. Cumberland, Roehampton co. Surrey and
    of Easby co. Cambridge   VI 222
Bowser of Tortworth and Stone co. Gloucester   XIX 109
Bowyer of Camberwell co. Surrey, connected with Ash and
    Wilson   V 42
————— Cropley and Wilson   XVIII 23
————— of Coles co. Herts connected with Owen   III 311

Bowyer of Combe in the psh of Elkstone, Minchin Hampton co.
    Gloucester and of London co. Middlesex   II 133
Bowyer of Coventry co. Warwick connected with Ashmole   III 134
Boyle Archbishops of Tuam and Armagh   II 328
———————— connected with Clifford and Bedingfield   V 318
Boyne of Titchfield co. Hants connected with Bargus   I 185
Boys connected with Bellingham   XXI 87
———————————— Dalison   XVIII 4
                                       XXI 295
———————— of Hawkhurst connected with Hickes   IV 391
Boyse of Wellesborne co. Warwick connected with Swan and
    Danvers   XIX 14
Brace of Bedford connected with Thurloe   VIII 153
Bracegirdle of Hampton connected with Wightwick   V 77
                                       XVIII 36
Bracken of Underbrough co. Westmorland, and of Greenwich,
    connected with Atkinson   II 41
Brackenbury Brakenbury of Roan and Caen in Normandy, Denton
    Sellabye co. Durham, Southwark, and Lambeth co. Surrey;
    London co. Middlesex, Burnhall, Softely, Kaverston, and of
    lands lying in Bolam, Heighington and Chester   VII 267
———————— lord of the Manors of Sellabie co. Durham, Glastonbury
    co. Somerset, and of Rumney Marsh   XIV 24
Brackus of Claughton co. Lancs connected with Leyburne   XXI 76
Bracy and Clark – certificate of marriage –   XIX 81
Bradborne M.I. at Morley co. Derby   VI 107
Bradburn of Henbury co. Gloucester connected with Webb   XX 259
Bradburne M.I. at Morley co. Derby   VI 108
———————— of Winchester and of Woodlands in Surrey   IX 42
Bradford, Bridgeman Baron   XV 10
———————————— armorial ensigns   VIII 454
———————————— connected with Newport   V 123
Bradford, Newport Earl of   I 315
———————— of London co. Middlesex, and of Philadelphia New
    York   IX 110
———————— of Warwick and of Dortwich   VIII 372
———————— of Wroughton, Can Court in the psh of Lydiard,
    Tregose co. Wilts, Midgehill, Shrivenham, Farnham co.
    Berks, London co. Middlesex and of the East Indies   IV 330
———————— went to America lived at New York many years   V 90
Bradley connected with Peach   I 269
———————— of Bradley co. Palatine Lancs and of Betham co.
    Westmorland   XXI 79
———————— of Hampnet, Combe End in the psh of Elkstone co.
    Gloucester, connected with Dallaway   VIII 26
———————— of Kirkland co. Lancaster, London co. Middlesex, and
    of Westham co. Essex   II 74
Bradney of Pinn co. Stafford connected with Hoare   IV 432
Bradsburn of the Hugh Park co. Derby connected with Babington XVI 91
Bradshaigh of Haigh co. Lancaster M.I.   XIV 4, 5, 9
Bradsham M.I. St Peter's Church Chester   XIV 9

Bradshaw connected with Barnham   III 453
———————————— Hall and Winchcombe   XX 153
————————————   XIX 208
———————————— Heath, Sims and Wollet   XXI 320
———————————— Jackson   XVII 20
———————— M.I. St Peter's Church Chester   XIV 9
———————— note as to will   XVI 27
———————— of Makeney co. Derby   XXI 136
Bragg of Somerset; Banbury co. Oxon, Retford in the psh of
    Clarboro co. Nottingham, Lincoln and of Teddington co.
    Middlesex   IX 80
Brailesford connected with Chandos   VIII 50
Brailsford of South Normanton, Rowthorne, Bolsover, co. Derby,
    Mansfield Woodhouse co. Nottingham and of New York   IX 108
Brain see Brayne
Braithwaite of Wakefield connected with Schofield and Watson IV 85
Brakenbury of Melsonby near Richmond co. York and of Upper
    Deal co. Kent   XXI 210
———————— of St Dunstan's West   IX 71
———————— see Brackenbury
Bramham of Stanley Ferry near Wakefield connected with Pearson III 42
Bramston connected with Turnor and Master   X 59
Branch connected with Sheldon   VII 46
Brand of Edwardston co. Suffolk   XIII 23
——   XVII 44
Brandfield connected with Haine   IV 75
Brandling M.I. St Nicholas Church Newcastle upon Tyne   VII 377
———————— of Spytton Newcastle upon Tyne, Felling, Alnwick co.
    Northumberland; Ipswich co. Suffolk, and of Leathley co.
    York   II 58
———————— of Yorkshire and of Felling near Newcastle; London
    co. Middlesex, and of Gosport   X 129
Brandon connected with Beddome   XV 79
———————————— Seckford   I 198
———————————— Sidney and Dormer   XVI 95
———————— Duke of Suffolk   XIV 18
———————————— Earl of Lincoln   XX 56ª
Brangwin connected with Bowers   XVIII 39
Branson of East Lodford co. Lincoln, connected with Benson   XXI 113
Brathwait of Ambleside, Burnishead and Warcup co. Westmorland XXI 50–2
Brawne M.I. in Kirkby Ravensworth Church   VI 122
Bray connected with de la Barre and Lyons   I 20
———————————— Sandis   XXI 22
———————— of Barrington   XX 54
Brayne connected with Mooner and Tucker   V 179
———————————— Winter   II 197
———————— or Brain of Hanham, Kingswood and of Barfield in the
    psh of Westbury co. Gloucester, of Great Dean and Little XV 74–8,
    Dean co. Gloucester   80–1
Breadalbane, Campbell Earl of, connected with Persall   XVI 19
Brecknocke, Lord of,   XIV 19

Breedon of Beere Court Pangbourne co. Berks; Rectors of
    Croughton co. Northampton, South Morton and of
    Pangbourne co. Berks   XIII 27
———— of South Morton and of Pangborne co. Berks   I 330
Bremar of Charles Town connected with Laurens   III 158
Brereton connected with Stanley   XIII 122
———— M.I.   XX 134
———— of Charlton Kings co. Gloucester, and of Mitcham co.
    Surrey   XX 135
———— of Mitcham co. Surrey, Turk Dean, Charlton Kings,
    and of Cirencester co. Gloucester   XIX 180
Brerewood connected with Gammull   V 80
                                       XVIII 38
Bret of South Moyerton co. Dorset connected with Morgan   VIII 179
Bretagne Earl of, connected with Poulton   XVI 18
Bretherton of Lancaster connected with Browne   III 239
Brett connected with Dacre and Bludworth   III 177
———————————— Marten   VII 99
Brett of Down and Connen, Moynalty and Ficullen in the Counties
    of Meath and Kildare   VII 249
———— of Dublin connected with Smith   IV 532
———— of Leicestershire and of Down Hatherly co. Gloucester   XIX 47
———— of Marvell co. Southampton   VI 102
Brewer als Briggwer, Baron of Adcomb   VIII 252
———— connected with Aldredge   XVII 56
Brewster ———— Darley   VI 375
———— of Lincoln's Inn co. Middlesex, and of Stoke Green co.
    Bucks, connected with Umfrevile   III 519
———— of London co. Middlesex   V 114
———— of Wrentham co. Suffolk connected with Croftes   IV 133
———— of York, and of the Borough of Southwark co. Surrey
    connected with Bigland   XVI 100
Brice afterwards Kingsmill   VII 125
———— connected with Roberts   XIII 104
———— of Kilroot Castle Chichester, Belfast, and of London
    co. Middlesex   VII 125
Brickdale – in the Spanish service –   I 505
———— of West Mankton and of Combe Flory co. Somerset   VII 393
Brickenden Master of Pembroke College Oxon connected with
    Thorpe   XXI 214
———— of North Tidworth co. Wilts connected with Yalden   I 176
Bricknill connected with Depden   VIII 180
Bridge of Shudy Camps and Harston co. Cambridge also of
    Bocking co. Essex   II 376
Bridgeman, Baron Bradford   XV 10
———————————— armorial ensigns of   VIII 454
Bridgeman Lord, connected with Newport   V 123
———— connected with Daston and Langston   XX 109ᵃ
———— Sir Orlando connected with Matthews   V 121
Bridger of Shoreham, Port Slade co. Sussex; Kingston by Sea,

Narborough co. Leicester, and of Thorpe — I 62
——————— of Isle of Wight in Virginia — IV 235
——————— of Warminghurst, Ashurst and of Combe Sussex — III 420
Bridges als Bruges of Neinde, Lovettwood, Woodchester, Crom-
 wal, Colesburn, Titherington co. Gloucester, and of
 London co. Middlesex — XIX 52
——————— connected with Bevis and Trapps — V 46
——————————————————————————————— — XVIII 92
——————————————— Jones of Treverne co. Radnor — I 112
——————— Duke of Chandos connected with Scudamore — XVII 33
——————— of Keynsham co. Somerset — XX 56
——————————————— Coborly co. Gloucester, Sudoley Castle;
 Tangley, Cornbury, Shorhampton, co. Oxon, and of
 Chidleigh co. Devon — IX 30
——————— of Keynsham connected with Speke — II 379
——————— of Up Leadon co. Hereford — IX 66
Bridgewater, Earl of, connected with Spencer — VI 55
Bridgman connected with Windsor — XIII 5
Bridoake of co. Oxon connected with Boucher — VIII 163
Briggs connected with Bromfield — XVIII 49
——————————————— Chandler and Brooke — II 369
——————— M.I. at Cheam — VI 128
——————— of Calmire co. Westmorland — XXI 77
——————— of Haughton connected with Wilbraham — V 129
——————— of London co. Middlesex, of Holt, Lord and Patron of — IV 164
 the Town, connected with Bromfield
Briggwer als Brewer Baron of Adcomb — VIII 252
Brigham of Cannon End — XIII 29
Bright connected with Beddome and Cooke — XV 76
——————— formerly Liddel — XVI 21
——————— of Carbrook co. Yorks connected with Westby — VII 511
Brinckhurst of the Moore in the County of Bucks — IX 21[b]
——————————————————————————— connected with
 Barnewall and Carson — III 181
Brindley of Mertham co. Cornwall connected with Totman — III 347
Brindsley co. Notts connected with Butler — VI 204
Brisco connected with Western — VII 505
Briscoe lord of Briscoe, of Crofton Westwood co. Cumberland,
 and of Aldenham co. Herts — XXI 12[c,d]
——————— of London and of Charles County in Maryland — IV 26
Bristow of Southrope co. Gloucester — XX 61[a]
——————— of the family of Bristow of Ayot St Lawrence co.
 Herts, of London co. Middlesex, and of Quidenham Hall
 co. Norfolk — XIII 25
Brittany, Earl of — VIII 249
Britten of Daventry co. Northampton, and of London — IX 146
Broc, de la, see Brooke — X 78
Brocas of Beaurepair co. Southampton and of Wokefield co. Berks — XXI 139
——————— of Beaurepei co. Southampton connected Webb and
 Nott — XIX 89

Brockbank M.I.   XIV 8
Brockholes formerly Fitzherbert of Claughton, & Heton co.
    Palatine Lancaster   V 4
────────── formerly Hesketh   V 3
Broderick of Wandsworth co. Surrey, and of Jamaica West Indies –
    Lord Middleton –   II 57
Brodway of Postlip and of Winchcombe co. Gloucester   XIX 256
Broke of Nacton co. Suffolk   IX 90
Brokushole connected with Lewis   IX 93
Brome of Coleshill co. Warwick and of Melton co. Leicester   IV 421
Bromfield of London co. Middlesex   IV 162
                                                                                  XVIII 48
────────── of Odomer Ewhurst co. Sussex, Suffolk Place co.
    Surrey, and of Barton under Need Wood co. Stafford   IV 149
────────── of Odemere; Suffolk Place co. Surrey and of Ilford in
    Barking co. Essex   VI 64
────────── of Odomer co. Sussex, Suffolk Place co. Surrey
    Burton under Needwood co. Stafford and of the City of
    London   XVIII 51
Bromilow of Risley near Warrington Prescott co. Lancaster and of
    Billings   V 215
Bromley connected with Worthington   III 449
────────── M.I. Worcester Cathedral   XIV 9
────────── of Thaworden co. Salop connected with Newport   I 316
Brompton of Tedstone co. Salop   IX 151
                                                                                  XI 180
Bromwich connected with Lewis and Nanson   XIX 170
────────── of Frampton on Severn and of Titherington co.
    Gloucester   XIX 159
Brook Brooks of York   VI 88
────────── connected with Grey   XXI 208
────────── Gulston   XV 10
────────── Pockley and Osbaldeston   XXI 234
────────── Knight of the Rhodes of Norton and of Meere   I 249
────────── York Herald   X 64
Brooke connected with Maude   IX 53
────────── de la Broc, of Leighton, Bertunley Norton in Cheshire
    and of Pukye in Lancashire   X 78
Brooke Earls of Warwick   XVI 82
────────── Greville Lord of Beauchamp Court co. Warwick and
    of Thorp Latimer co. Lincoln   XVI 20
────────── Lord see Willoughby   XIV 16
────────── of Aspall Hall, Athlington, and of Ufford co. Suffolk   III 366
────────── of Blacklands co. Stafford, and of Shiffnall co. Salop   II 369
────────── of Burton Hall in the psh of Gateforth co. York,
    connected with Hammond and Hawke   III 354
────────── of Grove House Brownsberrow co. Gloucester
    connected with Thackwell   XX 95[a]
────────── of Madeley co. Salop connected with Brudenell   XIV 22
────────── of Malden co. Essex connected with Crump   IV 1
────────── of Nacton co. Suffolk connected with Bowes   I 278

Brooke of Norton Bartby connected with Legh   III 309
———— of Norton in Cheshire Pukye in Lancashire connected
    with Audley   X 77
———— of Stepney co. Middlesex connected with Spurrell   IV 1
———— of the County of Cavan in Ireland   VII 472
———— Sir Fulke Grevill, Lord   XVI 82
———— Willoughby, Lord   XVI 82
Brooks afterwards Shene of Little Dunham co. Norfolk   III 485
———— of Bromley connected with Wilbie   II 451
———— or Brook of York   VI 88
Brough Lord of Brough co. York and of Hulford connected with
    Lawson   XXI 285
Brougham of Cockermouth, Dovenby, co. Cumberland afterwards
    Lamplugh   V 302
Broughton of Broughton co. Stafford and of Loudham co. Notts,
    Bart.   VI 57
———— of co. Denbigh called himself a Baronet   VI 2
———— of Kington co. Hereford connected with Jones and
    Chinn   I 112
Brown Browne of Haverhill co. Suffolk and of Halsted co. Essex   III 206
———— connected with Bathurst   XX 41[a]
———— Cuttel   IV 282
———— Duncombe   III 30
———— Mayne   XV 43
———— Walker   IX 69
———— of Betchworth Castle co. Surrey, Deptford co. Kent
    and of Caversham co. Oxon   IX 23
———— of Boltons   XXI 272[a]
———— of Brockley in the Shire of Berwick, Blackburn and of
    London co. Middlesex   II 15
———— of Carmarthen connected with Evans   VIII 457
———— of Frampton connected with Trenchard   VIII 188
———— of London co. Middlesex connected with Vernon and
    Nicoll   III 137
———— of Melton Mowbray, Loughborough co. Leicester,
    Little Leake co. Nottingham, London co. Middlesex, and of
    Derby   III 2
———— of Minty connected with Nott   XIX 88
———— of Newbury co. Berks   V 144
———— of Shidley co. Wilts connected with Angell   XI 55–6
Browne according to family tradition descended from the ancient
    and Knightly family of Browne, of Abbess Roding, Weald
    Hall and Wickham Hall in Essex, and of Brownes Hill in the
    psh of Catherlough   IV 525
Browne afterwards Duncombe   IV 291
———— Mill   XI 42
———— Selby   VI 224
———— als Duncombe   III 30
———— Brown of Haverhill co. Suffolk and of Halsted co.
    Essex   III 206
———— connected with Angell   I 77

Browne connected with Mabb and Acton   XIX 6
———————————— Paston   IX 113^b
———————————— Pym and Vernon also Nicoll   II 465
———————————— Savage   XVI 23
———————— formerly Eaton of Downham and Elsing co. Norfolk   VII 39
———————— Folkes of Grays Inn co. Middlesex and of Hillington
co. Norfolk   V 232
———————— of Antigua and of London co. Middlesex   VI 231
———————————— connected with Bretherton   III 239
———————— of Beckwith Castle Darking   IV 488
———————— of Beechworth in Surrey and of Singleton near
Ashford in Kent connected with Bourchier   XIX 48
———————— of Betchworth Castle in the psh of Darking co. Surrey
– Baronet   XVIII 1
———————— of Bodmin co. Cornwall, and of London co.
Middlesex   VI 177
———————— of Bristol connected with Tippetts   V 311
———————— of Buckland co. Surrey   XVIII 1
———————————————————— connected with Browne of
Beckwith Castle, Darking   IV 488
———————— of Campfield Place co. Herts, connected with
Barrington   IX 73
———————— of Catherlough and Browne's Hill, according to
tradition descended from the ancient & Knightly family of
Abbess Roding Wickham Hall co. Essex   I 462
Browne of Cowdrey, Midhurst Eatstbourne co. Sussex Caversham
co. Oxon, West Shifford co. Berks, Wickham Brewes co.
Kent, Elsing co. Norfolk, Kiddington co. Oxon, Pirbright
co. Surrey, & Methley co. Warwick – Viscount Montagu   VI 209
———————— of English Bicknor co. Gloucester connected with
Lane   XIII 119
———————— of Frampton, Forstan, Godmanston, Blandford St
Mary co. Dorset   VII 346
———————— of Frampton and St. Mary Blandford co. Dorset   X 162
———————— of Gatcombe Isle of Wight co. Hants, connected with
Urry   III 514
———————— of Gloucester and of London co. Middlesex   XIX 258
———————— of Kiddington co. Oxford connected with Pitt   X 23, 159
———————— of London co. Middlesex   IV 490
———————————— connected with Cooper and Drury   X 29
———————————— connected with Watts   XVIII 1
———————— of Northern Islands of Scotland, of Draffin co. Lanark,
and of Fowlford, see also Browne of Prior Hall   XV 13
———————— of Norwich co. Norfolk   III 522
———————————— and of Peckham Surrey   VII 124
——————————————————————————   VII 342
———————— of Oakingham co. Berks connected with Boak   VIII 351
———————— of Pitchford, Lawley, Sowbatch, Roden, Lond Stan-
ton, Shrewsbury co. Salop, Nantwich co. Chester and of
Bay Hall in Kent   VI 224
———————— of Prior Hall descended from the Brownes of Draffin

in Lanarkshire – see also Brownes of Northern Islands of
    Scotland   XI 1, 2
——————— of Shawdon, Branton, and Bolton co. Northumberland
    and of Rochester co. Kent   V 466
Browne of Sherdicote co. Stafford, Hungry, Bentley, co. Derby
    Withington and Upton co. Salop, St Ives co. Huntingdon
    and of London co. Middx   V 468
——————— of South Weald, Shenfield, and of Baddow co. Essex   II 127
——————— of Westerham co. Kent, and of Stoke Newington   VI 229
——————— of West Wycombe Bucks, Alford co. Lincoln,
    Debenham co. Suffolk, and of London co. Middlesex   I 64
——————— of Wickham Hall, Southweald, Hutton, Brentwood,
    Shenfield, and Baddow co. Essex   I 460
——————— Viscount Montague   IX 120
Browne-Mill   XI 42
Brownell of London, Whitechapel co. Middlesex and of Lambeth
    co. Surrey   II 316
Browning of Bermondsey co. Surrey, Blackheath co. Kent, and of
    Edinburgh   VII 192
——————— of Coaley and of Aust co. Gloucester   XIX 83
——————————— connected with Smyth   XIX 143
Brownlow co. Derby, High Holborn co. Middlesex, Kirby under
    Wood, Great Humby, Belton co. Lincoln, Baron Charleville
    and Viscount Tyrconnel   IX 9
Brownrigg of Brownrigg in Cumberland, Beccles, Rishangles,
    Clopton, Bury St Edmunds, and of Willisham co. Suffolk   XI 34–7
——————— of Park Annesley, Cranvilla, Norris, Mount, co.
    Wexford   VII 439
——————— of Park Annesley, Logan, Wingfield co. Wexford,
    Tubber Patrick Buckingham co. Wicklow and of Dublin   XI 38
Bruce of Kinloss, Earl of Elgin, Earl of Aylesbury connected with
    Rolle   VI 390
Bruce of London co. Middlesex connected with Johnson   III 113
Brudenel of Upton near Windsor connected with Dipden and
    Waller   XVIII 96
Brudenell connected with Entwisel   XI 26
——————— Earl of Cardigan connected with Bruce   VI 392
——————— of Dene co. Northumberland   XIV 22
Bruen connected with Joll or Jol   XVI 30
————————————— Martin   XXI 224–5
Bruges see Bridges   XIX 52
Bruin connected with Dennis   XIII 103
Brulie had large possessions in the County of Oxford, of
    Waverstock co. Oxford   XIX 14
Brumsell of Dover co. Kent   IV 99
————————————— connected with Bagster and Walker   III 350
Brusse of Gower connected with Hookes and with Lord Rees
    Prince of South Wales   XVIII 104
Bryan of Marklock co. Somerset; Weymouth co. Dorset, and of
    Westborne co. Sussex   IX 4
Bryant of Ryegate co. Surrey connected with Andrews   VIII 270

Brydgeman of Dean Magna and of Nympsfield co. Gloucester   XIX 214
Brydges connected with Creyghton   XIII 115
———————— of Old Colwall co. Hereford connected with Jones   II 418
Buck connected with Green   XXI 320
———————————— Greene   IX 142
———————— of Dambrooke in Craven co. York connected with
    Dawson   II 436
Buckee of Shoreditch connected with Thorowgood   IV 61
Buckhurst, Sackville Baron   XVI 53
Buckingham connected with Waldegrave   X 25
Buckingham, Duke of, Earl Stafford   XVI 50
Buckland connected with Fermour   VIII 497
———————————— and Benolt   V 6
Buckley formerly Forster   II 276
———————— of Ashton under Lyne and Manchester co. Lancaster   XV 60
———————— of Buckley in the psh of Rochdale co. Lancs   II 276
Bucknall of Oxey near Watford co. Herts, London co. Middx,
    Epsom co. Surrey, and of Bengal   II 139
Buckston of Bradbourne, Smalley co. Derby, Loughborough co.
    Leicester connected with Brown   III 3
Buckstone or Buxton of Coggeshall co. Essex extracts from
    Registers   VI 342
Buckton of Belyngeland and of Bucton co. York connected with
    Collingwood   XV 7
Budgell of St Thomas near Exeter   XV 10
Bugge of Leake co. Nottingham lord of Thurleston and Westerleck
    co. Leicester connected with Moton and Pole   VIII 53
Bull connected with Davys   I 149
———————— of Bromsgrove co. Hereford connected with Rees or
    Rhys   IV 348
Buller connected with Yard   XVIII 113
———————————— Yarde   III 507
———————— of Down co. Devon connected with Coxe   II 421
———————— of Shillingham, Morvall, Keverell co. Cornwall,
    Ospring co. Kent, Downes co. Devon afterwards Yarde
    Buller   XVIII 53
Bully of London co. Middlesex connected with Witham and Dean   IV 381
Bulman M.I. St Nicholas Church Newcastle upon Tyne   VII 376
Bulmer extract from Register   XVI 80
———————— of Newcastle co. Northumberland connected with
    Errington   IV 520
Bulstrode connected with Huncks   XIX 149
———————— of London co. Middlesex and of Tewkesbury co.
    Gloucester   XIX 198
Bulteel connected with Forterie   IV 485
                                                                 XVIII 145
Bundy in the psh of St Anne in the Island of Jamaica connected
    with Snowden   IV 399
Bunting of Hilborough, Sporle, and of Diglington co. Norfolk   IV 45
Burder of Bugden co. Huntingdon, Southwark, co. Surrey,
    Islington co. Middlesex and of Coventry co. Warwick   II 215

Burdet connected with Jones and Ernley	V 341
Burdett of Arrow co. Warwick connected with Conway	XI 16
———— of Hornsey, London co. Middlesex, and of Bracknell co. Berks	V 180
Burdon of South Shields, Newcastle, and Sedgefield co. Durham	X 130
Burge of Jamaica West Indies connected with Griffin	XXI 184
Burges connected with Wood	X 61
———— see Burgess	IV 338
Burgess of Berks; Odiham co. Hants, and of London co. Middlesex	XV 45
———— of Ludsdon co. Kent	II 373
———— of New York connected with Afflack	VIII 397
———————————————— Middleton & Hardy	II 244
———— or Burges connected with Somerville	IV 338
Burghall of Bunbury co. Chester	I 224
Burghall of Bunbury co. Chester	IV 194
Burgis see Burgess	XV 45
Burgoyne of Sutton Park co. Bedford connected with Burton	V 22
Burgum of Flaxley Bristol and of Little Dean co. Gloucester	XX 68–ᵃ
Burke connected with Skerrett	I 89
Burland connected with Popham	III 235
———————— and Portman	XVIII 131
———— of Wooton under Edge co. Gloucester	VIII 420
————————————————————————	XX 30ᵃ
Burley of Malhurst, Asterley and Shrewsbury connected with Hopton	VIII 27
———— M.I. at Pontesbury Church and St Aulkmonds Church Shrewsbury both co. Salop	VI 113
Burlington, Clifford Earl of, connected with Boyle and Bedingfield	V 318
Burnaby of Broughton Poges co. Oxford	IX 39
Burnel M.I. at Winkburn Church co. Nottingham	VI 116
Burnell connected with Hungerford	V 48
————————————————————————	V 235
————————————————————————	XIX 204
———————————— Strelley	XXI 323
———————————— Wombwell	III 292
———— of Bermondsey and Southwark co. Surrey also of Coventry co. Warwick	II 329
———— of London co. Middlesex Coddicote, Bury, co. Herts, and of Jamaica	II 203
———— of Twickenham, London co. Middlesex, and of co. Herts	IV 186
———— of Woodlesford, Leeds co. York, and of London co. Middlesex connected with Pearson	III 40
Burnell of Wootton under Edge co. Gloucester, Bath co. Somerset and of Shoreditch co. Middlesex	IV 56
Burnett of Kingston upon Hull co. York, and of London co. Middlesex, connected with Stanton	II 109
———— of Leys in the psh of Upper Banchory, Balmain co. Kincardine afterwards Ramsay	XV 55

Burnett of Thames Ditton co. Surrey, and of London co.
  Middlesex connected with Beverley   III 142
Burnford of London co. Middlesex connected with Feake   XVI 93
Burnham of Southwark co. Surrey connected with Meade   III 453
Burrell connected with Collingwood   XV 6
——————— of Cuckfield and of Lindfield co. Sussex   II 27
——————————————————————— and of Beck-
  enham co. Kent   II 195
——————— of Cuckfield Lindfield co. Sussex and of London co.
  Middlesex   II 417
——————— of Howtell co. Cumberland   XXI 33
———————   XXI 191ᵃ

Burrough of Clarendon Park near Salisbury, Devizes co. Wilts,
  Lymington co. Hants, and of Bristol co. Gloucester   IV 175
Burroughs M.I. St Peter's Church Chester   XIV 9
Burrow of Christ Church, Clapham, Starborough Castle co.
  Surrey, Leghorn, Marseilles, London co. Middlesex, and of
  Holwood Hill co. Kent   I 567
Burrowes connected with Hodges   V 283
Burrows connected with Gardner and Powell   I 564
Burslem of Packington, Stanton co. Derby; Market Bosworth co.
  Leicester and of Flintham co. Nottingham   V 196
Burt connected with Champneys   V 158
Burton ——————— Brereton   XX 135
Burton connected with Norton   VIII 537
——————————————— Ryder   X 19
——————————————— Wigley   XV 25
——————— of Bramley Hall in the psh of Handsworth   V 19
——————— of Cartledge and Apperknowle in the psh of Dronfield,
  Holmesfield, Chesterfield co. Derby Fanshaw Gate, London
  co. Middlesex, Putney co. Surrey, Royd Mill in the psh of
  Sheffield and of Bramley Hall in the psh of Hansworth co.
  York   V 21
——————— of Hotham, Hull, Bank co. York, connected with
  Christie   III 94
——————— of Luffenham co. Rutland connected with Pitt   X 23, 158
——————— M.I. St Nicholas Church Newcastle upon Tyne   VII 375
Bury connected with Taylor   III 224
Busby connected with Bromfield   IV 149
Bush of Bristol co. Gloucester   XX 59ᵃ
Bushell of Broad Merston, Dry Merston co. Gloucester, Prior
  Cleve co. Worcester, and of Wells co. Somerset   XIX 151
Busk of Bullhouse and of Leeds co. York connected with Rodes,
  Rich, and Milnes   XV 16–7
Bustle of London co. Middlesex connected with Lloyd   IV 190
Butcher came from Bedfordshire of Appleshaw co. Hants   II 319
——————— formerly of Cople and of Ravensden co. Bedford   VIII 367
Butler Baron of Coher   XVII 8
——————— connected with Pleydell   XIX 112
——————————————— Poole   XIX 80

Butler Earl of Ormond, will of   IX 161
——————— of Apletree in the psh of Aston in the Walls co.
    Northampton   XX 69
——————— of Aston in the Walls Lickborough co. Northampton   XXI 153
——————— of Boston New England   I 504
——————— of Byfleet near Shepperton, London co. Middlesex and
    of co. Kent   III 86
——————— of Crediton, Buckland Brewer co. Devon, connected
    with Haine and Rouse   IV 73
——————— of Hatfield connected with Waller   XVIII 98
——————— of London co. Middlesex connected with Dobson   III 408
——————— of Waresley co. Huntingdon, Stratford near Baldock,
    Finny Drayton, St Ives co. Cambridge, Tewing or Tew-
    ingbury co. Herts, Belterbel co. Cavan Lord Newtown,
    Viscount Lanesborough   VI 203
Butt connected with Driver   I 172
——————— of Bradford   XX 226ᵃ
Butteller of Yatton co. Somerset, and of Wiche, also of
    Shernebrooke co. Bedford   IV 218
Butterworth connected with Oakden and Chadwyk   XI 27
——————— of Rochdale or Windybank connected with Lodge   VII 474
——————— of Thorrock Green Hall near Blackburn Birmingham
    and Coventry co. Warwick also of London co. Middlesex   XVII 5
Button of Alton Prior, Tockenham Court co. Wilts and of
    Lyneham Court   V 429
——————— of Alton in Wilts and of Buckland near Limington   XX 64
——————— of Laindon Hills and of Mucking Hall co. Essex   VII 117
Button of Laindon Hill and of Mucking Hall co. Essex   VII 307
Buxton of Bakewell co. Derby, and of London co. Middlesex
    connected with Cowie   IX 106
——————— or Buckstone of Coggeshall co. Essex, extracts from   VI 342
    Registers
Byerley of Hardwick co. Palatine Durham connected with Frevile
    and Clerke   XII 29–47
——————— of Middleridge Grange, Hardwick co. Durham, and of
    Goldesborough co. York   VII 168–70
Byfield connected with de la Barre   I 19
Byles of near Blandford co. Dorset   III 166
Byndlose Bynelosse of Hailston co. Westmorland Borwick Hall
    co. Palatine Lancaster see also Bindlosse   VII 365
Byndlosse of Hailston co. Weston, Borwick Hall co. Palatine Lancs
    see also Bindlosse   XXI 49
——————— of Jamaica connected with Gregory and Beckford see
    also Bindlosse   I 192
Byne of Rowdel co. Sussex connected with Spence   IX 69
Byng of Wrotham co. Kent – Viscount Torrington   XXI 256
———   X 59
Bynks of Richmond co. York connected with Moore   V 10
Byrche M.I. Worcester Cathedral   XIV 9
Byrkin of St Briavels co. Gloucester connected with Davies   XIX 131

Byrne afterwards Leycester or Leicester   VI 156
──────── of Newry co. Wicklow and of Byrnes Grove co.
    Kilkenny   II 229
──────── of Newry co. Wicklow, co. Kilkenny, co. Leicester,
    Cappanteely co. Dublin, Knight & Baronet   I 119
──────── Sir Gregory Bart of Ireland   XXI 203
Byrom of Byrom in Lancs & of Dudleston near Chester   VIII 62–5

C

Cabell of Buckfastleigh co. Devon, Marshfield co. Gloucester and
    of London co. Middlesex   XX 89[a]
Cade connected with Whitworth   XX 242[a]
──────── of Sutton Bangor co. Wilts connected with Flower   I 328
Cadman of Tutbury co. Stafford connected with Parkes   III 5
Cadull connected with Hyet   X 69
──────── and Arthur   XIX 158
Caesar als Adelmare connected with Angell   I 79
Cage of London co. Middlesex   XIX 206
Caldwall of Didlick co. Salop, and of Beaudley co. Worcester   IX 61
Caldwell of Aston, Mitton, co. Stafford, Portbury co. Somerset,
    and of London co. Middlesex   XXI 131
Caley of Malton Brompton, Thormandby co. York and of New-
    lands co. Warwick   VI 73
Callis of Deptford, Bexley, Eltham, and of Foots Cray co. Kent   XXI 284
Callowhill connected with Jordan   I 526
Calmady of Combes Head in the psh of Stoke Climsland co.
    Cornwall connected with Hamlyn   II 286
──────── of Farwood in the psh of Colliton Wembury co.
    Devon, and of London co. Middlesex   VI 174
Calthorpe connected with Grose   IX 57
──────── of Calthorpe, Cockthorpe Antingham and of Hickling
    co. Norfolk   XVII 3
Calver als Carver als Calvert als Wright of Thorpe Abbots
    Needham co. Norfolk and of Brundish Lodge co. Suffolk   V 26
Calver als Carver als Wright als Calvert see Carver   VIII 40
Calverley of Calverley co. York afterwards Blacket   VII 217
Calvert als Calver als Carver als Wright see Carver   VIII 41
──────── Lord Baltimore of Ireland connected with Wyndham   I 544
──────── of Borrowbridge co. York – Lord Baltimore   XXI 181
──────── of Brundish co. Suffolk M.I.   VIII 44
──────── of Preston connected with Jackson   XVII 20
──────── of Redmire near Richmond   IX 24

Calvert see Calver	V 26
Cam connected with Ford	VII 184
———————— of Cam Dursley co. Gloucester and of London co. Middlesex	II 295
———————— of Coaley and Dymock co. Gloucester	XX 94ª–94ᶜ
———————————————— Sapperton near Michen Hampton co. Gloucester connected with Wilkins	XX 245ª
Cambell of Folsham co. Norfolk, London co. Middlesex, Woodford, Clayhall co. Essex, Baronet	VI 76
Cambridge of Quar and of Theesecomb in the psh of Hampton	IX 28
———————— of Wheatehurst and of Twickenham co. Middlesex connected with Small	II 96
———————— of Woodchester, Minchinhampton, Horsley co. Gloucester and of Twickenham co. Middx	XX 72ª
———————— of Woodchester co. Gloucester, extracts from will	VIII 508
————————————————————————————————	X 70
———————— Richard Earl of	XVI 9
Came of Bristol and of Compton Greenfield co. Gloucester connected with Gunning	XX 131
Camel connected with Stebbing	VII 320
Camerton, Gospatrick lord of	II 456
Campbell connected with Worsley and Troughear	VI 237
Campbell Earl of Breadalbane connected with Persall	XVI 19
———————— of Calder Milton Ernys co. Bedford and of Sweden Earls of Argyle	II 155
Campden, Noel Viscount, connected with Hickes	XIX 240
Campling afterwards Mayhew	XVII 53
Candish connected with Brandon	XX 56ª
Cann Knight and afterwards Baronet	I 10
———————— of Busselton co. Somerset	XX 96ª
Cannell of Kirk Michael Isle of Man	II 129
———————— of London co. Middlesex – came out of Northamptonshire	VII 404
Canning of the City of Bristol, Foxcote co. Warwick, Enston co. Oxon, Garvagh in Londonderry, London co. Middlesex, Bewdley co. Worcester, and of Elsenham co. Essex	XII 56–65
Cannynge of London co. Middlesex	XII 61
Cantelow see Cantilupe	XVI 18
Cantelupe of Snitterfield co. Worcester connected with Bushell	XIX 151
Canter connected with Thornborough	XXI 90
Cantillon connected with Newland	X 18
Cantilupe or Cantelow of Aston Cantilow, Lord Abergavenny, connected with Paulton	XVI 18
Capel of Hadham co. Herts connected with Bedell	V 454
———————— of Pitchecombe, Stroud, Wooton under Edge co. Gloucester, Warminster co. Wilts, and of Bermondsey co. Surrey	XX 81
Caper of Rugeley co. Stafford, and of Birmingham co. Warwick	XXI 176
Carbery Lord connected with Horton	II 177
Carboile Earl of, lord of Toring in Normandy	XXI 272

Cardale of Dudley, Hagley co. Worcester & of White Notley   I 334
Cardigan Brudenell Earl of, connected with Bruce   VI 392
Carew Carree or Carrio of Crocombe, Holcomb or Hacombe in
    Devonshire   X 77
———————— formerly Gee   XIII 6
———————— Lord of Carew, Mulfford and Odron, Beddington co.
    Surrey, Haccombe co. Devon, and of Anthony co.
    Cornwall   XIII 5, 6
———————— of Somerset   I 266
———————— or Throgmorton   XIII 6
Carey Earl of Dover connected with Cockaine   I 97
Carington connected with Bowles   VIII 172
Carleton of Swaffham co. Norfolk   IX 119
Carlisle, Howard Earl of, connected with Grahme   III 510
——————————————————————————— Visct. Preston   XVIII 54
———————— of Antigua connected with Payne   IV 170
Carlos of Broomhall co. Stafford   XXI 324
Carlton connected with Dillingham   IX 101
———————— of Lady Holton connected with Plowden   XXI 201
Carlyon of Tregrehan in the psh of St Blazey, St Just, St Austel,
    and of Truro co. Cornwall   I 530
Carnaby of Beaufront   X 146
——   XXI 1
——   XXI 120^q
———————— of Halton co. Northumberland connected with
    Errington   XVI 36
Carne connected with Windham   II 85
Carnes lived near Edinburgh migrated to Boston New England,
    thence to Jamaica of Demerara and Philadelphia   IX 97
Carpenter connected with Andrew   III 242
———————— of Huelsfield St Briavells co. Gloucester   XX 78^a
Carr connected with Biggs   X 136
———————— formerly Ellison   X 135
———————————————— Hay   IV 385
———————— of Cocken co. Durham, and of Deal co. Kent   X 135
———————— of Etall co.Northumberland connected with Hay Earl
    of Errol   IV 385
———————— of Iniskilling in Ireland and of Twickenham co.
    Middlesex connected with Short   IV 397
——   IX 74
———————— M.I. St Nicholas Church Newcastle upon Tyne   VII 375
——   VII 377
———————— of Suffolk   III 520
Carrant connected with Reed   XIX 254
Carree Carrio see Carew   X 77
Carrell connected with Howard   XIV 21
Carrick of Willington co. Warwick connected with Wigley   XV 25
Carrio Carree see Carew   X 77
———————— see Carew   XIII 5
Carrow of Lynn connected with Smith of Ely and Norfolk   VI 91

Carru see Carew	XIII 5
Carter connected with Harrison	IV 405
———————— of Barford co. Oxon connected with Ford	V 293
———————————————————————————	XI 39
———————— of Charlton Abbots co. Gloucester	XIX 77
———————————————— Alverscott, Brisenorton co. Oxford, and of Knolle in Blockley co. Worcester	XX 83
———————— of London co. Middlesex, and of South Weston co. Oxon	XVII 44
Carteret of Trinity Manor in the Island of Jersey	VIII 437
Cartwright M.I.	IX 49
———————— of Lyme from Lancaster connected with Gundry and Warren	I 488
———————— of the Bank House in the Township of Oddrode in the psh of Astbury in Cheshire	XV 82–4
———————— of Washbourne Tredington co. Gloucester and of London co. Middlesex	XX 92
and of Crickley in the psh of Badgworth	XIX 71
Carus M.I.	XIV 6
———————— of Esthwaite, Kirkby Lonsdale, Kendal co. Westmorland, and of Halton co. Palatine Lancaster	XXI 62, 104
———————— of Kirkby Lonsdale Kendal co. Westmorland connected with Thornborough and Bigland	VIII 319
Carver als Calver als Calvert als Wright of Thorp Abbots, Norwich, Needham co. Norfolk, and of Brundish Lodge co. Suffolk	VIII 42
co. Norfolk and of Brundish Lodge co. Suffolk	VIII 40
———————— see Calver	V 26
Cary claims the title of Lord Hunsdon	III 475
———————— connected with Mildmay	IX 33
———————————————— Stafford and Courteney	XVI 62
———————— of Castle Cary, Cockington Plashy co. Devon, Launceston co. Cornwall, Berkhampstead co. Herts, Levengrove co. York, and of Stanwell co. Middlesex – Viscounts Falkland	V 188
———————— of Charles Town near Boston in New England connected with Russell and Graves	III 157
———————— of Derry, Redcastle and of Castle Cary co. Donegal	IX 5
Cary of Plashy, Holway, Cockington co. Devon, Berkhampstead co. Herts, Viscount Falkland in Scotland	VIII 247
Casamajor connected with East	X 11
Cassamajor of Bristol Tockington and Stapleton co. Gloucester	I 380
Casson M.I.	XIV 8
Castelman of Bridgewater co. Somerset, London co. Middlesex, Beddington co. Surrey, and of Horseley co. Gloucester	XIX 105
Castile Ferdinando King of, connected with Hookes	XVIII 105
Castle Lion als Skeirne lord of Skeirne and Norththroppe connected with Hotham	XVIII 82
Castlemain, Child, Viscount	XIII 61

Castlemaine, Palmer Earl of	XIII 60
Castleman of Painswick Horsley, Barton End co. Gloucester connected with Skinn	III 146
———— see Castleman	XIX 105
———— of Warminster co. Wilts and of Langport co. Somerset	II 370
Caswell of Clifton upon Teme and Meadows Field co. Worcester	XX 88
Catchmay of Bigsware	XIII 37
———— of Biggesware co. Gloucester, Comehoy co. Somerset, and of Trelleck co. Monmouth	XIX 194
———— of Bigswear co. Gloucester	XX 10
———— of Biggesware co. Gloucester and of Trelick co. Monmouth	XX 79[a]
———— note as to pedigree	IX 82
Catchmayd of Monmouth afterwards Gwinnett	XX 128[a]
Cavan Earl of	XVII 7
Cave M.I. in Winkburn Church co. Nottingham	VI 116
———— of Yateminster Evershot co. Dorset and of Bristol co. Gloucester	III 281
Cavendish formerly de Gernon, of Glemsford, Grimston Hall, Trimley St Martyn co. Suffolk, Chatsworth, Moor Hall co. Derby, Tutbury co. Stafford and of Welbeck Abbey, Baron Cavendish of Hardwick, Earl of Ogle, Duke of Newcastle, and Duke of Devonshire K.G.	XVI 68
Cecil connected with Porter	XVII 34
———— Earl of Exeter	XX 139
———— Salisbury connected with Tufton	XVI 58
———— see Cecyll	XVI 76
Cecill of Walsington in Ashperton co. Hereford and of Bristol	XIX 82
Cecyll of Thornbury co. Gloucester	XVI 76
Cellam als Davies of Kellam co. Cardigan	XIX 131
Chadwick see Chadwyck	XI 26
———— of Haslingden co. Lancaster	XXI 249
———— and of London co. Middlesex – went to Ireland in the time of Cromwell	VIII 442
Chadwyck Chadwick of Heley co. Northumberland of Spotland and Honursfeld in the psh of Rochdale co. Lancaster, connected with Entwistle	XI 26
Chalfhunt of Chalfhunt co. Bucks, held the Manors of Ashurst and Frensted co. Kent connected with Waller	XVIII 96
Chalmers of Balnecraig and Cults	V 365
———— of Hatfield Peverell connected with Simpson	II 342
———— of London co. Middlesex, Edinburgh and of Portsmouth co. Hants	V 378
Chaloner of Denbigh, Chester and of London co. Middlesex connected with Mathew and Hookes	XVIII 109
Chamberlain connected with Luddington and Kirkby	XIII 97
———— of Astley in the County of Warwick, New House in Hereford and of Dymock co. Gloucester	XIII 74
———— of the Boyce in the psh of Dymock co. Gloucester, see also Chamberlayne	XIII 106

Chamberlaine or Chamberlen of Tankerville in Normandy, London co. Middlesex, and of Paris   II 254

———— see Chamberlayne   XX 80[b,c]

Chamberlan connected with Roberts   XVI 89

Chamberlayne of Newhouse co. Hereford, the Boyce in the psh of Dymock, and of Bristol co. Gloucester, see also Chamberlain   XIX 27

———— of Prestbury, Maugersbury, Oddington, co. Gloucester, and of Barking in Essex   XX 80[b,c]

Chamberlen see Chamberlaine   II 254

Chamberlin of London co. Middlesex connected with Owen   III 311

Chambers of London and Hackney connected with Monoux   XIX 93

———— of Newcastle upon Tyne connected with Wilton   IX 98

———— of Stapleford co. Derby and of London co. Middlesex   VI 99

———— of the City of Lincoln, and of Charles Town near Boston in New England, connected with Russell   III 156

Champain of Bengal and of London co. Middlesex connected with McIntosh   XVII 26

Champayne see de Champaigne   VIII 54

Champernown of Dertington connected with Trenchard   VIII 183

Champernowne formerly Harrington   IV 32

———— of Dartington co. Devon   IV 32

Champion letter as to the family –   X 63

———— of Bristol co. Gloucester connected with Bell and Dimsdale   III 264

———— of Guernsey connected with La Serre   VIII 403

———— of Guildford in Surrey and of the City of Winchester   IX 117

Champneis connected with William of Wickham and with Perrot   VIII 240

———— connected with Wickham   XIX 94

Champneys of Cams Hall, Penton Lodge co. Hants Orchardley co. Somerset, and of Con Hill co. Gloucester   VII 113

———— of Oosterhanger co. Kent   V 158

Chance or Chaunce connected with Gardner   II 25

Chandler connected with Bath   I 65

———— Bowes   X 131

———— Briggs   II 369

———— of London and Haggerstone co. Middlesex connected with Moss   IV 197

Chandos Brydges, Duke of   XVII 33

———— connected with Pole   VIII 50

Chantler ———— Merricks   I 71

Chantmarle of Chantmarle connected with Stoke   VIII 179

Chapman of Frocester co. Gloucester connected with Wilkins   XX 245

———— Rector of Bradford in Wilts and of Walcot   XIII 92

Charles I   XVI 9

———— copy of Warrant signed for the death of   XVIII 140[a]

Charleton of Hesleside co. Northumberland see Charlton   V 84

Charlton connected with Berriman and Stanhope   II 119

Charlton of Heselside Long Lea co. Northumberland, and of York   XI 63

———— of Lymington connected with Dawson   I 407

Charnock of Charnock Preston co. Lancaster, and of Newfoundland   IX 150
Charter of Bishop's Lideard co. Somerset connected with Mallet   VII 81
Charteris connected with Chute and Keck   XVII 15
Chastillion Earl of Flanders connected with St Paul   XIII 32–5
Chaston of Yarmouth co. Norfolk connected with Fortune   II 269
Chaunce see Chance connected with Gardner   II 25
Chauncey connected with Small   II 95
———————— of Yardley Bury Little Court, Cottond co. Hertford,
   and of Edmonton co. Middlesex   IV 272
Chaytor of Crofts co. York M.I. St Peter's Church Chester   XIV 9
Cheeks of Barbadoes   VI 140
Cheere Madryll – Cheere   VIII 457
———————— Sir Henry   XXI 180
Cheselden connected with Gloucester als Porter   XIX 158
Chester ———————— Cranmer   XIII 90
———————————————— Hewett and Robinson   IX 71
———————————————— Wollaston   III 381
———————— Earl of,   XXI 289
———————— Earls of,   VIII 251
———————— family of, dates of burial   XX 91ª
———————— of Bristol, Almondsbury, Barton Regis co. Gloucester
   and of London co. Middlesex   XIX 229
———————— of Royston Barkway co. Herts, Broadwater co.
   Sussex, descended from an ancient family in the County of
   Derby   VIII 368
Cheston of the Cities of Hereford Bristol and Gloucester   XX 85
Cheston of the Cities of Hereford Bristol and Gloucester also of
   Maryland   VIII 430
Cheverell of Chantmarle connected with Jorden   VIII 179
Chew of Hiningbay the Clifts, Sasquhannah, Sessafrass Maryland,
   Annapole, Annarundle, Mataponia, Virginia, Johnstown
   New York, Newcastle, Kent, and of Sussex Pensilvania   IX 131
Cheyney connected with Jackson   X 53
Chichele of Higham Ferrers co. Northampton connected with
   Tyndale   X 124
——————————————————————————————————— London co.
   Middlesex, Godwinstone co. Kent, and of Wimple co.
   Cambridge, Archbishop of Canterbury and Founder of All
   Souls College Oxford   XIX 56
———————— of London co. Middlesex   X 46
Chicheley connected with Norton   VII 398
Chichester ———————— Colley   IX 55
——————————————————————————   XXI 174
Child of London co. Middlesex   III 406
———————— Woodford co. Essex and of India connected with
   Corsellis   I 47
———————— of Portsmouth co. Hants Wanstead co. Essex, Baron of
   Newton Viscount Castlemaine and Earl Tilney   XIII 61
———————— of Yaxley co. Huntingdon and of London co.
   Middlesex   I 28

Childe of Northwick, Sheley, Pensax co. Worcester, and of
    Enstone co. Oxford   XIX 17
Childerow connected with Bolton and Pudsey   II 430
Chillock ————— Stebbing   VII 320
Chinn of Bristol connected with Harford   II 418
Chinn of Newnham and of the Moat in the psh of Newent co.
    Gloucester   XX 77[a]
————— of Newnham and of Bristol co. Gloucester   I 111
Chinnery of London co. Middlesex and of Gilwell in the psh and
    Hamlet of Seawardstone co. Essex   VII 61
Chippindall of Blackburn connected with Glover   VI 217
Chittenden of Hawkhurst co. Kent connected with Osborne   VIII 1
Chitton of Houghton le Spring and of Hanaton   XV 47
Chokke of Avington co. Berks connected with Lowe and Hale   II 87
Cholmondeley of Vale Royal co. Chester connected with Vernon
    and Atherton   III 279
Cholmondely connected with Pitt   X 160
Chorley of Southwark co. Surrey, a Lancashire family connected
    with Owen, Wragg, and Merrick   III 315
Chrilly ————————— Thorowgood   IV 58
Christian ————— Giles and Curtis   I 332
————————— Leigh of Thorley   VI 241
————— of Unerigg connected with Curwen   II 461
————————————————————————   VIII 35
Christie of Sheriff Muir near Stirling North Britian   III 95
Christmas of Waterford removed to Barnstaple co. Devon
    connected with Smith   IV 451
Chudleigh of Holydown co. Devon and of Kinsale Ireland   I 26
Church connected with Somerset   XVI 61
————————————— Tyrell   VI 408
———————————————————   VIII 103
————————————— Urry   III 516
Churchey ————— Westley   XIII 72
Churchill of Eaton co. Berks connected with Dore   VII 469
Churchus of Badgeworth co. Som. connected with Grinsteed   III 443
Chursdon connected with Porter   X 69
Chute connected with and afterwards Keck   XVII 15
————— of the Vine co. Southampton connected with Keck and
    Tracy   XIX 173
Cibber connected with Colley   IX 54
Clapham of Beamsley co. Gloucester connected with Thornbury   XX 222[a]
Clapperson in the psh of St Georges in the East co. Middx.   XVII 7
Claramond als Clere de Clermont Clarey or Clary   V 417
Clare and Hertford, Earl of,   XXI 272
————— of Hatchbury, Devizes & of Upton Lovell co. Wilts.   I 339
————— of Worcestershire, Ballyshanby, co. Tipperary, Carlow
    in Ireland, Maidford co. Northampton, and of Jamaica   I 21
Clarence Duke of, connected with Barrington   V 174
Clarey als Clare als de Clermont als Claramond als Clary   V 417
Clark and Bracy certificate of marriage   XIX 81

Clark connected with Jol   XVI 30

————————— Lynch   IV 510

———————————————————   XVIII 79

————— of Brickenbury co. Hertford and of London co. Middlesex connected with Colchester   XIX 153

————— of Bruken Denbury co. Hertford and of London co. Middlesex   XX 74[b]

————— of London co. Middlesex connected with Fletcher   IV 445

————————— and of co. Herts connected with Fletcher   XVIII 8

————— of Wells and Bale co. Norfolk   I 322

————————————— connected with Paston   III 331

Clarke connected with Bigland and Squire   XIII 12

————————— Clerke of Willoughby   VIII 45

————————— Errington   I 93

————————— Jervoise   IX 112[b]

————————— Marnes   III 18

————————— Scroope   III 409

————————— Turner   IV 109

————————— Wingfield Stanley and Hayford   I 508

————— of Barford, Hele & Salisbury connected with Bowles   I 143

————— of Belgrave, Layer co. Leicester and of Shirland co. Derby   IV 400

————— of Chipping and of Wickham co. Bucks   IV 401

————— of Derry, Glencallin co. Monaghan, and of Hitcham co. Bucks   XII 81–5

————— of Dymock connected with Smith   IV 266

————— of Godmanchester co. Huntingdon and of Hungerford co. Berks   II 28

————— of Hull co. York and of London co. Middlesex connected with Raikes   I 162

————— of Merton and Putney co. Surrey connected with Davie   II 421

————— of Smithfield co. Middlesex and of Sandridgebury co. Herts   V 216

————— of Snitterby co. Lincoln connected with Thompson   XIII 74

————— of Someshall, Chilcot, and Sutton co. Derby and of Ulcombe co. Kent   I 6

————————— in the psh of Brampton co. Derby connected with Byerly   VII 170

————— of Tetbury co. Gloucester   V 310

————————————— connected with Sloper and Croome   XX 226[a]

Clarke of Walpole in Norfolk, Wisbich St Peters in the Isle of Ely, and of London co. Middlesex   VIII 461

————— of West Bromwich co. Stafford, Idsworth Park co. Southampton, afterwards Clarke Jervoise   XI 70–3

————— Price Clarke

Clarke-Jervoise see Clarke of West Bromwich   XI 70–3

Clarkson connected with Comerford   III 403

————————— Dobson   III 409

Clary als Claramond, Clere, Clarey, or de Clermont   V 417

Clavering Bishop of Peterborough, Regius Professor of Hebrew at Oxford	XXI 144
———— connected with Errington and Widderington	X 145
———— extract from Register	XVI 80
———— M.I. St Nicholas Church Newcastle upon Tyne	VII 379
———— of Callaley Newcastle upon Tyne co. Northumberland	X 139
———————————— connected with Collingwood	X 45
Claxson of Woodcot in the psh of South Stoke co. Oxon, Bishops Sands in the psh of Sonning co. Berks and of the City of Gloucester	XVII 18
Claxton connected with Pearce	IV 476
————————————————————————————————	XVIII 32
———— of Oldpark and of Wynyard co. Durham connected with Jenison	XII 28–47
Clay of London connected with Harvey	I 570
Clayton connected with Paston	IX 113[b]
———— of Fulwood and of Liverpool co. Lancaster	I 230
———— of Newcastle	I 492
—————————	X 134
Cleasby of Cleasby co. York	VIII 5
———— of the Craighouse in the psh of Brough in Westmorland, descended from the family of Cleasby in the County of York	VIII 5
Cleaver of Weedon co. Bucks and of London co. Middlesex	VIII 493
Cleeve of the City of London, Hay Hill co. Bucks, Lord of the Manor of Foots Cray co. Kent, connected with Bourchier	IV 407
Cleland connected with Child	I 47
Clemensen arms and crest of the noble family of	VIII 227
Clement connected with Lloyd	XIV 19
Clements ———— Lock	XXI 306
———— Pruen	XX 185[a]
Clere als de Clermont or Clarey als Claramond Clary	V 417
———— of Ormesby connected with le Groos	VII 502
———— de St connected with Gage	XIX 64
Clerk of Balnegoch in Ross shire and of London co. Middlesex	IX 151
Clerke als Hammond of Willoughby co. Warwick Watford co. Northampton connected with Clarke of Somersall	VIII 46
———— of Somersall co. Derby connected with Frevile and Byerley	XII 29–31
———— of Watford co. Northampton	III 422
———— of Weston Hitcham co. Bucks, and of North Weston co. Oxon	IV 491
———— of Weston co. Oxon Hitcham co. Bucks and of London co. Middlesex	XVIII 2
Clevland of Tapley co. Devon	I 333
Cliborne of Hayclose co. Cumberland, Kellerby and of co. Westmorland	XXI 29
Cliff of Coripole co. Somerset connected with Mallet	VII 75
Clifford Baron, of Chudleigh connected with Blount	XVI 64
———— Barony of	IX 6

Clifford connected with Cressener   XI 10
Clifford formerly Winchcombe   I 30
——————— Lord, connected with Boyle and Bedingfield   V 319
——————— Hudleston   XXI 40
——————— of Shipton Castle connected with Pudsey   II 433
——————— of Frampton and of Swindon   IX 160
——————— Rector of Landbeach co. Cambridge and of
    Cockingham co. Lincoln; of Amsterdam and Haarlem   XI 40
Clifton Baron of Leighton, of Bromswould co. Hunts   XIV 24
——————— Barony of, Petition of Catherine Lady O'Brian   IX 16
——————— Lord connected with Darcy   VIII 468
——————— M.I. at Barton co. Nottingham   VI 112
——————— of Buckenham Castle connected with Knevet   XIX 259
——————— of Clifton co. Nottingham connected with Coote Earl
    of Bellomont   XVI 24
——————— of Clifton Lytham and of Westby co. Lancaster   VI 40
Clinton Earls of Lincoln, of Sourton Parva co. Lincoln and of
    Newfoundland   V 184
——————— Lord, Earl of Lincoln   IX 114
——————— of Coleshill and of Badesley Clinton co. Warwick   XIX 151
——————— of Wells   XIII 115
Clipsham connected with Swale   I 285
Clitherow of London co. Middlesex connected with Jennyns   III 110
Clotterbooke see Clutterbuck   II 468
Clowes of Langley co. Chester and of the Inner Temple co.
    Middlesex connected with Daniel   III 499
——————— of Namptwich co. Chester and of Shoreditch   XXI 130
——————— of St Leonards Shoreditch   XXI 165
Clutterbuck Clotterbooke of Mill End in the psh of Eastington,
    Kings Stanley co. Gloucester, and of Islington co.
    Middlesex   II 468–9
——————— connected with Browne   VI 177
Clutterbuck connected with Sheppard and Clifford   IX 160
——————— notes concerning the family of, by A Dunford   XX 57
——————— of Frampton connected with Bell   XX 67
——————— of Kings Stanley and of Leonard Stanley co. Gloucester   I 577
——————— Eastington, Bristol, Redborough co. Gloucester,
    Dunton co. Bucks and of London co. Middlesex   XIX 146
——————— of Warkworth   I 514
Coates connected with James and Walton   XVIII 92
———————————————— Mills and Bowles   VI 253
——————— of Middleham co. Yorks extracts from Registers   VI 341
——————— of Ripon   XV 71
—————————————————— co. York and of Bishopton   XVII 11
Coatsworth of Hermitage in Northumberland   XXI 1
Cobb of Hardresse in Kent connected with Clare and Skynner I 22
——————— of Lichfield   VIII 314
—————————————————— co. Stafford and of Twickenham co.
    Middlesex   XIII 65
——————— of Sandringham, Thornham, Hunston co. Norfolk and

of London co. Middlesex   II 354

Cobbe of Winchester connected with Godolphin   VII 353

Cobhan of Rochester connected with Higgins   IV 355

Cobley of Ide co. Devon, London co. Middlesex, and of Naples   III 20

Cock M.I. St Nicholas Church Newcastle upon Tyne   VII 375
     VII 377

Cockaine of London co. Middlesex, Rushton co. Northampton, Viscount of Cullen in the County of Donegal in the Kingdom of Ireland   I 97

Cockayn of Pooley co. Warwick connected with Marow   VII 25

——————— Ashbourn co. Derby connected with Marow and Ferrers   VII 369

Cockayn of Pooley co. Warwick connected with Marow   XXI 108

Cockerill of Scarborough co. York and of Bengal   III 145

Cocks als Cox of Longforth and Tugworth Bristol co. Gloucester and of Virginia   II 98

——————— Cox, Coxe of the Leigh in the psh of Ashton Keynes co. Wilts, Stour Easton, Downside co. Somerset, and of Calcutta   II 420

——————— Coxe of Castleditch in the psh of Eastnor co. Hereford, Crowle, Shuckburgh, Benow, co. Worcester, Bladon with Woodstock co. Oxon, Wootton Bassett, Cricklade co. Wilts, Cleave Dumbleton and Stone, Easton co. Gloucester, London and Acton co. Middlesex, and of Hawksted co. Suffolk   II 422

——————— Coxe of Tarleton Sudgrove in the psh of Miserdene, Stone Easton, Cleeve Dumbledon co. Gloucester, Castle Ditch co. Hereford, Leigh Aston Caynes, Wootton Bassett, co. Wilts Hankstead co. Suffolk, Crowle co. Worcester, Middle Temple co. Middlesex, Bladen with Woodstock, and Rollwright co. Oxon, and of Leavings als Purlant co. Bucks   V 356

——————— descended from a family of that surname in Kent, of Croale co. Worcester, London co. Middlesex, Castle Ditch co. Hereford, and of Dumbleton co. Gloucester   XIX 31

——————— of Eastnor co. Hereford, and of Dumbleton co. Gloucester – Baptisms etc.   VI 328

Cockshutt of co. Leicester and Chaddesdon co. Derby connected with Thisleton   I 423

——————— of Harford Magna connected with Dawson   II 436

Codrington of Bristol co. Gloucester, Bridgewater and Exeter co. Devon   III 498

——————— of Codrington, Dodington, Didmartin, and of Bridgewater   X 43

——————— of Pucklechurch co. Gloucester connected with Porter   X 69
     XVIII 62

——————— and Dodington co. Gloucester connected with Porter   XIX 158

Coel of Depden Hall co. Suffolk   X 67

Cofin connected with Cole   XIX 174

Cogan of Montagu connected with Lynus — XVI 59
——————— co. Somerset and of Manchester co. Lancaster connected with Symes — XIX 250
Coher Butler Baron of — XVII 8
Coke connected with Roberts — XVI 89
——————— Wilmot — IX 124
——————— formerly Roberts — I 485
——————— Lord Lovel, connected with Thanet — XVI 58
——————— of Melbourne co. Derby connected with Bedall and Leventhorpe — V 455
——————— of Thonington co. Suffolk, Longford co. Derby – Earl of Leicester Viscount Coke of Holkam in Norfolk — I 485
——————— Vice Chamberlain to George I, of Melbourne co. Derby connected with Lamb — V 70
——————— Viscount of Holkham connected with Tufton — XIII 68
Colby of Kensington co. Middlesex connected with Flewelling — IV 423
Colchester of London co. Middlesex, of the Wildern in the psh of Abbenhall co. Gloucester, and of Ulmington co. Warwick — XIX 153
Colchester of Westbury on Severn co. Gloucester — X 69
——————————— connected with Clark — XX 74[b]
Colclough of Tinturn Abbey co. Wexford — XI 58
——————— of Wexford connected with Beauchamp — XII 70
Cole of Bickington co. Devon, Standon co. Hereford and of Charlton in the psh of Henbury co. Gloucester — XIX 175
——————— of Cambridge connected with Harmer — XX 144
——————— of Charleton — XIII 103
——————— of Dicey, Bicester co. Oxon connected with Rigby — IX 83
——————— of Gloucester and of Colchester co. Essex — XIX 174
——————— of Kingston, Winchcliffe in the psh of Ashbury co. Bucks, and of Marlborough co. Wilts — I 180
——————— of Lisse co. Southampton connected with Ayde — XXI 211
——————— of London co. Middlesex — XXI 185
——————————— of Lyss or Lyle co. Southampton connected with Fauntleroy — XV 63
——————— of Magdalen Laver co. Essex, and of Islington co. Middlesex — VIII 438
——————— of Northay co. Gloucester — XIX 184
——————— of North Bovey, Morton Hempstead, Exeter co. Devon, London co. Middlesex, and of Baltimore in America — XV 37
——————— of Perran Uth co. Cornwall connected with Davis and Sandes — II 442
——————— of Slade in the psh of Cornwood, Buckland-tout-Saints, and of Buckes co. Devon — XX 82[a]
——————— of Tewkesbury co. Gloucester and of Stanley Hall als Salisbury co. Hertford — XIX 175
——————— of Westphalia and of Lambeth co. Surrey — XVII 27
——————— of Yate co. Gloucester connected with Neale — XX 176
Colebrand of Borham and of Lewes co. Sussex — V 456
Colebrond ——————— — VII 12

Coleman of Basingstoke co. Southampton connected with
  Harwood .... VIII 305
Coles of Pulborough co. Sussex connected with Cooper ... X 29, 30–1
———————————————————————————————— X 34–5
Collenridge connected with Dormer .... XVI 95
Collet Lord Mayor of London; Dean of St Paul's connected with
  Knevet .... XIX 259
——————— of Lechlade co. Gloucester, Southlye co. Oxford, and
  of Chelsea in the County of Middlesex .... XIX 249
Colleton of Exeter co. Devon and of London co. Middlesex ... VI 37
Collett of Tewkesbury and Bristol co. Gloucester .... XX 86ᵃ
Colley of Broomyard co. Hereford .... II 282
——————— of Glaston co. Rutland and of Dudford co. Northants;
  also of Ireland .... IX 54
——————— of Glaston co. Rutland and of Dadford co. Northants XXI 174
Collier connected with Bridge .... II 377
——————— of London connected with Lloyd .... IV 191
Collimore of Chipping Sodbury co. Gloucester and of London co.
  Middlesex .... XIX 117
Collin of Seton co. Rutland connected with Angell .... I 75
———————————————————————————————— XI 55
Collingwood connected with Brown and Blake .... X 155–6
——————————————— Hughes .... XXI 127ᵇ
——————————— M.I. .... VI 129
——————————— of Byker, Newcastle and of Unthank co. Northum-
  berland .... XIII 114
——————————— of Little Ryle, Unthank, & Prendwick in the psh of
  Alnham co. Northumberland .... IV 424
——————————— of Little Tyle co. Northumberland Brevet and of
  Unthank co. Cumberland .... X 45
Collingwood of Unthank co. Northumberland .... XXI 148ᵃ
——————————— Little Ryle, Great Ryle, Eslington, Wollore Tughill
  Hall Pendrick in the psh of Alnham co. Northumberland
  Hetton on the Hill Eppleton co. Durham and of Reveley ... XV 4–8
——————————— of Unthank and Little Ryle connected with Blake III 256
——————————— of Newcastle and of Chirton connected with Biggs X 136
Collins connected with Burroughs .... XVII 6
——————————————— Leach .... IX 101
——————————————— Rigby .... IX 83
——————————————— Rosse .... XX 194
——————————— name assumed by Wharton of Wharton co. York VIII 221
——————————— of Glyn connected with Browne .... VI 177
——————————— of St Christophers – descended from Devonshire and
  of St Vincents .... II 343
——————————— of Walthamstow co. Essex .... IX 61
Collis connected with Purser .... XVII 31
Collyer connected with Ash .... I 124
——————————————— Curzon .... X 9
Colserat of Exeter co. Devon .... IV 8
Colston as to the arms of, ... XX 90

Colston of Colston Hall Carham co. Northumberland, Bristol
  co. Gloucester, Felton, Preston and of Reybell   XIX 220
─────── of Corby co. Lincoln and of London co. Middlesex
  connected with Lowe   II 87
Colt M.I. at Shireborne Church co. Gloucester   VI 114
Colville Lord of Bitham Castle co. Lincoln connected with Basset   VIII 52
Colvin of Forbeck in the Shire of Inverness connected with
  Mackintosh   XIII 36
Colyard of London co. Middlesex connected with Randall   VIII 426
Combe connected with Davys   I 149
─────── of Bridistow co. Devon Newington co. Middlesex
  Hemel Hempsted co. Herts and of Chedington co. Bucks   XIII 54–7
Comber connected with Thornton   XV 24
─────── of Cambridge connected with Whish   IX 136
─────── of East Newton co. York, London co. Middlesex and
  of Allington co. Sussex; Rector of Stonegrave co. York   IX 10
Combers of Shenfield co. Essex connected with Browne   I 459
─────── Southweald and Baddow co. Essex   II 126
Comerford of Barcelona and Madrid from Tipperary   XXI 222
─────── of Cales in Spain and of London co. Middlesex   III 403
Commyns of Oratava in the Island of Teneriffe connected with
  Strickland   VII 296
─────────────────── list of children   VIII 340
Compeer of Wootton under Edge   I 104
Compton connected with Ayleworth   XIX 172
─────── of Bramble Teigh co. Sussex connected with Paston   XIV 22
─────── of Chittern co. Wilts   I 340
─────── of Wiltshire Hartbury and Alvington co. Glosc.   XIX 145
Comyn Lord of Bradenagh in Scotland connected with Walker als
  Walkfare   VII 328
Conan Earl of, Little Britain in France connected with Tate   VII 259
Conduit of the Mint and of Cranbury co. Hants connected with
  Barton   I 147
Congreve of Stockton near Bridgeworth co. Salop connected with
  Phillips and Grenius   III 93
Coningsby, Earl, connected with Jones – Earl of Ranelagh   XIII 7
Connop M.I. Kirkby Ravensworth Church   VI 123
Cons of Osnaburgh connected with Garnons   II 487
Constable connected with Lord Berkeley   XI 16
─────────────── Windsor   XIII 5
─────── formerly Sheldon, of Ditchford Winchester co. Hants
  and of Burton Constable co. York   VII 46
                                                                      XIV 21
─────── formerly Tunstall and again Constable see Tunstall   X 106
─────── of Burton Constable and of Halsam co. York   II 409
─────────────── connected with Fairfax   XIV 21
─────── of Everingham co. York   V 39
─────── of Shreweswell in Sussex connected with Roberts   IX 152
─────── of Yorkshire came into Cornwall, of Falmouth and of
  Woolwich co. Kent   IX 152
Constantine of Dodington, Whitchurch co. Salop, London co.

Middlesex, Merley in the County of Dorset and of Constantinople — VII 311

———— of Merley co. Dorset — XVIII 65

———— of the ancient family of that name, of Marley co. Dorset connected with Hawkins — XII 49–51

Consul Earl of Gloucester — XXI 272

Conway Lord connected with Popham and Seymour — XVIII 131

———— of Arrow connected with Burdett Stanley & Arden — XI 16

———— of Brynyryne connected with Puliston & Hookes — XVIII 107

———— of Portrivan and of Ruthland connected with Hookes, Stanley and Drihurst — XVIII 107

Conwyn connected with Rees — XIV 20

Conyers of Boultby co. York connected with Lambton — I 367

———— of Homby, Lord, connected with Darcy — VIII 468

Cook connected with Whalley — IX 104

Cook of Michael Church co. Radnor connected with Price — XXI 191

———— of Stanton co. Worcester connected with Cutler — XIX 118

Cooke connected with Leigh — XX 162

———————— Tyssen — VII 20

———— of Bristol co. Gloucester connected with Crisp — III 438

———— of Cleveland co. York — IV 262

———— of Highnam co. Gloucester and of Giddy Hall co. Essex — XIX 126

———————— connected with Guise — I 358

———— of Lezenes Abbey co. Kent connected with Lowe — XX 161

———— of London co. Middlesex connected with Constantine — XVIII 65

———— of Sandall near Doncaster Cartinghouse near Batley, Wheatley co. York, and of London co. Middlesex — VI 85

———— of South Cerney co. Gloucester, and of Kemble co. Wilts — XX 87ᵃ

———— of Stoke Newington connected with Fremeaux — III 80

———— of Thornbury co. Gloucester, London co. Middlesex, Rumford and Chelmsford co. Essex — VII 510

————of Trowbridge co. Wilts — VI 168

Cooksey connected with Summers and Blurton — II 425

———— of Evesham co. Worcester connected with Acton — XIX 6

Cookson of Crookhorne co. Somerset — III 123

———— of Leeds co. York connected with Fenton — I 480

Coombe connected with Chamberlain — XIII 74

———————— Chamberlayne — XIX 27

Coombs of London co. Middlesex connected with Bibbee — IV 62

Cooper connected with Broke of Nacton co. Suffolk — IX 90

———————— Bridger — III 421

———————— Browne — IV 489

Cooper connected with Browne — XVIII 1

———— Coles — X 35

———————— Paliser — VII 96

———————— Priaulx — IV 482

———————————— XVIII 143

———— Earl of Shaftesbury — X 46

———— formerly of co. Warwick of Farnborough co. Kent — III 520

Cooper of Bath co. Somerset connected with Leigh   XX 162
———— of Dicham in Hastings, Chichester and Pulborough co. Sussex   X 29, 31
———— of St Duffield in East Riding near Selby, and of Darran near Knaresborough co. York   XXI 195[a]
———— of South Weston co. Oxford   XX 66[a]
———— of Tetbury co. Gloucester   XX 192[a]
———— of Thurgarten co. Nottingham and of Lynn co. Norfolk   VII 402
———— of York connected with Allanson   III 502
———— of Cowper of Ditcham   X 30
———— Vicar of Loxley co. Warwick   XX 66[a]
Coote connected with Walkeden and Mansergh   XXI 47
———— of Ash Hill co. Limerick   II 104
————   IV 298
———— of Cote Hill co. Cavan connected with St George   VII 408
———— Earl of Bellamont and Baron of Caloony Lord of Birchmorton co. Worcester, of Coote Hill co. Cavan connected with Nanson   XIX 170
———— Earl of Montrath, Viscount Coote of Castle Coote, Earl of Bellomont   XVI 24
Cootes Patent from the Grand Mogul   XVIII 72–6
Cooth connected with Bowles   I 145
Copdowe or Copto of Flemyngs in the psh of Runwells co. Essex connected with Sulyard and Tyrell   VII 17
Cope connected with Spencer   VI 55
———— of Jacomb co. Gloucester connected with Escourt   XIII 108
Copeland of Plymouth co. Devon and of Launceston co. Cornwall connected with Dare   II 30
Copinger of Cork   VIII 197
———— connected with Galway and Goold   XII 53
Copley connected with West Lord Delawar   XII 51
———— of Exeter connected with Braithwaite   IV 85
Copner of Bristol connected with Bergum   XX 68
Coppinger George   XIII 93
Copto see Copdowe   VII 17
Corbet connected with Fitzwarren   XX 49[b]
————   XX 200[a]
———— formerly Flint   IV 515
———— Corbett of Longor co. Salop, Blacklands in Bobington, Elton co. Hereford and of London co. Middlesex   IV 512
————   XVIII 135
Corbet of Morton Corbet co. Salop connected with Bridgeman   XV 10
———— of Stanford co. Salop connected with Blount   XIX 219
———— of Sunder co. Salop connected with Browne   V 469
———— see Corbett
Corbett formerly Flint   X 20
———— Licence for confirming the name of   IX 14
———— of Damhall co. Chester   IX 26
———— of Moreton co. Salop   X 20

Corbett of Stoke co. Salop connected with Weld & Powell	V 65
———————————— Kynaston and Powell	XVIII 120
————— or Corbet of Longnor co. Salop London co. Middx, Bucklands co. Stafford and of Elton or Micklewood	IV 512
Corbett Corbet ———————————————————————	XVIII 135
Corbin of King and Queen County Porto Bacca Middlesex County in Virginia & of London	I 9
———————— of Westmorland connected with Tucker and Taylor	IV 221
Cordals M.I. in Winkburn Church co. Nottingham	VI 116
Corke connected with Oatridge	XX 177
Cornet of Wootten under Edge co. Gloucester connected with Harmar	XX 144
Cornewall connected with Hanbury and Tyndale	X 124
Cornwall of Bredwardine Castle and of Moccas co. Hereford	III 439
Cornwallis, Baron, of Eye co. Suffolk and of Malmesbury co. Wilts connected with Earle	XX 117[a]
——————— of Brome & of Fincham co. Norfolk connected with le Groos	VII 504
Corry of London co. Middlesex connected with Brice	VII 125
Corsbie of Scotland late of Ashwill Thorpe connected with Calver	VIII 42
Corsellis of Roussilier Flanders, London co. Middlesex, Layer Marney Wivenhoe co. Essex and of Hoddesden co. Hertford	I 48
Corthine of the Isle of Wight and of Kingston upon Hull co. York	VII 340
——————— of the Isle of Wight connected with Hartland and Harmar	XX 144
Cory of Waterbeech co. Cambridge connected with Lunn and Johnson	IX 43
Coryton formerly Goodall of Crockerton co. Cornwall	III 85
Cosby of the Kingdom of Ireland connected with Howard	VII 174
Cosens see Cozens	I 335
Costeker of Ashford co. Kent connected with Dobree	VI 245
Cosyn see Cousin	XIX 203
Cotes als Boardman took the surname of Bowman	VI 222
——————— connected with Struther	XXI 148
	XXI 161
——————— of Colshill Woodcote, Vice Admiral of the Red; Principal of Magdalen Hall and Public Orator of the University of Oxford	X 21, 22
Cotesworth connected with Newman	IV 260
Cotgrave of Guilded Sutton near Chester, the Borough of Southwark co. Surrey and of Philadelphia	III 170
Cother of Sandhurst	VIII 376
Cottingham, Baron de Stuteville	VIII 252
Cottington	XXI 155
Cotton connected with Bellingham	XXI 88
——————— Birch	X 79, 88
——————— Hanbury and Howard	X 124
——————— Taylor and Whithall	V 69
———————	XVIII 119
——————— Tyrell	VIII 99

Cotton from Bellaport co. Salop, of Chigwell Romford co.
Essex and of London co. Middlesex   III 47
——————— M.I. in Kirkby Ravensworth Church   VI 122
——————— of Connington co. Huntingdon and of Stretton co.
Bedford connected with Bowdler   VIII 213
——————— of Drayton co. Salop connected with Birch   X 77
Couger of Bristol connected with Peach   I 271
Coulter M.I. St Nicholas Church Newcastle upon Tyne   VII 378
Coulthurst went from Lancashire into Ireland, of Clithero co.
Lancaster, and of Melksham co. Wilts   III 81
Coun connected with Witchall   XX 238ᵃ
Court of Maplebury Green connected with D'Ewes   I 388
Courtenay Lord connected with Peverell   V 49
Courthope of Stodmarsh near Canterbury co. Kent and of Grays
Inn co. Middlesex   I 32
Courtney from Hull co. York, of Chelsea co. Middlesex connected
with Campling and Mayhew   XVII 53
Cousin Cosyn of Hellesley co. Gloucester and of Westberrie
connected with Tipping   XIX 203
Cousins of Trig Lane and of South Lambeth co. Surrey   X 126ᵃ
Covell or Colvil connected with Musgrave   XXI 59
Coventry formerly Darby   XVII 36
——————— of Cossington co. Oxford, and of Snitterfield co.
Worcester, Baron Coventry of Ailesborough and Viscount
Deerhurst   XIII 84
Coverall als Barker of Coverall Castle Coulshurst Hopton Castle   XIX 197
Hagmond co. Salop and of Fairford co. Gloucester
Cowan of Tailzourtown connected with Smith of Braco   I 482
Coward, Leonard   XIII 99
——————— of West Penard co. Somerset connected with Leigh   XIII 71
Cowgill of Fielding Clough near Earby in the psh of Thornton co.
York, connected with Shackleton   I 4
Cowie of Montrose and of London co. Middlesex   IX 106
Cowles of Cranham co. Gloucester and of London co. Middlesex   XX 180
Cowper M.I. St Peter's Church Chester   XIV 9
——————— of Ditcham connected with Coles & Ayliffe   X 34–5
——————— see Cooper of Ditcham
Cox als Cocks   II 98
Cox als Hayward of Forthampton Wellesthorp and of Quedgley
co. Gloucester   XIX 246
——————— connected with Grahme   III 511
——————————— Viscount Preston   XVIII 55
——————— Long   IX 49
——————— of Birderop co. Wilts   VII 401
——————— of Bishops Cleeve co. Gloucester connected with
Walter   XX 240
——————— of Hempton connected with Parnell   I 528
——————— of Oakley in the psh of Berkeley and of Stone co.
Gloucester   XX 74ᵃ
——————— of Quarley co. Hants, Clent co. Worcester, and of

London co. Middlesex   XXI 216
————— of West Haddon co. Northampton and of London co.
    Middlesex; co. Surrey also   II 474
Cox see Cocks   II 420
Coxe connected with Wintle   XVI 74
————— of Lypiate and of Kemble co. Wilts   XX 84
————— of Stone Easton co. Somerset   XX 97
————— see Cocks   II 422
                                                                V 356
Coxwell of Ablington Cirencester and of Turk Dean co. Gloucester XIX 116
————— of Cirencester Ablington —————   XVI 77
————————————————————————————————— and of London
    co. Middlesex   XX 73^a–5^a, 6
Coytmer of Coytmer in Penryn – took name of Pugh   V 162
Cozens of Yate Minster near Sherborne co. Dorset   I 335
Crackenthorp of Newbiggin co. Westmorland connected with
    Askew   XVI 82
Cracroft of Bardney co. Lincoln connected with Bennett   II 158
Cradoc ap Howell de Grono, lord of Newton, assumed the name
    of Newton   XIX 216
Cradock of Wolverhampton co. Stafford, Archbishop of Dublin
    and a General in the Army   VIII 82
Crafton of Southwark co. Surrey and of London co. Middlesex
    connected with Bell and Day   III 314
Crakenthorp of Newbiggen co. Westmorland connected with
    Mottram   VII 336
Crane connected with Pavey and Lovell   XIII 72
————— of Bristol connected with Selfe   II 352
Cranmer als Wood connected with Wood   XIII 90
————— of Aslacton co. Nottingham Archbishop of Canterbury   VIII 258
Craster of Craster co. Northumberland   I 108
Craven connected with Ireland   III 69
————— of Wakefield co. York, Craven Lodge in the psh of
    Hackney, London co. Middlesex, Nether House in the psh
    of Waltham Abbey co. Essex, and of Stamford Hall   XVII 19
Crawley of Flaxley Abbey, Bloxley in the Forest of Dean co.
    Gloucester, afterwards Bovey   XX 93^a
Crayle formerly Bellamy   I 564
————— of Newark upon Trent co. Nottingham and of London
    co. Middlesex   I 157
————————————— connected with Bellamy and Morgan   I 564
Creagh see Creigh
Credy als Perron connected with Mallet   VII 75
Creed connected with Pickering and Steward   IX 64
————— from Charing in Kent, of London co. Middlesex and of
    Canterbury co. Kent   III 60
————— of Charing, Greenwich, Canterbury and of Melton co.
    Kent   XXI 121
Creed of Lathbury co. Bucks connected with Rotherham   III 61
————— of Oundle co. Northampton   XV 33–5

Creigh of Newcastle upon Tyne and of Dublin connected with
Rogers .... I 307
————————————————————————————— connected
with Isaacson and Rogers .... XXI 147
———————— or Creagh of Newcastle upon Tyne & of Dublin ... XVI 69
Crekelade lord of Studley and Cadenham co. Wilts connected with
Sambourne .... XX 212ᵃ
Creketot of Ovesdenne connected with Le Blund .... XVI 64
Cressener of London co. Middlesex and of Earls Colne co. Essex ... XI 3, 10
Cresset connected with Pelham .... IX 69
Cresswell of Cresswell co. Northumberland and of London co.
Middlesex .... VII 413
———————— of Sydbury Bridgnorth co. Salop and of Pinkney co.
Wilts .... XVI 76
Creswich of Hanham Abbots co. Gloucester and of Langford co.
Somerset .... XIX 258
Creyghton connected with Waldron and Laying .... XIII 115
Crisp of London co. Middlesex .... III 438
Croft of Stillington co. York, London co. Middlesex and of
Cambridge .... III 432
Croftes of Bardwell Saxham Westow co. Suffolk London co.
Middlesex and of Norwich co. Norfolk .... IV 130
———————— see Crofts
Crofts als Croftes of Weston, Saxham, Bardwell co. Suffolk, and
of London co. Middlesex .... XVIII 71
———————— of East Appleton co. York descended from the family
of Croft of Clawton co. Lancaster .... XI 63
———————— of Saxham and West Stowe co. Suffolk see also Croftes ... VI 59
Croke M.I. in Salisbury Cathedral .... VI 131
———————— of Chilton co. Bucks connected with Unton ...... XVI 51
Croker connected with Can and Bayley .... XXI 47
———————— from Lincham co. Devon of Rawlinstone, Ballanguard
Dublin, Youghall Cork Dungarvon and of Corriglas .... II 380
Crompton of Chorley co. Chester and of Derby .... II 134
———————— of Fairwood near Bitton Ashwill Inskip West Haughton
co. Lancaster and of London co. Middlesex .... III 274
Cromwell als Williams .... XXI 242–3
————————————————— of Hinchinbrooke & Henyingforde
Ramsey co. Huntingdon stiled Protector of England, of
London co. Middlesex, Spinny Abby co. Cambridge and of
Putney co. Surrey .... XV 18–22
———————— connected with Russell .... VIII 244
———————— Earl of Essex, Lord Cromwell of Okham co. Rutland,
Viscount Lecale and Earl of Avglasse in Ireland .... XV 18, 19, 22
———————— Earl of Ardglasse of Okeham co. Rutland and of
Henchingbroke co. Huntingdon als Williams, Baron of
Okeham Viscount Lecale .... XXI 242–3
———————— Lord, connected with Rugge .... III 163
Croobie als Crosbie of Scotland late of Ashwell Thorp co. Norfolk
connected with Carver .... VIII 40
————————————————— Crosbie of Scotland late of Ashwell Thorpe co.

Norfolk connected with Calver   V 26
Crooke of the Island of St Kitts – from Gloucestershire   II 256
Croome of Beverstone co. Gloucester connected with Wicks and
    Clarke   XX 226ᵃ
Crop of Bremen Papton co. Bucks Westoe co. Cambridge and of
    London co. Middlesex   XIII 26
Cropley of Brandon co. Palatine Durham Soham co. Cambridge
    and of London co. Middlesex   VI 83
————— connected with Wilson and Ashe   V 42
————— of Brandon co. Palatine Durham   XVIII 23
Crosbie als Croobie of Scotland late of Ashwell Thorp co. Norfolk
    connected with Carver   VIII 40
————— of Crosbie Park co. Wicklow, Maryborough Queens
    County, Ireland, Bishop of Ardfert & Aghadae   XXI 4, 5
————— of Liverpool connected with Dawson and Pudsey   II 434
————— of the Hermitage Kings County   IX 41
————— see Croobie
Crosby of Ireland connected with Howard   XXI 269
————— see Crosbie
Crosfield of Middleham co. York connected with Wilson   III 14
————— of Seatle M.I.   XIV 9
Crosse of Broomfield and of Bristol co. Somerset connected with
    Clinton and Pope   XIII 115
Crossfield of Northallerton co. York   XXI 156
Crossman connected with Brickdale   VII 394
———————————————————————————————————————   I 506
Crouch connected with Fortune   II 269
Crow of Shadwell   VIII 390
Crowe connected with Marlowe   IX 88
————— of Malden co. Essex and Shadwell co. Middlesex
    connected with Sidney   XXI 323
Crowther of Doddington and of Chilwood in Acton connected
    with Belchier and Atwell   X 60
————— of Shillingford near Exeter Honiton, Alphington co.
    Devon and of London co. Middlesex   VII 454
Cruger connected with Peach   XIX 225
Crump of Stepney co. Middlesex and Great Henney co. Essex,
    connected with Spurrell and Brooke   IV 1
Crumpe of Bodley in the psh of Westbury co. Gloucester and of the
    City of Bristol   XIX 154
Crumpling afterwards Mayhew   XVII 53
Crundon of Eastbourne, Pittinghove, Ringmer co. Sussex,
    Hawkhurst, Hayes co. Kent, and of London co. Middlesex   III 194
Cruse of Ogbourn St George co. Wilts and of Sheering co. Essex   I 338
Cruys connected with Jermyn, Shortridge Mallet etc.   II 296
Crymes of London co. Middlesex, Peckham co. Surrey and of
    Virginia   VI 3
Cuching connected with Fletcher   IV 445
———————————————————————————————————————   XVIII 8
Cullen ————— Dillingham and Carlton   IX 101
————— M.I. at Shurborne Church co. Gloucester   VI 114

Cullen Viscount   I 97
Cullerne connected with King   III 273
Cullimore of Morton   XVI 88
Culver of Hoxton and of London co. Middlesex   I 337
Culwen or Curwen of Camberton, Workington, Sella Park in the
    psh of St Brides co. Cumberland, Grissiard, and Stubbe, see
    also Curwen   II 457–461
Cumberland, Clifford Earl of   XIV 18
——————— connected with Bernard and Cromwell   XV 21
Cumberlege connected with Hodges   V 280
Cunliffe High Sheriff of Cheshire   XXI 270
Cunningham of Boston connected with Fellows   Iv 429
Curling of Ramsgate co. Kent & of London co. Middlesex   I 138
Curr of Sannam connected with Stephens   IX 8
Currer of Brown Moor co. Selkirk; Holrule co. Teviotdale, the
    Town of Rule, Charles Town South Carolina and of
    Howick connected with Kerr   III 9
Curson M.I. at Morley co. Derby   VI 106
——————— of Kedleston co. Derby   III 276
——————— of Waterpury co. Oxon connected with Brinckhurst
    and Barnewall   III 182
——————— see also Curzon
Curteis of Glamorganshire, Bristol of Mardike in the psh of Clifton
    co. Gloucester   II 277
Curtis of Churton Mendip, Butcombe co. Somerset, and of
    Manchester co. Lancaster   I 169
——————— of Stamford co. Lincoln connected with Wildbore   II 107
——————— of Sutton co. Hants connected with Sheppard   II 484
——————— of Tenterden co. Kent and of Rye co. Sussex   I 332
Curwen connected with Musgrave   XXI 56
——————— M.I.   XIV 9
——————— of Camerton co. Cumberland   XXI 30
——————— of Workington ———————   XXI 62, 105
——————————————— Boltington in the psh of St Bees co.
    Cumberland, Weldon Peterborough, Kettering & Fenn
    Stanton co. Huntingdon   IV 18
——————— of Workington Hall co. Cumberland connected with
    Christian   VIII 35
——————— see Culwen
Curzon came out of Normandy with William the Conqueror, of
    Croxhall Kedleston co. Derby, Letheringset co. Norfolk
    Mursley in Bucks and of London co. Middlesex   XVI 53
——————— M.P. for Derbyshire   X 9
——————— see also Curson
Cusack of Gerardstown, Tirawly in Connaught, Killum co. Meath
    and of Duleck co. Drogheda   XIV 12–14
Cussans of Shrewsbury in the East in the psh of Clarendon in the
    Island of Jamaica   XXI 163
Cutcliffe of Ilfracombe, King's Ash, Hartland, Barnstable co.
    Devon, and of the Manors of Lincomb and West Warcombe   III 294
Cuthbertson of Alnwick and of Newcastle   X 135

Cutler of Fauwaite Darfield Stainborough, Barnsley Laming near
    Bedal co. York, and of Lechlade co. Gloucester   XIX 118
Cutt see Cutts   VIII 247
Cuttel of London co. Middlesex connected with Brown and Poole   IV 283
Cutling connected with Harmar   XX 144
———————— and Lester   I 360
Cutts or Cutt of Woodhall co. Essex Childesley co. Cambridge
    connected with Thurbane and Marshall   VIII 247

D

Dacre connected with Appleby   VII 175
———————— formerly ————————   X 140
———————— of Malfield als Mayfield co. Stafford Cheshunt, Tewin,
    Bedwell Park co. Herts London Clerkenwell co. Middlesex
    and of Letford co. Northampton   II 123
———————— of Malfield co. Stafford and of Cheshunt co. Herts   XVIII 40
———————————————————————————— Beswell Park,
    Marwell co. Southampton and of Stratford in Essex   III 175–7
———————— of Nathfield als Mayfield co. Stafford, Stratford co.
    Essex Cheshunt co. Herts Marvell co. Southampton,
    London co. Middlesex and of Bedwell Park   VI 102
Dacres see Dacre
Dalby of Castle Dunnington co. Leicester, Ockbrooke and of
    Hoppell co. Derby   IV 278
Dale connected with Andrews and Forbes   II 227
———————— of Brockminton co. Hereford connected with Wood
    and Duppa   II 339
———————— of Mark in the psh of St Briavels, and of Bristol co.
    Gloucester   XX 16[a]
———————— of St Briavels co. Gloucester   XX 112[a]
Dalison connected with Stanley   XXI 295
———————— see also Dalyson
Dallaway of Birmingham co. Warwick, and of Brinscombe in the
    psh of Stroud co. Gloucester   VIII 26
Dallway connected with Andrews   VII 92
Dallway connected with Andrewes   VIII 269
Dalston of Dalston and of Ulndale co. Cumberland   XXI 110
———————————————— co. Cumberland connected with
    Brathwayt   XXI 52
Dalton connected with Bingley   III 114
———————————— Grahme   XVIII 54
————————————————————————————————————   III 510
———————— M.I. At Hauxwell   XIV 12

Dalton in Beacon Ash Church co. Norfolk   VI 121
———————— of Byspham and of Thurn co. Palatine Lancaster
  connected with Bigland   VIII 319
———————— of Thornham Castle near Lancaster connected with
  More   V 11
Dalyson Dalison of Loughton, Greetwell co. Lincoln, Halling, and
  of West Peckham co. Kent   XVIII 4
———————— of Lawlen, Gretwell, Blesby, and of Laughton co.
  Lincoln   I 129
———————— of West Peckham co. Kent connected with Kirrell and
  Hodgskins   III 392
Dam, Van, connected with Reynst and Clifford   XI 40
Damarell of Hinton connected with Trenchard   VIII 178
Damer, Baron Milton, of Milton Abbey Dorset   XVI 21
Daniel connected with Bowles   I 146
———————— Draper   IV 23
———————— of Daresbury co. Chester   III 499
Daniell of London co. Middlesex   VIII 337
———————— of Yeovill co. Somerset and of London co. Middlesex   V 288
Dannet of Bosbury co. Herts connected with Stephens and
  Bourchier   XIX 49
Dansey of Brinsop connected with Reed   XIX 254
———————— Court co. Hereford connected with Mallet   VII 80
Danvers of Burton Calthrope, Banbury, Ippewell co. Oxon,
  Chamberhouse co. Berks, Upton co. Warwick, Blisworth
  co. Northampton and of London co. Middlesex   XIX 14
———————— of Cheslehampton, Banbury and of Crowthorp co.
  Oxford   XIX 10
———————— of Corsham co. Wilts said to be descended from
  Culworth co. Northampton   VIII 416
———————— of Cotherope connected with Unton   XVI 51
———————— of Culworth co. Northampton connected with Lord
  Say and Sele   VIII 241
———————— of Swithland co. Leicester, Chelsea co. Middlesex, the
  Forest co. Oxon and of Dantsey co. Wilts   VI 205
———————— of Swithland co. Leicester connected with Babington   XVI 79
Darby afterwards Coventry   XVII 36
———————— of Henley on Thames connected with Hawkins   XVII 36
———————— of Wombwell co. York   I 264
Darcey als Southwell, of Morton Horsham St Faith and of Spixworth
  co. Norfolk   II 130
———————— connected with Grey and Lawson   XXI 285
Darcy and Conyers, Lord, Earl of Holderness   VIII 468
———————— Lord   VIII 468
———————— of Chich, Viscount Colchester and Earl Rivers
  connected with Trenchard   VIII 181
Dare of Penn in the psh of Whittchurch near Lime co. Dorset,
  London co. Middlesex, Plymouth co. Devon, and of
  Madras   II 30
———————— of Taunton co. Somerset connected with George   VII 407

Darell of Chawcott co. Hants and of Cornwall, took the name of
    Trelawney   XVIII 7
———————— of Scotney co. Sussex, Collingborne co. Wilts and of
    Colehill co. Kent connected with Chichele   XIX 56
Darke of Cheltenham co. Gloucester connected with Ireland   III 70
Darley see Darleye   VI 371
Darleye of Darley co. Derby, Alderhouse Lee Wystowe Bittererame
    Bishop Wilton Audby and of Grays Inn co. Middlesex   VI 371
Darnell connected with Duke of Somerset and Hookes   XVIII 107
Darnley Hen Stewart Lord   XVI 9
Dartiquenave of Ilderton co. Northumberland connected with
    Bowerbanke and Dent   VII 480
Darvall of London co. Middlesex, Bencoolen Masutipatum East
    Indies and of Boulogne sur mer   XXI 11
Darwall of London co. Middlesex   XVI 99
Dashwood of Northbrook Leadwell co. Oxon and of Stanford Hall
    co. Notts   II 78
———————— of Wellhall co. Lincoln and of Heveningham co.
    Suffolk   II 77
———————— of West Wycombe co. Bucks Lord Despencer   XXI 288
Daston of Dumbleton co. Gloucester and of Hinton   XX 109[a]
Dath connected with Williams and Probyn   XX 151
Daubeny of Bristol connected with Baker   X 48
Daubigny, Lord, Duke of Lennox, connected with Darcy and
    Conyers   VIII 469
Daundelin connected with Champaigne   VIII 54
Daungers of Langford Parva, Maiden Bradley co. Wilts and of
    Moncton Parva   I 143
Daunt of Farhley co. Cork and of Owlpen co. Gloucester   XX 110, 111
———————— Ouldpen co. Gloucester   XIX 199
Davenport of Calveley   IX 100
———————— Petition as to change of name from Hulme   VI 384
David King of Scotland   VIII 251
———————— see Davies   III 397
Davidson of Newcastle co. Northumberland connected with
    Stodart   IV 522
Davie of Creedy co. Devon connected with Northleigh Clarke and
    Pollexson   II 421
Davies connected with Bird   VI 385
———————————— Jackson   VIII 60
———————————— Warburton   I 449
———————————— Wilbraham   V 130
———————— of Burnehall in the psh of Burien co. Cornwall   II 72
———————— Davis of Burnehill connected with Sandes and Noy   II 443
———————— of Bosworgy St Erth and Ednovean co. Cornwall
    connected with Noy   II 442
———————— of Chepstow co. Monmouth connected with Higford   XX 160[a]
———————— of Fawnhope Stretton Grantham co. Hereford   XVI 57
———————— of Gwasana co. Flint connected with Brockholes   V 5
———————— of Kellam als Cellam co. Cardigan   XIX 131

Davis of Langham and of Harwich co. Essex   XVIII 88
———————————— connected with Howell   III 397
————— of Llandovery co. Carmarthen and of Swansea co.
Glamorgan   IX 84
————— took the arms and surname of Howorth   VI 172
————— of Pontypool co. Monmouth connected with Moseley   VIII 13
————— of Slymbridge co. Gloucester and of London co.
Middlesex   XX 102ᵃ
Davis connected with Power and Owen   III 54
————— formerly Wood   II 339
————— of Bear Court in Tangbourn co. Berks and of Watlington
co. Norfolk   III 227
Davis of Chepstow connected with Higford   VIII 440
————— of Cliro in Radnorshire   VIII 376
————— of Ducklington co. Oxon   XX 208ᵃ
————— of Highworth co. Wilts and of London co. Middlesex
connected with Powers   II 374
———————————— afterwards Batson   XIX 253
————— of Tenby co. Pembroke connected with Rees or Rhys   IV 347
————— see Davies
Davison M.I. at Tredington co. Gloucester   IX 49
————— St Nicholas Church Newcastle upon Tyne   VII 375
                                                               VII 379
————— of Freshford co. Somerset connected with Ash   II 351
                                                               III 348
                                                               IV 93
————— of Richmond co. York connected with Gascoigne   XXI 217
Davy of Samford near Crediton co. Devon connected with Bidlake XIII 54
Davye connected with Bidgood   X 68
Davys connected with Meredith   VIII 80
————— of Chicksgrove co. Wilts   I 149
Dawbeney Lord, Earl of Bridgwater of Wayford co. Somerset and
of Gorwell co. Dorset   XVIII 67
Dawbeny ——————————————————————   III 328
Dawes connected with Bendish   I 114
————— of Moorfields connected with Sells   I 540
Dawney baptism and burial register   XIV 12
————— connected with Playdell   XX 214
———————————— Windham   II 86
————— of Aylesbury co. Bucks, London and of Hendon co.
Middlesex   VII 415
————— of Crownin, Aylesbury co. Bucks   VII 417
Daws connected with Thon   IX 1
Dawson of Ardee co. Louth   II 70
————— of Azerley near Ripon, London co. Middlesex
connected with Saville and Shepherd   VII 189
————— of Clare Castle co. Armagh co. Down and of Charles
Fort co. Wexford   II 71
————— of Lancliff Hall near Settle, Bolton, and of Holton Gill
co. York connected with Pudsey   II 434–6

Dawson of Newcastle & Tanfield co. Durham .... X 130
————————————— Tempsford co. Bedford, Little Hollesbury
    in Essex, and of Redriffe in Surrey .... XXI 124[a]
————————— of Terraby co. York .... I 406
Day connected with Crafton .... III 314
de Abbetot Lord of Elmley connected with Beauchamp .... VIII 253
de Abyngton flourished at Abyngdon co. Cambridge, Wyching-
    ford co. Worcester, and of Dowdeswell co. Gloucester .... XIX 169
de Aguilar, Baron of the Holy Roman Empire, of London co.
    Middlesex connected with de Costa .... IV 228
de Alphram connected with Legh and de Vernon .... II 168
Dean of Dennis Hall in Essex, and of the Inner Temple co.
    Middlesex .... IV 380
————————— of Gloucestershire and of Crutched Fryers co.
    Middlesex .... XIX 244
de Andeville Lord of Knebworth co. Herts connected with Hoo .... VIII 245
Deane of Dene of Awre, Bristol co. Gloucester, London co.
    Middlesex and of Newenham co. Herts .... XX 104
de Antioch of Tarent Rawson als Antiocheston Tarent Antioch co.
    Dorset connected with Lovell .... VIII 271
Dearling of Chichester connected with Parsons .... III 431
de Aslacton of Aslacton co. Nottingham connected with Cranmer .. VIII 258
de Aula see Hall .... XIX 208
Deaver connected with Cartwright .... XX 92
de Aylesbury co. Bucks of Edreston co. Warwick .... V 415
De Bass connected with Jol .... XVI 30
de Baynham afterwards Serjeaunt .... XIX 44
de Beauchamp Baron of Hache connected with Seymour and
    Mallet .... VII 74
de Beaufort Marquess of Dorset, Duke of Somerset .... VIII 249
de Beaumes connected with La Zouche .... VIII 249
de Belgrave connected with Grosvenor .... VI 155
de Bellomont Earl of Warwick .... VIII 254
de Belobee connected with Poulton .... XVI 18
de Brancion connected with Coulthurst .... III 81
de Braose Breos Braouse to whom William the Conqueror gave
    Brember Castle in Sussex, Lord Brecknock and Abergavenny
    connected with Poulton .... XVI 18
de Brian connected with Holway .... VIII 248
de Brockholes of Heton and Claughton Torresholme Merscough
    co. Palatine Lancaster .... V 4
de Brotherton connected with Stafford .... XVI 50
de Carew see Carew .... XIII 5, 6
de Carteret lord of St Oüen and Sark in the Island of Jersey, Baron
    Carteret of Hawnes in co. Bedford .... XIX 55
de Champaigne, came into England with William the Conqueror,
    of Thurleston co. Leicester .... VIII 54
de Chapeau of Picardy in France, London co. Middlesex, Shipton
    Solers co. Gloucester, Hurworth, Darlington co. Durham,
    Worcester, and of Shipton Olyffe .... I 72

de Chaucombe connected with Basset   VIII 51

de Clare came into England with William the Conqueror, Earl de
    Clare Earl of Pembroke, Lord Marshal of England connected
    with Poulton   XVI 18

de Clarmont als Clere als Claramond als Clary   V 417

de Clayton connected with Totleworth   XXI 263

de Clermont or Clarey Clere als Claramond als Clary of Ormesby
    Runham Blickling co. Norfolk   V 417

de Clinton lord of Bucksted co. Sussex   XXI 190

de Combe see Combe   XIII 54

de Conyers of Howton Conyers co. Durham   VIII 258

De Cotes connected with Moleins and Trenchard   VIII 178

de Courcy connected with Sadlier   I 348

————— Lord Kinsale connected with Blennerhasset   II 148

de Crespon Steward of Normandy connected with the Earl of
    Yvery   VIII 250

de Curzon see Curzon   XVI 53

de Dalston of the Barony of Dalston, the Manor of Ulndale and of
    Heath Hall co. York   XIV 30

de Eglesfield of Ellenborough Hall co. Cumberland & of
    Leckonfield co. York, Founder of Queen's College Oxon   XXI 200

de Ellol of Wyrdsall connected with de Molineux   VIII 257

de Engaine Lord of Graynsby co. Lincoln connected with de Welles   VIII 246

de Enys of Gluvias co. Cornwall   I 87

de Fraunkeville connected with de la Forterie   III 517

    IV 480

de Gernon afterwards Cavendish of Moor Hall co. Derby and of
    Grimston hall co. Suffolk   XVI 68

de Gernons Earl of Chester   VIII 251

Degge Knighted by Charles II, note as to   IX 13

————— of Derby connected with Walklate   XXI 305–6

————— of Stramshall in the psh of Uttoxeter co. Stafford and
    of Derby   XXI 112

de Gorges, co. Dorset and the Gascoignes, notes as to   VIII 536

————— lord of Wraxall   XX 200

de Grey of Merton co. Norfolk connected with Windham   V 43

————— De Gray —————   XVIII 22

————— of Cavendish Denardeston Stanfield co. Suffolk,
    Carbroke Gyrston Spikesworth Merton Wissingett co.
    Norfolk   VI 255

de Gwadir, Earl of the West Angles connected with Bellomont   VIII 250

De Handlo connected with Nigell and de la Pole   I 121

Dehaney of Jamaica and of London   I 194

de Hanslap connected with Mauduit   VIII 253

de Hastings connected with Champayne   VIII 54

————————————— de Windsor   XIII 1

de Heley ————————— Okeden   XI 27

de Heskaythe see Hesketh

de Holland connected with Molineux   VIII 257

de Hudleston lord of Millum   I 106

de Hungerford, Baron Hungerford and Hoytesbury of Down

Ampney co. Gloucester Cadenham, Calne co. Wilts and of
    Buscot co. Berks — XIX 204–5

de Kayton connected with Molineux — VIII 257

de Kyrkeshagh or Kyrshaw of Town Houses near Rochdale
    connected with Chadwyk — XI 26

de la Barre of Mons in Hainault in Flanders and of London co.
    Middlesex — I 20

de la Bech connected with Walker — VII 328

Delebere formerly Baghot — XIII 120

——————— of Southampton — XIII 120

Delabore of Southampton and of Prestbury co. Gloucester
    connected with Stephens — VII 142

de la Broc see Brooke — X 78

de la Est Court see Estcourt — XIX 230

de la Forterie connected with de Fraunkeville — III 517

——————— Fortray see Forterie — XVIII 143

——————— of Lisle in Flanders, settled at Canterbury of East
    Comb in the psh of Greenwich, Wombwell Hall in the psh
    of Northfleet co. Kent, Kew Green co. Surrey, Byall Farm
    co. Cambridge, and of Norton co. Leicester — IV 483

    — XVIII 143–5

de la Hall — XIX 208

Delamere, Booth Lord, connected with Clinton — IX 114

de Langley, Duke of York — XVI 9

de la Pole connected with Handlo and Rede — I 121

——————— see Pole — I 234

de la River, Rivers, of Tormorton — XX 200

——————— lord of Tormorton connected with Russell — XX 49[a]

de la Roche lord of Roche Castle — IX 76

de la Spencer see Spencer — VI 52

De Laune of London co. Middlesex, Sharsted and Doddington co.
    Kent — I 184

    — IV 70

Delaval of Dissington Seaton Delaval co. Northumberland and of
    Doddington co. Lincoln — XVI 78

——————— of Ford Castle — XXI 2

Delawar Thomas West, Lord — XIV 23

De la Warre, Baron, connected with Mallet — VII 76

de la Zouch of Codnore — I 445

——————— of Haringworth and of Ashby co. Leicester connected
    with Bamfield — XIX 97

de Lega, Leigh, see Legh — II 168

    — X 115

de Leycester of Toft Tabley, Aston Hayes, Stanthorne Hill,
    Wallasey, Worleston, and of Mobberley co. Chester — VI 153

Delgarno of Newport Isle of Wight connected with Dickinson and
    Troughear — VI 239

de Lima of Amsterdam connected with Norden — XXI 184

de Lisle connected with Tyes — VIII 255

de Louther see Lowther

de Lovanio Baron of Aye and of Askew — XIII 1

Delprat of Bristol and of the Island of Jamaica — VI 178
Delves connected with Huband — IX 144
————— of Dudington in Cheshire connected with Bushell — XIX 151
de Maigne Earl of Hereford — XIX 90
de Mendoza connected with Alvez and Rebello — III 317
de Meschines Earls of Chester — VIII 251
de Millum connected with Hudleston — V 345
de Molineux of Sefton co. Lancaster, Haughton Mansfield, Teversall co. Nottingham, and of London co. Middlesex — VIII 257
de Moorhouse connected with Joudrell — III 363
Demoulin of St Christophers in the West Indies connected with Arnold — III 153
de Nassau, Lord of Zulestein in the Province of Utrecht connected with Killigrew — VI 150
Dene of Awre see Deane or a Deane — XX 104
de Newburgh Earl of Warwick — XVI 82
de Newmarche – a noble Norman and conqueror of Brecknockshire connected with Paulton — XVI 18
Denford connected with Gunter — XIX 266
Denmar of the Farm Newington, and of Houndsditch, connected with Ware — II 240
Denne of Denne Hill Wye, Lyd co. Kent, London co. Middlesex, and of Winchelsea co. Sussex — II 22
Dennett connected with Pitt — X 62
Dennis Dennys of Dyrham Pucklechurch and of Siston co. Gloucester — XIX 159
————— — XX 99
————— — XX 200
————— of Beckford Bristol co. Gloucester and of London co. Middlesex — XIX 157
————— of Bristol connected with Brain — XV 79
————— of Chelworth in Cricklade connected with Ray and Fettyplace — I 152
————— of Pucklechurch co. Gloucester — XIII 103
————— of Waterford Dublin co. Kildare Carrown Tubber co. Galway — II 16
Dennison connected with Thirsk — IX 6
————— of Leeds co. York connected with Sunderland — VII 286
Denny of Giseton co. Gloucester connected with Porter — X 69
————— of Surrenden Denny co. Kent — XX 114
————— of Thurlton Langley Toft Monks Raveningham and of Great Yarmouth co. Norfolk — XXI 10
————— of Tralee and of Ballyvelly — II 313
Dennys of Barnstaple and Wolcot now Duryard co. Devon — I 126
————— of Erdicot Dirham Ogmor Marlow of the Manor of Knowgheless High Sheriffs of the County of Gloucester and of Wales — XIX 159
————— — XX 99
————— — XX 200
————— see Dennis — XIX 159
de Norbury connected with de la Horne — I 441

Dent of Halloughton co. Leicester Thornbury Park co. Gloucester,
    London co. Middlesex and of Newport Pond co. Essex   VII 482
———————— of Ipswich co. Suffolk   VII 480
———————— of London, Edmonton co. Middlesex, descended from
    Leicestershire, a Rear Admiral in the British Navy   VII 479
———————— of York and of Newcastle upon Tyne co. Northum-
    berland   VII 477
———————— Prebendary of Westminster   VII 478
Denton of Wilton, Weeting co. Norfolk and of Brandon in Suffolk   XXI 43
Denys connected with Fitzwarren   XX 200[a]
———————— of Alveston and of Dirham see also Dennys or Dennis   XIX 159
————————————————————————————   XX 99
————————————————————————————   XX 200

de Pascale, Marquis, connected with Frampton   I 452
Depden connected with Trenchard   VIII 178
de Perwynge connected with Walker and de Scaleby   VII 329
de Pull, Pull, see Poole   XIX 80
de Quincey Earl of Winchester connected with Lord of Galloway
    and La Zouche   VIII 250
——————————————————— connected with Poulton   XVI 18
de Quincy connected with de la Zouch   XIX 97
de Ramsay connected with Clerke   XVIII 2
Derby, Stanley Earl of, see Stanley
Derbyshire of Brackley connected with Grey and Thicknesse   I 148
Dere of St Athen and Tralhum co. Glamorgan connected with
    Roberts   II 10
Derehurst connected with Berewe   XIX 7
————————————————————————————   XIX 102

Derelove of the Borough Southwark connected with Dare   II 31
de Riddell lord of Wittening co. Northampton connected with
    Basset   VIII 51
de Ridlesford connected with Longspee   VIII 252
Dering of Surrenden Dering co. Kent connected with Barkham and
    De Laune   I 183
Derwentwater Earl of, connected with Webbe   XIII 118
——————————————— see Radcliffe and Ratcliffe
de St Clere seized of lands in Sussex, of Aston Clinton co. Bucks
    connected with Gage   XIX 64
de St Poll or Poole connected with Stanton   X 69
de Say lord of the Manor of Stoke co. Salop, and of Richards
    Castle, connected with Mortimer   XVIII 95
de Scaleby connected with Walker   VII 329
Deschamps of the City of Paris and of London co. Middlesex   XXI 179
de Schepden als Drake   XXI 277–80
de Sevenhouse see Senhouse   XXI 200
Desmadryll of Madryll of Trimnels co. Essex afterwards Madryll
    Cheere   VIII 457
de Sodington connected with Blount   XVI 64
————————————————————————————   XIX 219

Despencer, Le, Baroness   IX 6
de Stafford connected with Hesketh   XXI 263

de Strickland of Sisergh co. Westmorland, Cherick, Catherick, Thornton Bridge co. York, and of Lincolns Inn co. Middlesex   VIII 342

———— of Sisergh co. Westmorland; Heslington Catterick, Richmond, Boynton in the Would co. York, Lincolns Inn co. Middlesex, Hackelthorpe & Thornton Brigge   VII 292

de Stuteville Baron of Cottingham   VIII 252

de Talbot of co. Salop connected with Bowers   XVIII 39

Dethick connected with Hawley   VIII 453

———— M.I. at Barton co. Nottingham   VI 111

———— of Dethick co. Derby, London and Poplar co. Middlesex, and of Gretham co. Durham, Garter Principal King of Arms   XIX 153

———— of Leigh connected with Kinardsley   XXI 308

de Threhouse see Hotham   XVIII 82–7

de Throkemerton and de Throkemertona see Throckmorton   XVI 34

de Throkemertona and de Throkemerton see Throckmorton   XVI 34

de Tony, Lord Tony of Flamsted connected with Beauchamp Earl of Warwick   VIII 254

de Totleworth, Lord of Totleworth, connected with Hesketh   XXI 263

Devall of South River Maryland connected with Poole   III 492

de Valonys connected with Blount   XVI 64

Devenish of Hellingleigh co. Sussex connected with Tauke Smallpage and Wheatley   VIII 244

de Verdon connected with Pantulph Baron of Wem   XIX 90

de Vere Earl of Oxford connected with Scrope   XX 18

———— Lord of Bolebec and Stamford   XIX 25

Deverell of Westerleigh and Minchinhampton co. Gloucester   XX 113[a]

de Vernon connected with de Alphram and Legh   II 168

Devile connected with Gulston   XV 10

de Villiers of Crosby connected with Mollineux   VIII 257

de Vivonia of Acquitaine and Gascony also of Sellings co. Kent connected with Mallet   VII 74

Dew of Goodrich co. Hereford   XX 85

de Wake, Lord Wake of Lydell connected with Brewer   VIII 252

de Warburton als Dutton lord of the Manors of Arley co. Chester   XIX 181

Dewell of Lidyard Millicent co. Wilts connected with Dore   VII 466

———— of Lidyard Tregoz co. Wilts connected with Dore   VII 465

de Welles, Lord, connected with Hoo and Waterton   VIII 245

D'Ewes of Great Coughton co. Warwick Long Marston co. Gloucester and of Maplebury Green   I 387

———— to Granville, Petition   VI 382

de Wesenham M.I.   VIII 44

de Windesore, a Noble Baron connected with Hodenge and Scudamore   XVIII 57

de Windsor of Stanwell co. Middlesex, Baron Windsor connected with Andrews   VIII 266

———— see Windsor   XIII 1

de Workedsly see Worsley   XXI 296

de Wynston see Winston   XIX 32

Dexter of Flewitt Kegworth connected with Aynsworth	II 325
Deye of Eye co. Suffolk	I 229
Dicas of the City of Chester	XVII 60
Dickens of London co. Middlesex, Ripplington co. Southampton Cowling co. Suffolk and of Wollaston co. Northampton	II 121
———— of New Forest Riplington co. Hants Cowling co. Suffolk and of Wollaston co. Northampton	X 64
Dickenson connected with Tilby	I 125
———— of the Isle of Wight connected with Troughear	VI 240
Dickins connected with Sparke	III 479
Dickinson of Scarborough and of Hackness co. York	III 145
———— of Ware co. Wilts and of London co. Middlesex	III 284
Dickleston connected with Higford	XIX 210
Dickson connected with Collingwood	X 155
———— of Smolholm, Spittle, Roxburgh, Court Hill, Orchard in the psh of Cavers in the Shire of Roxburgh	I 88
Digby Bishop of Dromore and Limerick, Dean of Cashell, of Landens Town co. Kildare, Ring Mahon Castle co. Cork, Twickenham co. Middlesex, and of the City of Bristol	VII 258
Dillingham of Dean co. Bedfordshire and of Hampton	IX 101
Dillon certificate for livery	IX 15
———— certificates of marriage and burial	XIII 10
———— connected with Newland	X 18
———————— Wingfield	I 556
Dimock of Bisley Stonehouse co. Gloucester, and Rector of Uppingham co. Rutland	XVII 48[b]
Dimsdale connected with Bell and Champion	III 264
Dine of Lankhurst co. Sussex	IV 379
Dinsdale of Middleham co. York connected with Wilson and Crosfield	III 14
Dipden of Dipden near Christchurch co. Hants connected with Brudenel and Waller	XVIII 96
Dirwin connected with Hache	VII 75
Disbrowe ———— Dismadryl – letter as to marriage	XIII 82
Dismadryl ———— Disbrowe ————	XIII 82
Disney of Pontefract connected with Thorpe	III 46
Dixon connected with Hamilton of Silverton Hall	III 262
———————— Penith	X 72
———————— Sandis	XXI 15
———— of Frishope Burne in Wear Dorile co. Durham Swindon co. Wilts, and of High Huntrods in East Allimdorle co. Northumberland	XVI 54
———— of Newcastle and of Belford co. Northumberland	X 136
———— of Freshopeburn and Burnhope also of Belford co. Northumberland	X 141–4
Dobbs connected with Wyatt	X 44
Dobinson of Carlisle co. Cumberland connected with Curwen or Culwen	II 461
Dobree of Guernsey and of Hackney co. Middlesex	VI 246
Dobson of Bingley co. York connected with Ferrand	I 53

Dobson of London co. Middlesex	III 408
Dobyns afterwards Dobyns-Yate of Winchester, Bristol Bromsberrow co. Gloucester, Bishop Frome co. Hereford and of co. Cork	I 11
———— of the Middle Temple co. Middlesex assumed the name of Yate	XX 263[a]–5
Dobyns-Yate see Dobyns	I 11
Dockenfield of Dockenfield	XIV 4
Docminigua connected with Edwards	II 412
Dod of Calverhale als Calverhall Lord of the Manor of Cloreley; of Pixley co. Salop, Birmingham co. Warwick, Hegge co. Chester, and of Lea co. Worcs	XXI 301
	XXI 313–15
Dodge of Wrotham co. Kent and of Worrington co. Norfolk	XX 101
Dodingselles als Twenge	XXI 263
Dodington of Hants connected with Hoby	VII 65
Dodsworth of Barton co. York connected with Killinghall	VII 275
———— of Scarborough co. York and of London co. Middlesex	II 327
Dodwell connected with Fuller	XV 69
———— of Dublin and Sligo in the Kingdom of Ireland, Salisbury, Bishops Connongs co. Wilts, Maidenhead co. Berks, Welby, Harlexton Colsterworth co. Lincoln and of London co. Middlesex	I 118
———— of Sevenhampton and of Stroud co. Gloucester	XIX 119
———— of Souldern co. Oxon connected with Austin	XV 59
———— of the City of Oxford – wills etc.	VII 381–9
Dolben Bishop of Rochester connected with Sheldon	XXI 252
Domet of Lyme connected with Cartwright	I 488
Donald IV King of Scotland connected with Walker	VII 328
Donne of Ockington connected with Hookes & Dutton	XVIII 107
Donnellan afterwards Beauchamp connected with Boughton	VIII 410
Donovan of Antigua connected with Dobyns-Yate	I 12
Dore als Mabb of Burton co. Worcester connected with Acton	XIX 6
———— of Bourton in the psh of Shrivenham, Blewberry, Longcot, Ashbury co. Berks, London co. Middlesex, Onger co. Essex, Husborne Tarrant co. Southampton, Luddington als Liddenton, Hinton Parva, East Leaze Wickfield in the psh of Lidyard Tregose, Lidyard Millicent, Ramsbury, Mannington, West Leaze, Longcot and Earls Court in the psh of Wanbro' co. Wilts, Norroy King of Arms	VII 468
———— of Longcot co. Berks, Little Hinton co. Wilts, Thornbury co. Gloucester, Bluemantle, and Richmond Herald	XVI 28
Dormer of Grove Park co. Warwick, Lord Dormer	XXI 324
———— of Shipton Loe	XIII 101
———— of West Wycombe co. Bucks	XVI 94–8
———— Shipton Lee als Lee Grange, and of Lincolns Inn co. Middlesex	XX 103[a]
———— of the city of Antwerp, Lord Dormer, Baron of Wenge in the County of Buckingham	IX 13
Dorrington connected with Shellard	XX 207[a]

Dorrington of London co. Middlesex, Wittersham co. Kent, Tame
co. Oxon and of Camberwell co. Surrey | III 62
Dorset Grey Marquess of | XIV 18
———— Marquess of, | VIII 249
———— Sackville Earl of, connected with Tufton Earl of
Thanet | XIII 68
Dottin of Barbadoes connected with Estwick | II 303
Doughty of Snarfoot Hall co. Lincoln | I 86
——————————————————————————— | XXI 203

———— of Esher co. Surrey, Snarford Hall co. Lincoln con-
nected with Brownlow | IX 9
Douglas connected with Gough and Kingston | XIX 186
——————————————————————————— | XX 11, 13, 14[a]
———— Earls of Angus, a genealogical tree of the family | VII 449–52
———— of Newcastle upon Tyne | XXI 1
———————————— Governor of Hartlepool co. Durham | X 146
———— of Fowey co. Cornwall Baron Glenbervie of Kin-
cardine, of Midhurst co. Sussex, Fechil in the psh of Ellon
co. Aberdeen, and of Kilmonth | VII 456–7
———— of Halton Castle and of Newcastle co. Northum-
berland connected with Blackett | II 55
Dove of Salisbury co. Wilts connected with Jones | XIX 155
Dover Carey Earl of, connected with Cockaine | I 97
———— of Norfolk | XVII 9
———————————— and of Barton in the Heath co. Warwick | XIX 267
Dowdeswell of Pull Court co. Worcester and of the City of
Gloucester | XX 105
———————————— connected with Winnington | IV 124
Dowker of Chesterfield, London co. Middlesex, Liverpool co. Pal.
Lancaster, and of Duckmanton co. Derby | VIII 484
Dowling of Suffolk, Pensford co. Somerset and of London | II 358
Downe Earl of, M.I. in Sherborne Church co. Gloucester | VI 114
Downes of co. Derby, London co. Middlesex, Sheffield and
Ecclesfield co. York | I 8
———— of Greenfield, Letton co. Herefordshire, Tenbury co.
Worcester, Rainham, Ashford Carbonel co. Salop, and of
Basingstoke co. Hants | IX 116
———— of Wardly M.I. at Wigan co. Lancaster | XIV 9
Downey M.I. | XIV 9
Downish of Heath co. Devon connected with Cole | XX 82[a]
Downshire, Hill Marquess of | VIII 243
D'Oyley of Banbury, Alderbury and of Bodicote co. Oxon | VII 62
Doyne of Wells co. Wexford M.I. | XVI 49
Drage of Biggleswade co. Bedford, Greenwich co. Kent, London
co. Middlesex, and of Dublin | I 92
Drake als de Schepden of Horley Green in the psh of Halifax,
Dodworth, Thornton in Craven, Beverley co. York; Bray-
toft co. Lincoln, Bernoldswick Coates, and of London co.
Middlesex | XXI 277–80
———— connected with Colserat | IV 8

Drake connected with Seward of Lichfield see also Drake of
Salcombe — X 126[a]

—————— of Ash, Yardbury in the psh of Colyton, Trill in the
psh of Axminster co. Devon — IV 418

—————— of Buckland co. Devon connected with Pocock see also
Drake of Tavistock, Sir Francis Drake — VII 70

—————— of Bucks — IV 305

—————— of Dunscombe, Salcombe, and of Sidmouth co. Devon — IV 416

—————— of Otterton, Exmouth, Ashe, Mount Drake, and of
Trill — V 413

—————— of Salcombe, Dunscombe, Ash, Colyton Yardbury,
Trill in the psh of Axminster, Spratshays in the psh of
Littleham, Daleditch in the psh of East Budleigh co. Devon
see also Drake connected with Seward — XVIII 43–5

—————— of Shirley co. Surrey connected with Long — I 203

—————— of Spratshays, Dale Ditch in the psh of Budleigh,
Salcombe co. Devon, Middle Temple co. Middlesex, and of
Bystocke — IV 420

—————— of Tavistock, Buckland Monachorum co. Devon — V 411

—————— of Woodstock Park co. Oxon — VII 493

—————— Sir Francis – grant of arms by Queen Elizabeth — XXI 119

Draper connected with Sclater — II 151

—————— of Bedenwell als Kellam Crayford Erith Bexley Bromley Plumstead co. Kent, Beswick co. York, Netherwotten
co. Oxon, London co. Middlesex, co. Essex, and of
Bombay — IV 20

—————— of Coland als Culland co. Derby connected with Port
and Harper — I 251

—————— of Hampstead co. Middlesex — IV 353

—————— of Malmesbury co. Wilts and of London co. Middlesex — II 336

—————— of Newent co. Gloucester and —————— — XX 107[a]

—————— of Remenham Sunning Hill Park co. Berks and of
Agecombe Croydon co. Surrey — V 451

Drax of Charborough co. Dorset and of Ellerton Abby co. York
connected with Erneley — IV 184

Draycote connected with Blomer — IX 120

Drew —————— Waldron — XIII 115

—————— of Drew Court co. Limerick and of Dublin connected
with Prestwich and Ringrose — I 298

Drewry of the City of Lincoln, Hull co. York and of Derby — III 148

Driden of Staffehill in Cumberland Farndon Tichmarch Canons
Ashby co. Northampton Chesterton co. Huntingdon and of
East Hempstead co. Berks — I 135

Drihurst of Denbigh connected with Grimsditch, Conway and
Hookes — XVIII 107

Dring afterwards Thring — I 268

Driver of Gloucester — XXI 209

—————— of Rodborough co. Gloucester connected with
Holbrow — I 172

Drummond afterwards Pinkerton — I 256

Drummond connected with Smith of Braco	I 482
———— of Hawthornden	I 256
Drury connected with Lloyd	III 230
———————— Tyrell	VIII 97
———— of Nottingham and of Okeham co. Rutland connected with Lowe and Greatorex	III 28
———— of Watergate in the psh of Upmarden co. Sussex connected with Cooper	X 29
Dry of Bermondsey co. Surrey connected with Newton	III 495
Dubois connected with Mansergh	X 3, 5
Ducie, Moreton, Baron, of Moreton co. Stafford and of Tortworth co. Gloucester	XX 100[a]
———— of co. Stafford, London co. Middlesex, Viscount Down in Ireland	XX 100[a]
———— of Willanhall, Little Aston co. Stafford, London co. Middlesex, Viscount Downe in Ireland	XX 106
Duckett of Grayrigg co. Westmorland	XXI 69
Duckinfield of Bristol, Utkinton co. Chester, London co. Middlesex, and of Jamaica	I 484
Duckworth of Bucksand, Stoke and Rislip co. Middlesex and of Manchester co. Lancaster	III 221
Ducy see Ducie	XX 106
Dudley of Yeanwith co. Cumberland and of Newington co. Middlesex, Lord Dudley	XXI 36
———— Sutton Lord connected with Blount	XIII 1
Dugdale Sir William, Garter	III 131
Duke of Otterton St Mary co. Devon connected with Taylor and Young	III 105
Dumaresq of St Ouen Brelades in the Island of Jersey	III 463
Dumbleton of Bourton on the Hill co. Gloucester	VIII 375
Dun see Dunn connected with Sheldon	VII 46
Dunbar connected with North	I 551
———— Earl of	II 454
———— of Mocknen and of Liverpool co. Pal. Lancaster	VIII 391
Dunch connected with Hungerford	V 256
————————————————————	V 56
Duncombe als Browne	III 30
———— formerly Browne	IV 291
———— of Drayton co. Bucks and of London co. Middlesex	IV 291
———— of Moreton co. Bucks and of Dodington co. Oxon connected with Colchester	XIX 153
———— of Whitchurch and of Drayton co. Bucks	III 31
Dundas of Dundas Castle connected with Lord Forbes	II 228
Dundee Viscount, title claimed by Graham	XVII 54
Dunford of the City of Bristol and of Cramlington co. Northumberland connected with Stodart	IV 516
Dungate of Reigate, Croydon, Bermondsey co. Surrey, and of London co. Middlesex	IV 410
Dunmore of Hackney co. Middlesex, and of Eversley co. Hants – Baptisms etc.	VI 286

Dunn afterwards Dunn-Gardner of Houghton near Darlington co.
    Durham, London co. Middlesex and of Chatteris in the Isle
    of Ely & County of Cambridge   VIII 290
————— connected with Sheldon also Dun   I 321
————— Dun of Garnish Hall in Essex and of West Heath co.
    Worcester connected with Sheldon   VII 46
——   III 330
————— of Leamington co. Warwick connected with Strother   XXI 148
————— of Newton and Leamington connected with Strother   XXI 161
————— of Stella in the County of Durham and of Newcastle
    upon Tyne co. Northumberland   XVII 65
Dunn-Gardner formerly Dunn of Houghton near Darlington co.
    Durham, London co. Middlesex, and of Chatteris in the Isle
    of Ely and County of Cambridge   VIII 290
Dunne of Grays Inn connected with Errington   I 94
Duppa of Longvile co. Salop, Bromyard and Batchley co.
    Hereford   II 338
Durham connected with Buckland and Whitehead   VIII 372
————————————————— Temple   XVII 30
————— of Postlip near Winchcomb co. Gloucester   XX 108ª
Durling connected with Allen and Thompson   XXI 157
Durnford connected with Isaacson   I 308
—————————————————————   XVI 69
—————————————————————   XXI 147

Dutton lord of the Manors of Dutton and of Arley co. Chester als
    de Warburton   XIX 181
————————————— M.I. at Loughcrew co. Meath   VI 115
————————————— at Shireborne Church co. Gloucester   VI 114, 290
————————————— of Dutton connected with Donne and Hookes   XVIII 107
————————————— of Sherborne co. Gloucester   XX 98ª
Dycer of Wrentham co. Suffolk Uphall co. Herts and of Hackney
    co. Middlesex   VI 63
Dycher connected with Hill of Hawkstone co. Salop   XVIII 118
Dyck of Vries in Drenthe and of Groningan connected with
    Koostray   IV 317
Dyer connected with Griffin   VIII 515
————————————————— Stonestreet   VIII 520
————————————————— of Leicestershire   VIII 2
————————————————— of Newton Hall and of Spains Hall
    Thrasted co. Essex   II 405
Dykes afterwards Ballantine of Warthole, Gilcruse, Shadwell, and
    of Crookdale Hall in the psh of Bromfield co. Cumberland   II 406
————— of Bishops Lideard near Taunton, Clive Abbey near
    Watchet, Frome co. Somerset, and of Cardiff co.
    Glamorgan   VIII 489
————— of Warthole or Wardhole and of Crookdale Hall in the
    psh of Bromfield co. Cumberland   V 303
Dykes-Ballantine   V 303
Dymer of Fyfield co. Wilts, of the City of Bristol, and of Redlands
    in the psh of Westbury super Trim co. Gloucester   XIX 206
Dymock of Nottingham connected with White   II 3

Dymock of Sweyton co. Lincoln, Sesses in Cranfield, Ampthill
    co. Bedford, and of Newport   VII 354
Dymond of Brierley in the psh of Felkirk, Cramb, Jamaica, Blith
    co. Nottingham and of London co. Middlesex   III 160
Dynghill connected with Hawker   XIX 158
Dynham ———————— Handlo and Rede   I 121
Dyon of New London connected with Chew   IX 131
Dyott of Dyott Street ——————— Meadows and Skip   II 141
Dyson connected with Glover   VI 215
———————————————— Philipps   IX 105
———————————————— Savage   XIX 102
—————————————————   XIX 129

E

Eades of the Devizes co. Wilts and of London co. Middlesex   I 58
Eagles of Bristol connected with Perkins   I 29
Earl of Winton   I 500
Earle connected with Read   IX 118
——————— formerly Benson   XXI 116
——————— of Craglethorpe and Scragelthorpe   V 409
——————— of Crudwell co. Wilts   XX 117[a]
East of London co. Middlesex, Peckham co. Surrey, Hall Place in
    the psh of Hurley co. Berks   X 10, 11
——————— of Peckham co. Surrey and of London co. Middlesex   X 26, 27
Eastwell connected with Sperring   XIII 91
Eaton afterwards Browne of Downham and Elsing co. Norfolk   VII 39
——————— of Halford Hall near Sandbatch, Branch-a-Wood,
    Wrembury Namptwich co. Chester, and of Bristol co.
    Gloucester   IV 340
——————— of Lane in the Lordship of Whitley, Mobberley and
    Grappenhall co. Chester connected with Port   I 250
——————— of Rainham co. Essex connected with Pell   I 285
Eburne of Coventry co. Warwick   XVIII 138
——————————————— connected with Makepeace   IV 471
Echingham of Echingham co. Sussex   XIII 1
Eddy connected with Carpenter   XX 78[a]
Eden ——————— Lowth   X 53
———————————————————————————   X 62
——————————————— Shaftoe   XXI 124
Edgar of Bristol co. Gloucester   I 343
Edge connected with Fane   V 208
Edmonds of Preston Deanery Alstone co. Northampton and of
    America   II 288

Ednevet Vachan   XIV 20
Edolphe of Brenset co. Kent connected with Wilcocks and May   VIII 267
Edward I   XVI 9
——————— connected with Philip of France and with Hookes   XVIII 105
——————————— Stafford   XVI 50
——————— II   XVI 9
——————— connected with Stafford   XVI 50
——————— III   XVI 9
————————————————————————————————————   XXI 229
——————— connected with Barrington and Lowndes   V 174
————————————————— Hudleston Eyre and Neville   II 390
————————————— Stafford   XVI 50
——————— IV   XVI 9
——————— connected with Woodvile and Gray of Groby   XXI 242
Edward V   XVI 9
——————— Prince of Wales   XVI 9
Edwardes of Rhydgorse in the Borough of Carmarthen Glentery
    co. Cardigan afterwards Gwynne connected with Jones of
    Tyglyn   XV 26–32
——————— Edwards of Greete and Frodesley co. Salop   III 97
Edwards connected with Allen   I 517
————————————————— Freeman   XVII 15
————————————————— Urry   III 388
——————— Edwardes of Greete and Frodesley co. Salop   III 97
——————— M.I. at Westbury upon Severn co. Gloucester   VI 116
——————— of Cirencester co. Gloucester connected with Timbrell   III 51
——————— of Croggen in the psh of Llanderdville co. Merioneth,
    and of London co. Middlesex   VIII 85
——————— of Filkins co. Oxford   XVI 52
——————— of Haverfordwest co. Pembroke created Lord
    Kensington   VIII 81
——————— of Highgate co. Middlesex connected with Holford   XX 147[a]
——————— Huntingdon   IX 103
——————— of Llawag and Cerrigllwydion in the psh of Llanynnys
    co. Denbigh Bodlewyddan in the psh of St Asaph co. Flint   XVII 45
——————— of Newbury, Wingfield co. Berks, Kilworth Beau-
    champ co. Leicester, and of London co. Middlesex   II 412
——————— of Wales   XVIII 14, 15
Edwin formerly Windham   II 85
Egerton connected with Saunders   XXI 171[a]
————————————————— Skinner   III 226
————————————————— Walker   VII 329
————————————————— Warburton   XIII 14
——————— Lord Ellesmere and Earl of Bridgewater connected
    with Spencer   VI 55
——————— of London co. Middlesex and of Bombay, Bishop of
    Durham   III 225
——————— of Wrunhil co. Chester connected with Griffith   XIV 16
Eglesfield of Elenbrough or Alnbrough in Wales, and of Oxford   VII 177
Eglington, Earl of, connected with Macdonald   XXI 204
Egremont, Wyndham Earl of   I 544

Eliott or Elyott extracts from wills	X 55
Ellerker formerly Manwaring connected with Dixon	X 144
—————— of Ellerker, Risby & Youlton co. York	I 132
Elletson of Stannerley M.I.	XIV 9
Elliot connected with Keble	IV 258
—————— of Port Elliot connected with Fleming and Willis	XXI 218
Elliott connected with Lettsom	VIII 11
—————— formerly Ovens	II 466
—————— of Dursley, Edgworth, Bristol, Eastington, Stonehouse co. Gloucester, Binfield co. Berks and of London co. Middlesex	II 466
—————— of Gatacre Park in the psh of Claverley and County of Salop, Stratford co. Hereford and of Radnorshire	XXI 202
—————— of Lariston in the psh of Castleton in the County of Seddlesdale; Brough and Southfield in the psh of Hawick co. Tivodale in Scotland	IX 153
—————— of Plymouth co. Devon connected with Bidlake	XXI 150
—————— Register of the psh of Claverley co. Salop	XIV 12
Ellis connected with Bowles	VII 91
—————————— Cartwright	XV 82
—————————— Long	I 202
—————— of Aley co. Flint connected with Fiennes	I 423
—————— of Elbey in Stonehouse co. Gloucester	XX 187
—————— of Jamaica, and of London co. Middlesex connected with Beckford	I 190
—————— of Minstonworth connected with Vyner	IX 163
—————— of Orford co. Suffolk	IX 39
—————— of Stow on the Would co. Gloucester connected with Margetts	II 322
—————— of Yorkshire and of London co. Middlesex connected with Peers	V 86
—————— to Rodbard petition as to change of name	IX 17
Ellison afterwards Carr	X 135
—————— of Ebburne Park House near Gateshead	X 132
—————— of Newcastle connected with Carr	X 135
Ellsworth of Knowle co. Somerset, Redland and Bristol co. Gloucester	XIX 82
Ellwood of London co. Middlesex connected with Bell and Sargent	III 268
Ellys of Grantham Wyham Noeton co. Lincoln and of London co. Middlesex	XVII 35
Elmes of Aldworth co. Berks and of London co. Middlesex	II 63
Elphinstone connected with Warburton	I 450
	VII 287
Elphinstone date of births in pshs of Aldgate, Peckham, Westminster, Plymouth etc	IX 68
Elton als Baker	XIX 18
—————————	XX 116
————————— of Munslow, Much Marcle, Ledbury co. Hereford, Salisbury co. Wilts, and of Newent co. Gloucester	I 109
—————— of Bristol connected with Peach	I 271
—————————	XIX 225

Elton of Ledbury and of Munslow co. Hereford — XIX 18

———— of Nether Hall Ledbury Munslow co. Hereford, Newent and Bristol co. Gloucester — XX 115ᵃ–16ᵃ

———— of the Hasle in the psh of Ledbury co. Hereford connected with Cocks — XIX 31

Elwes Helwish see Helwis

———— of Stoke College co. Suffolk Binfield co. Berks, Aldershot co. Hants and of Isleworth co. Middlesex — II 485

Elyott connected with Wyndham and Janes — X 55

———— Eliott extracts from wills — X 55

Emerson of Irestone connected with Dixon — X 142

Emmerton formerly Westcomb — XVII 66

Emmet of London co. Middlesex — VII 214

Emmett connected with St George — VII 407

Emmott Emot co. Lancaster extracts from wills etc — VII 202

———— formerly Wainhouse — VII 221

———— of Emmott in the psh of Colne Wycoller Clitheroe co. Lancaster Goldings in the psh of Bengoe co. Herts and of Bolton in Bolling co. York — VII 222

Emms connected with Beale and Haywood — XX 66ᵃ

Emot see Emmott

Emuss of Bromsgrove co. Worcester — IX 86

Englefield connected with Huntley — XIX 237

English of Arkelby co. Cumberland and of Kingswood co. Wilts connected with Hodges — XIX 255

———— Prebend of Gloucester descended out of Worcestershire, Rector of Taynton co. Gloucester — XIX 245

Ennlee or Annlee connected with Jol — XVI 30

Entwisel Viscount, and Baron of Brykbeke in Normandy — XI 26

Entwisle connected with Millikin — III 154

———— formerly Markland — XI 25

———— of Entwisle Hall in the psh of Bolton, Foxholes in Huddersfield in the psh of Rochdale, Wigan and of Preston co. Lancaster — XI 17–26

———— of Foxholes, Middle Temple co. Middlesex and of co. Palatine Lancaster — I 439

Enys of Enys co. Cornwall connected with Penrose — II 226

Erisey of Erisey co. Cornwall connected with Killigrew — VI 150

Erle of Charborough co. Dorset connected with Ernley — IV 184

Ernele Ernley of Ernele, Chichester co. Sussex, Burton in All Cannings, Sutton Benger Hanley, Whitham, Brimslade Park, Echelhampton, New Sarum and of Madington co. Wilts — V 338

———— see Ernley

Ernley of Ernley co. Sussex, Borton in Cannings, Whetham, Conock, Echillhampton als Ashlington co. Wilts — VI 36

———— of Maddington co. Wilts connected with Drax — IV 184

Errington afterwards Stapleton — I 94

—————————————————————— X 16, 17

———— connected with Babington — XVI 26

Errington connected with Babington — XVI 37

Errington connected with Carnaby   X 146
————— formerly Ward   I 94
————— of Battle Bank   XIII 88
————— of Beaufront   XXI 1
————— Errington Walwich Grange Pontisland co. Northum-
berland   X 14, 16, 17
————— of Denton, Holy Isle Beaufront, Benwell, Newcastle
upon Tyne connected with Bigland   VIII 321
————— of Errington   X 75
————— in the psh of St John Ley, Beaufront, Benwell co.
Northumberland and of Newcastle upon Tyne   XVI 36
————— of Errington and of Beaufront, Benwell Newcastle
upon Tyne co. Northumberland   IV 519
————————————————— & of Sandoe   XVI 11, 12
————— of Newcastle co. Northumberland   X 152
————— of Pont Island Newcastle upon Tyne and of Preston co.
Northumberland   I 94
————— of Wessington and of Bingfield co. Northumberland   XIV 1
————— of West Denton co. Northumberland   X 1
————————————— Pont Island, Holy Island co. Northum-
berland, and of London co. Middlesex   VIII 317
Errol Hay Earl of, connected with Carr   IV 385
Erskine of Alva afterwards St Clair connected with Wedderburn   VII 167
Esch, Vander, of the Hague in Holland and of London co.
Middlesex   XVI 22
Escourt of Newenton, Pinkney co. Wilts, London co. Middlesex
and of Shipton Moyne co. Gloucester, see Estcourt   XIII 108
Escudamore Skeydemore Skydmore see Scudamore   XVIII 56–61
Escudamour of Home Lacy connected with de Huntercombe   XIII 1
Esk, Baron of, see Grahme   III 511
Essex Earl of Ardglasse connected with Southwell   XIII 68
————— connected with Williams   XIII 7
Essington of Essington Coaley   XX 118, 118ᵃ
Estcourt M.I. in Bracon Ash Church co. Norfolk   VI 119
————— of Cam co. Gloucester   VIII 388
————— of Shipton Moigne, Newton Bagpath, Lashborow and
of Tetbury co. Gloucester   XIX 230
————— of Shipton Moyne connected with Earle   XX 117ᵃ
————— see Escourt
Estuteville see Stuteville
Estwick of Barbadoes, and of London co. Middlesex connected
with Rouse   II 303
Etches of Ashbourn co. Derby and of London co. Middlesex
connected with Cadman and Parkes   III 5
Ethelred King of England connected with de Maigne and Boteler   XIX 90
Etherington of York connected with Glover   VI 216
Eton of Warwickshire connected with Langley and Stratford   XIX 261
Ettrick connected with Middleton   II 441
Euleston formerly Scaresbrick   XXI 152
Eure of Lincoln and of Shoreditch   III 416
Eures Lord, connected with Willoughby of Eresby   XIV 16

Eustace of Roberts Town co. Kildare	XIII 63
Evance Evans of Oswaldestre and of Treveleth co. Salop	VIII 473
———— Rectors of Newtown co. Montgomery, Hanwood, Westbury co. Salop, Aston co. Hereford and Vicar of Llanmeriewig; of Buckhurst Hill and of Chigwell co. Essex	VIII 479
———— Vicar of Llanmerywig co. Montgomery Rector of Westbury co. Salop and of Aston co. Hereford, of Buckhurst Hill in the psh of Chigwell co. Essex	VIII 471
Evans connected with Parry	VIII 457
———— Rawlinson	I 472
———— Lord Carbery connected with Horton	II 177
———— of Great Ealing connected with Hughes	II 306
———— of Montgomery and of the City of Gloucester	XIX 43
———— of Peterwell connected with Popkin	IX 91
———— of Windsor College connected with Stonestreet	VIII 523
———— see Evance	
Evelyn afterwards Glanville	XV 1
———— of Godstone Nutfield in Surrey, Tott Farm in the psh of Hurst Pierpont Norwood co. Sussex and of Elmsley in Ireland	XV 1, 2
Everard connected with Grey and Balch	VIII 25
———— of Long Ashton co. Somerset connected with Hill	IV 308
———— of Waltham in Essex connected with Cromwell	XV 21
Everingham of Billingboro	IV 376
Every connected with Mosley	VIII 335
———— of London co. Middlesex, Egginton co. Derby, and of Burford co. Stafford	V 390
Ewe in Normandy Earl of, connected with Poulton	XVI 18
Ewens of Wincanton co. Somerset, and of Deptford co. Kent	II 279
Ewer of London connected with Elwes	III 251
Exeter Cecil Earl of	XX 139
———— connected with Wilson	XXI 173
Eyner connected with Thorold	X 76
Eynion see Oynion	XIII 100
Eyre afterwards Archer	II 392
———— Gell	II 392
———— als Archer of co. Berks	V 137
———— connected with Whalley	IX 104
———— M.I. in Bracon Ash Church co. Norfolk	VI 118
———— of Fareham Titchfield co. Hants connected with Bargus	I 186
———— of Glossop, Hathesage, Newbolt and Highfield co. Derby, Manchester co. Lancaster, and of Sheffield co. Yorks	XV 3
———— of Hasop co. Derby	III 287
	I 322
———— of Hope Woodhouse Padley Bunhill near Chatsworth, Hylow, Holm Hall near Chesterfield, Hassop near Bakewell, Hathersage, Thorpe Newbolt, Routh co. Derby, Regton, Nether Hirst, Rampton Normanton Blith Spittle, Brookfield co. Nottingham, and of Keeton co. York	II 391

Eyre of Keeton co. York, Rampton co. Nottingham and of
    Derby   V 136
——————— of Kew in Surrey connected with Russell   VIII 244
——————— of Lanford near Salisbury connected with Penrose   II 226
——————— of Warkworth Castle and of Hassop co. Derby   III 369
Eyton of Eyton co. Salop connected with Talbot & Dod   XXI 301, 313

F

Fagg of Grinley co. Sussex connected with Woodyer   I 71
Fagge connected with Spence   IX 69
Fairfax Lord, connected with Forster   II 61
——————— of Gilling and Walton co. York, Viscount Fairfax of
    Emley in Ireland   XIV 21
Fairman related to Sir Thomas Gooch and Sir William Parker II 34
Falkoner of co. Rutland connected with Hudleston   XXI 42
Fallows of Heywood co. Chester and of co. Derby   I 440
Fancourt connected with Hollester   I 523
——————— of Rutland and of Woodford co. Essex   II 475
Fane Baroness Le Despencer   IX 6
——————— Earl of Westmorland connected with Dashwood   XXI 288
——————— extracts from Parish Registers and M.I in Church of
    Westbury on Trim co. Gloucester   XX 121
——————— of Ashton in Yorkshire and of Henbury   XIII 103
——————— of New Windsor co. Berks and of Whitechapel co.
    Middlesex   V 205
——————— of Wormesley co. Oxon connected with Chamberlaine II 254
Fannen of Ratcliffe Culey co. Leicester connected with Harcourt
    and Perkins   III 509
Fanner connected with Perkins   XVIII 28
Farington of Werdon, Shaw Hill, Warrington, Preston co. Lancas-
    ter connected with Gardner   V 217
Farmer connected with Jephson   I 95, 96
——————— Fermor of Somerton co. Oxford connected with
    Middleton   XIV 22
Farquharson of St Petersburgh in Russia connected with Ketelbey I 39
Farrell of Sussex & of London connected with Tuffnell   V 143
Farrington Consul at Grand Cairo connected with Gethin and
    Roberts   III 436
Farrow of Newbury co. Berks   IV 253
Fastolse connected with Fitzgrasse etc   VII 502
Faulkner connected with Eyre and Bargus   I 186
Fauntleroy of Crundall in Hants   XXI 10

Fauntleroy of Hedley, Boreham co. Essex, and of Isleworth co.
    Middlesex connected with Cole   XV 63–6
Fawcet of Durham   IX 71
Fawkes connected with Acton   XIX 6
Fawkner connected with Woodhouse   IX 29
Fazakerley connected with Tarlton   I 384
Feake of Croydon, Godstone co. Surrey, Whighton co. Norfolk,
    London co. Middlesex, Darrington in the psh of Shering co.
    Essex, and of the City of Salisbury, President & Governor
    of Bengal   XVI 33
———— of Godstone co. Surrey, Salisbury co. Wilts, and of
    London co. Middlesex   VI 214
———— of London co. Middlesex, Durrington in Essex
    Whigton co. Norwich, Jamaica West Indies, Bengal, and of
    the City of Salisbury   XVI 93–93[b]
———— of Salisbury M.I.   XVI 49
Fearon of Belliborough in Ireland Coote Hill co. Cavan and of
    London co. Middlesex   III 165
Featherstone of Hathery Clough in the psh of Stanhope co. Palatine
    Durham, London co. Middlesex, Blakeway in the psh of
    Ware co. Hertford, Basingske Hall, Stanford Le Hope, and
    of Terling co. Essex   VIII 512
Feattus connected with Brett   VII 249
———————— Smith   IV 533
Feild of Pagenhall and of Stroud co. Gloucester   XIX 183
Feilden of Cheshire connected with Mosley   VIII 324
Felbrigge of Felbrigge co. Norfolk connected with le Groos   VII 502
Fell of Over Kellet, Swarthmore Hall co. Lancaster, Baltimore in
    Maryland, and of Whitehaven   I 516
Fellowes of London co. Middlesex, Carshalton co. Surrey, Park
    Place near St Ives, and of Ramsay, both in the County of
    Huntingdon, Eggsford co. Devon, and of Nacton near
    Ipswich co. Suffolk   III 301
———— of London co. Middlesex, Carshalton co. Surrey,
    Eggesford co. Devon, Park Place near St Ives, and of
    Ramsey co. Huntingdon   VIII 463
———— of Odingley co. Worcester and of London co.
    Middlesex connected with Newton   III 494
———— of the Island of Jamaica, Sidmouth co. Devon, Jersey,
    and of Holyhead in the Island of Anglesea   VIII 459
Fellows of Ipswich in the Province of Massachusets Bay, Kensing-
    ton in the Province of New Hampshire, Boston New
    England, and of Gloucester co. Essex   IV 427
Felton connected with Hoo   VIII 245
———— of Oswestry co. Salop connected with Evance   VIII 478
Fenn Fenne of London co. Middlesex, and of Wotton under Edge
    co. Gloucester   XIV 23
Fenne of Yorkshire, Braintree in Essex, Resing, Warlingworth, co.
    Suffolk, Walkworth, Wootton-under-Edge co. Gloucester
    and of Calais   XIX 13
———— see Fenn

Fenner connected with Bellingham   XXI 88

Fenoulhet of London co. Middlesex   I 104

Fentham of West End Finchley and of London co. Middlesex
connected with Blicke   XV 36

———— supposed to be of Birmingham, Packington
Elmington, Bentley Heath co. Warwick and of London co.
Middlesex   II 66

Fenton connected with Cleaver   VIII 490

———————————— Drake   XXI 277

———————— of Leeds, Hunslet co. York and of Underbank   I 480

Fenwick connected with Errington   I 94

———————————————————————————— XXI 2

———————— Strother   XXI 161

———————— of East Dudder, Monk Seaton, Morpeth co. Northumberland and of Stepney co. Middlesex   XXI 122

———————— of Lambton co. Durham connected with Addison   XVII 1

———————— of Matfin and of Stanton, Constable of Newcastle   X 75

————————of Newcastle, Lemington co. Northampton and of
Brancley   X 134

———————— of Newcastle, Alnwick co. Northumberland,
Lemington co. Northampton, and of Brancley   I 491

Fenwyes connected with Sandis   XXI 22

Ferdinando King of Castle connected with Hookes   XVIII 105

Fergus of co. Mayo connected with Skerrett   I 89

Ferguson of Evenin in Scotland – afterwards settled in Poland   XVI 14

Fermor Farmer of Somerton co. Oxford connected with Middleton   XIV 22

———————— of Somerton, Tusmore, Banbury co. Oxon, London
co. Middlesex, Whitfield in the psh of Deerhurst co.
Gloucester, and of Worcester, see also Fermour   II 83

Fermour als Ricardes of Minster Lovel co. Oxford, lived at the
Staple at Calais, settled at Eston Neston near Toucaster co.
Northampton, Whitfield in the psh of Deerhurst co. Glou-
cester, London co. Middlesex and of Tusmore & Somerton   VIII 497

———————— als Ricards of Somerton, Minster Lovel, Whitney,
Tusmore, Banbury, Fritwell co. Oxon, Easton Neston co.
Northampton, the City of Worcester, London co. Middlesex, Whitfield in the psh of Deerhurst co. Gloucester, Yarm
co. York, and of Rome   V 7

Fern of Poswick Green and Hognaston co. Derby connected with
Beresford   II 207

Ferrand of Bingley, Harden Beck co. York Blythe co. Nottingham,
Messingham co. Lincoln and of Southwell   I 54

———————— formerly Waddington   I 55

———————— of Bingley co. York, Baptisms etc   VI 269

Ferrers connected with Hungerford   V 51

———————————————————————————— V 235

———————————————— Huntley   XIX 237

———————————————— Cockayn and Merow   VII 25

———————————————— Marow   VII 369

———————————————————————————— XXI 109

———————— Ferris connected with Scudamore   XVII 33

Ferris of Badsley Clinton co. Warwick connected with Bird — II 50
——————————————————— Blunsden, Corsham co. Wilts,
    London co. Middlesex, Fiddington co. Gloucester, and of
    Peckham co. Kent — XIX 73
——————— Shirley Earl, connected with Bathurst — XX 42[a]
Ferris Ferrers connected with Scudamore — XVII 33
Ferron of Soho co. Middlesex connected with Hughes — II 306
Ferry of Ferry Hill and of Wooller co. Northumberland — XXI 133
Fetherston of Hathory Cleugh in Stanhope psh; London co.
    Middlesex and of Blackesware in the psh of Ware co. Herts — VI 8
Fetiplace of Shefford, Chilrey co. Berks, Lincolns Inn co. Middlesex,
    and of Swynbrook co. Oxon — VI 69
Fettyplace of Castle Eaton, Childrey and Cricklade co. Wilts — I 152
Fhittyplace or Phettiplace — XVI 51
Fichett see Mallet — VII 74
Fido of Cold Ashton co. Somerset connected with Gunning — IV 53
——————————————————————————————— XVIII 103

Field afterwards Parker of Moorhouse Hill in the psh of Heskett in
    the Forest co. Cumberland — I 170
——————— connected with Thorowgood — IV 58
——————— of Kingston upon Hull co. York connected with
    Thornton — XII 91
——————— of Newnham, Hitchen, and of Tempsford co. Bedford
    connected with Foskett — VIII 176
Fielding of Horton and of Bristol co. Gloucester — XIX 238
——————— of Lutterworth connected with Palmer — IV 321
Fienes Lord Layard afterwards Lord Say and Sele connected with
    Danvers — VIII 241
——————— Viscount Say and Sele — IX 113
Fiennes of Broughton co. Oxford connected with Fermour — VIII 499
——————— see Fynes
——————— Viscount Say and Sele — I 423
Fifield als Lowe of Camberwell co. Surrey and of London co.
    Middlesex — XX 161
——————— of Coln St Aldwyn and of Auldsworth co. Gloucester — XX 123[a]
Finch came from Kent to Buskshey near Wickham in Bucks and of
    Kempley co. Gloucester — XX 29
——————— Lord Maidstone connected with Windham — XVIII 22
——————— of Valentines co. Essex — VIII 220
——————————————— Stifford co. Essex and of Canwell co.
    Stafford connected with Schoen — VII 252
Finderne of Finderne co. Derby — I 249
Fines, Baron, see St Paul — XIII 32–5
Finnemore of Halberton Rockbeare co. Devon London co. Middle-
    sex Horsley Down co. Surrey and of the Isle of Wight co.
    Hants — III 71
Finney of Durham connected with Burden — X 130
Fiott of Jersey and of London co. Middlesex — III 179
Firth of Barnsley connected with Glover — VI 218
Fish M.I. — XIV 9
Fisher afterwards Jeddere Fisher — X 165

Fisher connected with Armroid .... I 412
—————————————————— Stallwood and Jeddere ... X 165
————————— of Alderways co. Stafford, Lottesford co. Herts,
   Mickleton co. Gloucester, London co. Middlesex, Childrey
   co. Berks, and of Elliston co. Bedford .... XIX 15
————————— of Bellchamp St Pauls co. Essex connected with
   Sicklemore .... VI 190
————————— of Cumberland and of London co. Middlesex ... I 182
————————— of Dottell co. Salop, Lord of the Manor of Packington,
   of Welch Hall near Meriden and of Radford co. Warwick ... XXI 245
————————— of London co. Middlesex connected with Wilson ... III 16
Fishpool aged 103 .... VIII 431
Fiske of Norton, Lavenham, Rattlesden Bury St Edmunds Bard-
   well co. Suffolk, Diss co. Norfolk Walden co. Essex,
   Thorpe Halstead and of Lamash .... IV 135
Fitch connected with Leigh and Fleming .... XXI 218
Fitton lord of Harwood and half of Rufford connected with Nowell
   and Hesketh .... XXI 263
Fitzalan Earl of Arundel connected with Lovell .... VIII 248
Fitz Allen Earl of Arundel connected with Holland and with
   Hookes .... XVIII 105
————————— Earl of Arundel connected with Spencer ... VI 52
Fitzallen Lord Maltravers ————————————— ... VI 51
Fitz Dering of Kent connected with Mortimer & Waller ... XVIII 95
Fitzer of London co. Middlesex connected with Bigland ... XVI 100
Fitzgeffry Baron of Kirtling connected with Beauchamp Earl of
   Warwick .... VIII 254
Fitz Geoffry of Crookers in the County of Bedford connected with
   Osborne .... VII 302
Fitzgerald connected with Baron King .... XXI 273
————————————— Clare Earl of Gloucester and Hertford . XXI 272
————————— Earl of Kildare .... XIII 1
————————————— Earl of Desmond, had the Barony of
   Ophaly .... XIII 3
————————— of Turlogh, Dalgan co. Mayo, and of Woodlands co.
   Hants .... XVII 43
Fitzherbert afterwards Brockholes of Claughton Heton co. Palatine
   Lancaster .... V 4
————————— connected with Port .... XII 28–47
Fitz Herbert lord of Midsomer Norton co. Somerset connected
   with West and Mallet .... VII 76
Fitzherbert of Padley and Norbury co. Derby connected with Eyre II 396
Fitz James connected with Strode and Thynne .... XX 159
————————————— Stroud and Greville .... XVI 20
————————————— Trenchard .... VIII 180
Fitz Lucas see Lucas .... I 464
Fitz Man connected with Blofield .... XVII 4
Fitz Maurice .... XIII 1
————————— Lord, of Kerry .... XIII 2
Fitz Nicholl connected with Browninge .... XIX 83
Fitz Osborn Earl of Hereford .... VIII 250

Fitz Other Baron of Estaines   XIII 1
———————— Fitz Walter took the name of Windsor   XIII 4
———————— took the name of Windsor   XIII 4
Fitz Paine Earl of Mershewode Vale connected with St Lo   XVIII 11
Fitzpatrick of Evreux Earl of Salisbury   VIII 252
Fitz Peter Lord of Llanlovery connected with Vivonia   VII 74
Fitz Reginald connected with Fitz Peter and Vivonia   VII 74
Fitzroy afterwards Scudamore   XVII 33
Fitzwalter, Barony of   XVII 8
———————— Fitz Other afterwards Windsor   XIII 4
Fitzwarren lord of Alveston and Olveston   XX 200ª
Fitzwilliam Earl connected with Stringer   V 139
———————————————————————— and Newton   XX 175
———————— Lord   XXI 7
———————————————— connected with Hunter als Perry   XIX 13
Flanders, Chastillion Earl of, connected with St Paul   XIII 32–5
Fleetwood M.I. Worcester Cathedral   XIV 9
———————— of London co. Middlesex and of Cadiz   V 380–2
———————— of Penwotham co. Lancs, and of Colwicke co. Stafford
connected with Langton   XXI 31
Fleming ———————— Appleby   X 140
———————————————— Leycester and Byrne   VI 158
———————— formerly Willis of Water Hall and Stoneham Park   XIX 143
———————— of Mounton co. Glamorgan and of Peullyn connected
with Mathew   XIX 63
———————— of North Stoneham co. Hants   XXI 218
———————————————— connected with Hooper   X 46, 47
———————— of Wakefield co. York connected with Wingfield and
Roe   I 197
———————— of Whitehaven co. Cumberland, Rydal, Cogarth, and
of Fellfoot, Bishop of Carlisle   X 151
———————— of Woodhall in Methley connected with Waterton   VIII 246
Flemyng of Flemyngs in the psh of Runwells co. Essex, connected
with Copdowe and Sulyard   VII 17
Fletcher formerly Vane   VII 171
———————— M.I. at Cheam   VI 128
———————————————— in Thurston Church co. Norfolk   VI 118
———————— of Derby, Manchester co. Lancaster and of London I 181
———————— of Field Broughton M.I.   XIV 7
———————— of Hutton co. Cumberland connected with Fleming X 151
———————— of Manchester co. Palatine Lancaster   II 53
———————— of Monmouth connected with Hoskins   II 9
———————— of Plymouth co. Devon connected with Mooring   I 218
———————— of St Bridgetts co. Cumberland, Harwarden co. Flint,
and of Bangor co. Carnarvon   II 56
———————— of West Terring, Steyning, Chichester co. Sussex,
Middle Temple co. Middlesex, Colchester co. Essex,
Boston New England, and of the Island of Eustatia – York
Herald   IV 444
———————— of West Terring, Steyning, Chichester, Findon co.

Sussex, London co. Middlesex, Colchester co. Essex, and of
    the Island of Eustachia – York Herald ... XVIII 8
Flewelling of London connected with Aspeley and Colby ... IV 423
Flight of Woolwich co. Kent, connected with Knackston ... IV 306
Flint afterwards Corbet ... IV 515
————————— Corbett ... X 20
————— connected with Corbet ... XVIII 135
————————————— ... XX 62
————————— of Cruckton, Muklewood, Longnor, and of
    Shrewsbury co. Salop ... X 20
Flower of Paddington co. Middlesex connected with Drage ... I 92
————————— of Sutton Bangor co. Wilts, and of London co.
    Middlesex ... I 328
Floyer of Floyer Hays co. Devon, connected with Martin ... XXI 224
————————— of Stratton co. Dorset, Trusham co. Devon, Esher co.
    Surrey and of Risby co. Lincoln ... I 117
Fluck of the Oke in Apperley in Deerhurst co. Gloucester and of
    London co. Middlesex ... XX 124
Fogg of Damscourt co. Kent connected with Norwood ... XIX 209
Foley Lord, connected with Jol ... XVI 30
————————— of Prestwood co. Stafford connected with Hogetts ... IV 500
————————— of Stoke Edill co. Hereford, and of the Inner Temple
    co. Middlesex, connected with Hoare ... XX 116
————————— of Stourbridge co. Worcester and of London co.
    Middlesex ... XX 242
Folkes of Grays Inn co. Middlesex, Hillington co. Norfolk
    assumed surname and arms of Browne ... V 232
————————— of Illingdon co. Norfolk connected with Taylor ... III 319
Folliott of Pyrton Yardley co. Worcester, and of Ballyshannon in
    Ulster ... II 495
Fones a Norman, came into England with the Conqueror, of Saxby,
    Twesdon co. Kent, and of Bromsgrove co. Worcester, Baron
    of Holby in Scotland ... XXI 106
Foot of Royston co. Cambridge connected with Onslowe ... VI 7
Foote and Begbie note as to marriage ... XVII 40
————— connected with Goodere ... III 286
————————————— Newte ... I 319
————————— of Charlton co. Wilts, London co. Middlesex and of
    Ware co. Devon ... I 38
Forbes connected with Mackintosh ... XIII 36
————————— Lord, of the Kingdom of Scotland ... II 228
————————— of Newhall connected with Rae ... XXI 206
Forcer of Kello co. Durham ... X 145
Ford connected with Kemble ... VII 184
————————— of Ewelin co. Oxon, Ardley, Buckingham, and of
    Slade End co. Berks ... XI 39
————————— of Ford Abby co. Devon and of Codenham co. Suff ... IV 111
————————— of Sladend co. Berks, Evelin co. Oxon, Ardley co.
    Bucks, London co. Middlesex, Duntsborne, Bristol co.
    Gloucester North Moels co. Lancaster and of Southampton ... V 291

Forder of Barton co. Hants, Pitt in the psh of Hursley and of
    Merden   II 275
Forshew als Taylor   XX 198[a]
Forster afterwards Buckley   II 276
——————— connected with Stafford   III 130
——————— formerly Bacon   XXI 202
——————— of Balmborow & Edderston co. Northumberland   II 61
——————— of Bamborough Castle co. Northumberland and of
    Edderstone   III 290
——————— of Castle Caulefield co. Tyrone, and of Tullaghan co.
    Monaghan   XXI 212
——————— of Etherston co. Northumberland   X 6
——————— of Harpden in the County of Oxford and of
    Aldermaston co. Berks   XXI 250
——————— of Northamptonshire, Dymock co. Gloucester,
    Castlecomb co. Wilts, and of Pershore co. Worcester   XIX 92
——————— of West Indies and of Halesworth co. Suffolk   II 29
Fort of New Sarum co. Wilts and of London co. Middx   II 101
Forterie, de la, see de la Forterie
——————— Fortray or de la Forterie of Lisle in Flanders, Kew
    Green, Godalming co. Surrey, Byall Fen co. Cambridge,
    Wombwell Hall in the psh of Northfleet, Canterbury, East
    Comb in the psh of Greenwich co. Kent, see also Fortrie and
    Fortrey   XVIII 143–5
     IV 483
Fortescue of Fallowpit co. Devon connected with Sandes   II 443
——————— of Fillegh co. Devon, Baron Clinton   IX 114
——————— of Husbands Bosworth co. Leicester connected with
    Turville   V 100
Forth of Kings Sutton co. Northampton, Portcullis Pursuivant of
    Arms connected with Sheppard & Elwes   II 485
Forth of Wigan co. Lancs and of London co. Middlesex connected
    with Essington   XX 118[a]
Fortray see Forterie
Fortrey of Eastcomb co. Kent connected with Ayde, see Forterie   XXI 211
——————— see de la Forterie   IV 483
Fortrie of Northfleet, Rochester co. Kent, and of Kew co. Surrey,
    see Forterie   XXI 304
Fortune of Haverfordwest, Lueston Castle, Walwyns Castle, and
    of Mote co. Pembroke   VII 123
——————— of London co. Middlesex and of Great Marlow co.
    Bucks   II 269
Foskett of Moore Place co. Middlesex connected with Field   VIII 175
Fossett connected with Seccombe   II 115
Foster of Bedford connected with Senior   II 476
——————— of Holborn co. Middlesex connected with Griffiths   III 135
Fothergill of Murthwaite in Westmorland and of Northampton   X 157
——————— of Shap in Westmorland, Wensley, West Witton,
    Middleham co. York, Newcastle upon Tyne co. Northum-
    berland, and of London co. Middlesex   VII 240

Fothergill of Waingarth, Croftsbank, Lockholm in Ravonston-
    dale co. Westmorland, Vice Chancelor of Oxford   X 73
Foucher connected with Bugge   VIII 53
Foulhurst connected with Vernon   XIV 2
Foulke of Gunston co. Stafford of Tewkesbury co. Gloucester and
    of London co. Middlesex   XIX 203
Foulkes of the psh of Clarendon in the Island of Jamaica   VI 175
Fountayne connected with Carew   XIII 6
Fountayne-Wilson see Wilson   XVII 14
Fowell descended from John de Foghull by the daut and heir of
    Comb, of Fowell's Comb in the psh of Ugborough, Ply-
    mouth, Black Hall in the psh of North Huish co. Devon,
    and of the City of Bath   XV 38, 39
Fowell of Fowelscomb and of Plymouth co. Devon   VI 72
Fowke als Wheeler of Laverton in the psh of Buckland co.
    Gloucester and of London co. Middlesex   VIII 263
———— of Brewood, and of Gunston co. Stafford, see also
    Fowkes   XX 138ᵃ
Fowkes of Brewood see also Fowke   XIII 101
———— of Dry Merston co. Gloucester connected with Pelham
    and Bushell   XIX 151
Fowler of Gloucestershire   X 35
———— of Moor Hall, Stonehouse, Stanley Kings, and of
    Eastington co. Gloucester   XVI 99, 101–2
———— of Saperton, Quinington, Wootton under Edge co.
    Gloucester, and of London co. Middlesex   XX 122
———— of Stretton on the Fosse co. Warwick, and of Hampton
    co. Gloucester   XXI 158–9
Fownes afterwards Lutterell of Nethway co. Devon, connected
    with Yarde   III 506
———— Fowns of Nethway co. Devon connected with Yard   XVIII 113
———— of Nethway, Kittery Court co. Devon, connected with
    Seale   II 145
Fowns see Fownes
Fox afterwards Lane connected with Benson   XXI 116
——————————— created Lord Bingley   XVII 59
———— connected with Hope   III 151
——————————— Le Vieux   IV 74
———— M.I.   XIV 8
———— of Graigie co. Tipperary, East Ham co. Surrey,
    afterwards Fox Lane   XVII 59
———— of Stradbrook co. Suffolk, London co. Middlesex and
    of Thorpe co. Essex   I 167
———— of Whitehaven co. Cumberland connected with
    Bigland   VIII 326
Fox Lane see Lane   XVII 59
Foy of Bristol co. Gloucester connected with Edgar   I 343
Frampton connected with de Pascale   I 452
———— of Lower Donhead co. Wilts   I 149
———— of Moreton co. Dorset connected with Paston   III 331

Frampton Rector of Donhead of Bremhill co. Wilts, Oxford and
    of Bradpote co. Dorset | VIII 426
Francis of Chester and of London co. Middlesex | VII 100
Francke of Alwoodley near Harwood co. York connected with
    Hatfield | IX 129
Francland connected with Laying and Bloomberg | XIII 115
Frankaville or Fraunkeville connected with Forterie | XVIII 142
Frankland connected with Cromwell | XV 21
Franklin connected with Roberts | II 382
———— of Cork connected with Adderley | IV 165
———— of Hall Place and Deans Place in the psh of Hurley,
    Lawrence Waltham, co. Berks | VIII 228[a]
Franks connected with Dyer | VIII 2
———— of London co. Middlesex | I 515
Fraunkeville Frankaville of London connected with Forterie | XVIII 142
Frazer of Aberdeen | I 538
Freake of Searn connected with Trenchard | VIII 184
Frederick connected with Spence | IX 69
———— Prince, Elector Palatine, and King of Bohemia | XVI 9
Freeling connected with Newbery | IX 75
Freeman connected with Ashby | IV 458
———— Keck | XVII 15
———— of Batesford and Cropthorn co. Gloucester | XX 222
———— connected with Curtis | I 169
———— of Buckley co. Worcester and of Oxendon co.
    Gloucester | XVI 24
———— of Gains co. Hereford | II 473
Freeman of Ringsted, Peterborough co. Northampton, Rutland,
    Hawksworth co. Kent, and of Cambridge, connected with
    Purchas | III 417
———— to Thomas – change of name | VI 382
Freeth of Smithwick near Wolverhampton co. Stafford, Birming-
    ham, Coventry co. Warwick, Guildford co. Surrey, London
    co. Middlesex & of Worcester | III 220
Freind Prebendary of Westminster, of Witney co. Oxford con-
    nected with Walker | VIII 74
Freke of Devon connected with Gunston and Thomas | II 252
Fremaux see Fremeaux | III 80
Freme of Lypiate connected with Coxe | XX 84
———— Cirencester and of Cheltenham co. Gloucester | XIX 166–[b]
Fremeaux or Fremaux of Kingsthorpe co. Northampton connected
    with Bodington | III 80
French connected with Cromwell | XV 21, 22
———— Knapp | I 410
———— Roberts | II 236
———— M.I. at the Church of Holy Cross Pershore with coat
    of Arms | XX 117
———— of Arundell, Upper Barpham, Angmerin co. Sussex,
    and of London co. Middlesex | V 209
———— of co. Galway connected with Blake | IX 2
———— of Ruhusane co. Galway connected with Blake | III 259

Freshfield of Colchester co. Essex, and of Norwich co. Norfolk, connected with Gurney   IV 79

Frevile of Hardwicke co. Durham connected with Lambton   I 367

———— of Hardwick co. Palatine Durham connected with Jenison   XII 29–47

Frewen of Gesley Northiam Rye co. Sussex and of Thorington co. Essex   I 32, 2

Frewen Rector of Northiam Vicar of Fairlight; of Rotherbridge Brickwall co. Sussex, Putney co. Surrey and of Lincolns Inn co. Middlesex   VII 309

Friend of London and of Whitney co. Oxon   III 428

Frith of Wiltsford co. Wilts   III 401

———— supposed of England was at the Siege of Derry which first brought him to Ireland, of Inch, Kilkhaven and of Ballilum co. Wexford   III 208

Frowd of Brixton Deverill co. Wilts, Frampton co. Dorset, Frome Croscombe co. Somerset   II 346

Frowick of London co. Middlesex and of Caverley connected with Fisher   XIX 15

Fryer of Bristol connected with Fielding   XIX 238

Fulford in the psh of Dunsford co. Devon   IV 416

———— of Fulford in the psh of Dunsford co. Devon   XVIII 43

Fuller connected with Alcock and Dodwell   XV 69

———————— Clare   I 339

———— of Caldecot co. Huntingdon connected with Mingay   I 288

———— of Norton co. Suffolk and of Dedham co. Essex connected with Fiske   IV 140

Fulnetby of Fulnetby co. Lincoln and of Glenford co. Suffolk connected with Master   XIX 51

Furney of Gloucester, Bristol, and of Surrey   III 445

Furs of London co. Middlesex and of Lambeth co. Surrey connected with Dorrington   III 63

Fynes or Fiennes of Rooton co. Lincoln Mackton & of Hampstead co. Devon connected with Moorhouse   III 82

G

Gage Lord connected with Hall   XX 249[a]

———— of Cirencester co. Gloucester and of Halling co. Surrey, K.G.   XIX 12
   XX 125[a]

———— of Firley, Bentley co. Sussex, Healing in the psh of Croydon co. Surrey and of Wormley co. Hereford   II 490

———— of Furle co. Sussex, Henthorp co. Norfolk, Hengrave,

Stoneham co. Suffolk, Haling in the psh of Croydon co. Surrey, Packington co. Stafford, Sherborne Castle co. Oxon, and of London co. Middlesex — V 431

——————— of London co. Middlesex, Wormesley co. Hereford, Bentley, Framfield, Furley co. Sussex, Healing or Haling in the psh of Croydon co. Surrey — III 370

——————— of Northampton, Cirencester co. Gloucester, Bentley Furle in Sussex, London co. Middlesex Halling co. Surrey Wormsley co. Hereford and of Hengrave in Suffolk — XIX 64

Gale connected with Thornber — IV 89

Gall of Norton co. Suffolk connected with Fiske — IV 141

Galloway connected with Growden — IV 302

——————— Earl of connected with Paulton — XVI 18

——————— Lord of, connected with Quincey — VIII 250

Gallway see Galway

——————— Galway of Kinsale co. Cork — VIII 195

——————— of Maulbrack and Burnalow in the Barony of Carbery co. Cork — VIII 198

Galway Gallway of Kinsale co. Cork, of Limerick — VIII 195

——————— of Maulbrack and Burnalow in the Barony of Carbery, Kinsale, co. Cork and of Limerick, connected with Goold — XII 52–3

——————— note as to arms — VIII 200

Gam Sir David connected with Aubrey and Herbert — XX 160

Gamull of London co. Middlesex — V 80

——————— of the City of Chester — XVIII 38

Gandy of Exeter — IX 36

Gapper of Shipton Mallet co. Somerset connected with Smith of Alton — IV 173

Gardiner of Bermondsey, Dorking Lagham co. Surrey, Daylesford co. Worcester and of Guiting Power co. Gloucester — XIX 120

——————— of Dublin — II 100

——————— of London co. Middlesex and of Beaumaris in the Island of Anglesea — VI 20

——————— of Thundridge Bury co. Herts connected with Pettiwood — II 471

——————— Vicar of Henbury Aust and Northwick co. Gloucester — XX 133

——————— William — III 57

Gardner of Chatteris in the Isle of Ely and County of Cambridge connected with Johnstone — VIII 291

——————— of Coleraine co. Londonderry and of Dromore in Ireland — V 221

——————— of Gurton Grange, Minchin Hampton co. Glos and of Jamaica, connected with Hastings — II 25

——————— of London co. Middlesex connected with Powell — I 565

——————— see Dunn-Gardner

Garland of Malverley and of Slape in the psh of Wem co. Salop — II 408

Garland of Newton Melverley, Wem co. Salop, and of Rhandryvingen co. Montgomery — XVIII 140b

Garlick of Frocester co. Gloucester connected with Stodart — IV 521

——————— of Liverpool co. Lancaster connected with Whaley — IV 237

Garnault of Bulls Cross, Enfield and of London co. Middx   VIII 169

Garnet lord of the Manor of Espee co. Lancaster connected with Molineux   VIII 257

Garnett of Nantwich co. Chester connected with Peake   IV 285

Garnhams connected with Potter   IV 144

Garnons of the City of Hereford, the Hay co. Brecon, Horsley Down, co. Surrey, and of London co. Middlesex   II 487

Garrard als Gerrard or Garrett of Sittingbourne co. Kent, Dorney co. Bucks, London co. Middlesex, and of Lamar in the psh of Wheatampsted co. Herts   V 427

———————— connected with Port   I 249

Garrat of Walton Mason M.I.   XIV 7

Garrett see Garrard

Garrick came from Bourdeaux and settled in England – David Garrick   III 435

Garton of co. Sussex connected with Dent   VII 482

Gartside of Prestwich Manchester co. Lancaster and of Wrexham co. Denbigh lord of the Manor of Little Bolton   XXI 136

Gascoign of Middleton Thorpe and of East Ardisley connected with Ingram   VIII 538

Gascoigne an independent Captain of Marines   XXI 217

Gaskell connected with Milnes   XV 17

Gastrell of Tetbury, Shipton Moyne co. Gloucester   XIX 54

Gataker of Gataker Hall co. Salop   XXI 240

Gatonby of Howdon Pans co. Northumberland connected with Tucker   VII 332

Gaunt John of, connected with Neville Eyre etc   II 390

Gaunt John of, Duke of Lancaster connected with Barrington and Lowndes   V 174

———————— connected with Stafford   XVI 50

———————— of co. Leicester connected with Dyer   VIII 2

Gawdy connected with de Grey and Le Neve   VI 256

———————— of Harlslon, Gawdy Hall, Redenhall West Herling co. Norfolk, Crowes Hall in Debenham, Mendham co. Suffolk   VI 78

Gawen of Northington, Grittleton, Tichborne, Westbury, Tetbury co. Wilts, Oldbury, Bristol co. Gloucester, and of London co. Middlesex   XIX 78

———————— of the Wood see Johnston   VIII 287

Gay of Goldsworthy co. Devon connected with Bidlake and Combe   XIII 56–7

———————— went from Devon and settled in Dublin in Ireland, of Gaybrooke co. Westmeath, Drogheda and of Collinston co. Kildare, connected with Molineux   IV 367

Gayer connected with Rolle   VI 388

Gaywood of Wickham co. Essex, and of London co. Middlesex   IV 405

Gazelee of Burnham Thorpe co. Norfolk, London co. Middlesex and of Gosport co. Hants   II 290

Gee afterwards Carew   XIII 6

———————— connected with Hadfield   II 271

———————— of Bishop Burton, Beverley Mapleton in Holdeness, East Riding co. Yorks   XXI 156[b]

Gefford of Castle Jordan co. Meath   VI 47
Geffry of Chiddinglery co. Sussex connected with Whitfield   I 545
Gele Gell of Hopton co. Derby and of London co. Middlesex   V 444
Gell formerly Eyre   II 392
—————— of Hopton co. Derby connected with Beresford   II 207
Gell see Gele
George I King of England   XVI 9
—— II ——————   XVI 9
—— III ——————   XVI 9
Gerard connected with Dacre   II 122
——   III 175
—————— of Bryn co. Palatine Lancaster connected with Jenison   XII 28–47
—————— of Ince, Kingsley Brine, Baron Gerard of Gerards
   Bromley, co. Stafford   XIII 2
Gerrard see Garrard   V 427
Gethin of co. Sligo and of London co. Middlesex   VII 390
Ghibbs Gibbey see Gibby   XX 114
Gibb to Scott letter as to change of name   XVII 35
Gibbes of Barbadoes   XXI 212
—————— of Bristol, Bedminster co. Somerset, London co.
   Middx, Southwark co. Surrey, and of the Island of
   Barbadoes   VII 422
—————— of Gibbes Farm in Bedminster and of Bristol   XIX 189
—————— of Honyngton co. Warwick   XIII 71
—————— of Wicken Park, Lillingston Darrel and of Stony
   Stratford co. Bucks   IX 40
Gibbey Gibby Ghibbs   XX 114
Gibbons connected with Bentley   IV 61
—————— Extract from Register of Wroughton co. Wilts   XVI 48
—————— of co. Bucks, Pomfret co. York connected with Ley
   and Rudyard   III 448
—————— of Wolverhampton, Sadgeley, Kings Swinford, and of
   Tettenhall co. Stafford   IV 24
Gibbs connected with Bladen   I 67
Gibby Ghibbs or Gibbey   XX 114
Gibson connected with Culver   I 337
—————— of Goldenstanes Restalrig Hairlow in the Lordship of
   Wemyss, Durie, Saintford, Clatto co. Fife, Glasgow, Gran-
   ton, Carnbec, Nether Liberton in Edinburghshire, Pent-
   land, Portsmouth co. Hants, and of Nova Scotia   II 444
Gibson of South Waldon connected with Atkinson   IV 204
Giddy of St Erth co. Cornwall connected with Davies   II 443
Gideon connected with Wilmot   IX 124
Gidley of Gidley co. Devon – arms and crest   IX 40
Giffard of Chillington and Black Ladies, Madeley co. Stafford see
   Gifford   V 15
Gifford connected with Poulton   XVI 18
——————————————— Williams   VII 119
—————— Lord of Winterbourne and Bremesfield connected with
   Scudamore   XVIII 56

Gifford of Chillington co. Stafford connected with Port and
    Hawkins   XII 28–51
———— of Chillington connected with Parker & Roberts   IX 102
———— of London co. Middlesex, Burstall co. Leicester and of
    France   VII 244
Gilbank – came from the North of the Borough   IV 243
Giles connected with West   IV 207
———— of Biddenden co. Kent connected with Curtis   I 332
———— of Birmingham co. Warwick, London co. Middlesex,
    and of Dulwich co. Surrey, connected with Hopkins   VIII 349
———— of Birmingham co. Warwick and of London co.
    Middlesex connected with Hopkins   VIII 408
Gilkrist connected with Browne   XI 42
                                                                           XV 13
Gill of Charles Town New England and of Castle William con-
    nected with Nutting   III 376
Gilliam of Manchester connected with Percival and Greaves   XIV 1
Gillot of Pinley co. Warwick   XIX 149
Gilmore of Ramsbury and Marlborough co. Wilts connected with
    London   III 106
Gilpin of Scaleby Castle, Whitehaven, and of Carlisle co.   X 140
    Cumberland
Girdler connected with Pym   II 465
Girling of Camberwell co. Surrey and of Whitechapel co.
    Middlesex   VIII 156
Girlington of Girlington Hall near Richmond   X 105
Gisborne of Derby, Radborne in Dorset, Rothley Temple co.
    Leicestershire, connected with Packer and Stephens   VII 134
Gisburne of Derby   VIII 22
Gladman connected with Fane   V 206
Gladstanes connected with Christmas   IV 453
Gladwin of Tupton Hall, Stubbing near Chesterfield co. Derby,
    Plymouth co. Devon, London co. Middx, Ipswich co. Suffolk,
    Mansifeld Woodhouse co. Nottingham, Birmingham co.
    Warwick, and of co. York   II 32
Gladwyn connected with Stanton   II 108
Glanvill connected with Bourchier   I 557
Glanville formerly Evelyn   XV 1
———— of Elmsett co. Suffolk connected with Blair   VII 187
Glasse of Wansted co. Essex, and of Hanwell co. Middx   II 468
Gleadowe of the City of Dublin, Carrickclass co. Longford in
    Ireland, created a Baronet of Ireland, took surname and
    Arms of Newcomen in addition   VIII 279
Gleadowe-Newcomen formerly Gleadowe   VIII 279
Glean of Hardwick co. Norfolk connected with Rodney of Stoke
    Rodney   XX 32
Glegg of Calde Grange   XXI 312
Glen connected with Alsopp and Lowdham   XVII 67
Glendower, Owen, connected with Scudamore   XVIII 57
Glenny of Monymusk in the shire of Aberdeen, London co.

Middlesex, Liverpool co. Palatine Lancaster, Sydenham co. Kent, Ware co. Devon and of Dominica   I 38

Glesney connected with Brandon   XX 56[a]

Gloucester als Porter   XIX 158

———— Consul, Earl of   XXI 272

———————— and Hertford, Clare Earl of, connected with Fitzgerald   XXI 272

Glover of Osset co. York   VI 215

———————— of Silkston co. York, and of Blackburn co. Lancaster   VI 105

———————— of Thornbury co. Gloucester   XVI 28

Glubb of Bickton connected with Smith   IV 450

Glyn of Ewell connected with Lewen and Lewes   I 402

Glynn of Burford co. Oxon   I 220

Goad of Grange M.I.   XIV 9

Goate of Bottisdale co. Suffolk connected with More   V 12

Gobyon of Waresley connected with Butler   VI 203

Goddard connected with Gregory   I 193

———————————— Marlowe   IX 88

————————————————————————   XXI 322

———————— of Hartham Wills and of Berwit Basset   XIII 104

Goden M.I. in Chatham Church   VI 126

Godfrey of Hoddiford   XVIII 63

———————— of Minety co. Wilts   III 523

Godolphen of Godolphin and Walsingham co. Norfolk, Trevenage co. Cornwall, Windsor co. Berks, London co. Middlesex, Colston co. Wilts Lord Godolphin of Ryalton, Viscount Godolphen   VI 82

Godolphin of Sparg co. Cornwall connected with Mapletoft   VII 353

———————— Governor of Scilly connected with Burslem   V 197

Godstone connected with Holmes   VI 237

Godwin   XXI 231

Gold see Goold Gould

Goldesburgh connected with Brackenbury   VII 272

Goldfinch of Peckham co. Surrey   XVII 26

Golding connected with Spaw and Aldus   II 317

———————— of Poslingford and Thorrington co. Suffolk connected with Graves   I 503

Goldingham of London co. Middlesex and of the Divizes co. Wilts connected with Williams   V 185

Goldeney of Bath connected with Rundall   I 41

Goldsmid of London co. Middlesex and of Roehampton co. Surrey   V 460

Goldsmith connected with Dacre   II 125

———————————————— and Scott   III 177

Gonning of the City of Bristol   IV 51

———————— see Gunning

Gonvelde connected with Paston   IX 113[b]

Gooch ———————— Miller   IV 158

———————— of London co. Middlesex, Bungay in Ilketshall, Mettingham co. Suffolk, Bishop of Ely   XXI 253

Good connected with Hampson   XII 51

———————— of Cambridgeshire connected with Hookes   XVIII 108

Goodall afterwards Coryton of Foy co. Cornwall, and of London
   co. Middlesex   III 84
———————— of Normanton co. Derby connected with Dalby   IV 281
Goodchild of Vauxhall co. Surrey connected with Strickland   VIII 519
Goodenough of London co. Middlesex, Broughton Poges co.
   Oxford, and of Longford & Hanley co. Berks   IX 39
Goodere of Charlton, Hampton Magna co. Worcester and of
   Burghope co. Hereford   III 286
Goodeve of Gosport co. Southampton – memorial as to Arms   XVII 25
Gooding connected with Leach   IX 101
Goodrick first settler in Virginia, of the Isle of Wight in Virginia
   connected with Bridger   IV 234
Goodwin of East Grinstead co. Sussex   I 262
———————— of Horley co. Oxon connected with Ford   V 294
                                             XI 39
———————— of Winchendon co. Bucks connected with Babington VIII 322
———————————————— Throckmorton XVI 34
Goold, Gould, Gold of the City of Cork, Old Court co. Cork, and
   of Clonmore co. Tipperary, connected with Hawkins   XII 49–54
———————— Gould of Cork   VIII 194
———————— records of Wardships and Liveries – lists of Wills VIII 199
Gordon to Trenchard petition as to change of name   IX 13
Gore lord of the Manor of Sandon of Tring co. Hertford and of
   Godalming co. Surrey   VIII 164
———————— of Dublin and of Bath co. Somerset connected with
   Gorges   I 60
———————— of Ireland connected with Warre   II 4
Gorges connected with Gore   I 60
———————— of Leominster and of Eye co. Hereford   VII 242
———————— of Wraxall co. Somerset connected with Russell XX 49[a]
Gormanston Lord   I 303
Gort Viscount limitation as to succession   XVII 24
Gosnold of Stow Market co. Suffolk connected with Cobb   II 354
Gospatrick Earl of Northumberland   XIV 19
———————— lord of Camerton connected with Curwin   II 456
———————— Lord of Workington connected with Curwen   II 457
Gostling of Dedenham Leostaff co. Suffolk and of co. Surrey III 404
Gough connected with James   XX 157[a]
———————————————— Mawhood   IX 53
———————— letter as to family   IX 82
———————— of London co. Middlesex   XX 128
———————— of Willsbury, St Briavels, Wollaston, Hewelsfield,
   Flaxley, Newland, and of Bristol co. Gloucester, afterwards
   Aubrey   XX 1, 2, 3, 4
                                           XX 11, 13, 16[a]
                                           XX 19[a]–21[a]
                                           XX 22–5
———————— of Wollaston, Huelsfield, Wilsberry in the psh of St
   Briavels, and of Newland co. Gloucester   XIX 186
———————— see Smart   XX 215

Gould – came from Dorset – of Newington, Hackney, and of Woodbury co. Devon   IX 4

———— Goold Gold of the City of Cork, Old Court co. Cork, and of Clonmore co. Tipperary, connected with Hawkins   XII 49–54

———— Goold of Cork connected with Galway Coppinger O'Callaghan and Bourke   VIII 194

———— Goold records of Wardships and Liveries, lists of wills   VIII 199

———— of Dover co. Kent connected with Shaw   IV 287

Gourney connected with Trye   XIII 97

Gower formerly Hawkins   XII 48–9

———— Leveson connected with Thanet   XVI 58

———— of Ludlow and Glandovan connected with Stedman   XVII 48

———— of Richmarle Olives and Ridmarley co. Worcester connected with Sheldon   VII 43

Gowland connected with Chamberlaine   XX 80^b, 80^e

Graham connected with Gorges   VII 242

———— of the Scots Greys, Solicitor in Chancery, of Deptford, claimed title of Lord Graham and Viscount Dundee   XVII 54

———— see Grahme

Grahame sometime Privy Purse to King James II   XVI 32

Grahame Graham Viscount Preston and Baron of Esk, of Norton Conyers co. York, Southchurch co. Essex, and of Netherby co. Cumberland   III 511

———— Viscount Preston of Netherby co. Cumberland   XVIII 54

Grainger of Crurs Morchard, Sowton, Exeter co. Devon, and of Withicombe in the Moor   I 60

Grantesmenil Steward of England connected with Bellomont   VIII 250

Grantham connected with Pettiwood   II 472

Granville from D'Ewes – petition   VI 382

Grave, Graves of Clock Heaton in the psh of Burstal, Beamsley in the psh of Adingham in the West Riding of Yorkshire, London co. Middlesex and of Mickleton co. Gloucester   XIX 28

Gravenor of London co. Middlesex connected with Whorwood   IV 534

Graves Baron Graves connected with Budgell   XV 10

———— of Charles Town near Boston in New England connected with Russell   III 157

———— of Chiswick co. Middlesex   I 503

———— of Mickleton co. Gloucester connected with Swan and Danvers   XIX 14

———— see Grave

Gravett of Carrickfergus and Londonderry in the Kingdom of Ireland, and of Bristol co. Gloucester   XXI 236

———— of Chittingfold co. Sussex, Godalming co. Surrey and of London co. Middlesex   II 357

Gray, Lord   II 136

———— of Berringham Newcastle upon Tyne co. Northumberland and of Schives   I 57

———— of London co. Middlesex, Southwark co. Surrey, and of Hitchen co. Herts connected with Bell & Walker   III 267

———— of London co. Middlesex, Springwell Place near

Rickmansworth co. Herts – took surname of Ross –
  connected with Emmott   VII 221
Graye Lord M.I. at Barton co. Nottingham   VI 112
Greatorex of West Hallom, Merrybower, co. Derby and of
  London co. Middlesex   III 28
Greaves connected with Percival and Gilliam   XIV 1
————— of Sheffield and of Attercliffe co. York   I 574
     II 35

Green connected with Addison and Curwen or Culwen   II 462
————————— Dillingham   IX 101
————— of Boxley and of Newent co. Gloucester   XIX 228
————— of Buckton, Norton Danie, Maudilit co. Northampton
  connected with Paulton   XVI 18
————— of Dublin, Colerain, Belfast, and of Lanbeder co.
  Denbigh   VII 118
————— of Dublin, Rector of Llanbeder co. Denbigh   VII 305
     IX 143

————— of Hill House near Tenbury co. Worcester and of
  Ludlow co. Salop connected with Turner   IV 275
————— of Leversage, Leeds co. York, connected with Newton   III 282
————— of London and of Preston Northumberland connected
  with Errington   I 94
————— of Newport, North of Ireland, connected with
  Blennerhasset   II 148
————— of Oundle co. Northampton and of Great Kingshill in
  the psh of Hitchendon co. Bucks   XXI 226
————— of Trowbridge co. Wilts, Southwick and of Brook   XXI 320
Greene of Walton and of Stoford   IX 142
Greenfield of Petersfield co. Hants and of Medhurst co. Sussex   IV 209
Greenhalgh of Tevershall co. Nottingham connected with
  Molineux   VIII 256
Greening connected with Petty   XVIII 15
————— of Didbrooke, Alderton, Lechlade, Stanway, Gretton
  co. Gloucester, London co. Middlesex and of Hendred co.
  Berks   I 195
Greenland connected with Denne   II 23
Greenlaw of Elgin in the County of Morray in Scotland connected
  with Hodgskin and Bathurst   XIII 31
Greenous connected with Angell   I 79
Greentree of Shoreham co. Sussex and of Scarborough co. York,
  connected with Cockerill   III 145
Greenwallers Greenwollers of Wem co. Salop connected with
  Garland   II 408
Greenwollers of Wem co. Salop connected with Garland   XVIII 140[b]
————— see Greenwallers
Greenwood connected with Merttins   XXI 235
————— of Brears Norton connected with Whorwood   XX 249[a]
Greetham of Liverpool co. Palatine Lancaster – change of name of
  Wright   XVII 65
Gregg of Minhouse Cumberland M.I.   XIV 8

Gregory of Ashfordby co. Leicester, Eyton co. Nottingham,
    Styvechale co. Warwick, old Woodstock co. Oxon and of
    Rochester and Chatham co. Kent   XIX 122
———— of Cheltenham co. Gloucester   XX 29
———— of Hordley co. Oxon and of Jamaica   I 193
———— of Styvechale or Stivie Hall co. Warwick   VII 246
———— of Wallingford co. Berks connected with Angell   XI 55
———— of Wootton under Edge, Bitton, Nibley in the psh of
    Westerleigh co. Gloucester, East Grinstead in Sussex, and of
    Clevedon co. Somerset   XX 127–7ᵃ
Greinfield of Stow connected with Cole   XX 82ᵃ
Grendour connected with Tiptoft   XIII 121–2
———— of Clerewell in the Forest of Deane   XIX 45
Grene of Grenes Norton co. Northampton, Tanworth co.
    Warwick, and of the Middle Temple co. Middlesex   XIX 228
Grenfeld Grenville of Barnbow co. York connected with
    Stevenson   VIII 232
Grenius of Bridgenorth co. Salop connected with Phillips   III 93
Grenville connected with Smyth   VI 97
———— Grenfeld of Barnbow co. York connected with
    Stevenson   VIII 232
———— see Grenfeld
Greswold connected with Eburne   XVIII 139
———————————————— and Makepeace   IV 471
———————————— Wild and with Kynaston   XVIII 115
Grevile of Beauchamp Court connected with Verney   XIX 154
———— of Bristol, Tewkesbury and of the City of Gloucester
    connected with Brereton   XX 135–5ᵃ
———— of Campden co. Gloucester and of Drayton near
    Banbury co. Oxon   XIX 76
Grevill Baron Brooke see Greville   XVI 82
Greville Lord Brooke, of Beauchamp Court co. Warwick, and of
    Thorp Latimer co. Lincoln   XVI 20
Grey connected with Hogge   XXI 208
———————————— Thicknesse   I 148
———————————— Top and Everard   VIII 25
———————————— West   IV 206
———————————— Wolrich   V 198
———— Duke of Suffolk   XIV 18
———— Lord, of Codnore connected with de la Zouch   I 445
———— Lord Powis connected with Vernon and Curson   III 276
———— of Kingston co. Dorset and of Apsley co. Warwick   II 364
———— of Ruthin Lord   XVI 59, 60
———————————— connected with Pryor   XXI 242
———— see de Grey
Gribble of Boevey Tracey co. Devon and of London co. Middx   VIII 3
Grieve of Alnwick and of Swarland co. Northumberland   XXI 272ᵃ
Griffin Baron Griffin of Braybroke   XXI 262
———— connected with Jepson and Farmer   I 95
———— formerly Whitwell   XXI 262

Griffin Lord of Bran connected with Jones of Hendre   VII 254
───────── of Ewell and of Southwark co. Surrey connected with
Stonestreet   VIII 512
───────── of London co. Middlesex, and of Kingston Jamaica
West Indies   XXI 184
Griffith als Griffyn of the City of Worcester and of Great
Barrington co. Gloucester connected with Loggan   IX 113ᶜ
───────── ap Ednevet, Lord of Llandsadome co. Carmarthen   XIV 20
───────── Rees   XIV 20
───────── connected with Davies   III 395
───────── formerly Gwillim connected with Humphrys   II 80
───────── Lord of Bromfeld connected with Scudamore   XVIII 57
───────── of Glan Gwendrath als Colebrooke afterwards Jones   IV 216
───────── of Laneravon in the psh of Lanvrechva, New Port co.
Monmouth and of Keven-Lila   XVI 75
───────── of Lanaraven co. Monmouth connected with Bell   XX 67
───────── of Llanoyndyrne connected with Read   IX 76
───────── of Mountain Hall co. Carmarthen, Broadway co.
Worcester, and of Buckland   VIII 427
───────── of St Briavells co. Gloucester   XX 17ᵃ
───────── of Wichnore co. Stafford and of Burton Agnes co.
Yorks   XIV 16–20
───────── of Wollaston co. Gloucester, London & Antigua
connected with Crayle   I 157
───────── Uarwn Gwyn Lord of Yale connected with Scudamore   XVIII 57
───────── Uychan connected with Scudamore   XVIII 57
Griffiths of Cheshunt co. Herts and of Enfield co. Middlesex   IX 62
─────────────────── Enfield co. Middlesex and of South Wales   III 135
─────────────────── of Llangolman Llynderwan co. Pembroke
connected with Rhys   IV 346
Griffyn als Griffith of the City of Worcester and of Great
Barrington co. Gloucester connected with Loggan   IX 113ᶜ
Grimes or Parker arms to be taken by Bourke   XIII 15
───────── see Bourke   XIII 15
Grimshaw of Droylsden, Gorton, Audenshawe co. Lancaster   III 468
Grimsteed of Balsbury or Yatton co. Somerset, and of Bristol co.
Gloucester   III 443
Grimston connected with Shaw and Eyre   XVI 95
Grimstone, Viscounts, of the Kingdom of Ireland and of Oxhey
co. Herts connected with Bucknall   II 138
Grimwood of Chelsea and of Kensington   VIII 300
Groos, le Groos
Grose of Berne in Switzerland London co. Middlesex and of
Wandsworth co. Surrey   XXI 230
───────── of co. Surrey   IX 56
Grosset of Logu and Bredisholm in Scotland also of Brislington co.
Somerset   III 207
Grosvenor connected with Stanley   XXI 291
───────── Grosvenour of Hulme near Rudheath co. Chester
connected with de Leycester   VI 155

Grosvenor of Bishopsbury and New Bridge co. Stafford
    connected with Hawe and Parker   XXI 170
Grosvenour see Grosvenor
Grove of Clayton in Suffolk connected with Coles   X 35
———— of Fordhill in Wotton Waren co. Warwick connected
    with Sheldon   VII 44
———— of Thornbury connected with Thurston   XX 132ᵃ
Growdon of Cornwall connected with Galloway   IV 302
Grubb connected with Hutton   II 47
———— of Pottern co. Wilts connected with Bourchier   I 561
Gruffeth of Pentryn connected with Stanley & Hookes   XVIII 107
Grufith son of Rees ap Tudor the Lord Rees Prince of South Wales
    connected with Puliston and Hookes   XVIII 104
Grundie of Gorton, Collingham, Upton near Southwell, Holme
    Hall co. Nottingham, London co. Middlesex, and of
    America   III 288
Gryndom connected with Aburhall   XIII 100
Guidot co. Southampton and of London – entries as to date of
    deaths in the family   XX 132
Guildford connected with Throckmorton   XVI 34
———————— West Lord Delawar   XII 51
———— of Halden in Kent connected with Waller   XVIII 96
Guillim of Langston co. Hereford connected with Atherton of
    Atherton   III 280
Guise of Aspeley Guise co. Bedford, Sandhurst Elmore, Rencombe,
    Upton St Leonard, co. Gloucester, Blackdown co. Devon
    and of Lincolnshire   XIX 227
———— of Winterbourne, Upton St Leonards, and of Higham
    co. Gloucester   I 357
Guldeford connected with Gage   V 431
Gullan of . . . in Scotland   IX 150
Gully connected with Knight   XXI 156ᶜ
Gulston Deans of Chichester, Bishop of Bristol; of Portugal XV 10
———— of co. Herts connected with Stebbing   VII 317
Gundry of Lyme Regis co. Dorset connected with Warren I 488
Gunman connected with Hanson   III 64
————————————————————————— VIII 537
———————————— Wyvill   IV 269
———— of Govardin co. Norfolk, Deptford and of Dover co.
    Kent   VII 351
————————————   XXI 167
Gunning connected with Whish   IX 136
———— Gonning of Bristol   XVIII 102
———————— Cold Aston co. Gloucester and of
    Waterhouse near Bath co. Somerset   XX 130–1
———— of Bristol and Lord of Cold Aston co. Gloucester VIII 389
———— of Gravesend co. Kent, Vicar of Hoo, Bishop of Ely XXI 318ᵃ
———— of Langridge, Swanswick, Lord of the Manor of
    Turneys Court in the psh of Cold Ashton, Talwich co.
    Somerset, and of Sheffield co. York   IV 53
———— of Langridge, Talwick and of Swainswick co. Som. XVIII 103

Gunning of Waterhouse near Bath, Swainswick co. Som. and of
    Cold Aston co. Gloucester   IV 52
———————— see also Gonning
Gunston of Bishops Hull co. Somerset and of Knoyle co. Wilts   II 252
Gunter of Gunters Town in Wales, St Silliens, Abergavenny co.
    Monmouth, Andover in Hants, Milton co. Wilts and of
    Reading and Kintbury co. Berks   XIX 266
Gurdon connected with Dillingham   IX 101
Gurney of Norwich   IV 78
Guy of Frocester co. Gloucester connected with Wilkins   XX 244
Guydickens connected with Chute   XVII 15
———————— of London co. Middlesex Minister at Berlin Stockholm
    and St Petersburgh   XXI 175
Gwatkin of Bristol co. Gloucester   III 412
Gwillim ap Griff ap Gwillim afterwards Griffith connected with
    Humphreys   II 80
———————— connected with Steward   IX 64
Gwin of Horton co. Gloucester connected with Fielding   XIX 238
Gwinnett formerly Catchmayd   XX 128ª
———————— of London co. Middlesex, Badgworth Bristol and of
    Shurdington co. Gloucester   XX 128–8ª
Gwyn of Ystlysycoed in the psh of Llanon Gwempa in the psh of
    Llangendeirn Carmarthen   II 446
Gwynne connected with Essington   XX 118
———————— of Monachly co. Cardigan connected with Jones of
    Tyglyn, Edwardes, and Thomas   XV 26–32
Gyles of London co. Middlesex – Grant of Arms   XXI 281
———————— William, note as to family   XIII 105
Gywney of Heveringland connected with Fastolfe   VII 502

H

Habington see Abyngton   XIX 169
Hache of Wolley co. Devon connected with Mallet   VII 75
Hacket connected with Stebbing   VII 317
———————— of London and Litchfield connected with Reynolds   I 255
Hackett of Barbadoes connected with Dottin and Estwick   II 303
———————— of Moxhull co. Worcester connected with Bridgeman   XV 10
Hacon of Ipswich connected with Angell   I 76
Hadden of Haddington   I 57
Hadfield of Tideswell Chapel of Frith co. Derby and of Manchester
    co. Lancaster   II 271
Hagar or Agar of Bourne co. Cambridge connected with Hewitt VII 3
Haggerston of Haggerston and of Hellingham co. Northampton   X 147

Hague connected with Shackleton	I 1
Haine of London co. Middlesex and of Bishops Hull near Taunton co. Somerset	IV 74
Haines, Haynes connected with Clifford	IX 160
Hake connected with Seward	X 126[d]
—————— of Peterborough co. Northampton Plimpton near Plymouth co. Devon London co. Middlesex, Lisbon and of Virginia	VII 132
—————— went from Northampton to Devonshire, was of Plimpton near Plymouth and of Lisbon	VII 120
Hakeman connected with Angell	I 76
Hale connected with Bourchier	I 559
————————————— Mills	XX 164
————————————— Watts	XX 230
—————— of Alderley, Bradford co. Wilts, Bristol, and of North Nibley co. Gloucester	I 221
—————— of Alderly, Hillesley co. Gloucester, Evelin co. Oxon, Acton, Lincolns Inn co. Middlesex, and of Cottels in the psh of Alford co. Wilts	II 89
Halford of Lyminge	I 231
————————————— Elham Ightham and of Canterbury co. Kent	III 73
Halfpenny connected with Drage	I 92
Halket of Pitfirran formerly Wedderburn	VII 165
Hall, connected with Bickley	IV 2
——————————— Crekelade	XX 212[a]
——————————— Hatfield	IX 128
——————————— Hodges	V 276
——————————— Huxley	XV 9
——————————— Oades	I 243
——————————————————————————	XXI 159[b]
————— de la	XIX 208
————— of Bradford co. Wilts connected with Rogers	XIX 101
————— of Harding co. Oxon connected with Constantine	VII 311
————— of Highmead co. Gloucester	XX 249[a]
————— of Highmeadow, lord of the Manor of English Bicknor	X 43
————— of Highmeadow co. Gloucester	XX 153
————————————————————— connected with Winchcombe	IV 364
————— of Highmeadow in the psh of Newland in the Forest of Dean co. Gloucester	XIX 208
————— of Ledbury and of Hereford connected with Elton	I 109
————— of Lewnthorpe in Swillington co. York	IX 128–9
————— of London co. Middlesex	VIII 109
—————————————	XXI 318
————— of Manchester co. Lancaster connected with Pilkington	IV 315
————— of Oxford connected with Browne	XX 235[a]
————————————— London co. Middlesex Jamaica and of India connected with Bourne and Wilkins	II 341
————— of Richmond co. York connected with Bagster	I 212
—————————————————————————	IV 96

Hall of St Lawrence Wotton and of Moundesmere co. Southampton
    connected with Oades   VII 306
————— of Skirwith co Cumberland, Barklow co. Essex,
    London co. Middlesex, and of Madras   II 211
————— of Skirworth near Penrith and of Romford in Essex   X 8
————— of Southwick and of Burghill co. Sussex   I 61
Hallam of Dublin, London co. Middlesex, and of Okewood co.
    Surrey   II 216
Halle see Hall   XIX 208
Hallett of London co. Middlesex   X 164
Halliburton of Morislaw connected with Johnston and Elliott   IX 153
Halliday Holliday Holyday Halyday of Rodborough Stonehouse,
    Minchenhampton Stroud co. Gloucester, and of London co.
    Middlesex   XX 136–7
Halloran to Blakeney suggested change of name   XIII 16
Halloway connected with Cary   VIII 248
Hallyday connected with Pury   XIX II
Halstead connected with Playdell   VII 360
Halsted of Kirby Underwood co. Lincoln, Tamworth co. Stafford,
    and of Gosport co. Hants   VIII 163
Halton Baron of, and Constable of Chester   XIX 181
Halton heir to Sir William Holton Baronet,   IV 43
————— of London co. Middlesex   XIII 11
Halyday Holliday Holyday see Halliday   XX 136–7
Hambyns of Lea co. Gloucester connected with Brayne   XV 77
Hames, connected with Hawkins   XII 48–50
Hamilton afterwards O'Hara of Port Glenone and of Crebilly co.
    Antrim   XI 28–33
————— connected with Browne   XV 13
————————— Chamberlayne   XX 80[b,c]
————————— Onslow   I 209
————— Earl of Abercorne connected with Mackworth and
    Huddleston   III 341
————— of Letham co. Sterling connected with Montgomery
    and Thompson   II 37
————— of Muselburgh in the Shire of Edinburgh and of
    London co. Middlesex   XXI 275
————— of Silverton Hall Cadzour, Newton in the Barony of
    Drumsargart and psh of Cambuslang, Goslington Cats-castle
    in Lanarkshire, Hull co. York, and of Jersey   III 261
Hamlyn als Prust   XV 23
————— of Paschoe in the psh of Colebrooke, Exeter, and of
    Tinmouth co. Devon   II 287
————— of Wolfardisworthy co. Devon connected with Prust   XV 23
Hamlyne see Hamlyn
Hammersley of Roxby co. Lincoln and of London co. Middlesex   III 278
Hammond connected with Browne   VII 342
————— Leeke   XIII 92
————— Lucy   I 420
————— of Battle and of Ninfield co. Sussex   XVII 12
————— of Chertsey co. Surrey connected with Knollys   XVII 30

Hammond of Croydon co. Surrey connected with Carr   IV 384
———————— of Dibden co. Essex connected with Hinson   II 179
———————— of Greenwich co. Kent   XXI 252
———————— of Ingatestone in Essex   VII 124
———————— of Scarthingwell in psh of Saxton co. York and of
 Freston   III 355
———————— of Teddington co. Middlesex, lord of the Manors of
 Milton and Gravesend co. Kent   IV 412
———————— of Woolaston co. Gloucester   XX 17
———————— Rector of Gawsworth co. Chester connected with
 Lucy   I 13
Hamond Hayman connected with Tyrell   VIII 103
———————— of Hayling co. Surrey connected with Parker   III 197
Hampden connected with Cromwell   XV 19, 21
———————————————— Dacre   III 175
Hampson connected with Good   XII 51
———————— M.I. in Salisbury Cathedral   VI 131
Hampton connected with Walshe   XVIII 13
———————— of Minchenhampton in Gloucester, and of London co.
 Middlesex   XX 153ª
———————— of Westbury connected with Symons   XVI 65
Hamund als Clerke of Willoughby co. Warwick   VIII 46
Hanbury of Feckenham co. Worcester. Preston co. Gloucester and
 of Little Marcle co. Hereford   X 124
———————— of Hanbury, Elmesley Lovet co. Worcester, London
 co. Middlesex, Watton Mitton and of East Maple Durham
 co. Southampton   XIX 42
———————— of Kelmarsh co. Northampton connected with Waller   XVIII 99
———————— of Pont-y-pool co. Monmouth   III 17
                                                                IV 30
Hancock connected with Phillips   III 92
———————————————— Sperring   XIII 91
———————— of Twyning in the County of Gloucester descended out
 of Devon, of London co. Middlesex, Plaistow in Essex, and
 of Norton co. Worcester   XIII 97
Hankey of London, Poplar co. Middlesex, Richmond co. Surrey,
 East Bergholt co. Suffolk, and of Oxford   II 161
Hannah of Wadhingham   XIII 74
Hannes see Hans   VII 133
Hanover George Duke of   XVI 9
Hans or Hannes of Suffolk connected with Willis Packer and
 Stephens   VII 133
Hanson afterwards Inglish of Wakefield co. York Hampstead and
 of London co. Middlesex   VIII 507
———————— came from Coventry, of Osmanthorpe near Leeds
 Leventhorp in Swillington, of Milton in the East Riding co.
 York and of Normanton   IV 55
———————— connected with Gunman   XXI 167
———————————————— Ingram and Smith   IV 268
———————————————— Norton   VIII 536
———————— of Blewberry co. Berks, London co. Middlesex,

Coventry co. Warwick, and of Jamaica West Indies — III 64
———————— of Maryland connected with Briscoe — IV 26
Harbin connected with Bell — IV 402
Harby als Hardeby — XIV 12
Harcourt connected with Darel — IX 41
———————————— Perkins — III 509
———————————————————————————————— XVIII 28
Hardcastle of Leeds co. York connected with Potts — III 124
Hardeby als Harby of Evedon co. Lincolnshire M.I. — XIV 12
Hardeby Harvey of Evedon co. Lincoln connected with Willoughby — XIV 21
Harden of Burnham co. Somerset, Cirencester co. Gloucester and of Northampton — I 177
Harding connected with Akerman — IX 135
———————————— Johnston — III 112
———————————— Windham — II 86
———————— of Kings Newton, Farnsfield co. Nottingham, Cley Pool co. Lincoln, and of Holland — III 476
———————— of South Molton, Upcott in the psh of Pilton, and of Barnstaple co. Devon — III 424
———————— son of King of Denmark connected with Kingscote — XVI 29
Hardman connected with Pilkington — IV 315
Hards ———————— Hall — I 61
Hardware ———— Hunt — V 75
————————————— of Boreaton — XVIII 34
Hardwick ———— Cocks — II 422
Hardwicke of Chipping Sodbury and of Bristol co. Gloucester — XX 142ᵃ
Hardy memorial of — XI 2
———————— of Nedlington near Hull co York, Liverpool co. Lancaster, London and Edmonton co. Islington — II 245
Hare formerly Leigh — I 408
———————— of Serecroft co. York, Islington co. Middlesex, and of Tuxford co. Nottingham — II 360
Harford connected with Jones of Treverne co. Radnor — I 112
———————— of Bosbury co. Hereford — II 418
———————— of Bristol co. Gloucester — II 185
Harget connected with Lynch — III 298
Hargrave ———————— Bonner — VIII 421
Harington of Bourton on the Water co. Gloucester, Abergavenny co. Monmouth – took name of Champernoun — VI 230
Harley Earl of Oxford — XVI 30
Harman als le Groos — VII 505
———————— of Wood Dalling co. Norfolk connected with le Groos — VII 505
Harmar of Chalford co. Gloucester London co. Middlesex and of Manchester co. Lancs. — XX 144
Harnage connected with Blackman — II 482
Harneis of Hatherby co. Lincoln connected with Bennett — II 155
Harold Lord of Ewias in Herefordshire supposed to be the son of Harold that was Earl Godwyn's son, connected with Scudamore — XVIII 57
Harper of Bath and Calcutta connected with Rundall — I 41

Harper of Gosport co. Hants   XVII 63
————— of Manchester co. Warwick connected with Sir Guy de
Mancester and Brokushole   IX 93
————— of Swarkston Mickleover and of Littleover co. Derby   I 252
Harpur M.I. at Morley co. Derby   VI 107
Harrington connected with Hudleston M.I.   V 325
————— of Aigburth and Huyton co. Lancaster connected with
Tarlton   I 383
————— of Powderham co. Devon afterwards Champernowne   IV 32
————— of Wolferge co. Northampton and of Westley
connected with Stanley   XXI 291–3
————— of Wregshem in Cartmel in Furness co. Lancs. Wollax
co. Cumberland, and of Ubey Hall   XXI 32
Harris afterwards Barrington, of Worcester, Bestbrook in the psh
of Old Radnor co. Radnor and of co. Montgomery   VII 57
————— connected with Bowles   I 144
————————— Hopkins   IX 112
————————— Windsor   I 317
————— of Abergavenny connected with Lysons   I 45
—————————————————————————   XIX 138
————— of Cryglase co. Pembroke connected with Bowen   IV 193
————— of Glastonbury co. Somerset connected with Slade and
Roach   IV 523
————— of London co. Middlesex and of the East Indies
connected with Soame   I 495
————— of Lymington co. Hants connected with Voysey   III 441
————— of Old Woodstock co. Oxon connected with Sandes   II 442
————— of Oxford   XXI 186
————— of Prickley co. Worcester Haydon Deerhurst Walton   XIX 72
co. Gloucester and of Devizes co. Wilts
Harrison connected with Bayley   XXI 47
————— of Barnby, Howden, and of Brayton co. York   II 326
————— of Caverton and Orchard in the Shire of Roxburgh
connected with Dickson   I 88
————— of Coleshill co. Warwick and of London co. Middx.   IV 404
————— of Jamaica connected with Tomlinson   XV 85
————— of Middlesex   III 455
————— of Ripon and of York   XVII 49
————— of Stanley in the psh of Wakefield co. York   XII 17–27
————— of Stockton in the Bishopric of Durham, Elton co.
York, and of London co. Middlesex   III 90
————— of Stubhouse co. Durham connected with Brunshall   XXI 164
————— of Tar Point near Plymouth   III 352
————————————————— connected with Horne   IV 95
————— of Teignmouth near Plymouth connected with Horne
and Arundell   I 211
————— of Winandermer M.I.   XIV 9
————— of Wyfordby, Old Dalby, Claybrook, Sheepy co.
Leicester, Chelsea, London co. Middlesex, and of Daventry
in Northamptonshire   IV 180
Harryman of Bermondsey co. Surrey connected with Harrison   IV 404

Hart of Tockington co. Gloucester and of Boston co. Lincoln   XIX 53
———— of West Winch co. Norfolk   VIII 43
———————————— connected with Turner   V 28
Hartland connected with Corthine   VII 349
———————————— Harmar   XX 144
Hartley of Buckelbury and Donnington Castle co. Berks connected
    with Packer and Stephens   VII 135
———— of Grassington connected with Peart   III 490
Hartop of Little Dalby co. Leicester afterwards Wigley   XV 25
———————————— in Melton Mowbray co. Leicester   XXI 226
Hartopp of Burton Lazers, Rotherley, Woodhouse co. Leicester,
    and of Manstowe co. Devon   XXI 312
———— of Quarendon co. Leicester connected with Bennett   XV 10
Hartshorne of Long Whatton   II 324
Hartwell of Greenwich Hospital and of the Royal Navy   III 464
Harvey Hardeby of Evedon co. Lincoln connected with Willoughby   XIV 21
———— connected with Skinner   X 58
—— of Folkestone in Kent, Twickenham co. Middlesex,
    Rockhampton co. Gloucester, and of Combe Nevil co.
    Surrey   IX 133
———— of Folkestone in Kent, Rockhampton co. Gloucester,
    Combe Nevil and Clifton co. Dorset   VII 338
———— of Killiane Castle Bargey Castle co. Wexford Wigan
    co. Lancaster, Duffield co. Derby, and of Farnham co. York   XII 66–80
———— of London and Islington co. Middlesex   I 570
———— ———————————— Wokingham co. Berks,
    Strood, Rochester co. Kent, Bermondsey and Southwark
    co. Surrey, Baptisms etc.   VI 287
———— of Northampton and of Stafford   I 507
———— Suffolk and of London connected with Borrow   II 200
———— of Winchcombe co. Gloucester connected with
    Willoughby   III 168
Harwood connected with Feake   XVI 33
————————————————————————————————————   XVI 93
———————————— Hill   V 68
———— from Hackbourn and Streckley co. Berks and of Tern
    near Shrewsbury connected with Kynaston   XVIII 117
———— of Deane, Rector of Ewhurst, and of Laverstoke co.
    Southampton   VIII 304
———— of Norwich co. Norfolk connected with Tooke   VIII 226
Haslerton, lord of West and Castle Haslerton, Marton and Severby
    co. York, Lord of Bondby co. Lincoln connected with
    Hotham   XVIII 82
Hassard afterwards Short of the City of London   IV 396
———————————— East Keele and Edlington co. Lincoln,
    London co. Middlesex, and of Bealings co. Suffolk   IX 74
Hassenden of Hassenden, Rye, Benenden, Bethersden, and of
    Ashford co. Kent   I 280
Hastings Earl of Huntingdon connected with Hungerford   V 251
———— formerly Rawdon   V 261
———— Lord Abergavenny connected with Spencer   VI 52

Hastings connected with Hungerford — V 57
——————————— Talbot and Port — XII 28–47
——————————— of Dailesford co. Worcester — II 24
——————— of Woodford co. Northampton connected with Smith of Alton — IV 173
Haswell of Newcastle upon Tyne co. Northumberland and of Sunderland co. Durham connected with Anderson — III 136
Hatch connected with Jull — I 32
Hatchet Hatchett of Lee in the psh of Elsmere co. Salop — II 280
Hatchett of Edwinstone co. Nottingham connected with Ferrand — I 53
——————— of Ellesmere, Lee, and of Tedsmore in the psh of Felton co. Salop — XII 1–4
——————— of Ellesmere, Tedsmore Hall, West Felton, Lee co. Salop connected with Owen — VII 368
——————— of Penkerry co. Monmouth — IX 66
——————— see also Hatchet
Hatfield of Willoughby co. Nottingham, Follerton, and of Hatfield Hall Stanley co. York — IX 128
Hatsell connected with Walker and Mitford — XXI 188
Hatton als Newport connected with Gawdy — VI 78
——————— connected with Taylor and Romney — XIX 132
——————— of Weverham co. Chester connected with Williamson — I 250
Haughton of Westmorland connected with Blake — III 378
Haveningham see Heveningham — XXI 223
Havers of Thelverton als Thelton co. Norfolk, Grays Inn co. Middlesex, Maryland in Virginia, and of Dunkirk — II 479
Hawe connected with Grosvenor and Parker — XXI 170
Hawke of Lincoln's Inn co Middlesex lord of the Manors of Scarthingwell, Towton, Little Fenton, and of Barkston co. York connected with Bladen & Brooke — III 354
——————— of Sunbury co. Middlesex connected with Turner — XX 162
Hawker of Dudbridge and of Ulley co. Gloucester connected with Holbrow — I 171
——————— of Rodborough co. Gloucester connected with Small — II 92
Hawkesbury co. Gloucester extracts from Registers — VI 340
Hawkey of Llanlawren co. Cornwall — XXI 8
——————————————————————————————— XXI 11
Hawkins afterwards Gower of Colmers co. Worcester — XII 48–9
——————— connected with Nutt — XX 49
——————— of Holderness co. York Nash Court, Selling Whitstable co. Kent, London co. Middlesex and of Blackington co. Oxon — XII 48–51
——————— of Mill End in the psh of Hambledon co. Bucks — XVII 36
——————— of Nash co. Kent connected with Constantine — VII 314
Hawksworth of Thornbury co. Gloucester connected with Heynes — XIX 242
Hawkyns of Keldon co. Essex, Dorchester co. Dorset, and of London co. Middlesex — II 17
Hawley of Auler; Buckland co. Somerset, Corfe Castle co. Dorset, Boston near Brentford, and London co. Middlesex — VIII 451
——————— of Sturminster co. Dorset, Wyvelscomb co Somerset — VIII 451
Hawtayne connected with Strickland — VIII 514

Hawtrey connected with de Grey — VI 256
Hay connected with Pelham — IX 69
——————— Earls of Errol — IV 385
——————— of Glynde Bourne co. Sussex connected with Tutte — VII 199
——————— to Carr – change of name. — IV 385
Haycock connected with Woodhouse — IX 29
Haydock connected with Mollineux — VIII 257
Haydon of Grove in the psh of Walford co. Herts & of Shipton Solers co. Gloucester connected with Twinihoe and Peachey — I 72
Hayes connected with Cooper — X 29
——————— of Holliport near Windsor — XXI 125
Hayhurst of Melksham, Wilton co. Wilts connected with Bell — III 266
Hayles of Hollyse co. Stafford, Birmingham co. Warwick, and of Worcester, connected with Hopton — VIII 27
Hayman Hamond connected with Tyrell — VIII 103
——————— connected with Bridger — I 63
——————— of Deal, Somerfield, and of Selling co. Kent — V 176
——————— of St Mary Ottery co. Devon, Evershot near Yeovil co. Somerset, London co. Middlesex and of Liverpool co. Lancaster — IV 360
Hayne connected with Stone of Upcott — III 178
——————— of Auborne co. Wilts, and of Kintbury Eaton co. Berks. — II 300
——————— of Burton on Trent co. Stafford, and of Ashborne Green co. Derby, connected with Tildesley — I 386
Haynes Haines connected with Clifford — IX 160
——————— connected with Field and Tewkesbury — XVI 74
——————— of Copford Hall connected with Bowes — I 277
Hayter connected with Short — VI 367
Hayward als Cox of Forthampton, Wallesthorp, and of Quedgley co. Gloucester — XIX 246
——————— als Howard of Whitchurch co. Salop, and of Aldersey in the psh of Kings Tettenhall co. Stafford — VIII 298
——————— connected with Beale — XX 66[a]
——————— Juliet — IV 455
——————— Saunders — V 268
——————— Wintle — VI 186
——————— Wood and Thompson — XXI 156[c]
——————— of Blakeney co. Gloucester connected with Pick — XX 186[a]
——————— of Bourton in the psh of Shrivenham co. Berks connected with Dore — VII 462
——————— of Brimsfield co. Gloucester — VIII 392
——————— of Forthampton co. Gloucester, and of London co. Middlesex, see also Hayward als Cox — XIX 255
——————— of Frocester co. Gloucester — XVI 74
——————— of Gloucester, Huckle Court, Wallsworth Hall, co. Gloucester, and of London co. Middlesex — XIX 115
——————— of Tewkesbury connected with Neast — XX 172
——————— Rector of Broomberrow & Vicar of Dymock — XX 196
Heale see Hele — V 397
Healey connected with Tolson and Paine — XIII 112

Healy connected with Lovell	XIII 124–5
Heard ————— Michell	XVIII 62
	X 43
————— of Bridgewater co. Devon and of London co. Middlesex, Norroy King of Arms	XIX 166[c]
Hearst of Salisbury connected with Knatchbull	XIII 66
Heart of Stroud	XVI 89
Heath connected with Byne	IX 69
————— M.I. in Bracon Ash Church co. Norfolk	VI 119
————— of Fordhill in Wotton Waven co. Warwick, connected with Grove and Sheldon	VII 44
————— of Hatchlands co. Surrey connected with Nicholas	IV 256
————— of Stafford co. Nottingham and of London	II 320
Heathcote connected with Parker	IX 102
————— of Lea co. Hants, connected with Thorpe	XXI 214
Heaven of Kings Stanley co. Gloucester connected with Deverell	XX 113[a]
Heaveningham of Aston in Staffordshire connected with Symeon and Middlemore	IX 70
Heber of Marton in Craven connected with Atherton of Atherton	III 280
Hedger of Whitehaven Newcastle on Tyne and of Roborough co. Northumberland	XXI 216[a]
Hedges of Finchley co. Middlesex connected with Tate	I 204
————————————————— and of the Hague connected with Nicoll	III 138
Hedworth connected with Ayton of Errington, Musgrave and Milbank	X 131
————————————————— Huddleston	XXI 176
Hegarty of Scilly connected with Jarratt	IV 14
Heighington of Durham and of Bristol co. Gloucester	I 265
Hele came from Devonshire of London co. Middlesex	I 416
————— or Heale of Fleet co. Devon	V 397
Heley, de, connected with Okeden	XI 27
Helme of Chaseley and Eddisfield co. Worcester connected with Neast	XX 172
Helwis Helwish Elwes of Hublesthorpe, Asham co. Nottingham Worlaby, Gainsborough co. Lincoln, Brockston; Woodford co. Essex, Stoke Park co. Suffolk, Grove House near Fulham, Barton Court co. Berks, Hyde Hall Cheshunt, Throckton Hall co. Herts, and of Isleworth & London co. Middlesex	III 244
————— see also Elwes	
Helwish Elwes see Helwis	
Helyer of East Coker co. Somerset, Salisbury co. Wilts connected with Cozens	I 336
Heming of Jamaica; co. Warwick, co. Worcester, and of Chichester co. Sussex	II 253
Hemsworth of Monk Friston connected with Inglish & Hanson	VIII 506
Henderson M.I. St Nicholas Church Newcastle upon Tyne	VII 376
Hendley of Coorshorne in the psh of Cranbrook co. Kent and of Cuckfield co. Sussex	VI 70
Heneage connected with Hunlock	XX 138[a]

Hening of Tavistock co. Devon connected with Bidlake   XIII 54, 58
Henley connected with Hungerford   V 58
Henniker of Newton Hall and Stratford co. Essex, afterwards
    Major   XI 64–9
Henry I connected with Bedingfield   V 319
———————————— Stafford   XVI 50
——— II ————————   XVI 50
———————————— Bedingfield   V 319
——— III   XVI 9
———————— connected with Bedingfield   V 319
———————————————— Hookes   XVIII 104
———————————————— Stafford   XVI 50
——— IV   XVI 9
——— V   XVI 9
——— VI   XVI 9
——— VII   XIV 18
——————————   XVI 9
——— VIII   XVI 9
———————— of Broad Oak co. Flint and of London co. Middx.   IX 99
Henshaw connected with Whithall & Hill of Hawkstone   XVIII 119
Herbert connected with Hunt   V 75
——   XVIII 34
———————— Stanleigh or Stanley   XXI 12ᵃ
———————— Earl of Pembroke connected with Gam   XX 160
———————— of Colebrook co. Monmouth, Blackhall Montgomery,
    Aston Bromfield co. Salop, and of Doleog co. Montgomery   VI 14
———————— of Glamorgan connected with Dodington and Hoby   VII 65
———————— of Island of Nevis connected with Fenton   VIII 490
———————— of Kingsey co. Oxon connected with Hallet   X 164
———————— of Montgomery Castle Island and Cherburg co. Salop,
    Bemington near Salisbury co. Wilts and of Woodford   IV 409
Herdein connected with Ward   X 165
Hereford, Earl of, connected with Poulton   XVI 18
———————— Fitz Osborn Earl of   VIII 250
———————— of Sufton, Cannon Pym, Bullingham co. Hereford,
    Clifton co. Gloucester, and of Priors Court, Mayor of
    Dunkirk   VII 315
———————— Price Viscount   I 434
———————— Seymour, Earl of   XIV 17
———————— Yereford, connected with Cecil Earl of Exeter   XX 139
Hereward de Wake   VII 253
Herey of Crutchfield   III 500
Heritage of Edge Hill connected with Watts   XX 230, 232
Hern connected with Lowe of Goadby   III 204
Herne connected with Hall and Hodges   V 276
Heron connected with Mead and Wilmot   IX 126
———————— of Daresbury connected with Brook   I 249
———————— of Hamsterley co. Durham connected with Peat   VIII 167
Herring connected with Watlington   IX 101
Heselden of Great Grimsby co. Lincoln connected with Bennett   II 155
Heskaith see Hesketh   XXI 260–8

Heskaythe de see Hesketh
Hesketh afterwards Brockholes   V 3
———— Heskaith de Heskaythe lord of Heskaythe and Beconsawe, Rufford Holmes and Holmeswood, Martholme, Great Harwood and of Houghwick   XXI 260–8
———— of East Ratcliff Highway connected with Hamilton   XXI 275
———— of Hesketh, Rufford Aughton, Paulton Maines co. Palatine Lancaster, connected with Brockholes   V 2
Hester connected with Andrews   XIV 24
———————— Peachey   I 71
———— of London Islington co. Middlesex and of Cheshunt co. Herts   II 266
Hethe connected with de Grey   VI 255
Hetherington of Bletton and of Watton co. Cumberland   XXI 33
Heveningham or Haveningham of Haveningham co. Suffolk   XXI 223
Hewett connected with Hampson   XII 51
———————— Hayward   XIX 115
———— of Stretton   IX 71
Hewitt connected with Jekyll   I 291
———— of Headley Hall co. York St Neots co. Huntingdon and of Clare Hall   VII 4
———— of Pishiobury in the psh of Sabridgeworth co. Herts Viscount Hewitt of Gowran and Baron Jamestown in Ireland   VII 2
Heygate of London co. Middlesex, Husbands Bosworth co. Leicester, and of West Haddon co. Northampton   IV 225
Heynes of Southmead in the psh of Westbury   XIX 242
Heywood connected with Cannell   II 128
———— of Chesterfield connected with Milnes   XV 16, 17
———— of Crumpsall near Manchester co. Lancaster and of London co. Middlesex   III 458
———— of Heywood co. Palatine Lancaster Governor of the Isle of Man   XVI 92
———— of Westminster, Godmanchester, Paxton co. Huntingdon, Maristow in the psh of Tamerton Foliot co. Devon, and of Jamaica   I 52
Hibbett connected with Martin and Wight   V 333
Hickes of Bugshill and of Town Malling   IV 390
———— of Court House   VIII 437
———— of Cromhall and of Bristol co. Gloucester   XIX 239
———— of Tortworth the City of London, Campden, Beverston Castle, Widcombe, co. Gloucester, and of Wilde co. Hertford, Lord Hickes of Wilmington   XIX 240
———— of Tortworth, Pedington in the psh of Berkeley co. Gloucester, and of Pitt co. Monmouth   XX 143[a]
Hickman connected with Windsor   XIII 1
    XIII 5
Hide connected with Russell and Butler   VIII 436
Hieron of Kidderminster, Moor Close in the psh of Hampton co. Worcester, Sherborne co. Dorset, Bristol co. Gloucester,

and of Nailsworth in the psh of Avery   II 183
Higford als Huggefford Hugford of Edmondscot Henwod co.
    Warwick and of Dickleston co. Gloucester   XIX 210
———————— connected with Griffith   VIII 427
———————— of Dixton co. Monmouth   XX 160ᵃ
———————— of ———————— & of Alvington, lord of the Manor of
    Alderton   VIII 440
Higgons of English Bicknor co. Gloucester, connected with
    Burgum   XX 68ᵃ
———————————————————— of London Ratcliff co. Middlesex,
    Rochester co. Kent connected with Cobham   IV 354
Higgins connected with Powell   V 64
———————————————————— Baldwin & Kynaston   XVIII 119
Higman of Scarrington and of Mansfield co. Nottingham   XXI 201
Hignell connected with Turton   I 379
Hill als Hull see Hyll   XIX 195
Hill connected with Browne   I 64
———————————————— Jones Viscount Ranelagh   XV 10
———————————————— Sutton   IV 507
———————————————— Willet and Abrahams   III 59
———————— Marquess of Downshire   VIII 243
———————— M.I. Worcester Cathedral   XIV 9
———————— of Crackenthrop   XXI 103
———————— of Hawkstone and of Leightwick co. Salop   V 68
———————————————— co. Salop connected with Harnwood and
    Kynaston   XVIII 118
———————— of Olveston co. Gloucester, Bedminster and of Long
    Ashton co. Somerset   IV 307
———————— of Pevensey connected with Wheatley   VIII 244
———————— of Pounsford co. Somerset   XXI 160
———————— of Rotherhithe co. Surrey and of Exeter co. Devon
    connected with Hegarty   IV 14
———————— of Taunton co. Somerset connected with Symes   XIX 251
———————— Thomas, M.I. for Shrewsbury   XXI 212
Hillier of Cirencester co. Gloucester connected with Colley II 282
———————————————————————————————— Edwards   III 51
———————— of Maidford Farm in the psh of Norton co. Wilts, West
    Birt co. Gloucester, London co. Middlesex, and of Philpots
    in the psh of Hatfield Broad Oak in Essex   VIII 127
Hillman of Wolverhampton co. Stafford and of London co.
    Middlesex   XV 86
Hilton of Hilton   X 131
Hilyard of Taunton co. Somerset connected with Cabbell   XX 89ᵃ
Hinchcliffe of Waterside near Holmforth co. York, connected with
    Hadfield   II 270
Hinchinbrooke connected with Popham   XVIII 130
Hinchinbroke Edward Lord   III 233
Hinchliffe of London   I 228
Hind M.I.   XIV 9
Hinde connected with Sowles   IX 110

Hinde of Kendal co. Westmorland   III 523
———————— of Theobalds co. Hants, London co. Middlesex, and of
  Langham Hall co. Essex   III 336
Hindle connected with Glover   VI 218
Hinson of Fordham, Snailwell co. Cambridge, Finchingfield,
  Rowley Hall, and of Little Sandford co. Essex   II 179
———————— of Fordham co. Cambridge, and of Dublin, afterwards
  Powell   VI 29
Hinton of Hanbury co. Stafford, Baptisms etc.   VI 278
———————— of Hinton co. Salop connected with Dod   XXI 303–15
Hippesley of Stow in the Wold co. Gloucester, connected with
  Coxe or Cocks   II 421
———————— see Hippisley
Hippisley of Cameley and of Stone Easton co. Somerset connected
  with Cox   II 419
Hippon connected with Sunderland   VII 282
Hoare of Greens Norton co. Northampton and of London
  connected with Elton   XX 116
———————— of London co. Middlesex   IV 431
                                                                         XVIII 20

Hobart connected with Hampden Earl of Buckinghamshire   XV 19
Hobbs of Gosport co. Hants   XXI 193
Hobhouse of Westbury upon Trim co. Gloucester connected with
  Gwatkin   III 412
Hobling of St Budeaux and of Saltash Cornwall   I 216
Hoby connected with Dodington and Rice   VII 65
Hockley connected with Hamilton   XXI 275
Hockly of Marlborough co. Wilts, and of Wickwar co. Gloucester   XX 145^a
Hodenge lord of Burnham Bekonesfelde, co. Bucks connected
  with de Windsore and Scudamore   XVIII 57
Hodges formerly Parry   I 476
                                                                         VI 228
———————— from formerly Parry petition – change of name   VI 383
———————— M.I. in Bracon Ash Church co. Norfolk   VI 119
———————— of Cotherstock, Aston near Oundle co. Northants,
  London, Bethnal Green co. Middlesex, Bicester, Solderne
  co. Oxon, Saxham co. Suffolk, Homewood co. Surrey,
  Upton co. Essex, St Elizabeth Jamaica, and of the Kingdom   V 272, 277,
  of Spain   278, 281
———————— of Puddimore co. Somerset connected with English   XIX 255
———————— of Shipton Moigne co. Gloucester and of Shuston
  Magna co. Wilts   VI 228
———————————————————————————————— and of
  the Inner Temple co. Middlesex   I 476
———————— of Shipton Moyne co. Gloucester, Baptisms etc.   VI 289
———————————————————————— and of Shuston Magna co.
  Wilts   XIX 160
———————— of Shipton Moyne co. Gloucester, and of Shipton
  Dovell   XIII 102
———————— Thomas   VIII 378

Hodgett of London co. Middlesex, and of Shackerston co.
    Leicester   IV 502
Hodgetts Hogetts Hogets Hojetts or Hodyetts of Corbins Shutt
    End, Holbeach Hall in the psh of King Swinford, Ashe-
    wood Bridge in the psh of Kinver co. Stafford, Coleshill co.
    Warwick, and of London co. Middlesex   IV 494
——————— of Hamysworth   IV 493
——————— Hogetts Shutt End, Prestwood, Holbeach Hall in the
    psh of Swinford Regis co. Stafford   XXI 287
——————— Hogetts of Shutt End in the psh of Kings Swinford and
    of Prestwood co. Stafford   VI 179
——————— of West Bromwich co. Stafford   IV 503
Hodgkin of Tattenhall co. Chester London co. Middlesex and of
    Philadelphia connected with Arris and Blackburn   IV 358
Hodgkinson of Horwich co. Lancaster connected with Pilkington   IV 314
Hodgshon M.I. St Nicholas Church Newcastle upon Tyne   VII 378
——————— of Helborne co. Palatine Durham   V 13
Hodgskin of Goudhurst in Kent connected with Bathurst   XIII 31
Hodgskins connected with Dalyson   III 393
                                                                  XVIII 5
Hodgson of Lancaster   III 44
Hodington connected with Winter   II 196
Hodleston see Hudleston
Hodshon M.I.   VII 379
——————— of Newcastle co. Northumberland and of Poland   VII 248
——————— of Newcastle co. Northumberland, Hebburne co.
    Durham, and of Poland   IX 132
Hodsoll of St Mary Cray and of Dartford co. Kent   XVII 42
Hodson of the Town of Huntingdon Broughton co. Hunts, Fort St
    George East Indies, Wellingborough co. Northampton and
    of London co. Middlesex   III 478
Hodyetts see Hodgetts
Hogan of Clayns, Stone Hall co. Clare and of London   II 265
Hogben of Baughton under the Blean near Faversham co. Kent
    connected with Denne   II 22
Hogets see Hodgetts
Hogetts see Hodgetts
Hogg of Clifton in the psh of Ashborne co. Derby connected with
    Ellis and Cartwright   XV 82
——————— of Sion Walk Twickenham co. Middlesex connected
    with Jenkinson   XXI 171[a]
Hogge of Northampton connected with Saunders   XXI 208
Hoghton connected with Ashurst and Majendie   I 345
Hojetts see Hodgetts
Holbach of Lyons Court co. Somerset connected with Coxwell   XIX 116
Holbech connected with the Marquess of Winchester   XIII 95
Holbrook of the psh of Bromyard and of Bishops Frome Ledbury   XV 68
Holbrow of Kingscot, Bagpath, Uley, Stanley Leonard, Dursley
    co. Gloucester, Luggershall co. Wilts. Hampton and of
    London co. Middlesex   I 171

Holcroft of Holcroft co. Lancaster connected with Birch   X 88
Holder connected with Ware   II 240
———————— of Northwold co. Norfolk connected with Graves   XIX 30
Holford of Holford co. Chester and of Churchdown in the City of
    Gloucester   XIX 38
———————— of Holford and of Iscoid co. Denbigh   XXI 220
———————— of Lincolns Inn co. Middlesex, Avebury in Wilts, and
    of Weston Birt co. Gloucester   XX 147ª
———————— of Wotton Hall co. Warwick connected with Wright   IX 158
———————— Sir William   I 432
Holland Earl of Kent   VIII 249
——   XVI 39
———————————————————— and Duke of Surrey connected with
    Hookes   XVIII 105
———————— of Callice connected with Bellingham   XXI 87
———————— of Conway connected with Griffith and Hookes   XVIII 109
———————— of Warminghurst and of Arundel co. Sussex connected
    with Lear and Eades   I 59
Hollester of Bristol, Saltmarsh in the psh of Almondsbury, Little
    Sodbury, and of Nibley in the psh of Westerleigh co.
    Gloucester   I 523
Holliday Holyday Halyday see Halliday   XX 136–7
Hollings of London co. Middlesex, and of Shrewsbury co. Salop,
    connected with Merry   I 489
Hollister connected with Hollester   I 524
Holloway of Wells   XIII 96
Hollowell of Harleywood co. Lancaster connected with Ridgway   III 121
Holman of Downham connected with Smith of the City of Ely   VI 91
———————— of Wirksworth co. Derby connected with Eyre and
    Stafford   II 395
Holmer of co. Derby   XXI 159
Holmes connected with Wharton   VI 240
———————— of Birmingham co. Warwick, and of London co.
    Middlesex, connected with Laurie   IV 106ª–7
———————— of New Sarum co. Wilts, Yarmouth, Newport, Isle of
    Wight co. Hants, Killmarnock co. Limerick and of Mallon
    co. Cork   VI 238
———————— of Twyford co. Derby and of Wandsworth co. Surrey   II 366
———————— of Upholland and of Winstanley co. Palatine Lancaster
    afterwards Bankes   XV 14
———————— Sir Robert   X 50
Holt of the Manor of Chesham and of Stubley co. Lancaster
    connected with Entwistle   XI 27
Holtham connected with Harrison   VIII 375
Holton connected with Green   XXI 320
Holway of Holway co. Devon connected with de Brian and Cary   VIII 248
Holwell connected with Newte   I 319
Holyday Holliday Halyday see Halliday   XX 136–7
Holyland of London co. Middlesex connected with Elton   XX 116ª
Homden of London co. Middlesex connected with Taylor   XIX 167
Honning of Eye connected with Wingfield   IV 293

Honywood of Evington co. Kent   III 325
————————————— connected with Buller   XVIII 53
————————— of Horsham co. Sussex   I 268
Hoo and Hastings Lord, connected with Devenish   VIII 245
Hood connected with Taylor and Palmer   VIII 528
————— of Thorncomb co. Somerset, Portsmouth co. Hants.
    Viscount Bridport   III 122
Hook of Crokes in the psh of Pauntley and of Balsdon in the psh of
    Newent co. Gloucester   XIX 108
Hooke of Marshfield and of Bristol co. Gloucester   XIX 109
Hookes of Hookes co. Lancaster, Flint, Aberconway co. Carnarvon,
    Swapham in Norfolk, and of Yorkshire   XVIII 104–9
Hoole connected with Horton   VII 507
Hooper connected with Fuller and Clare   I 340
————————————————— Somerset   I 259
————————— of Boveridge co. Dorset, connected with Manners Earl   X 46, 47
    of Rutland
————————— of Caswell in the psh of Much Marcle, Kingston and of
    the Whitton co. Hereford connected with Whitcombe   XV 57
————————— of Gloucester connected with Webb   XX 240
————————— of St Budeaux co. Cornwall connected with Lawrence   I 217
Hooxe connected with Edwards of Wales   XVIII 15
Hope of Charing Havisham co. Kent, and of Naseley co. Lincoln   III 151
Hoper of Stayning, Lewes co. Sussex, and of London co.
    Middlesex   II 13
Hopkin or Popkin of the Forest   IX 91
Hopkins afterwards Probyn of London co. Middlesex   XX 151
————————— connected with Chamerlen   II 254
————————————————— Kiblewhite   I 532
————————————————— Skinner of Lyd co. Kent   II 23
————————————————— Williams   IX 38
————————— of Haverfordwest in Wales, & Bideford co. Devon
    connected with Smith   IV 452
————————— of London co. Middlesex   VIII 349
————————————————————————————   VIII 407
————————————————————————————   IX 112
————————— of Stifford co. Essex   XII 30
Hopkinson of Heath near Wakefield co. York connected with Legh   III 309
Hopton connected with Browning   XIX 33
————————— of Cockfield, Westwood co. Suffolk, and of London
    co. Middlesex   XVI 25
————————— of Huntley connected with Probyn   XIX 40
————————— of Stanton Lacey co. Salop, descended according to
    family tradition from Sir Walter de Hopton founder of
    Hopton Castle co. Salop, of Chalford in the psh of Bisley
    co. Gloucester and of the City of Worceter connected with
    Dallaway   VIII 26
Horlock of Blandford co. Dorset, Trowbridge co. Wilts, and of
    Ashwick co. Gloucester   XIX 156
Horn of Bristol connected with Ford   XI 39
Hornby connected with Winckley   XIII 94

Horne of Evesham connected with Heritage and Watts   XX 230–2
——————— of the Isle of Wight   I 211
————————————————————— connected with Arundell Harrison
and Bagster   III 352
——————— of the Isle of Wight connected with Bagster and
Harrison   IV 95
Horner connected with Fortescue   XX 146
Horniman of Abingdon co. Berks connected with Thompson   XIII 74
Horninge connected with Fastolfe and Le Groos   VII 502
Horseley of Thorley co. Hertford   IX 67
Horseman connected with Shorswell   I 197
Horton connected with Whittington   XIX 35
——————— of Bath co. Somerset   XIII 99
——————— of Catton, Smithersfield co. Warwick, Hadley and of
London co. Middlesex   II 177
——————— of Catton and Cowley, Coole in the County of
Chester, Dunstable co. Bedford, Chaville, Broughton,
Ilford, Westwood, Elston co. Wilts, Lullington, Wolverton
co. Somerset, Radder near Cardiff co. Glamorgan, Stanton
co. Worcester, Crayford co. Kent, and of London co.
Middlesex   V 30
——————— of London co. Middlesex   VII 507
Hosdeng connected with de Windsor   XIII 1
Hosier of Wickham Park co. Northampton connected with Sharp   VIII 418
Hoskins of Beaminster co. Dorset, and of Crookhorne co.
Somerset connected with Cookson   III 122
——————— of London co. Middlesex and of Wrexham co.
Denbigh   II 9
——————— of Pantee co. Monmouth   VIII 446
————————————————————— connected with Hill als Hull   XIX 195
——————— of Stow Clewerwell Longhope co. Gloucester, and of
Uxbridge co. Middlesex, connected with Rogers   II 311
——————— of Stowe Grange St Briavells and of Clowerwall in
Newland   XX 149
————————————————— of St Briavells Rector of Abenhall co.
Gloucester   X 122
——————— and of Platwell in Newland co. Gloucester   XX 237
Hoskyns of Harwood co. Hereford   XX 162
Hotham als de Threhouse lord of Kyrkenny in Ireland, of the
Castle and Manors of Wilton in Pickering Lithe, West
Haslerton, Marton and of Sewerbye co. Lincoln   XVIII 82–7
Hough connected with Whitmore and Cromwell of Leighton in
Worrel   XXI 242
——————— of Northen, Torkington, Stockport co. Chester,
Manchester co. Lancaster, Jamaica West Indies, and of
Chadomoss   III 270
Hougham or Huffam of London co. Middlesex, the Manor of
Langport als Barton and of Ash near Sandwich co. Kent   XI 43–5
Houghton M.I.   XIV 4
——————— of Houghton co. Lancs. connected with Stanley   XXI 291
——————— of Reddleton in the psh of Winwick   VIII 21

Houkeston connected with Egerton and Walker   VII 329
Houlton connected with Green   IX 142
Hovell of Hillington co. Norfolk connected with Folkes   V 232
——————— of Wyverston co. Suffolk; Bradlee; Iffeley co. Oxford, Soulgrave co. Northampton and of co. Wilts connected with Bohun   VIII 48
How connected with Coel   X 67
——————————— Degge   XXI 112
——————————— Pole   I 234
————————————————————   II 132
——————————— Walklate   XXI 112
————————————————————   XXI 305
————— see Howe   XIX 4, 5
Howard als Hayward   VIII 298
——————— connected with Nevinson   XXI 148ª
——————— Duke of Norfolk   XIV 24
————————————————————   XVI 64
——————————————— connected with Mortimer   XII 51
——————————————————— Stafford   XVI 50
——————————————————— Tyndale & Vere   X 124
————— Earl of Arundel connected with Daubigny   VIII 469
————————— Carlisle connected with Grahme   III 510
————————————————————— Viscount Preston   XVIII 54
————— Earl of Surrey and Duke of Norfolk connected with Orfeur and Palliser   VII 94
————— of Corby Castle co. Cumberland   IX 12
————————————————— and of Newark Castle   XIV 23
————— of Great Bookham co. Surrey   XIII 30
————— of Greystock co. Cumberland   XXI 227
————— of London co. Middlesex   I 102
————— Marlow co. Bucks, Chersey co. Surrey and of London co. Middlesex connected with Butler   III 87
————— of Naworth Castle co. Cumberland connected with Fairfax   XIV 21
————— of Overacres in the psh of Elsden co. Northumberland   VII 174
————— of Overacres co. Northumberland connected with Crosbie   IX 41
————— of Overacres in the psh of Elsden co. Northumberland   XXI 269
Howe of Mistley Thorne co. Essex and of Havant co. Hants, connected with Stephens   VII 152
————— Viscount Howe   XX 152
————— or How of Stanligh, Hunspel de la Heies co. Somerset, South Wokingdon in Essex, Compton co. Gloucester, Langar co. Nottingham, Hanslop co. Bucks, Viscount Howe, Baron of Clenawley in Ireland, and Baron Chedworth   XIX 4, 5
Howel King of South Wales connected with Edwards   XVIII 14
Howell ap David ap Griffith Vychan of St Albans co. Herts afterwards Powell   I 562
————— ap Howell of the ancient Abbey of Lanturnum co. Monmouth   VIII 10
————— formerly Jones of Llannon Brin y mane co. Carmarthen,

Llandebye, and of Pinknash Park co. Gloucester   IV 216
———————— of Brinkurch Gellch Cyny co. Cardigan connected
with Davies   III 396
———————— of Isle of Ely near Wisbech   I 499
———————— of Wales connected with Davies   XVIII 88
———————— see Powell   V 64
Howland of Streham in Surrey connected with Child   XIII 61
Howle of co. Montgomery connected with Russell   IV 344
Howorth formerly Davies   VI 172
Howse of Cheekendon co. Oxon connected with Woodward   XVII 30
Hoyle connected with Robinson   III 415
———————— of Cromhall connected with Yate   XX 194
Huband connected with Daston   XX 109ª
———————————————— Wright and Delves   IX 144
———————— of Ipsley co. Warwick   VI 32
                                                                                III 32
Hubbald Lord of the Manor of Stoke, of Tetenhall co. Stafford and
     of London co. Middlesex   XXI 274
Huddlesford connected with Stephens   VII 143
Huddleston Hodleston Hudleston Lord of Millum, Hoton John co.
     Cumberland, Pinchbeck co. Lincoln, Salston co. Cambridge,
     Farrington co. Lancs, and of Boynton co. Yorks   XXI 38–43
———————— Hudleston connected with Wells and Bigland   XVI 45
———————— M.I. at Millum   XIII 89
———————— of Millum co. Cumberland Farrington co. Lancs. and
     of Hoton John   XXI 176–7
———————— of Millum Castle co. Cumberland, Sawston co. Cam-
     bridge Elford co. Stafford and of co. Lancs.   XXI 23–5
———————— of Millum Castle and of Warleston connected with
     Askew   XVI 82
Huddlestone of Millum Castle co. Cumberland connected with
     Neville and Eyre   II 390
———————— of Millum Castle co. Cumberland connected with
     Wells and Bigland   VIII 325
———————— of Sawstone co. Cambridge and of London co. Middx   XXI 283

     lord of the Manors of Sawston, Danford, Payrets and Deal,
     all in co. Cambridge   III 340
Hudleston a Brief of the Family and their ancestors taken from the
     Records at York before the Conquest   V 324
———————— de, lord of Millum, of Hooten John co. Cumberland,
     Sawston co. Cambridge Farringdon co. Lancs and of
     Boynton co. York   I 106
———————— lord of Anys in Millum, of Millum Castle, Hutton
     John co. Cumberland, Boynton co. York, Farington co.
     Lancaster, London co. Middlesex, Kelston near Bath co.
     Somerset, Down Place near Windsor co. Berks, Tame
     Park co. Oxon, Elford co. Stafford, Newendon co. Kent,
     Tirley co. Gloucester, Lord of the manors of the
     Danford, Sawstone, Wilbraham, Payrets, and of Deall co.
     Cambridge   V 344

Hudleston see Huddleston

Hudlestone Lord of Millum of Hutton John co. Cumberland
    Sawstone co. Cambridge, Farringdon Hall co. Lancs.
    Bamton co. York, Bath Wells and of Kelston co. Somerset   V 372

Hudson M.I.   XIV 8

———————— of Gloversham and Gildersome co. York   III 488

———————— of Glovershaw ————————   II 274

———————— of London co. Middlesex connected with Deschamps   XXI 179

Huffam see Hougham   XI 43–5

Hugford Higford Huggefford   XIX 210

Huggefford see Higford   XIX 210

Huggett of Dover   IX 65

———————— of Eton College connected with Randloph   X 109–12

———————— of Tiddenham co. Gloucester connected with Webley   XX 237

Hughes connected with Bridges   XX 56

———————————— Callis   XXI 284

———————————— Collingwood   X 155

———————————— Sayer   IV 214

———————— of Carnarven and Uxbridge connected with Williams
    and Brickenden   I 176

———————— of Ealing from Wiltshire near the Devizes see Hughes
    of Warminster   II 306

———————— of Haverfordwest co. Pembroke, Radway co.
    Warwick, and of Loughborough co. Gloucester   VIII 433

———————— of Penryn connected with Coytmer   V 162

———————— of Portsmouth   XXI 205

———————— of Queinton co. Gloucester, Stretton upon Foss co.
    Warwick, connected with Rutter   XIX 68

———————— of Ringleden in the psh of Wye co. Kent connected
    with Champneys   V 158

———————— of Southampton, Baronet   XXI 127[a]

———————— of Trostrey co. Monmouth   I 25

———————————————————— and of Cheltenham co.
    Gloucester   XIX 196

———————— of Vineg co. Carmarthen or co. Cardigan, and of
    Longborough co. Gloucester   III 405

———————— of Warminster and Devizes co. Wilts connected with
    Hodsoll see Hughes of Ealing   XVII 42

Hulbert of London co. Middlesex, Chatham, Rochester, co. Kent,
    and of Bristol   VI 247

Hull als Hill als Hyll of Inst in the psh of Olveston, Cam, and of
    Alveston co. Gloucester   XIX 195

———————— connected with Mallet   VII 76

Hulme to Davenport – change of name – petition   VI 384

Hume of Hackshaw and Creighton in Scotland   I 225

———————— of London co. Middlesex and of Bilton Grange co.
    Warwick connected with Boughton   VIII 413

———————— of Wormleybury co. Herts connected with Frederick   IX 69

———————— Sir Abraham, Bart.   XXI 244

Humfreston M.I. St Aulkmonds Church Shrewsbury co. Salop   VI 113

Humphreys connected with Trimmer   I 160

Humphries of Highwath co. Wilts connected with Bridges   XX 56
Humphry of Place y Bellen co. Flint   II 81
Humphrys of London co. Middlesex   VII 494
Huncks of Aspeley Pleyn co. Bucks, Northwick co. Worcester and
      of Redbroke co. Gloucester   XIX 149
Hungate of York, Chelmsford co. Essex and of Jamaica   II 264
Hungerford connected with Escourt   XIII 108
————————————————— Pollen   V 155
————————————————— Topper   V 66
——————————————————————————————————————   I 537
————————————————— Winter   XIII 122
M.I. Yattesbury near Calne co. Wilts, Salisbury Cathedral, and of
      Bremhill co. Wilts   VI 131–4
——————— of Cadenham and of Studley co. Wilts   I 44
——————— of Castle Hungerford, Heytesbury, Cadenham, South
      Marstin, Standen, Corston, Calne co. Wilts, Cadenham
      House and Buscot co. Berks, Winrush, Down Ampney co.
      Gloucester, Black Burton, Farley Castle co. Oxon. Compton
      Dands co. Somerset, Canon Leigh in the psh of Burlescombe
      co. Devon, and of London co. Middlesex   V 48
——————— of Castle Hungerford, Calne Heytesbury, Cadenham,
      Studley, Lea Blacklands, Trowbridge, Corsham, Standen
      co. Wilts, Cowley Winrush, Down Ampney, Bristol co.
      Gloucester, Exeter co. Devon, Wellow, Farley Castle,
      Compton Danes co. Somerset, Black Burton, Henley on
      Thames co. Oxon, Nutfield co. Surrey, Buscot, Reading,
      Burfield co. Berks, Middle Temple and Chelsea co.
      Middlesex, Market Harborough co. Leicester, Dingley Hall
      co. Northampton, of Maloes in France   V 236
——————— of Chisenbury near Bedwin and of Fifield connected
      with Thorpe   XXI 214
——————— of Kelloe Melloe co. Somerset   V 62
——————— of Lea or Legh in the psh of Ashton Reynes, Hankerton
      co. Wilts, Lincoln's Inn co. Middlesex, Bath co. Somerset,
      and of Horseley co. Gloucester   V 60
Hunloke of Wingerworth co. Derby and of Pensylvania   I 253
————————————————— connected with Tyrwhitt   XIII 7
Hunsdon, Lord, see Cary   III 475
Hunt connected with Beale and Palmer   IV 477
——————— Owen   V 74
——————— Roberts   VII 86
——————— of Basingstoke and of Harefield co. Middlesex   II 2
——————— of Camberwell co. Surrey Hildslveston co. Norfolk
      and of London co. Middlesex   IV 36
——————— of Charlton Kings co. Gloucester, connected with
      Stephens   VII 145
——————— of Reepham co. Norfolk   IV 35
——————— of Shrewsbury, Boreaton, Betton co. Salop,
      Gouldstone co. Stafford, Harrow on the Hill co. Middlesex,
      and of Mollington co. Chester   XVIII 35

Hunt of Shrewsbury, Betton, Boreaton co. Salop, Walles-
borough, and of Mollington co. Chester   V 72
———————— of Shrewsbury, Boreaton co. Salop, Oundle Stoke
Doyle co. Northampton, London co. Middlesex, and of
Lisle in Flanders   VII 88
Hunter als Perry born in the County of York, came into Glo-
ucestershire and assumed the name of Perry of Wootten
under Edge, Henbury, Winterbourn co. Gloucester,
London co. Middlesex, and of Kingswood in Wilts.   XIX 13
    XX 150
Hunter als Perry of Wotton under Edge co. Gloucester connected
with Fenn   XIV 23
———————— of Wall Town in Northumberland   XXI 143
Huntercombe connected with Hosdeng   XIII 1
———————— of Wansted co. Essex, Burnham, and Bekenesfelde co.
Bucks, connected with Scudamore   XVIII 57
Huntingdon, Earls of,   VIII 251
———————— of Lancashire, Derby, Mortlake co. Surrey, and of
London co. Middlesex   III 152
Huntington connected with Tyrell   VI 407
Huntley of the Ree Standish, Boxwell, Frocester co. Gloucester   XIX 237
Hurford of Washfield, Tiverton co. Devon, and of London co.
Middlesex, connected with Stone   III 76
Hurlestone of Picton co. Chester connected with Pindar   V 65
———————————————————— and Kynaston   XVIII 121
Hurst of Upton connected with Ayerigg   XX 37[a]
Husband of Little Harksley co. Essex, connected with Glanville
and Blair   VII 181
Hussey connected with Blount   XIX 60
Hussy connected with Cusack   XIC 13
Hutchenson of Boston co. Lincoln, connected with Mottram   VII 336
Hutchinson connected with Tyrell   IX 89
———————————— Wrottesley   IV 345
———————— of Owthrop co. Nottingham connected with Poulton   XVI 18
———————— of Owthrop co. Nottingham connected with de la
Zouche   I 447
———————— of Wood Hall co. Herts   XX 162
Hutton Kin of the Founder of New College connected with Coles   X 31,
and Sacheveral – notes as to pedigree –   32, 38
———————— of Cockerton, Newsam, Woodham, and of Eldon co.
Durham, connected with Jenison   II 47
———————— of London co. Middlesex, descended from Scotland,
connected with Featherstone & Thomason   VIII 515
———————— of Penrith co. Cumberland and of Goldesbrough co.
York   X 148
———————— of Thorpinsty M.I.   XIV 6, 9
Huxley connected with Benson Tatem etc.   XV 9
———————————————— Dent   VII 481
———————— of Eaton Park   I 279
———————— of Poole Hall co. Chester   XXI 188

Huxley of Wyer Hall Edmonton connected with Becher   VIII 338
Huxtable of Ratcliff Highway   III 129
Hyde connected with Levinz   VII 409
——————— of Ashmount co. Wexford   V 178
——————— of Rushia Hall in the psh of Hondley co. Chester
    connected with Williams and Giffard   VII 119
Hyet connected with Cadull   X 69
———————————————— and Arthur   XIX 158
Hyett of the City of Gloucester and of Painswick co. Gloucester   XX 140–ª1
          XX 158

——————— of Lidney, New Place, Rodley in the Forest of Dean,
    Westbury on Severn, and of Newent co. Gloucester   XIX 177
Hyll als Hill see Hull   XIX 195
Hynde connected with Mansergh   XXI 47

I

Ibbotson of St Anthonys Newcastle upon Tyne   VIII 421
Idnevth ap Edred   XIV 20
Ilderton of Ilderton and of Newcastle upon Tyne   I 104
———————————————————————— co. Northum-
    berland, and of the City of Durham   III 190
Iles of Tetbury connected with Estcourt   XIX 231
Iliff of Exeter co. Devon connected with Cozens   I 335
Ilive formerly Ayliffe   IX 42
Impey of Saffron Waldon co. Essex connected with Atkinson   IV 203
Ince M.I. Chester, St Peters Church   XIV 9
Inckley of East Indies and West Indies   IV 303
Ingelo connected with Archer and Evans   VIII 522
Inglethorpe M.I. Worcester Cathedral   XIV 9
Inglish connected with Hemsworth   VIII 506
——————— or Hanson Inglish, formerly Hanson of London and
    Hampstead co. Middlesex   VIII 507
Ingloysse of Pylham connected with le Groos   VII 502
Ingoldesby of Dinton and Waldridge co. Bucks, connected with
    Limbrey and Poulett   VIII 12
Ingram connected with Halliday   XX 138
——————————— Hanson   III 65
————————————————————————   IV 267
————————————————————————   VIII 538
——————————— Smith   VIII 538
——————————— Noel   XXI 215
——————— of Barrowby and Hutton co. York connected with
    Mallory and Cary   VIII 259

Ingram of Glynhafren co. Montgomery — III 100
————— of Glynhafren co. Montgomery connected with Lloyd and Lewis — I 437
————— of Wakefield — V 18
Innes see Innys
Innys Rector of the University of St Andrews in Scotland removed to Feathard in co. Tipperary in Ireland — X 48
Inwood of Send, West Horsley, Napphill co. Surrey, and of Houndslow co. Middlesex — III 213
Ireland of Northampton, Forthampton co. Gloucester, connected with Pansum — III 69
Ireton connected with Cromwell — XV 19, 22
————————— Lloyd — IV 125
Irton of Irton co. Cumberland — XXI 13, 27
Irwyn of London co. Middlesex connected with Chamberlayne — XX 80[b,c]
Isaacson of Fenton Newcastle co. Northumberland — I 308
—————————————————————— XVI 69
———————————————————— connected with Creigh — XXI 147–7[a]
Isham of Pichley Lamport co. Northampton connected with Poulton — XVI 18
Isles of Hill Martin and afterwards of East Leaze co. Wilts, connected with Dore — VII 463
Ivor Lord of Iscoed connected with Lewelyn last Prince of Wales and with Hookes — XVIII 105
Ivy of Exeter connected with Michell — IV 37
Izod notes as to family of — XX 250
————— of Todington and of Staunton co. Gloucester — XIX 120

J

Jackson als Jasson of Green Street near Enfield co. Middlesex connected with Wollaston — III 380
————— connected with Franks — I 515
————— of Berwick upon Tweed and London co. Middx — IX 149
————— of Christchurch and Overton co. Hants — X 53
————————— co. Hants connected with Lowth — X 62
————— of Cotham co. Durham, Cowes Isle of Wight, London co. Middlesex and of Mogadore Morocco — II 267
————— of Cotham in the psh of Preston co. Durham and of Wood Plumpton co. Lancs — XVII 20
————— of Crayford co. Kent and of London co. Middx — III 144
————— of Forest Hill co. Oxon connected with Ford — XI 39
————— of Hackney, Mile End co. Middlesex, Carlisle co.

Cumberland, Long Melford co. Suffolk and of the Isle of
Man   IX 63
———————— of Newcastle upon Tyne, Hickleton co. York, and of
London co. Middlesex   VI 24
———————— of Saperton in the psh of Broughton co. Derby, and of
London co. Middlesex, Vicar of Twyford co. Hants   VIII 57
———————— of Yorkshire and of Mile End Stepney   IX 152
Jacob of Norton, Hallavington co. Wilts, connected with Packer
and Stephens   VII 135
Jacobs connected with Cooke   XX 87[a]
James II   II 146
James IV   XIV 18
————— V   XIV 18
————— VI   XIV 17
                                                                                           XVI 9
———————— afterwards Keck connected with Wyles   III 461
———————— connected with Gibbons   IV 25
———————————— Jarrett   VII 194
———————————————— Walton and Jarman   XVIII 92
———————— of Abberley co. Worcester   IV 403
———————— of Bristol connected with Brayne   XV 79
———————— of Denford co. Berks   XXI 304
———————— of Eastington co. Gloucester and of Frogmil connected
with Pruen   XX 185[a]
———————— of Kent, Baronet   XXI 225
———————— of Lanthowell in Carmarthenshire, Vicars of Longney
Elmore and of Aston Blank co. Gloucester   XX 157[a]
———————— of Lidney connected with Warren   XX 11
———————— of Reigate and of Isham co. Kent connected with
Halford   I 231
———————— of Reigate and Ightham co. Kent connected with
Halford   III 74
———————— of Soylwell co. Gloucester   XX 158
———————— of Wales and of Eltham co. Kent   II 407
———————— of Wallingford connected with de la Pole Handlo and
Rede   I 121
———————— of Wollaston, Bristol, Soylwell in the psh of Lidney co.
Gloucester, and of Lugwardine co. Hereford   XIX 39
———————— of Wollaston, Tidenham co. Gloucester, and of Lin-
colns Inn co. Middlesex   XX 160–[a]
———————— of Wollaston co Gloucester   XX 154
Jane of Huelsfield Bristol co. Gloucester and of Chepstow co.
Monmouth   XX 17
Janes connected with St John   X 55
———————— of Catlidge in Cambridgeshire connected with North   XXI 319
Jans connected with Rolle and Wrey   VI 388
Janson connected with Soulegre   VI 249
Jansson connected with Clifford   XI 40
Jarman connected with Walton   V 47
                                                                                           XVIII 92
Jarratt of Bury Barton in the psh of Bury Pomeroy connected with

Hegarty and Newell   IV 14
Jarrett of Westmorland, of Orange Valley in the psh of Trelawney
   in the Island of Jamaica, Freemantle near Southampton co.
   Hants   VII 193
Jarvis connected with Stonehouse   XX 82ᵃ
——————— of Wicken co. Cambridge connected with Hinson   II 178
Jason of Hinton co. Gloucester connected with Partington   XX 156
Jasson als Jackson   III 380
Jauncey of Munslow co. Hereford connected with Elton   XX 116
Jaye of Farnham co. Surrey, Rothercombe co. Southampton, and
   of Whiteley Park co. Gloucester   XIX 100
Jeddere afterwards Jeddere Fisher connected with Stallwood   X 165
Jefferies of Ham Castle co. Worcester connected with Walshe   XVIII 12
Jefferson of Witney co. Oxon and of London co. Middx   VI 139
Jefferyes of Redborough co. Gloucester   XIX 105
Jeffries of Bristol connected with Cann   I 10
——   XX 96ᵃ

Jeffryes of Acton co. Denbigh, Bulstrode co. Bucks, and of Alicant
   in Spain   V 151
——————— of Bayly cum dwyr in Lhewell Kevenrhollan
   Bedwelthey co Monmouth and of London co. Middx   V 148
Jekyll of Halsted and Clavering co. Essex   I 291
Jenison of Elswick co. Northumberland and of Wolsingham co.
   Durham   X 147
——————— of Newcastle upon Tyne and of Quebec   II 46
——————— of Yokeflete, Bennet Land, Quenaki co. York, Winter-
   ton co. Lincoln, Walworth, Carlebury and Woodham co.
   Palatine Durham, Irchester co. Northampton, and of
   Newcastle upon Tyne co. Northumberland   XII 28–47
——————— Jennison
——————— M.I. Sᵗ Nicholas Church Newcastle upon Tyne   VII 377
Jenken connected with Mathew   IV 435
——   XVIII 80

——————— or Jenkin of Holme co. Norfolk, Sutton co. Lincoln,
   Ufford co. Northampton, and of London co. Middlesex   III 481
Jenkin descended from the Jenkins of the North of Folkestone   III 482
——————— see Jenken
Jenkins connected with Frewen   VII 310
——————— Mason   X 102
——————— of Gladlys in the psh of Llangynwyd co. Glamorgan   XVIII 17
—— connected with
   Vaughan and Phaer   III 398
——————— of Strabane in the Kingdom of Ireland, connected with
   Heywood   II 128
Jenkinson connected with Raikes   I 163
——————— of Cubley co. Denby connected with Saunders and
   Hogg   XXI 171ᵃ
Jenkyns connected with Tucker and Monro   V 179
Jenner connected with Tyrell   VI 401
——   VII 19
——————— of Shrivenham co. Wilts connected with Dore   VII 469

Jenner of Slymbridge, Berkeley co. Gloucester connected
    with Davies   XX 102[b]
Jennings connected with Warren   XX 252[a]
——————— of Acton co. Middlesex connected with Davies   VI 172
——————— of Shiplake co. Oxon, Puddle Trenthide co Dorset
    connected with Constantine   VII 313
Jennison M.I. St Nicholas Church Newcastle upon Tyne   VII 377
——————— of Elswick co. Northumberland M.I. St Nicholas
    Church Newcastle upon Tyne   VII 376
——————— see Jenison
Jennyns of Hayes co. Middlesex   III 110
Jepson of co. Palatine Lancaster and of Bristol   I 96
——————— of Gloucester connected with Wilkins   XX 245
Jerningham of Cossey co. Norfolk, connected with Stafford and
    Plowden   IV 474
——————— of Cossey co Norfolk connected with Plowden   XVIII 3
——————— of Somerleighton co. Suffolk, and of Cossey Hall co.
    Norfolk, connected with Scrope   XX 5, 18
Jervice M.I. in Salisbury Cathedral   VI 131
Jervis connected with Pooley and Butler   VI 204
——————— of Chatkill Darlaston co. Stafford, and of Ollerton co.
    Salop   I 415
——————— of Darlaston co. Stafford connected with Bendish   I 116
Jervoise connected with Byerley   VII 170
——————— of Britford co. Wilts and of Heryard co. Hants
    afterwards Purefoy   I 175
——————— of co. Salop, Frefolk, Heriot co. Southampton, and of
    Britford co. Wilts   IX 112[b]
——————— of Herriard co. Hants connected with Clarke   VIII 45
                                       XI 73
Jervys connected with Tudor   X 66
Jesson of Langley Sutton Coldfield co. Warwick, connected with
    Ash and Ashby   IV 457
Jocelin connected with Dacre   III 177
——————— Knight of the Bath   II 125
Jodrel Jodrell see Joudrell   XVIII 136
Jodrell of Lincolns Inn co. Middlesex connected with Vanderplank   III 109
——————— Jodrel see Joudrell
John afterwards Jones, came to Brin ȳ mane in co.
    Carmarthenshire, of Llhuynon   IV 216
——————— King of England   XVI 9
——————————— connected with Bedingfield   V 319
——————————————— Stafford   XVI 50
——————— of Gaunt Duke of Lancaster   XVI 9
                                       XXI 229
Johns formerly Beldam   VIII 422
——————— of Great Dunmow and of Littlebury co. Essex   VIII 422
——————— of Helstone in Cornwall   XXI 181
Johnson afterwards Ketelby, of Bitterley and Steple Hall co. Salop,
    also of the Middle Temple co. Middx   I 40
——————— connected with Bowles and Lisle   I 141

——————————————— Clarke and Walsh   I 5

——————— M.I. St Nicholas Church, Newcastle upon Tyne   VII 379–80

——————— of Cheshire, Kerford and of Petworth co. Sussex   I 179

——————— of Chippenham connected with Rogers   I 100

——————————————————— Tipping   III 470

——————— of Fordwick co. Kent   IX 43

——————— of Layton Buzard co. Bedford and of Widford co. Gloucester   XIX 184

——————— of Middleton in Teasdale co. Durham connected with Thornborough   XXI 90

————————— of Pebworth co. Gloucester   IX 37

——————— of Retford co. Nottingham, and of Oxford connected with Wilkins   II 340

——————— of Stock co. Essex connected with Richardson   XXI 163[a]

——————— of Westlecut in the psh of Wroughton co. Wilts connected with Dore   VII 463

————————— see Johnston

Johnston connected with Elliott   IX 153

——————— Gawen, of Elsi Shields in Scotland, commonly called Gawen of the Wood, of Triplo and Red Hall near Dumfries, Kellonbanke, Laird of Castle Milke in Scotland, of Pontefract co. Yorks, Ealing co Middlesex, connected with Dunn-Gardner   VIII 287

——————— Johnson of Embledon, Cockermouth co. Cumberland, and of London co. Middlesex   III 112

——————— of Dumfries and Annadale also of the Colony of Virginia   XVI 38

Johnstoun als Souter – as to change of name   VII 23

Jol or Joll   XVI 30–1

Joll or Jol   XVI 30–1

Jolley connected with Hill of Hawkstone co. Salop   XVIII 118

——————— of the Bothoms in the psh of Chedleton co. Stafford Coston Hall co. Worcester connected with Lowe   XX 161

————————— see Jolliff

Jolliff als Jolley of Leek co. Stafford, Buglawton co. Chester, Ewell co. Surrey, Heytesbury co. Wilts, and of London co Middlesex, connected with Tufnell   XI 3–11

——————— formerly Tufnell and Milner   XI 3

Jones afterwards Howell   IV 216

——————— Archdeacon of Lismore, Bishop of Cloyne and of St Asaph connected with Parker   VIII 225

——————— connected with Bradford   VIII 372

————————————— Brockholes   V 4

——————————— Dawkins   II 114

——————————— Einley   V 341

————————— Gough   XIX 187

————————— Owen of Llunillo   VII 367

————————— Pitman   I 320

————————— Roberts   XIII 104

————————— Seccombe see Jones of Swansea   II 114

————————— Warren   XX 252[a]

——————————— Wood   X 61
——————————— York   X 73
Jones Earl of Ranelagh in Ireland connected with Willoughby
    of Parham   XIII 7
——————— formerly Griffith of Glan Gwendrath als Colebrooke   IV 216
——————————————— John   IV 216
——————————————————— Thomas and Gwynne   XV 26
——————— of Avebury co. Wilts and of East Wickham co. Kent
    connected with Pelham   IV 7
——————— of Chepstow co. Monmouth and of Hanham co.
    Gloucester   XIX 155
——————— of Dingeston co. Monmouth   III 334
——————— of Dursley co. Gloucester connected with Purnell   XX 183
——————— of Gloucester   XVI 22
——————— of Guven y marl in Carefallurch in the psh of Northop
    and St Asaph co. Flint   III 527
——————— of Hendre a true and authentic Pedigree   VII 253
——————— of Llanvarne co. Hereford connected with Powell   IV 44
——————— of Llhuynon in Wales, Colebroke, and of Brin ȳ mane
    in Llannon co. Carmarthen   IV 216
——————— of Ludlow co. Salop connected with Davies   XVI 57
——————— of Middleton co. Lancs connected with Essington   XX 118ᵃ
——————— of Oldbury co. Gloucester connected with Hill als Hull XIX 195
——————— of South Cerney, Painswick and of Cirencester co.
    Gloucester   XX 155ᵃ
——————— of Swansea co. Glamorgan connected with Seccombe   VIII 16
——   VIII 294
——————— of the Temple co. Middlesex connected with Linley
    and Dymond   III 160
——————— of Tetbury co. Gloucester connected with Wills   I 284
——————— of Thornbury co. Gloucester   XX 160ᵃ
——————— of Todds in the psh of St John in the Island of
    Barbadoes   V 163
——————— of Treverne, Prestaign co. Radnor, and of Antigua,
    from Carmarthen, connected with Jones and Chinn   I 112
——————— of Treverne co. Radnor, and of Kington co. Hereford,
    connected with Harford and Brydges   II 418
——————— of Tyglyn co. Cardigan   XV 26–32
——————— of Waley connected with Crowther   X 60
——————— Viscount Ranelagh of the Kingdom of Ireland
    connected with Gulston   XV 10
Jopson connected with Witham of Ledstone   X 148
Jordaine of Leicestershire from Huntingdonshire   III 524
Jordan connected with Cusack   XIV 13
——————————————————— Hollister   I 526
——————— of the psh of Crawley or Highfield co. Sussex and of
    Chelsea co. Middlesex   II 262
Jorden of Dunsley co. Stafford connected with Wightwick   V 78
——   XVIII 36
——————— of Wolverton near Dorchester connected with Mohun   VIII 179
Joudrel see Joudrell   III 362

Joudrell Jodrel or Jodrell of the High Peak co. Derby Wheston co.
    Leicester, Yardsley near Macclesfield in Cheshire, Moor
    House, and Lane End   XVIII 136
————————— of Wilkinhill Bugsworth, Coumbs Whithill Milntown
    Hayfield co. Derby, Yeardsley near Macclesfield Hundred,
    the Manor of Hawkhurst in Wales, and of Jerdese Wayle   III 362
Jouret of London co. Middlesex and of Holland connected with
    Laurie   IV 107
Joyce of Newland connected with Gryndon and Aburhall   XIII 100
Joyes of Denyhoule co. Mayo connected with Lynch   I 146
Judde of London co. Middlesex connected with Chichele   XIX 56
Juliet left France at the Revocation of the Edict of Nantz came to
    Barnstaple and settled at Bideford co. Devon   IV 455
Jull of Ash near Sandwich, Woodnesborough als Winsborough co.
    Kent, and of Goldstone in Ash   I 32
Jullion a French Refugee of London and Brentford co. Middlesex,
    and of Portsmouth co. Hants   II 307
Jurin of Trinity College Cambridge well known in the learned
    world   XXI 1
Juxon extracts from Registers   XX 241
————————— of London co. Middlesex, Chichester co. Sussex, Little
    Compton co. Gloucester, and of Albourne co. Wilts,
    Archbishop of Canterbury   XIX 38

K

Kaye Keay of Woodsom, Thorpe, Milshawe, Okenshaw and of
    Heath near Wakefield   XVI 56
Kay of Woodsom co. York connected with Marow   VII 27
————————————————————————   VII 370
————————————————————————   XXI 109
Keane of the Island of St Vincent connected with Payne   X 100
Keate of Hoo, London co. Middlesex, Bath co. Somerset,
    Hungerford, Studley, Calne co. Wilts, connected with
    Hungerford   I 43
————————— of Wells co. Somerset – whose family came out of
    Dorsetshire   III 275
Keating connected with Chadwick   VIII 443
————————— of Ireland, Stratford upon Avon co. Warwick, Bengal,
    Madras, East Indies and of London co. Middlesex   III 162
Keay see Kaye   XVI 56
Keble of Portland co. Dorset   IV 258
Keck formerly James   III 461
————————— M.I. at Shirborne Church co. Gloucester   VI 114

Keck of Long Marston co. Gloucester and of Great Tew in
    the County of Oxon   XIX 173
———————— Sir Antony   XVII 15
Keeling of Somershill in the psh of King Swinford co. Stafford,
    connected with Hogetts   IV 496
Keeting M.I. in Bracon Ash Church co. Norfolk   VI 119
Keilway of Weck in the psh of Wootten Rivers   VII 445
Keith of Pensylvania connected with Senior and Digges   II 477
Kekewich of Knatchfrench, Pollmarken, Trehawke, co. Cornwall,
    Rumford in Essex and of Hackney co. Middlesex   XVIII 25
Kellet of Hackney connected with Hudlestone   V 349
———————— of Weltonhow M.I.   XIV 5
Kelley of Kelley co. Devon see also Kelly   II 6
Kelly of Kelly, Holdsworthy, and of Burrington co. Devon, see
    also Kelley   I 23
Kemble M.I.   XVI 88
———————— of the psh of St Winniards, Kimpton co. Hereford,
    Lidbrook in the Forest of Dean co. Gloucester, and of
    London co. Middlesex   VII 183
Kemeis of Monmouth and of Keven Madley co. Glamorgan   XIII 116
Kemp connected with Read   IX 118
———————————————— Stonestreet   VIII 535
———————————————— Viscount Monticute   XXI 146
———————— of Dorrington and Lewes co. Sussex, also of Pangdean
    in the psh of Pyecombe   XXI 276
Kempe of Ollantigh co. Kent   I 209
———————————————— Gennes New Forest co. Southampton, and
    of Chenston co. Hereford   XIX 56
———————— of Ollantye connected with Shirley   IV 102
Kendall connected with Taylor and Crayle   I 157
Kene connected with Chichele and Tyndale   X 124
Kennet connected with Bigland   XIII 12
———————— Vicar or Minister of Postling co. Kent   XVI 13
Kennett als Kinnick of Battersea, Putney, and of London co.
    Middlesex   IV 296
Kensington of London co. Middlesex   I 305
Kent Holland Earl of,   VIII 249
——   XVI 39
———————————————— connected with Hookes   XVIII 105
Kenyon of Casan co. Denbigh connected with Lloyd   I 438
Ker connected with Collingwood see also Kerr   X 155
———————— of King and Queen County in Virginia connected with
    Tucker   IV 222
———————— of Russia descended from Ker or Car Duke of Rox-
    burgh Marquess of Lothian   XVIII 30
Kerby of Gloucester connected with Brewster   V 115
Kerle of co. Hereford connected with Waller   XVIII 99
Kerne als Tresillian – notes as to wills.   IX 166
Kerr connected with Collingwood – see also Ker   X 45
———————— of Llanden co. Selkirk, Edinburgh and of Calcutta East
    Indies   III 8

——————— of the psh of St James in Jamaica   VII 194
Kerswell of Penwarden co. Cornwall   XXI 318
Ketelbey formerly Johnson   I 40
——————— Kettilby of Henley, Steple, Ludlow, Bitterley co Salop
   and of New Inn co. Middlesex   I 40
Ketelby of Great Wratton, Stonham co. Suffolk, Southwark co.
   Surrey, Willingale Doe co. Essex, Luton co. Bedford, and
   of London co. Middlesex   I 331
Kettilby see Ketelbey   I 40
Kettleby of Heen Savage co. Salop and of Bewdley co. Worcester VIII 439
Kevelix Earl of Chester   VIII 251
Key of Stafford or Salopshire and of Hampstead co. Middlesex   VIII 217
Keys of Upledon co. Gloucester connected with Compton   XIX 145
Keysall of Orleton, Richards Castle co. Hereford, Heston near
   Osterley, and of London co. Middlesex   I 34
Keyt of the psh of Ebrington co. Gloucester Lord of the Manor of
   Bishampton co. Worcester, and of Wolford Magna co.
   Warwick   XIX 57
Kibblewhite of Fawley   IX 8
Kiblewhite of Fawley co. Berks   I 532
——————————————— connected with Packer and Gibbes   VII 426
Kidd connected with Dixon   X 141
——————— of Welhope and Wolsingham co. Durham   XXI 195
Kidney of Market Harborough, Little Stretton Hall and Gumley
   co. Leicester, Knutsford Hall co. Northampton, and of
   London co. Middlesex   I 352
Kildare Fitzgerald Earl of,   XIII 1, 3
Kilham of Shadwell and of Plaistow co. Essex   II 75
Kill connected with Jepson   I 96
Killegrew Killigrew of Arwenack near Falmouth co. Cornwall   VI 17
Killigrew Lord of Killigrew, of Arwenick co. Cornwall, & of
   London co. Middlesex   VI 142
——————— see Killegrew
Killinghall of Middleton St George in the County of Durham   VII 274
Kilner connected with Bigland   VIII 327
Kilvington of Barrowby in the psh of Leake, Thirsk,
   Boroughbridge, Wakefield, and of Ripon co York   VII 347
Kinardsleygh see Kinardsley   XXI 308
Kinardsley of Coleaton Brockton co. Derby, Loxton & of Lee   XXI 308
King connected with Clarke   VIII 460
——————— Isaacson   I 308
———————————————————————————————   XVI 69
———————————————————————————————   XXI 147
——————— M.I. at Shurborne Church co. Gloucester   VI 114
——————— of Abingdon co. Berks, Highworth co. Wilts, Bristol
   co. Gloucester, and of Whitchurch co. Bucks   III 273
——————— of Alkerton co. Oxon connected with Shurmer   XX 102ᶜ
——————— of Billeek co. Mayo in the Province of Connaught Earl
   of Kingston, Viscount Kingsborough   XXI 273
——————— of the Borough of Southwark connected with Potts
   and Hardcastle   III 125

King of Haverhill co. Suffolk connected with Greatorex   III 28
——————— of Sampford Peverell near Tiverton co. Devon and of
   Bristol co. Gloucester   V 38
——————— of Sandhurst in Kent, Ninfield, Lewes, Wartling,
   Willingdon co. Sussex, and of Lambeth co. Surrey   XVII 12
——————— took in addition the name of Simpson   XVII 12
Kingscote connected with William the Conqueror and King of
   Denmark   XVI 29
——————— of Kingscote co. Gloucester connected with Barnesley XIX 23
                                                                    XXI 204
Kingsmill formerly Brice   VII 125
Kingston connected with Bourchier and Douglas   XIX 186
—————————————— Goodenough   IX 39
——————— of Rotheley co. Leicester, Flaxley Abbey co.
   Gloucester, Clopton, and of Russhe co. Berks, K.G.   XX 2, 5
                                                                    XX 8, 9, 13
                                                                    XX 14–16, 18
——————— of Tortworth and of Flaxley Abbey   XX 219[a]
Kingston-upon-Hull, Pierrepont Earl of,   XVIII 124–9
Kingstone – note as to Pedigree.   IX 82
Kinnardsly of London co. Middlesex connected with Baker   XX 206
Kinnick als Kennett   IV 296
Kinsale connected with Roberts   XXI 316
——————— De Courcy Lord   II 148
——————— Lord connected with Sadleir   I 348
Kinsey connected with Saunders   I 226
                                                                    XXI 171[a]
Kipp connected with de la Barre   I 20
Kirby of Cromer co. Norfolk and of London co. Norfolk   VI 166
Kirkby connected with Luddington   XIII 97
——————— of Kirkby connected with Comber   XV 24
Kirke connected with de la Barre   I 20
Kirkham connected with Carew   XIII 5
Kirklie M.I. St Nicholas Church Newcastle upon Tyne   VII 380
Kirrell of Hadlo in the County of Kent   III 392
——————————————— connected with Dalyson   XVIII 5
                                                                    XXI 295
Kirsop or Kirsope of Hexham co. Northumberland   IX 61
Kirsope see Kirsop
Kirwan afterwards Lyster   III 425
——————— of Scilan co. Galway of Castlehacket Nantz   I 91
Kitchen of Ewell in Swirey   XIII 69
Kitchin of Bonsall co. Derby   V 212
Klockenbrinck of London co. Middlesex   XXI 194
Knackston of Suffolk connected with Hill and Flight   IV 306
Knapp connected with Hartop   XV 25
——————— of Swinbrook co. Oxon, Little Linford, Shenley co.
   Bucks, and of London co. Middlesex   I 409
Knatchbull of the Law, Wickford co. Wilts, Highgate co.
   Middlesex, and of Babbington House co. Somerset   XIII 66

Knee of Wootton-under-Edge co. Gloucester connected with
   Watts   XX 230

    XX 232

Knevet connected with Tyrell   VIII 103
————— of Mendesham, Buckenham co. Norfolk, and of
   Charleton co. Wilts   XIX 259

Knight of Barrells co. Warwick connected with Rawlins   XIII 101
————— of Langold co. York connected with Thompson &
   Gully   XXI 156ᶜ
————— of Somerset House   IX 41
————— of the Isle of Wight connected with Priaulx   IV 483

    XVIII 144

Knightley als Whitwick of Offchurch co. Warwick see Knightly   XXI 109
Knightley als Whitworth of Oschurchbury co. Warwick connected
   with Marow   VII 370
————— of London co. Middlesex connected with Dent   VII 482
Knightly als Whitwick of Oschurchbury co. Warwick connected
   with Marow   VII 27
Knipe of Cirencester   I 391
————— of Coln Deans co. Gloucester, Baptisms etc.   VI 277
————— of Preston co. Lancaster Baptisms etc.   VI 273
————— of Warton co. Lancaster, London co. Middlesex,
   Epsom Imber Court co. Surrey, Fairbank, and of Kirby
   Kendall co. Westmorland   IV 115–20
————— of Wood Broughton M.I.   XIV 7, 8
Knollis Earl of Banbury   III 236
————— see Knollys
Knollys connected with Fleming   X 47

    XXI 218

————— Knollis als Knowles of Rotherfield Greys co. Oxon
   Stanford, Reading co. Berks Earl of Banbury, Viscount
   Wallingford   XXI 309–11
————— of Fearnhill in the psh of Wingfield, Lower Winche-
   don, Reading co. Berks, London co. Middlesex, and of
   Mortlake co. Surrey   XVII 30
————— of Reading co. Berks, and of Thame co. Oxon,
   connected with Hinde and Thayer   III 337
————— of Rotherfield Greys co Oxon, Stanford, Reading co.
   Berks, Lord Knollys of Grays, Earl of Banbury   II 247
Knott of Margate Minster, Isle of Thanet, Ashford co. Kent, and of
   London co. Middlesex   III 218
————— of Rydal co. Westmorland connected with Fleming   X 151
Knowles see Knollys   XXI 309–11
————— supposed to descend from the family in Vincents
   Norfolk, of Aylsham, Reepham and of Holt co. Norfolk   VIII 155
Knyfton came from Derbyshire and settled at Uphill near Wells co.
   Somerset   III 195ᵇ
Koostray of Oudega in Friesland, Groningan, and of London co.
   Middlesex   IV 316
Kynaston connected with Powell   V 64

Kynaston of Shrewsbury, Lord of the Manors of Hordley and of Hardwick co. Salop   XVIII 115–9

Kynnersley connected with Trye   XIII 97

Kyrshaw or de Kyrkeshagh of Town Houses near Rochdale connected with Chadwyk   XI 26

L

Lacey of Winchester co. Hants   II 149

Lacy connected with Appleby   X 140

———————————— Fifield als Lowe   XX 161

La Faussille connected with Barron   XIII 112

Lake of Chippenham co. Wilts connected with Tipping   III 470

———————— of Wisbech in the Island of Ely connected with Eaton   VII 39

Lakon connected with Stanley and Banvile   XXI 289

Lamb of Brocket Hall co. Herts Lord Melbourne, of London co. Middlesex, see also Lambe of Fairford   V 70

Lambe of Coulston co. Wilts Clifton co. Gloucester and of London co. Middlesex   XIX 119

———————— of Fairford co. Gloucester, and of Brocket Hall co. Herts, connected with Benson and Holmes – see also Lamb.   IV 106ª–7

Lamberd of Greenwich in Kent connected with Dalyson   XVIII 4

Lambert Earl of Cavan   XVII 7

———————— of Ferry Bridge co. York connected with Taylor   III 223

———————— of Twiford co. Southampton connected with Andrews and Walshe   XVIII 12

Lambton connected with Chitton   XV 47

———————— of Lambton and of Biddick co. Durham   I 367

Lamego of Jamaica connected with Lousada   XXI 287

Lamplew connected with Porter   XXI 34

Lamplough of Lamplough and Shellesmore co. Cumberland see also Lamplugh of Lamplugh   XXI 27

Lamplow connected with Burder   II 214

Lamplugh formerly Brougham   V 302

———————— of Lamplugh co. Cumberland, Archbishop of York, see also Lamplough of Lamplough   V 305

———————— of York and of Lebberson Vicar of Dewsbury   IX 3

Lancaster connected with Fanning and Willox   IX 66

———————— Earl of, connected with Bedingfield   V 319

———————— Henry Plantagenet Earl of, connected with Bedingfield   V 319

———————— John of Gaunt, Duke of   XVI 9

   XXI 229

Lane connected with Brown   XIII 119

———————— Lodge   VII 475

Lane formerly Fox of East Horsley co. Surrey, Lord Bingley XVII 59
——————— formerly Fox connected with Benson XXI 116
——————— of Haresfield co. Gloucester connected with Seale and
Pansum III 67
——————— of the City of Gloucester and of Apperley co. Glosc. XIX 53, 174
Lang of Clapton co. Middlesex connected with London III 107
Langdale of Haughton, Cliffe, Easthorpe & Lowthorpe co. York X 105
——————— of Haughton co. York connected with Repinder
Pierson and Howard I 396
—————————————————————————————————————— IX 12
——————— of Sunderland connected with Hutton II 48
Langdon connected with Gwinnett I 422
——————— went to America about 1650 of New York New Hants
and Portsmouth III 326
Langley M.I. at Morley co. Derby VI 106
——————— of Christ Church co. Monmouth, and of Mangotsfield
co. Gloucester XIX 212
——————— of Woodhall co. Essex connected with Marshall VIII 247
Langston of Sedgeborrow co. Worcester XX 109[a]
Langton Baron of Newton and Lord of Walton co. Lancs XXI 31
——————— connected with Gonning or Gunning IV 51
—————————————————————————————————————— XVIII 102
—————————————————————————————————————— XX 131
——————— connected with Winter XIII 122
——————— of Langton, Cumberworth co. Lincoln, Bristol co.
Gloucester, Brislington co. Somerset, and of London co.
Middlesex XX 95[b]
Lankester of Stockbridge and of Kendal co. Westmorland XXI 95
Lant of Exeter co. Devon, Thorpe Underwood co. Northampton,
London co. Middlesex, and of the City of Oxford, Windsor
Herald XIX 157
Larkin of Bristol co. Gloucester connected with Walter VIII 418
Larpent of London co. Middlesex connected with Porter I 301
Lasceles connected with Windsor XIII 1
Lascelles of Lisburn co. Antrim Killough co. Devon and of London
co. Middlesex I 33
——————— of Northallerton and Stank in the psh of Sigstone in
connection with Mitford I 309
——————— of Richmond, Northallerton, and of Hanwood for-
merly Gawthorpe, co. Ebor I 310
La Serre fled from France at the Revocation of the Edict of Nantes
and settled in the Island of Guernsey VIII 401
Lateward of London co. Middlesex I 392
Latham of Bexley in Kent connected with St George VII 407
——————— of Eltham co. Kent connected to Ashby IV 457
——————— of Harlington co. Palatine Chester XXI 168[a]
——————— of Sandon and Southweld Hall co. Essex, connected
with Staunton XIX 174
Lathom connected with Steel and Barnesley XIX 23
——————— Lord of Lathum Founder of the Abbey of Lathum in
the County Palatine of Lancaster connected with Worsley XXI 296

Lathom of Denbigh and of Lewney Green connected with Hookes
    and Mathew   XVIII 109
Lathum see Lathom
Latimer, Nevil Lord connected with Danvers   VI 208
Laton M.I. in Kirkby Ravensworth Church   VI 122
———————— of Berford connected with Pudsey   II 431
Latton M.I.   X 65
Latus connected with Huddleston   XXI 23
Launcelin connected with Dormer   XVI 95
Laurence of St Budeaux co. Devon and of Loo co. Cornwall   I 216
Laurens a French Refugee of South Carolina and of Charles Town   III 158
Laurent of the Island of Granada   X 9
Laurie of Dumfries in the Kingdom of Scotland, Cheshunt co.
    Herts, and of London co. Middlesex, connected with Jouret
    and Holmes   IV 106–6ª
Lavers of Crookhaven in Ireland and of Bristol co. Gloucester
    connected with Gravett   XXI 236
Lavington connected with Jackson   VIII 60
———————— of Bideford co. Devon connected with Shepherd   VII 191
Law connected with Burton   V 22
La Warre or Warre   I 465
Lawford of Stoke Gifford co. Gloucester and of the County of
    Warwick   XIX 194
Lawley of Canwell Spoonhill, and of Ealing co. Middlesex con-
    nected with Lolley   VII 197
———————— of Wenlock co. Salop, Luton Mortimer co. Bedford,
    and of Canwell Hall Spoonhall   V 117
Lawrence als Wardeboys the last lord Abbot of Ramsey   XVII 47
———————— connected with Barrow   X 74
———————— connected with Keble   IV 259
———————— of Manchester co. Lancaster connected with Atkinson   IV 205,
———————— of New York connected with Willett   VII 489
———————— of Ramsey St Ives co. Hunts. Sᵗ Margarets co. Herts,
    Wavertree co. Lancs, Brokedish, Emneth co. Norfolk,
    Selscombe in Sussex, and of Jamaica in the West Indies   XVII 47
———————— of St Ives co. Hunts, St Margarets co. Herts,
    Ironshore, Fairfield and of Belfield in Jamaica   VIII 111
———————— of Shardington House   X 12, 13
Lawry connected with Bennet and Rashleigh   XIII 23
———————————————————— and Morden   XVII 44
Laws of Jamaica connected with Long   I 202
Lawson of Burwell, Usworth co. Durham, Cramlington, Allen-
    dale, Heaton, and of Rock co. Northumberᵈ   XXI 285
———————— of Chirton and of Cramlington co. Northumberland   X 131
———————— Sir Wilfred, Bart.   V 323
Lawton connected with Chandos and Pole   VIII 50
Layard Lord see Fienes   VIII 241
Laybourne connected with Preston of Leavens Hall co.
    Westmorland   XXI 53
———————— of Cunswick co. Westmorland   XXI 53
Layer of Norwich connected with Rugge   III 163

Laying connected with Creyghton and Franckland   XIII 115

Layton of Delmayne   XXI 30

Lazenby of the City of York, Burlington co. York, and of London
    co. Middlesex   III 474

La Zouche Lord of Ashby Zouche see Zouch   VIII 249

Leach connected with Dillingham and Gooding   IX 101

Leadley of Aisenby near Thirsk co. York connected with Wilson   III 12

Leake connected with Thorold   X 76

————— of Bath   XIII 92

————— of Newark Eperston co. Nottingham Great Snoring
    and of East Deereham co. Norfolk   XXI 261

Lean of Graystone connected with Browne   XI 42

—————————————————   XV 13

Leaper of Osmaston near Derby   I 36

Lear of Arundel Chichester Angmaren Park Batter Park co. Sussex,
    connected with Eades   I 59

Leathart of Haltwisle co. Northumberland and of London co.
    Middlesex   VI 261

Leatherbarrow of Wigan M.I.   XIV 9

Leatherland see Lytherland   I 353

Le Blond Le Blund see Blount

Le Blund Le Blond see Blount

Le Breton of Jersey   I 188

Lechmere of Hanley Castle   II 365

le Clere connected with de la Barre   I 20

————— extract from baptism register   XVI 5

Le Despencer, Baroness   IX 6

————— Dashwood Lord   XXI 288

Ledwell connected with Bridges   XX 56

Lee als Leigh   V 284

————— connected with Curtis and Hockly   XX 145[a]

————————————— Harrington   XXI 32

————————————— Parker   II 289

————————————— Powell and Kynaston   XVIII 119

————— of Billesley co. Warwick connected with Elwes   III 248

————— of Deer Park co. Waterford   XIV 26

Lee of Great Delce near Rochester co. Kent connected with Watson
    and Dormer   XXI 324

of Quarendon co. Bucks, Baron of Spilsbury co. Oxon, Viscount
    Quarendon, and Earl of Litchfield connected with Pope   XIX 21

————— of Selby, Knaresborough co. York, Acomb, S[t] John
    Lee co. Northumberland   XXI 198

Leech M.I.   XIV 9

Leeds, Duke of, Baron Conyers by descent   VIII 469

————— Osborne Duke of, connected with Danvers   VI 208

Leeke connected with Murfen   VII 403

————— of Newark co. Nottingham, Baron of Deincourt, Earl
    of Scarsdale, of Sandiacre co. Nottingham Governor of the
    Forts of Tilbury and Gravesend   VIII 142

————— of St Johns in the Isle of Wight connected with Bargus   I 186

Lees of Plat – petition as to taking the names of Carill and Worsley   IX 14

Leese of Milton, Canterbury co. Kent and of London co. Middlesex — VIII 447

le Espek of Wernworth Whitelacking and of Bath — II 163

Le Geyt of Jersey connected with Fiott — III 180

Legh of Adington or Adlington and of Battlefield co. Salop — III 357

————— of Alpram, Northwood, High Legh, and of Easthall co. Chester — X 115

————— of East Hall in High Legh in psh of Rosthorne co. Chester — III 309

————— Leigh of Legh, High Legh Alphrem co. Chester West Hall Northwood and of Barton — II 168

————— see also Leigh

Le Grand of Frankfort on the Rhine connected with Southwell — XVI 58 / XX 48ª

le Groos als Harman — VII 505

————— of Sloley & Crostwick co. Norfolk — VII 502

Leicester, Bellomont Earl of — VIII 250

————— Earl of, connected with Lewelyn last Prince of Wales and with Hookes — XVIII 105

————— formerly Byrne — VI 157

————— see de Leycester

————— Sidney Earl of — III 185 / X 52

Leigh afterwards Hare of London co. Middlesex, Iver co. Bucks, and of Stow Bardolph co. Norfolk — I 408

————— als Lee of Asfordby Walton in the Would co. Leicester, London co. Middlesex, and of Plaistow in the psh of Canford co. Sussex — V 284

————— connected with Fitch and Fleming — XXI 218

————————— Hooper — X 47

————— lord of Crofton connected with Fitton and Hesketh — XXI 263

————— of Adlestrop co. Gloucester, Lanchurch co. Worcester connected with Wight — V 330

————— of Adlestrop co. Gloucester, Rectors of Harden co. Oxon, Llanwarne co. Hereford, and of Little Ilford co. Essex — XX 162

————— of Bank in the co. Palatine of Lancaster connected with Leycester — VI 156

————— of Inner Temple co. Middlesex, and of Over Darwin co. Palatine Lancaster – change of name to Trafford – — VI 383

————— of Leigh co. Devon and of Wells co. Somerset — XIII 71

————— of London co. Middlesex and of Lymm co. Chester — III 385

————— of Oughtrington; Jamaica; & Liverpool co. Lancs. — II 223

————— of Ride in the psh of Sutton, Macclesfield, and of London co. Middlesex — VIII 405

————— of Tamyn co. Chester Combe Wotton Bradley and of Pucklechurch co. Gloucester — XIX 235

————— of Thorley Yarmouth — VI 184

————————— connected with Troughear — VI 241

————— of West Hall co. Chester connected with Joddrell and Doughty — XX 163

Leigh of Whitechurch co. Salop descended from Leigh of
    High Leigh co. Chester and of London co. Middlesex   III 486
———————— see Legh
Leighton connected with Smyth   XX 48
——————— of Watlesborough co. Salop connected with Dodge   XX 101
————————————————————————————————— Maude   XVII 57
Leightonhouse of Oxford House in the psh of Ugley als Oakley   IX 66
Leith Lieut. Gov. of Prince of Wales' Island   VII 437
Lemoine of Plymouth co. Devon, of the Royal Artillery   XVII 37
Le Neve connected with Fox   I 168
Leneve of Great Whichingham co. Norfolk connected with
    Gawdy   VI 80
Le Neve ————————————————————————————   VI 257
    and with de Grey
————————— of Tivetshall, Norwich, North Tuddenham, Ringland,
    Great Whitchingham als Wichingham, Dereham co.
    Norfolk, London co. Middlesex, Messina in Sicily, Rouge
    Croix Pursuivant of Arms, Norroy Kings of Arms   VII 109
le Newcomen of Saltfletby Soleby, Nether Taynton, Skrelesbye,
    Gaudbie, Hagnaby, Bag-Enderby, Witherne co. Lincoln,
    Haydon co. Essex, Stratford co. Herts, and of London co.
    Middlesex   VIII 231
Lennox Duke of   VIII 469
le Norris of Normington co. Wilts   VIII 177
Lenox Stuart Duke of   XIV 24
————————— Mat. Stewart Earl of   XVI 9
————————— M.I. at Lougherew co. Meath   VI 115
————————— Stuart Duke connected with Clifton & Howard Earl of
    Arundel   XIV 24
Lenthall of Hinton St George co. Somerset, and of Langford in
    Fiford   III 373
Leofric Earl of Chester connected with Jones of Hendre   VII 253
le Palmer see Palmer   XIX 74
Le Roche of Thurleigh co. Bedford connected with Wells   IX 137
Lescaleet of Shoreditch and Stepney co. Middlesex, also of
    Walthamstow co. Essex   II 238
————————— of Shoreditch co. Middlesex and of Low Leyton co.
    Essex, Baptisms etc.   VI 282
Leslie formerly Anstruther of Great Driffield   VII 130
le Speke, Speke see Le Espek   II 163
Lesse connected with Andrewes   IX 35
Lester of London co. Middlesex Poole co. Dorset and of
    Rotherhithe co. Surrey   VIII 219
Lethicullier of London co. Middlesex connected with Burrow   I 568
Lettsom of City of London, Sambrook Court, and of Camberwell
    co. Surrey   VIII 11
Leventhorpe of Shingle Hall co. Herts connected with Bedall   V 455
Levett a German by birth or Dutchman – changing of name from
    Levy –   XVII 22
Le Vieux of Dorsetshire, came from France, connected with Slade
    and Haine   IV 74

Levinz connected with Hyde   VII 409
————— of Levins Hall, Crooke in the psh of Kendal co.
Westmorland Evenley co. Northampton and of Oxford   XXI 80
Levy of Southwark co. Surrey connected with Akerman   IX 135
————— to Levett   XVII 22
le Warren Earl Warren and Surrey Founder of the Priory of
Copledon   XVIII 94
Lewelyn ap Grufeth last Prince of Wales connected with Hookes   XVIII 105
Lewen of Wimborne, Poole co. Dorset, London co. Middlesex,
and of Ewell co. Surrey, connected with Glyn   I 401
Lewer of New Castle connected with Middleton   II 440
Lewes of Rowdell co. Dorset, Tortington co. Sussex and of co.
Stafford   IV 103
————— of Tredwed, Newport co. Pembroke, Whippingham
co. Hants, and of London co. Middlesex   I 403
Leweston of Leweston co. Dorset   XX 159
Lewis connected with Aubrey   I 122
————————— Bell   IV 402
————————— Dashwood and Phillips   II 79
————————— Greswold   IV 470
——————————————————————————————————————   XVIII 139
————————— Grevile   XX 135ᵃ
————————— Hopkin or Popkin   IX 91
————————— Lewthwaite   XVII 1
————————— Powell   I 361
————————— Rhys   IV 346
————— VIII connected with Stafford   XVI 50
————— IX —————   XVI 50
————— of Cardiff co. Glamorgan connected with Grimsteed   III 444
————— of Carmarthen connected with Read   IX 76
————— of Glasgow Exeter and of Kingston in the Island of
Jamaica   XVII 52
————— of Hengel co. Carmarthen, Llanirnhangel co. Mon-
mouth, and of London co. Middlesex   II 297
————— of Higga co. Monmouth connected with Morgan   XX 167ᵃ
————— of Jamaica connected with Gregory   I 194
————— of Mancester co. Warwick and of Stanford co.
Nottingham   IX 92
————— of Monmouth, London co. Middlesex, Dodman Hall
co. Worcester, Corby in the psh of Witherell co.
Cumberland, Moss Hills in the psh of Stratford, and of
Leominster co. Hereford   IV 113
————— of New Brentford co. Middlesex, and of Jamaica,
connected with Hughes   II 306
————— of Radnorshire, Montgomeryshire, co. Salop, and of
Plymouth co. Devon   XXI 321
————— of Terracoed co. Carmarthen connected with Gwyn   II 447
————— of Tynroes Rhydalt co. Denbigh, connected with
Lloyd   I 437
————— of Wolverhampton co. Stafford, connected with
Wrottesley   IV 344

Lewthwaite of Breadgate in the psh of Millum co. Cumberland XVII 1
Ley of Mayfield and of Ilam co. Stafford III 447
——————— of Yeos and of Lanes Exeter connected with Colby III 20
Leyburne of Cunswick co. Westmorland XXI 75
Leycester Leicester formerly Byrne VI 157
——————— of Toft and of Stoke co. Salop XVII 9
Lezburne of Cunswick M.I. XIV 29[b]
le Zouch or le Zusche see Zouch
le Zusche see Zouch
Lhwyd of Lhanvorda III 335
Liddel afterwards Bright connected with Ravensworth XVI 21
——————— Baron Ravensworth of Ravensworth Castle co.
Durham XVI 21
——————— of Red Heugh Durham connected with Tucker VII 332
Liddell baptisms – extract from the Register XVII 30
——————— of Newton Hall near Durham connected with Bowes X 131
Ligney Earl of, connected with St Paul XIII 32–35
Limbrey of Upton and of Tangers Park co. Hants VIII 12
Limbrick of Charvill Ashwick and of Westerley XVII 6
Lincoln, Lord Clinton, Earl of IX 114
Lindley of Kegby co. Nottingham connected with Wilkinson VIII 481
Lindores, Lord, connected with Anstruther VII 130
Lindsey connected with Long I 202
Linley of Brierley in the psh of Felkirk co. York connected with
Dymond III 160
Linskill connected with Ward and Errington I 94
Linwood of Cogenho-c co. Northampton connected with Whalley IX 104
Lippincott of Bristol connected with Jeffries and Cann XX 96[a]
Lisle descended from the Lisles of Wodeton in the Isle of Wight XIX 204[b]
——————— M.I. St Nicholas Church Newcastle upon Tyne VII 377
——————— of Evenley co. Northampton connected with Bowles XXI 188
——————— of Gosford co. Northumberland, Lord of Woodborne,
of Felton Barnston, Brackley and Evenley co. Northampton I 139
Lister afterwards Neville of Sysonby co. Leicester, and of Holbeck
co. York I 18
——————— connected with Bellomont VIII 250
——————— Bolton and Pudsey II 430
——————— of Horton near Gisburne co. York, Hornsey and
Brentford co. Middlesex I 282
——————— of London co. Middlesex I 306
——————— of Roughton, Westbury co. Salop and of London co.
Middlesex IV 100
——————— of Westby, Arnolds Bigg, Pathnole Green, Horton
Green, Newholme in the psh of Gisburne Kighly co. York,
London, Hornsey, and Brentford co. Middlesex III 466
Little of Elmston & Hardwick connected with Pearce VIII 429
——————— of Halsted co. Essex connected with Bridge II 376
Littlebury connected with Vernon XIV 2
Littledale of Whitehaven co. Cumberland connected with Walters XXI 45
Littlefield of Kingston near Portsmouth connected with Roche VIII 229[b]
Littlehales of Winchester connected with Parry and Hodges I 475

Littleton, Lord, of Litchfield co. Stafford, and of Coventry co. Warwick — I 246

Livingston connected with Hamilton of Silverton Hall — III 262

——————— Earl of Newborough — XVI 32

Llewellyn ap Jerwith Prince of Wales connected with Hookes — XVIII 105

——————— connected with Briscoe — IV 27

Lloyd afterwards Salusbury connected with Thelwall — XIII 41

————————————— Topp of Pontesbury co. Salop — V 67

——————— connected with Bridgeman — XV 10

————————————— Mears — XXI 159[a]

————————————— Morse — IV 125

————————————— Owen of Llanillo — VII 367

——————— descended of the Lloyds of the Forest co. Carmarthen — I 66

——————— Loyd lived in or near Wrexham Denbighshire — III 230

——————— of Bristol connected with Gibbes — VII 422

————————————— co. Gloucester connected with Bond and Gibbes — XIX 189

——————— of Cheam co. Surrey and of London co. Middlesex — I 66

——————— of Duffryn in the psh of Bettus co. Salop — III 19

——————— of Finant in Montgomeryshire, Cheam, Parsons Green, and of Islington co. Middlesex — IX 154

——————— of Garth co. Montgomery descended from the family at Leyton — VI 86

——————— of Holy Rood Ampney co. Gloucester, Spersholt co. Berks, and of London co. Middlesex — XIX 235

——————— of Holy Rood Ampney, Wheatonhurst, and of Marshfield co. Gloucester — XIX 236

——————— of Jamaica, Bylaugh, Oulton, and of Swaffham co. Norfolk — III 194[b]

——————— of Laton Hall and of Gregory co. Berks — IV 322

——————— of Lhoydiartch in Anglesea and of Dublin — II 315

——————— of Llanstiffa connected with Phaer — III 400

——————— of Llanstyffa — XVIII 16

——————— of Plas Madock, and of Penllan co. Denbigh connected with Kenyon and Ingram — I 438

——————— of Shrewsbury and of London co. Middlesex, connected with Spriggs — IV 190

——————— Sir Griffith — XIV 19

Loader of Deptford co. Kent — XXI 205

Lock of Nowton and of Milden Hall co. Suffolk connected with Ray — XXI 306

Lockey of Aldbury Hatch co. Essex, Tetbury Eastington co. Gloucester and of London co. Middlesex — II 294

Lockman connected with Peachey — I 70

Lockwood of Killinghall and Leeds co. York connected with Wilson and Lodge — VII 474

Locky connected with Beard — II 181

Loder of Lechlade co. Gloucester — XX 41

Lodge of Leidsin Kirk Heaton co. York London co. Middlesex and of Darking co. Surrey – the celebrated engraver — VII 474

Logan connected with Hartwell — III 465

Loggan of Little Few, Idbury co. Oxon, and of Millend co. Bucks IX 113[c]

Loggin of Beoley co. Worcester connected with Cole XX 82[a]

Loggins of Newent co. Gloucester XX 107[a]

Lokier of Horsley co. Gloucester connected with Deverell XX 113[a]

Lolley of Hull in Yorkshire and of Liverpool co. Palatine Lancaster, connected with Lolley and Mather VII 196

Lomax of Pilsworth, Manchester co. Lancaster, London and Hackney co. Middlesex I 24

Lomb of Norwich, Great Yarmouth co. Norfolk connected with Walford IV 311

London of Brentford co. Middlesex, Clapham co. Surrey Lee co. Kent, and of Queenhithe III 107

Long connected with Child XIII 61

———————————————— William of Wickham VIII 240

———————————————— M.I. at Spanish Town Jamaica VI 113

———————————————— of Bodington and of Stoke Orchard in Bishop Cleeve IX 49

———————— of Draycot-Cerne Wrexhal co. Wilts London co. Middlesex VI 68

———————— of East Tredudwell connected with Tate VII 266

———————— of Grittleton near Chippenham co. Wilts connected with Phipps II 219

———————— of Longville in Jamaica and of London co. Middlesex connected with Pocock VII 71

———————— of Melksham co. Wilts VI 288

———————— of Nether Haven co. Wilts, Saxmundham co. Suffolk London co. Middlesex Carshalton co. Surrey Tredudwell co. Cornwall and of Chichester co. Sussex I 201

———————— of Tredredwel co. Cornwall and of Jamaica connected with Tate III 201

———————— of Whaddon, Bart VI 65

———————— see Longe

Longden connected with Wallbanke XX 257[a]

Longdon of Doctors' Commons co. Middlesex connected with Crawley XX 93[a]

Longe Long of Clerkenwell co. Middlesex, Edlington, East Kirby co. Lincoln, and of Carshalton co. Surrey, connected with Short IV 397

——— ——— of Berkhampstead, Aldenham co. Hertford, London and Clerkenwell co. Middlesex, Holme Hall co. Derby, Edlington East Kirby co. Lincoln, and of Carshalton co. Surrey IX 74

Longford of Haresfield co. Gloucester connected with Trye XIX 134

Longspee Earl of Salisbury VIII 252

Lord of Ticehurst and Ore, Wilmington, Alfriston, Northiam, Pitt, Fairlight co. Sussex, and of London IV 232

Lott of Wrax Hall co. Somerset connected with Hollester I 524

Lotterell connected with Beaumont XIII 1

Lottrell connected with Morgan VIII 181

Lousada of Jamaica West Indies and of London co. Middlesex IV 178

———————————————————————————————————— XXI 287

Louther de Louther see Lowther

Lovanio see de Lovanio   XIII 1

Love of Baing Farm in the psh of Frockfield co. Hants connected
    with Tate and Wynne   IV 145

Loveday of Atherston, Wolvey co. Warwick, and of London co.
    Middlesex   X 56

Lovel Coke, Lord, connected   XVI 58

———————— of Boveney near Windsor connected with Huntercombe   XIII 1

Lovelace Baron Lovelace of Hurley connected with Wentworth   XIX 21

Lovell connected with Stafford and Fitzalan Earl of Arundel   VIII 248

———————— connected with Tanfield   VIII 256

———————— notes from survey of Dorsetshire   XIII 79

———————— of Bristol co. Gloucester connected with Gwatkin   III 413

———————— of Ireland connected with Cole   XX 82ª

———————— of Philadelphia and of the Island of Antigua   VI 176

———————— of Tarent Rawson als Tarent Antioch als Tarent
    Antiocheston, Tomstone co. Dorset, Wells, Rectors of
    Pitney co. Somerset, and of Rookley House Crawley co.
    Southampton   VIII 271

———————— of Tarrant Rushton als Antiocheston co. Dorset, of the   XIII 72,
    City of Wells, & of Pitney co. Som.   124–5

Lovering of Sandhurst co. Berkshire connected with Salcombe   VIII 420

Lovesey of North Leach co. Gloucester   II 333

Lovet Lovett of Kingswell co. Tipperary, and of Liscombe co.
    Bucks, connected with Mansergh   X 4

Lovett of Liscombe co. Bucks, and of Kingswell in Tipperary,
    connected with Mansergh   XXI 46

———————— of Liscombe co. Bucks see also Lovet   III 484

Loveyn of Penhurst in Kent connected with St Clare and with Gage   XIX 64

Low Leyton, Extracts from the Registers of   VI 298

———————— of Alderwasley, Hasland co. Derby, and of Oulgrave,
    connected with Gell and Beresford   II 207

———————— of Gloucester co. Essex New England, connected with
    Fellows   IV 429

Lowdham connected with Barwell and Stratford   XIX 261

———————————— Glen   XVII 67

Lowe als Fifield of London co. Middlesex, Bromley co. Kent, and
    of Newark co. Gloucester   XX 161

———————— connected with Jol   XVI 30

———————— Lord Mayor of London, of Newark co. Gloucester   II 87

———————— of Chelsea co. Middlesex, Claverton near Bath, Black-
    house Farm near Bromsgrove, High Sheriff of Worcester   XXI 228

———————— of Denby, Stoke co. Derby, and of London co.
    Middlesex, connected with Greatorex   III 29

———————— of Goadby co. Leicester   III 203–4

———————— of Jamaica and of Goadby   I 202

Lowle of Yardley co. Worcester, Clivedon co. Somerset, Toc-
    kington, and of Woodhouse in the psh of Olveston co.
    Gloucester   XIX 265

Lowndes connected with Hopper Martin and Dalston   I 365

———————— Osborne   VII 304

Lowndes of Chesham co. Bucks, and of London co. Middlesex,
    connected with Barrington   V 175
———————— of London co. Middlesex, Chesham, Brickhills and
    Winsloe co. Bucks   II 45
———————— of Palterton co. Derby, and of Hampstead co.
    Middlesex, connected with Milnes   XV 16
Lowth Bishop of Oxford   X 62
———————————————— connected with Jackson   X 53
Lowther de Louther of Lowther, Whitehaven, Stockbridge co.
    Westmorland, Greystock, Penrith co. Cumberland, and of
    London co. Middlesex   XXI 65–8
———————— de Louther of Louther in Westmorland, of Widehope,
    Harcley, Penrith, Stockdale, High Raughton, and Raughton
    Hall co. Cumberland, Ingleton Hall co. York, Lord of the
    Manor of Louther co. Fermanagh, Downamtor co. Meath
    in Ireland, and of Lincolns Inn co. Middlesex   VII 323
———————— of Lowther co. Westmorland, and of Ingleton co.
    York   XIV 31
———————— of Lowther, Greystock, Penrith, Whitehaven co.
    Cumberland, Cadby Lath Meburn co. Westmorland,
    Acworth Park, Swillington co. York, London co.
    Middlesex, Viscount Lonsdale   XVI 70–73
———————— M.I.   XIV 4, 5, 7
Loyd see Lloyd   III 230
Lucas connected with Thorold   X 76
———————— of Hasland and of Chesterfield co. Derby, also of
    Timberland co. Lincoln   III 169
———————— of Leeward Islands connected with Pinckney   I 522
———————— of Saxhum, Horniger, Bury St Edmunds co. Suffolk,
    Colchester, Ramsay and Shenfield co. Essex, Baron Lucas
    of Shenfield   I 464
Luccombe or Luckombe of Plymouth Exeter co. Devon, London
    co. Middlesex, and of Russia   III 212
Luckman connected with Stephens   IX 8
Luckombe see Luccombe   III 212
Lucy of Charlcot, Hampton Lucy; and of Henbury co. Chester   I 13
———————— of Charlcote co. Warwick, Pembroke in Wales, Cley-
    brooke co. Leicester, Bickering, Sharpenoe Richmont co.
    Bedford Henbury co. Chester, Barley End co. Bucks, and
    of Castle Cary co. Somerset   I 420
———————— of St Davids, Castle Cary co. Somerset, Salisbury co.
    Wilts, and of Herts   I 293
Luddington connected with Kirkby and Chamberlain   XIII 97
———————— M.I. Worcester Cathedral   XIV 9
———————— of the Manor of Leadon Court co. Gloucester, Powick,
    and of Defford co. Worcester connected with Wylde   XIX 152
Ludlow connected with Vernon and Grey Lord Powis   III 276
————————————————————————————   XIV 3
———————— of Devizes co. Wilts   X 125
Ludlowe M.I. in Hamildon Church co. Bucks   VI 124
Ludwell of Brewton co. Somerset, and of Greenspring in Virginia,

Secretary of State for the Province of Virginia, and Governor of South Carolina — VII 333

———— of the Town and psh of Brewton co. Somerset, and of Greenspring in Virginia — XXI 155

Lumley connected with Dawes and Bendish — I 114

Lunn connected with Booth — VII 107

———————————————————————————— VIII 158

———————————————————————————— VIII 216

———— of Canterbury connected with Johnson — IX 43

Lupton of Ringmer co. Sussex connected with Davies — VI 171

Lupus Earl of Chester — VIII 251

Luther connected with Chamberlaine — II 254

Lutterell formerly Fownes — III 506

Luxemburgh Guy of, Earl of Ligney connected with St Paul — XIII 32–5

Lydall of Hampton co. Middlesex connected with Zouche — III 344

Lymington connected with Conduit and Barton — I 147

Lynch of Grimley co. Worcester connected with Yarranton — IV 48

———— of Groves in Staple co. Kent — IV 508

———————————————————————————— XVIII 78

———— of Shruel and of Seville — I 146

———— of Weald in Essex and of Tonbridge Wells co. Kent — III 298

Lyne connected with Draper — IV 352

———— of Little Compton co. Warwick, Batsford co. Gloucester, and of Lyde — VIII 425

Lynus of Chard — XVI 59

Lyons connected with de la Barre and Kipp — I 20

Lysaght M.I. at Cheam — VI 128

Lysons M.I. at Westbury upon Severn co. Gloucester — VI 116

———— of Nether Lay in the psh of Westbury, Bristol, Hempstead, Rodmarton, Cherington co. Gloucester, the City of Worcester, Hull co. York, and of the Inner Temple co. Middlesex — I 45

———— of Nether Lay, Hempsted, Bristol co. Gloucester, Hull co. York, Bath co. Somerset, and of the City of Worcester — XIII 97

———— of Nether Lay Hempsted and Bristol co. Gloucester — XIX 138

Lyster formerly Kirwan of Dublin — III 425

Lyte of Lytes Cary co. Somerset — IV 523

Lytherland of Disworth and Swannington in the psh of Whitwick, Ashby de la Zouch co. Leicester, Ripon co. York, London co. Middlesex and of Ireland — I 353

Lyttelton letter as to family — IX 156

Lyttleton M.I. Worcester Cathedral — XIV 9

M

Mabb als Dore of Burton co. Worcester connected with Acton   XIX 6
Mablethorpe connected with Nevil and Newdigate   XVI 95
Mac Arthur of Miltown and Ascog connected with Stewart   XVIII 147
Macbride connected with Harrison   III 352
Mc Bride connected with Harrison and Horne   IV 95
Mc Culloch of co. Antrim and of London co. Middlesex   IX 61
MacDonald of the Isle of Skye in Scotland, Rodney Stoke and
    Wells co. Somerset, and of London co. Middlesex   I 254
Macdonald, Sir Alexander   XXI 204
Macdonell of Glengarie co. Inverness, evidences relating to the
    family of   VIII 356
Macfie of Glasgow and of Kilmarnock in the County of Ayr,
    afterwards Shaw   XV 53
Mc Gregor of the Shire of Perth   I 341
Machell M.I.   XIV 8
Machen connected with Mucklow   XIX 155
———— of Crickley co. Gloucester and of Benshington co.
    Oxford   XIX 234
———— of Eastbatch Court in the psh of English Bicknor co.
    Gloucester   XX 167
Machin connected with Prout and Hockley   XX 145ᵃ
———— of Seabridge co. Stafford   I 36
McIntosh connected with Browne   V 468
———————— Patterson   XVII 26
Mackintosh of Mackintosh in the psh of Moy, of Daviot, Castle
    Leathers, Balnespick all in the Shire of Inverness, New-
    brough in the Shire of Fife, and of Sandwich in Upper   XIII 36,
    Canada North America   38–40
Macklin of Wirral Barnston and of Derby   X 15
Mackworth connected with Huddleston & Hamilton   III 341
McLean of the Isle of Mull in Scotland settled in Ireland   III 241
McLellan of Bomby, Borgue and Auclane Balmangane, Baron of
    Kirkcudbright   I 453
McNeal Dean of Down connected with Brett   IV 532
Maddison of Hilton Birtley, Silkworth in the County of Durham,
    and of Newcastle upon Tyne co. Northumberland   XIII 44–53
———— of Townaby, Alvingham, Gainsborough co. Lincoln,
    and of London co. Middlesex   V 182
Maddocks of Ross connected with Powles   XX 188
Madoc Lord of Powys connected with Jones of Hendre   VII 254
Madock ap Meredith connected with Scudamore   XVIII 51
———————————— Prince of Powis connected with the Lord
    Rees Prince of South Wales and with Hookes   XVIII 104
———— of Alvington, Hartpury, Walleston, Tidenham co.
    Gloucester, and of Ashley Abbots co. Salop   XIX 110
Madox from co. Salop, of Greenwich co. Kent and of co. Surrey   VIII 455

Madox of London co. Middlesex, Boughton, Mencherry co.
　　Kent and of Wormley co. Herts   V 447
Madryll or Desmadryll of Trimnels co. Essex, afterwards Madryll
　　Cheere   VIII 457
Magnus of London co. Middlesex, connected with Anstruther   VII 130
Maidstone Church co. Kent M.I. Beale of Maidstone   VII 412
Maidstone, Finch Lord, connected with Windham   XVIII 22
Main of Kent connected with Waller   XVIII 99
Mainwaring connected with Maude   IX 53
————————— of Whitmore co. Stafford   IV 326
Maire of Hardwick co. Durham connected with Collingwood   XV 6
————————— of Hartbushes or Harrbushes, Hardwick co. Durham,
　　and of Lartington co. York   XX 170
Maismore of Wantage co. Berks connected with Warren   I 302
Maisterson connected with Joudrell   XVIII 136
Maisterton —————————————   III 362
Majendie of Exeter co. Devon, Windsor co. Berks, Salisbury co.
　　Wilts, and of Weston near Bath co. Somerset   I 346
Major formerly Henniker   XI 67
————————— of Worlingnorth Hall co. Suffolk, came from Nor-
　　mandy in the Kingdom of France and settled at Bridlington
　　co. York   XI 67–9
Makepeace connected with Eburne   XVIII 139
————————————————— Greswold   IV 470
Malbane connected with Wilbraham   V 127
Malcolm Canmore King of Scotland   VIII 251
————————— King of Scotland connected with Walker   VII 328
————————— Scots connected with Curwen   II 456
Malet see Mallet
Maleverer connected with Jackson   VI 24
Malherbe connected with Tate and Allard   III 201
Mallet of Combe Flory, St Audrey, and of Enmore co. Somerset   XX 166
————————— of Corye Mallet, Enmore, Deandon, Grendon, Walton
　　or Dalton, Coripole, St Audries, Comb Flory co. Somerset,
　　Middle Temple co. Middlesex & Maiden Newton co.
　　Dorset, Lord of Durburgh & Lord of Eye co. Suffolk   VII 72
————————— of Enmore co. Somerset, St Audries co. Cornwall &
　　Normandy   VII 397
————————— of Iddesly and Mevy co. Devon   XXI 172
————————— who named himself Fichett   VII 74
Mallory of Studley co. Yorks connected with Tempest and Ingram VIII 258
Malmaines connected with St Omer   VIII 245
Malory connected with Moton   VIII 51
Malson M.I. at Westbury upon Severn   VI 116
Man connected with Carpenter   XX 78[a]
————————— of London co. Middlesex, Lindsell, Hatfield, and
　　Broad Oak co. Essex, connected with Feake   XVI 93
Manby co. Lincoln connected with Stote   I 576
Manigault of Bourdeaux and of Charles Town in South Carolina,
　　also of London   I 213

Manistre of Norton co. Suffolk, & Wretham co. Norfolk, con-
    nected with Fiske   IV 136
Manley of Earleigh Court in the psh of Sunning co. Berks and of
    co. Wilts connected with Pryce   II 220
Manlove connected with. Blofield   XVII 4
Mann connected with Read   IX 118
Manners Earl of Rutland connected with Montague   X 46
———————————————————————————— Pierrepont   XVIII 129
Manning connected with Hollister   I 523
———————————— Lawley   VII 197
———————————— Raymond   XVI 88
———————— of High Hall in the psh of Blimhill co. Stafford   III 36
———————— of Stinchcombe and of Uley co. Gloucester   XX 169
———————— of Thetford and of Santon co. Norfolk connected with
    Mingay   I 287
———————— of Tormarton co. Gloucester connected with Fielding XIX 238
Mansel of Cosgrove near Stony Stratford co. Northampton con-
    nected with Biggen   I 258
Mansell connected with Narborough   V 449
———————— of Llanelty connected with Stepney   V 422
———————— of Margam co. Glamorgan connected with Shovell   VII 400
Mansergh of Berwick Hall in the psh of Kirby Lonsdale co.
    Westmorland, Grenan, Kingswell co. Tipperary, Limerick,
    Macroney, and of Ballybur   XXI 45–7
———————— of Macroney co. Cork connected with St George   X 3, 5
Manwaring connected with Dixon assumed the name of Ellerker X 144
———————— of Carincham co. Chester   VIII 223
———————— of Smallwood co. Chester connected with Ashmole   III 132
Mapleston of London connected with Haine   IV 75
Mapletoft Prebendary of Chester   VII 353
March Mortimer Earl of connected with Waller   XVIII 94
Marchant connected with Credy als Perron   VII 15
Marche and Dunbar, Earl of, connected with Merley   XIV 19
Mareshal Earl of Pembroke, Lord Marshal, surnamed from his
    Office, connected with Paulton   XVI 18
Margetts of Enstone Woodstock co. Oxon, and of London co.
    Middlesex   II 323
Markham M.I. in Winkburn Church co. Nottingham   VI 116
———————— of Markham Allerton, Cotham co. Nottingham
    Oxford, Okeley, and of Claxby   X 103
———————— of St Albans co. Herts, Winsloe co. Berks, Staines co.
    Middlesex, Stanton St John co. Oxon, Marlow co. Bucks,
    and of Cotham co. Nottingham   VII 484
———————— of Yatton co. Somerset connected with Grimsteed   III 443
Markland afterwards Entwistle of Wigan, Foxholes in Hud-
    dersfield in the psh of Rochdale and of Manchester co.
    Lancaster   XI 25–6
Marlborough, Duke of, connected with Hedges Nicoll & Trevor III 138
———————————————————— as to installation at Windsor   XVII 6
————————, family titles   IX 15

Marley of Newcastle	X 72
	X 150
———————————— connected with Dixon & Perith	X 143
	X 144
Marlow of Flemyngs in the psh of Runwells co. Essex connected with Tyrell and Sulyard	VII 19
———————— of London, from Reading co. Berks, and of Shirley in the psh of Milbrooke Southampton	I 513
Marlowe a goldsmith	IX 88
———————— connected with Sidney and Goddard.	XXI 322
Marnes of Hinton co. Hants	III 18
Marney connected with Bedingfield	V 312
Marow of Stebenhithe, Hoxton co. Middlesex, Rudsin Berkswell co. Warwick and of Elmdon	VII 25
———————— of Stebenhithe, Lord of the Manor, of London, Hoxton co. Middlesex, Berkswell and Rudsin co. Warwick	VII 369
———————— of Stebenhithe, Hoxton co. Middlesex, Rudsin and Berkswell co. Warwick Baronet	XXI 108
Marratt of Utoxeter co. Stafford and of London co. Middlesex	XXI 181
Marriot connected with Angell	XI 55
Marriott of Chatteris in the Isle of Ely and County of Cambridge connected with Gardner	VIII 291
———————— of Northampton connected with Williamson	XVII 31
Marrow see Marow	VII 25
Marsden of Pendleton co. Lancaster	VIII 133
Marselis connected with Clifford	XI 40
Marsh connected with McNeal	IV 532
———————— of Brompton co. Kent – Rear Admiral	IX 141
———————— of Hendon co. Middlesex	I 199
———————— of Thornbury and of Bristol co. Gloucester	III 99
Marshal connected with Bucknall	II 140
———————— of Lidyeard Tregose co. Wilts, and of Eastington co. Gloucester	XXI 158
Marshall connected with Cutt or Cutts and Langley	VIII 247
———————— M.I.	XIV 8
———————— at Barton co. Nottingham	VI 112
———————— of Aynsome M.I.	XIV 9
———————— of co. Durham, Bedell and Middleham, connected with Snaith and Becket	II 273
———————— of Knaresborough co. York connected with Herey	III 500
———————— of London co. Middlesex, Hampton near Windsor co. Berks, Charing co. Kent and of Edinburgh	II 281
———————— of Sculpins co. Essex and of Huntingdon	IX 4
Marten als Martyn of Furness co. Lancaster, Somerton, Rowsham, North Aston, Steeple Aston, Radford, Tackley co. Oxon, Shellesley, Beauchamp co. Worcester, and of Lavington co. Wilts	VII 98
———————— connected with Byrom	VIII 62
Marter of . . . . near Stoke Dabernon, Cobham, Talworth Court, and of Long Ditton co. Surrey	IV 537

Martin and Wight, extracts from Registers, see Martin of London V 332
————————————————————————————————————— VI 351
———————— of Blasbury co. Somerset and Trowbridge co. Wilts I 318
———————— of Baltonburgh co. Somerset and of Athelhampton co.
Dorset XXI 224–5
———————— of Calcutta VII 182
———————— of Donkerton co. Somerset connected with Floyer I 117
———————— of East Langder co. Kent connected with Byng XXI 256
———————— of East Moulsey co. Surrey connected with Greening I 196
———————— of Hardwicke and Slymbridge co. Gloucester XX 30
———————— of Kensington co. Middlesex connected with Lolley VII 195
———————— of London co. Middlesex connected with Wight V 332
———————— of Pebworth co. Gloucester IX 37
———————— of Stanton, Thetford co. Norfolk Palgrave co. Suffolk
and Rector of Livesmore IX 155
———————— of Woovvern connected with Field I 170
Martyn see Marten
Marwood of Nunthorp & Little Buskby in Cleveland co. York also
of London co. Middlesex VI 22
Mary Queen of Scots XIV 18
————————————————————————————————————— XVI 9
Mascall of Aldgate co. Middlesex connected with Anderson III 102
Mason connected with Hunt XVIII 34
——————————————— Jenkins X 102
———————— of Boreham Wood co. Herts and of Bengal connected
with Roberts II 10
———————— of Chichester co. Sussex connected with West IV 207
———————— of co. Lancaster III 184
————————————————————————————————————— IV 309
———————— of Deeping co. Northampton I 214
———————— of Marshgibbon connected with Ford XI 39
———————— of Shrewsbury connected with Hunt V 73
Massey Baron, of Dunham Massey co. Palatine Chester connected
with Rudde XXI 296
———————— of Eccleston co. Chester I 219
Massham of Bradwell Ash, Shakerland Hall co. Suffolk Otis
Manor, Matchyn, High Laver co. Essex, Baron Masham VII 8
Massingberd of South Ormesby co. Lincoln and of London co.
Middlesex I 304
Master came out of the West country and settled in Kent, of
Willesborough, Canterbury co. Kent, Hitherset in Norfolk,
Cirencester co. Gloucester, Lambourn Woodford co. Essex,
Woodchurch and of London co. Middlesex XIX 50
———————— of Croston co. Palatine Lancaster connected with
Mosley VIII 336
———————— of East Langdon, Ospringe co. Kent connected with
Pocock VII 68
———————— of East Langdon connected with Turnor see Masters X 59
———————— of London co. Middlesex and of Portsmouth co. Hants II 112
Masters connected with Durham XVII 30

Masters of East Langdon co. Kent see Master   XXI 135
Masterson of Biddenden co. Kent connected with Beale   III 103
Mather connected with Martin and Lolley   VII 195
Mathew of Hymeadow in Newland co. Gloucester connected with
    Hall   XIX 208
———————— of Lewney Green connected with Hookes   XVIII 109
———————— of Llandaff and of Ardar connected with Throkmorton   XIX 63
———————— of Pennitenny in the psh of St Kew co. Cornwall
Jamaica and of the Leeward Islands   XVIII 80
———————— of St Christophers, the Leeward Islands and of
Pentitenny in the psh of St Kew co. Cornwall   IV 435
———————— of St Kew and Tregoid co. Cornwall extracts from
Registers   VI 344
———————— of Tortworth, Huntingford in the psh of Wootton
under Edge, and of Thornbury co. Gloucester   XX 165[a]
Mathews M.I. St Nicholas Church Newcastle upon Tyne   VII 375
———————— of Lint, Buscot co. Berks, and Clapham co. Surrey,
connected with Paul and Oatridge   V 308
———————— of Tufley co. Gloucester connected with Mills   XX 164
Matthew of Northamptonshire connected with Lloyd   III 231
Matthews of Antigua, Demarny & of Demarara   VIII 84
———————— of Birchington, Minster in the Isle of Thanet co. Kent
and of London co. Middlesex   IV 231
———————— of Blodwell co. Salop   V 121
———————— of Lint co. Gloucester, Buscot co. Berks and of
Clapham co. Surrey   III 193
Maude als Mawhood of Ardesley, Snaith, Wakefield co. York,
Auchley, Helthwayte Hill near Harwood, and of Finchley   IX 52
———————— came from Ripon in Yorkshire and settled at Dundrum
co. Tipperary, Baron Montalt of Ireland   XVII 57
Maudit Earl of Warwick   XVI 82
Mauduit Lord and Baron of Hanslap connected with Beauchamp
Lord of Elmley   VIII 253
Maule of Ringwood co. Hants connected with Holbrow   I 171
Maulee de lacu one of the Founders of Bridlington Watton and
Groman Abbeys, Lord of Sutton Southcotts and Stonefer-
rie, also of the Manor of Crognall Banks   XVIII 82
Maunder connected with Hurley   XIII 85
Maunsell of Berryend co. Bedford, Wellingborough co.
Northampton. Chicheley, Haversham co. Bucks, Bally-
voreen, Monkstown, Mount Sion co. Limerick, and of
Roxborough   VIII 307
Maurice of Whittington, London co. Middlesex and of Woodford
co. Essex   XVI 63
Mautby connected with Paston   IX 113[b]
Mawhood see Maude   IX 52
Mawson of East Barnet co. Herts   VII 411
Maxfield of Wadsworth co. York   IX 150
Maxwell of Falkland in the Kingdom of Ireland connected with
Massingbred   I 304
May of Bibroke in the psh of Kennington co. Kent   VIII 267

May of Sodbury co. Gloucester and the neighbourhood — IV 196
———————— of Twickenham co. Middlesex Thunderley cum Wimbish in Essex connected with Moorhouse — III 82
Maycock of Hendon co. Middlesex and of Richmond co. Surrey — II 264
Maye of Blackwall connected with Anderson — III 136
Mayfield of Holme connected with Grundie — III 289
Mayhew formerly Crumpling — XVII 53
———————— of Colchester — XVII 53
Mayl Lord of Meleinoth connected with Evance — VIII 473
Maylin connected with Wood — III 368
Maynard of Barbadoes and of London co. Middlesex connected with Martin — VII 182
Maynarth Lord of Brecknock — XIV 19
Mayne of Powis Logie in the County of Clackmannan in the Shire of Perth, descended from the Maynes of Lockwood, Baronet of Great Britain and Peer of Ireland, of Moulsey co. Surrey — XV 40–3
Mayo of the City of Hereford and of London co. Middlesex connected with Watts — IX 21
Mazine connected with Rawlinson — I 473
Mead connected with Wilmot — IX 126
Meade connected with Wilkes — I 502
———————— of Kirush near Limerick Ireland, and of London — I 42
———————— of Southwark co. Surrey, connected with Whitworth and Burnham — III 453
Meadows Sir Philip connected with Dyott — II 142
Meakin of Eccleshall co. Stafford and of Hinstock co. Salop — VII 55
Meallin of Frankton near Rugby co. Warwick and of Southampton — VIII 228[b]
Meares of Pierston co. Pembroke connected with Lloyd — XXI 159[a]
Mee connected with Lysons — I 46
— XIII 97
———————————————— and Trye — XIX 135, 139
Meecham of London connected with Burgess — II 373
Meeke of Wighill Park co. York afterwards Meyer and Thompson — IV 529
Meik of Drumney in Forfar and of Alyth in the Shire of Perth — XXI 201
Mellish co. Sussex and of Shadwell co. Middlesex — VII 102
Mellor connected with Buckston — III 3
Melsom connected with Voysey — III 441
Melvill collector of Customs at Dunbar, Deputy Governor of Pendennis Castle — XIII 64
Mendes de Costa connected with de Aguilar — IV 227
Mercer connected with Frith and Napper — III 208
Mercier connected with Bradford — V 90
— IX 110
Mere of Mere co. Chester, Rawstone co. Derby & Bewbridge co. Salop — XXI 233
Meredith of Brecknock — VIII 80
———————— son of Jevan ap Robert of Gwither connected with Puliston and Hookes — XVIII 106
Merley Lord of Morpeth in Northumberland connected with Somervile — XIV 19

Merrick of Southwark co. Surrey connected with Chorley and
    Wragg   III 315
Merricks connected with Woodyer   I 71
Merry of Whitby co. York, Yarmouth in Norfolk, Watford co.
    Herts, and of London co. Middlesex, descended from the
    Merrys of Redburne and Barton co. Derby   I 489
Mershewode Vale, fitz-Paine, Earl of, connected with St Lo   XVIII 11
Merttins of London co. Middlesex President of Christs Hospital   XXI 235
Mervin of Fonthill co. Wilts   I 149
Merwin of Heinton & Puncharden co. Devon   IV 245
Merydith ap Tudor, Sir Owen   XVI 9
Metcalfe of Brig co. Lincoln connected with More   V 11
Methley of Methley near Wakefield connected with Waterton   VIII 246
Methold of Northaw co. Herts, London co. Middlesex, and of
    Bath co. Somerset connected with Theed   IV 324
Methuen of Bradford, Bishops Canneys, Lucknam House co.
    Wilts, Bromsgrove co. Worcester, Cheddon, Fitz-pain,
    Withington and Beckington co. Somerset, Lord Chancellor
    of Ireland, Ambassador to Germany, Morocco, Spain,
    Portugal and Savoy   II 285
Meux of Kingston in the Isle of Wight and of London   V 446
Mews of Winchester afterwards St John   I 25
Meyer formerly Meeke   IV 529
Meynick connected with Pitt   X 160
Michaelson of Greenbank M.I.   XIV 8
Michel or Mitchell of Angram Grange   I 294
Michell connected with Rowe   XVIII 62
———— of Branscombe co. Devon and of Bilboa descended
    from Michell of Dorsetshire   IV 37
———— of Doncaster co. York and of London co. Middlesex III 53
———— of Warnham co. Sussex connected with Miller   IV 161
—————————————————————   XVIII 18

Middleton, Alan Broderick Lord   II 57
———— connected with Erington   X 75
———— formerly Ryred ap David connected with Boulder VIII 485
———— Lord connected with Edwards   XVI 52
———— M.I.   XIV 4
———————— Worcester Cathedral   XIV 9
———— of Belsoe co. Northumberland Silksworth co. Durham
    and of Offerton   II 440
———— of Bolham co. Durham extracts from Registers   VI 327
———— of Chirk Castle co. Denbigh   XV 10
———— of Denbigh connected with Hookes and Mathew XVIII 109
———— of Gwyninoge North Wales and of Denbigh   V 443
———— of Kirkby Lonsdale co. Westmorland   XXI 93
———— of Middleton Hall Bethom co. Westmorland   XXI 70–4
———— of Middleton co. Salop connected with Bowldler VIII 485
———— of New York   II 244
———— of Shipton, Hart co. Durham and of London   II 344
———— of Stockheld co. York connected with Farmer or
    Fermor   XIV 22

Middleton, Sir John Lambert   II 494
Midgeley M.I at Thirsk   VI 126
Midhope connected with Pudsey   II 431
Milbanke of Yorkshire connected with Marten   VII 99
Mildmay connected with Halliday   XX 138
——————— originally written Mildme, Mildeme Mildmey of
   Stonehouse co. Gloucester, Hambleton, Cretingham co.
   Suffolk, Athery co. Northampton, Sanbridge co. Herts, and
   of Woodham Water co. Essex   IX 31
Miles of Hawknest co. York connected with Ward   IV 239
——————— of London co. Middlesex, Wanstead co. Essex, and of
   Eyarth House in the psh of Llanfair in the County of
   Denbigh, assumed the name of Wynne   XIII 17
——————— of Shay connected with Andrews   XX 36ᵃ
Miles-Wynne see Miles   XIII 17
Mill Browne-Mill   XI 42
——————— formerly Browne   XI 42
——————— of Newton Berry and of Motsfont co. Hants connected
   with Sandes   II 443
Miller connected with Borlace   V 403
——————— connected with Webb and Horlock   XIX 156
——————— of Bridy connected with Trenchard   VIII 180
——————— of Bristol co. Gloucester connected with Burrough   IV 175
——————— of Brunswick in the Jerseys connected with Willett   VII 489
——————— of Chichester co. Sussex and of the City of Chester IV 158
————————————————— Warnham Shapwick co. Sussex   XVIII 18
——————— of Dorsetshire, Southampton, Emsworth co. Hants,
   London Ratcliff Highway co. Middlesex, and of Cheltenham
   co. Gloucester   I 14
——————— of Dunstable House   V 465
——————— of Fairleigh in Kent and of Blackfriars co. Middlesex VII 87
Milles Mills   XV 61
——————— of Melvord and Mickleton co. Gloucester   XIX 248
Millikin of Port Glasgow in Scotland and of London co. Middlesex III 154
Mills als Blunt of Bridgewater co. Somerset   VI 254
——————— of Highhampe co. Hants   XV 61-2
——————— Milles   XV 61
——————— of Bridgewater co. Somerset extracts from Registers VI 360
————————————————— and Bishops Hull co. Somerset, Twickenham co. Middlesex, Richmond co. Surrey, Lower Slaughter
   co. Gloucester, Woodford co. Essex and of the Island of St
   Christopher   VI 250
——————— of London co. Middlesex and of Glenton Pike co.
   Northumberland   II 39
——————— of Mickleton   XX 29
——————— of Newcastle upon Tyne co. Northumberland connected with Fothergill   VII 239
——————— of Wishanger, Bidfield, Miserden, Painswick co.
   Gloucester, and of London co. Middlesex   XX 164
Millum Lords of, connected with Hudleston   XXI 23
Milner afterwards Joliff of the City of York   XI 3-11

Milner connected with Wilcocks   IV 413

Milnes afterwards Rich and reassumed the name of Milnes   XV 16

———————— of Ashford in the Water, Chesterfield co. Derby, Wakefield, Hull, Cottenham, Bawtry co. York, Governor of the Island of Martinique, Lt Governor of Canada   XV 16, 17

Milson of London co. Middlesex   IX 1

Milton Damer, Baron, of Milton Abbey co. Dorset   XVI 21

Mingay of Shottisham co. Suffolk, connected with Beaumont   IV 382

———————— of Shottisham; Woodstock co. Oxon, Norwich co. Norfolk, Woodbridge co. Suffolk, Hull co. York, Edinburgh, and of the Inner Temple co. Middlesex   I 287

Minors of Triago co. Hereford connected with Reed   XIX 254

Mitchell connected with Parry   III 173

———————————————— Umfreville   III 518

———————— Michel of Angram Grange   I 294

———————— of Branscombe and Salcombe co. Devon   XIX 166^c

———————————————————— co. Devon connected with Rowe & with Codrington   X 43

Mitford connected with Hatsell and Walker   XXI 188

———————— of London co. Middlesex, Richmond co. Surrey, Petworth, Tillington co. Sussex, and of Madras East Indies   I 206

———————— of Mitford Castle, Newcastle, and of Burnhall co. Durham, see Mitfort   IV 257

———————— of Newhaven co. Berks connected with Edwards   II 413

———————— of Northallerton co. York and of London co. Middlesex   I 309

———————— of Seghill co. Northumberland   X 132

Mitfort of Mitfort Castle co. Northumberland connected with Osbaldeston see Mitford and Midford   XXI 234

Mitton connected with Smyth and Leighton   XX 48

Modyford connected with Norton   VIII 536

———————— of Devon London and Chiswick co. Middlesex   VI 38

Mogg of Cholwell in the psh of Cameley and of High Littleton co. Somerset   VIII 423

Mohun Baron of Dunster of Ham Mohun co. Dorset   VIII 177

Mole of Denham co. Bucks connected with Lescaleet   II 239

Moleins connected with De Cotes and Trenchard   VIII 178

Molineux of Castle Dillon and of the City of Dublin connected with Gay   IV 369

Mollineux of Septon co. Palatine Lancaster   XIV 23

Molloy of Greenwich co. Kent and of Roscommon   X 8

Moncaster Muncaster, Lord, see Pennington   I 344

Monck connected with Saunders   XXI 208

———————— Duke of Albemarle connected with Rawlinson   XVI 82

Monington connected with Webbe see Monnington   V 195

Monk M.I.   XIV 5

Monke Duke of Albemarle connected with Payne   IV 168

Monnington connected with Webbe see Monington   I 50

Monoux of Berkhampsted co. Herts   XIII 107

———————————————— Cirencester co. Gloucester and of London co. Middlesex   XIX 93

Monoux see Monox

Monox of Samford co. Worcester London co. Middlesex and of
    Wotton co. Bedford   VI 13

———————— see Monoux

Monro connected with Tucker and Jenkyns   V 179

Montagu connected with Charlton   I 407

———————————— Evans   VIII 523

———————————— Rogers   I 308

——————————————————————— XVI 69

——————————————————————— XXI 147

———————— of Boughton co. Northampton connected with Geffry I 545

Montague, Browne, Viscount   IX 120

———————— of Boughton co. Northampton Lord Montague con-
    nected with Roper   X 46

Montford of Ashwood Lodge in the psh of King Swinford   IV 496

Montgomery of Coalsfield co. Ayr connected with Hamilton II 37

Montrath Coote Earl of   XVI 24

Mooner connected with Tucker and Monro   V 179

Moore Archbishop of Canterbury, of Brasted co. Kent   VII 121

———————— connected with Clowes   XXI 130

———————————— Eden   XXI 124

———————————— Lane   III 67

———————— M.I. of Douglas in the Isle of Man   XIV 9

———————————— Worcester Cathedral   XIV 9

———————— of Barbadoes   I 208

———————————— and of Moor Hall in Jamaica West Indies XXI 235

———————— of Bath connected with Draper   IV 23

———————— of New York connected with Long and Lowe I 202

———————— of Oxfordshire connected with Hardwick   III 142

———————— of South Fawley co. Berks connected with Hale II 88

———————— of Spargrove co. Somerset or of Haychurch co. Devon II 283

Moorhouse of Beamsley Hall Bolton Bridge, and of Skipton
    Craven co. York   I 237

———————— of Beamsley House near Bolton in Craven, Hud-
    dersfield, Heaton co. York, London and Islington co.
    Middlesex   III 82

Mooring of Chelsea co. Middlesex and of Plymouth co. Devon
    connected with Lawrence   I 218

Moorsom of Whitby co. York connected with Errington and Ward I 93

Mordant of Ormskirk co. Lancaster connected with Viscount
    Howe   XIX 4, 5

Mordaunt Earls of Peterborough of Hallsall   VI 160

More Judge of the Kings Bench, Chancellor of England of London
    co. Middlesex, Gubbins als More Hall in the psh of North
    Mims co. Herts, and of Barnborough co. York   V 11

Mores connected with Bathurst   XX 43

———————— of Low Layton co. Essex connected with Windsor XIII 5

Moreton of Moreton, Engleton co. Stafford connected with Ducie XX 106

———————— of Moreton and Ingleton co. Stafford afterwards Baron
    Ducie of Moreton co. Stafford and of Tortworth co.
    Gloucester   XX 100[a]

Morgan afterwards James   XX 160
————— connected with Colchester   XIX 153
——————————————————— and Clark   XX 74[b]
————— of Ardagh and of Dublin connected with Warburton –
see Morgan of Loughgilley   I 200
————— of Carmarthen connected with Thomas and with the
Earls of Leicester   X 52
————— of Court Blethin co. Monmouth, and of Newland co.
Gloucester connected with Bond   XX 52
————— of Glamorgan connected with Colchester   X 69
————— of Hurst in Lidney co. Gloucester   XX 167[a]
————— of Loughgilley in the County of Armagh and Dean of
Ardagh in the Kingdom of Ireland change of name to
Warburton see Morgan of Ardagh   VI 384
————— of Morgans Hayes co. Devon, and of South Maperton
co. Dorset   VIII 179
————— of Pembroke, Swindon co. Wilts, and of London   XVII 8
————— of St Georges co. Somerset, connected with Master   XIX 51
————— of Tredegar co. Monmouth, Ruspirra co. Glamorgan,
and of Therow co. Brecknock   IV 270
————— of Yelling co. Huntingdon connected with Austry   XX 34
Morgangame connected with Turbevile   XIV 19
Moring of Twyford in Hants and of Walworth co. Surrey   XVII 64
Morley connected with Pockley and Osbaldeston   XXI 234
————— formerly Wilson   VIII 3
————— of Giggleswick co. York connected with Wilson   VIII 3
————— of Hallerstone, Ravensthorpe co. Northampton and of
Foolesworth co. Leicester   VIII 293
————— of Horsley co. Derby and of London co. Middlesex   I 511
Morpeth M.I. St Nicholas Church Newcastle upon Tyne   VII 379
Morris connected with Portrey   XX 1
——————————————— Wilmot   IX 122
————— of Middleton Stony, Bletchington, Elsfield co. Oxon,
and of Cumnor co. Bucks, connected with Phillips   IV 155
————— of Newton St Loe co. Wilts connected with Webb   XIX 156
————— of Nonesuch co. Wilts connected with Selfe   II 353
Morse connected with Lloyd   IV 125
————— of Cam, Bristol, and of Dursley co. Gloucester   XX 192
————— of Gosport co. Southampton connected with Marlow   I 513
————— of Hereford connected with Hereford   VII 316
Mortimer connected with Browne and Acton   XIX 6
————— Lord of Wigmore Chelnerth and of Richards Castle,
Earl of March connected with Waller   XVIII 94
————— of Essex connected with Howard Duke of Norfolk   XII 51
Morton of Newcastle connected with Bonner   VIII 421
————— William Earl of connected with Macdonald   XXI 204
Morville connected with Rowland Lord of Galloway   VIII 250
Moseley connected with Thorowgood   IV 59
————— descended according to family tradition from Oswald
Moseley of Garret near Manchester co. Palatine Lancaster,
of London co. Middlesex, and of co. Essex   VIII 37

Moseley of Dublin, the Inner Temple co. Middlesex, and of
  Garret   II 135
————— of Mere, Ludlow co. Salop, and of Leighton Hall co.
  Stafford   VIII 13
————— of Owsden and Drinkston co. Suffolk   I 509
Mosley Rector of Rolleston co. Stafford and of the Inner Temple
  co. Middlesex   VIII 334
Moss of Leghorn connected with Patrick   II 299
————— of Norwich co. Norfolk, and of Spitalfields co.
  Middlesex   IV 199
Mostyne M.I. Worcester Cathedral   XIV 9
Moton of Peckelton and Stapleton co. Leiceter connected with Pole
  and Bugge   VIII 53
Mottram of Cawthorp, Thorp, Addlethorp, Osgardby, and of
  Stamford co. Lincoln   VII 335
Mould of Dunnington co. Salop, Costhall co. Stafford, and of
  Cotswall   VIII 386
Moulson connected with Vaughan   III 91
————— of London co. Middlesex, Milton and Gravesend co.
  Kent connected with Vaughan   IV 414
Mounteney formerly of London co. Middlesex and of Kew Green
  co. Surrey   X 51
————— of Kent   X 98, 101
————— of London co. Middlesex, Kew Green co. Surrey,
  Baron of the Exchequer in Ireland   XXI 169
Mousel of Moxon in Newland co. Gloucester   XX 168
Mowbray Duke of Norfolk connected with Fitzalan and with
  Stafford   XVI 50
Moyer connected with Jol   XVI 30
Moyles connected with Botreaux   V 50
————————————— and Hungerford   V 243
Mucklestone of co. Salop connected with Harnwood and Kynaston   XVIII 118
Mucklow of Winchcombe co. Gloucester   XIX 155
Mucleston of Muchelstone co. Stafford connected with Bret and
  Trenchard   VIII 179
Mukins of the City of Kilkenny   I 417
Mulgrave, Phipps, Lord   II 146
Mullins of Bath connected with Woodhouse   IX 29
Muncaster Moncaster Lord see Pennington   I 344
————— of Millum and of Cockermouth co. Cumberland   IX 64
Munday of Pangbourne co. Berks connected with Breedon   XIII 27
Mundy of Mackeaton co. Derby and of Osbaston co. Leicester   VIII 449
Munn of Greenwich Ashford co. Kent, and of London co.
  Middlesex   III 24
Murray connected with Collingwood and Bennett   X 155
————— of Black Barony in Scotland connected with Digby   VII 257
Murrell of Thetford Abbey co. Norfolk and of Stepney co.
  Middlesex   XVII 32
Musgrave connected with Hilton of Hilton   X 131
————— connected with Lord Dacre of Gillesland and Mar-
  tindale of Newton co. Cumberland   XXI 145

Musgrave of Eden Hall co. Cumberland Hartley Castle co. Westmorland Beach Hill co. Berks connected with Beckford and Turton   XII 91–100
————— of Hartley Castle co. Westmorland, Norton Conyers co. York, and of Hayton co. Cumberland   XXI 54–9
Musters of Colwick co. Nottingham connected with Heywood   I 51
Muttlebury of Creech Somerset connected with Westley   XIII 115
Mylles of Bittern Court co. Hants   XXI 207

N

Nairn connected with Drummond   I 256
Nalldrett of Waldrit House in the psh of Rudgwick co. Sussex   III 222
Nance of Grampound co. Cornwall and of Aylesford co. Kent connected with Bonythan   III 83
Nanson of Birchmorton, Hanley Castle co. Worcester, and of Tewkesbury co. Gloucester   XIX 170
Naper connected with Dutton   XX 98^a
————— M.I. at Lougherew co. Meath   VI 115
Napper connected with Frith   III 208
————— of Rudgwick Wisborough Green co. Sussex   I 35
Narborough of Blakney co. Norfolk, Knowlton co. Kent, connected with Shovell – Sir Cloudsley   V 448
————— of Knowlton co. Kent   VII 399
Nash connected with Kingscote   XVI 29
————— of Bridge End Stonehouse co. Gloucester, and of London co. Middlesex, connected with Elliott   II 467
————— of Miserden co. Gloucester connected with Mills   XX 164
————— of Old Stratford co. Warwick connected with Baugh   XIX 72
Nassau Powlet Lord   XVI 58
Naylor of Bureton Hall co. Chester, Windsor co. Berks, Manchester, Newton Hall co. Lancaster, London co. Middlesex, and of Ashburton co. Devon   III 214
Neale connected with Dean   X 43
————— descended from the Neals of Bedfordshire connected with Hanbury   X 124
————— of Allesley co. Warwick   I 267
————— of Exeter co. Devon connected with Radford   III 25
————— of Goosegreen in the psh of Yate co. Gloucester   XX 176^a
————— of Hertford and of London connected with Crayle   I 158
————— of Ipswich co. Suffolk connected with Baylis   VIII 395
————— of Plassy in Scotland connected with Seton   I 500
Neast Nest of the family of Nest of Chaceley co. Worcester

Twining Tewkesbury co. Gloucester and of London co.
    Middlesex   XIX 246
———————— of Chaseley co. Worcester Twyning and Tewkesbury
    co. Gloucester   XX 172
Neave of Needham and Framlingham co. Suffolk   VII 250
Need of Arundel co. Nottingham   II 18
Needham of Cheshire and of Sheffield co. York   IV 42
Nelson connected with Speed   I 314
Nelthorpe of Saxby connected with Coxwell   XIX 116
————————————————————————————————   XVI 77
————————————————————————————————   XX 75ᵃ, 76

Nepuen a native of France, of Elms, Hougham co. Kent, and of
    Twickenham co. Middlesex   XXI 321
Nest see Neast   XX 172
Netting of Little Ash near Salt Ash co. Cornwall, connected with
    Lawrence   I 216
Nevell of Rolston co. Nottingham connected with Babington   XVI 91
Nevil Earl of Westmorland connected with Stafford see Neville   XVI 50
———————— entry as to burial   XXI 239
Nevile connected with Newdigate   XVI 94–6
———————— of South Deverton co. Notts, connected with de la
    Zouche   I 445
Nevill Earl of Warwick connected with Spencer   VI 53
———————— Lord Abergavenny   II 493
———————— Lord Latimer connected with Danvers   VI 208
———————— of Forness, Newcastle co. Kildare, and of London   I 418
Neville als Smyth   XVI 66
———————— Earl of Westmorland connected with Eyre   II 390
———————————————————————————— and Earls of Salisbury con-
    nected with Barrington see Nevil   V 174
———————— formerly Lister   I 18
———————— of York connected with Brewster   V 114
Nevinson of Newby Hall co. Westmorland   XXI 148ᵃ
New of New Barnes co. Herts and of London co. Middlesex   I 250
Newark, Lord of the Kingdom of Scotland connected with
    Anstruther   VII 130
Newbery connected with Wooldridge   VIII 301
———————— of London co. Middlesex and of Heathfield Park co.
    Sussex   IX 75
Newborough Earl of, standing orders as to ascertaining Descents
    of Peers   XVI 32
———————— Livingston Earl of   XVI 32
Newburgh, Earl of, date of daughter Anne's birth   IX 16
Newby of Barbergreen   XIV 9
Newcastle upon Tyne St Nicholas Church M.I.   VII 375
Newcome Dean of Gloucester, Vicar of St Nicholas Abingdon co.
    Berks. Rectors of Penmark co. Gloucester and Wimpole co.
    Devon, Bishop of Dromore   XIX 238
Newcomen Gleadowe-Newcomen
———————— of Carrickclass co. Longford, Baroness Newcomen

and Viscountess Newcomen of Moss Town co. Longford	VIII 279
Newdigate of Harefield co. Middlesex, connected with Dormer	XVI 94–6
Newell afterwards Port	I 251
————————————————————————	IV 241
—————— M.I. Kirkby Ravensworth Church	VI 123
—————— of Ardwell and of Henley on Thames co. Oxon	XX 66
—————— of Cheltenham co. Gloucester connected with Blackman	VII 406
—————— of Scilly connected with Hegarty	IV 14
Newhergh Earl of Warwick	VIII 254
Newland Capt. Thomas	XIII 106
—————— connected with Loader	XXI 205
—————— of Calcutta and Bengal	II 79
———————————————— connected with Feake	XVI 93
—————— of Gatton co. Surrey	X 18
Newman connected with Edmonds	II 288
———————————— Fletcher	IV 445
————————————————————————	XVIII 8
———————————— Gilmore	III 106
—————— of Gatton in the Isle of Wight connected with Urry	III 388
—————— of London co. Middlesex	XXI 5
—————— of New House Wrotham co. Kent, connected with Davies	VI 171
—————— of Weekly	IV 260
Newnham of Streatham co. Surrey connected with Ryder	X 18
—————— of Wapley and Boxwell co. Gloucester	VIII 424
Newport als Hatton connected with Gawdy	VI 78
—————— connected with Wilbraham	V 131
————————————————————————	V 123
—————— of Burnt Pelham and Furneux Pelham co. Herts	III 497
—————— of High Ercall co. Salop afterwards Earl of Bradford	I 315
—————— of Walton connected with Windsor	I 317
Newsted of North Somercoats co. Lincoln connected with Mottram	VII 335
Newte connected with Foot	I 319
Newton als Cradoc of East Hartery co. Somerset and of Bitton co. Gloucester	IX 113[b]
————————————————————————	XIX 216
—————— connected with Eyre	II 394
———————————— Rodney	IX 139
—————— M.I. at Barton co. Nottingham	VI 112
———————————— at Morley co. Derby	VI 109
—————— of Bar Court in the County of Gloucester connected with Eyre and Stringer	V 137
—————— of Colsworth – Sir Isaac Newton	I 147
—————— of Easton, Berhake co. Northampton, and of London co. Middlesex	VI 23
————————————————————————	VI 30
—————— of Gloucester, Vicars of Sandhurst co. Gloucester and of Melksham co. Wilts	XX 173–5
—————— of Hartery co. Somerset connected with Paston – see	

also Newton als Cradoc – .... IX 113[b]

———————— of Hasker in Lincolnshire Lord of Bitton & Hunham XIII 103

———————— of Moreville and of Hartshill in the psh of Manceter co. Warwick .... III 282

———————— of Newton Hall co. Lincs and of London co. Middx XXI 153

———————— of Norfolk connected with Tucker .... IV 221

———————— of Whittimore Bleaklands co. Salop and of Shoreditch co. Middlesex .... III 495

———————— Wills proved at Stafford .... III 48

Niblett of Haresfield Colthrop in the psh of Standish co. Gloucester I 238

———————— of Haresfield and Standish co. Gloucester .... XX 202

Nicholas M.I. Shireborne Church co. Gloucester .... VI 114

———————— of West Horsley and Allcannings co. Wilts .... IV 256

Nicholl of Barham co. Kent connected with Barling .... IV 77

Nicholls of South Weald co. Essex, Maltby co York, & of London XXI 134

———————— of Chaston connected with Bowles .... I 145

Nichols of New York connected with Middleton and Hardy .... II 244

Nicoll connected with Keck .... XVII 15

———————— Pym .... II 465

———————— of Ridgeway in Hendon .... III 137

Nicolson of Aversholme co. Cumberland .... I 239

Nigell of Borestall .... I 121

Noble of London from Boroughbridge in Westmorland .... II 192

———————— went from Carlisle in Cumberland to Ireland of Cadiz VIII 310

Noel connected with Allen .... I 518

———————— Ingram .... XXI 215

———————— Viscount Campden connected with Hickes .... XIX 240

Norbury, de, connected with de la Home .... I 441

———————— M.I. Minster Isle of Sheppey .... VI 125

Norden of Amsterdam and of London co. Middlesex .... XXI 184

Norfolk Duke of, connected with Standish & Bickerton .... XIV 24

———————————————— Vere and Tyndale .... X 124

———————— Howard Duke of .... XVI 64

———————————————— connected with Mortimer ...... XII 51

———————————————————— Stafford .... XVI 50

———————— Mowbray Duke of Stafford .... XVI 50

Norreys of Prestbury co. Gloucester and of Reynham co. Kent XIX 152

Norris of Speak co. Lancaster M.I. .... XIV 9

———————— of . . . . near Canterbury and of . . . . near Deal co. Kent .... III 205

North of Mildenhall Laxfield co. Suffolk .... I 552

———————— of Walkeringham co. Nottingham, London co. Middlesex, Everton co. Nottingham, Lord North. XXI 3

———————— of Walkeringham co. Nottingham .... XXI 319

Northcote of Buckerell co. Devon .... XV 70

Northey connected with Jol .... XVI 30

Northleigh of Peamore co. Devon .... II 420

Northmore of Cleeve co. Devon .... VIII 302

Northumberland Earl of .... XIV 19

———————————————— connected with Bedingfield ...... V 319

———————————————————————— Stafford .... XVI 50

Northumberland Earls of   VIII 251
——————————————————————————————   VIII 254
———————————————— connected with Talboise   II 455
North Weald Basset co. Essex extracts from Registers   VI 335
Northwoode of Northwoode in the psh of Midleton near
    Sittingborne co. Kent and of Leckhampton co. Gloucester
    afterwards Norwood   XIX 209
Norton connected with Walker   XXI 111
——————— of Coventry connected with Hanson   IV 268
——————— of East Tisted co. Hants and of Southwick co. Sussex
    see also Norton of Shoreham   V 459
——————— of Mincly, Bath co. Somerset, and of Charlton VIII 434
——————— of Norton Conyers and of Allesley near Coventry co.
    Warwick   VIII 537
——————— of Old Alresford co. Hants and of Southwick co.
    Sussex   VII 398
——————— of Purton co. Wilts connected with Dore   VII 467
——————— of Shoreham, Chichester, Broadwater, Southwick and
    Hangleton co. Sussex, connected with Bridges and Hall   I 62
——————— of Williamsburg in Virginia connected with Walker IV 220
Norwood connected with Rogers   I 99
——————— see Northwoode   XIX 209
Notley of Chillington co. Somerset   I 366
Nott of London co. Middlesex Bradon co. Wilts Obden co.
    Worcester and of Minty co. Gloucester   XIX 88
——————— of Sheldesley Beauchamp co. Worcester connected
    with Walshe   XVIII 12
——————— of Worcester connected with Hodgetts   IV 497
Nottidge of Booking co. Essex   VII 22
Nottingham of Cirencester co. Gloucester   XX 153ᵃ
Nourse of Chilling Place Woodeaton co. Oxon, Milton co. Bucks,
    Weston under Penyard co. Hereford and of Porters Place in
    the psh of Newent co. Gloucester   XIX 243
——————— of Longhope co. Gloucester connected with Yate V 20
Novel Novell of London co. Middlesex, Hillington, and Northwold
    co. Norfolk   XIII 59
Novell see Novel
Nowell Lord of Read and a 3rd part of Harwood connected with
    Fitton   XXI 263
——————— M.I. in Bracon Ash Church co. Norfolk   VI 120
——————— of Gawthroppe Read and Manchester co. Lancs III 43
Noy of Carnonton co. Cornwall connected with Davies   II 72
——————— of Carnonton connected with Davies and Sandes II 443
Noye of Burian co. Cornwall   VI 380
Noyes of Marlborough co. Wilts and of London co. Middˣ   III 240
Noyse of Bristol connected with Chamberlain   XIII 106
Nugent connected with Cusack   XIV 13
——————— Count, Marquis de Valdesotto, of Vienna in Austria
    connected with Brangwin   XVIII 39
——————— Knight and Baronet   I 242

Nugent of Mount Nugent near Chesham co. Bucks connected
    with Blake   III 256
Nurse of Frocester co. Gloucester   XX 243^a, 245^a
Nutt of London co. Middlesex connected with Hawkins and
    Woolball   XX 49^c
———————— of Marshals in Maresfield in Sussex   XXI 173
Nutting of Cambridgeshire went to Cambridge in New England,
    of Halifax Nova Scotia, Spanish Town West Indies, Salem,
    Georgia, Reading, Waterton co. Middlesex New England
    and of Medford   III 374
Nycholas of Prestbury co. Gloucester   XIX 229

O

Oades of Mountsmere   XXI 159^b
——————————————— co. Southampton and of London   VII 306
——————————————— London co. Middlesex Reading co. Berks
    and of Rotherhithe   I 243
Oakes connected with Tyrell   IX 89
———————— of Chester Portsmouth co. Hants and of London
    Middlesex   IV 312
Oatridge connected with Corke   XX 177
———————— of Coaley co. Gloucester connected with Wilkins   XX 245
———————— of Doughton in the psh of Tetbury co. Gloucester
    connected with Mathews   V 306
———————— of London Whitechapel and Poplar co. Middlesex   II 310
———————— of Tetbury co. Gloucester connected with Matthews   III 192
O'Brien Catherine Lady   IX 16
O'Callaghan of Dromnine co. Cork – note as to arms and pedigre   VIII 200
———————— or O'Callahan   XII 54
O'Callahan see O'Callaghan
O'Carrol connected with Jervoise   IX 112^b
O'Carroll of the Kingdom of Ireland connected with Jervoise and
    Clarke   VIII 45
Ochterlony connected with Fancourt   II 475
Ockold of Upton St Leonard co. Gloucester and of the Ford in the
    psh of Lanmartine co. Monmouth   XIX 249
O'Connor went from the County of Limerick to Carrick Foyle in
    Jamaica and so named his estate   VIII 118
Odell in the psh of Hanover in the Island of Jamaica connected with
    Hough   III 271
Odwell of Epping co. Essex and of Deptford co. Kent connected
    with Chandler   IV 198

Offaley Gerald Lord   XIII 1
Offwood of Hepworth connected with Persey & Fiske   IV 140
Ogden connected with Bradford   V 92
Ogdin ———————————   IX 110
Ogle connected with Morse   IV 126
————— Cuthbert Lord   XXI 11
————— M.I. St Nicholas Church Newcastle upon Tyne   VII 377
————— of Cawsey Park   I 281
O'Hara formerly Hamilton of Port Glenone and of Crebilly co.
    Antrim   XI 28–33
————— of Crebilly co. Antrim   XI 28
Okeden of Heyley co. Northumberland connected with
    Butterworth and Chadwyk   XI 27
————— of Mere Crickell co. Dorset connected with Parry   I 296
Okes of Bedford connected with Butcher   VIII 367
Okewold of Sudgrove and of Oddington co. Gloucester   XX 92
Oldesworth of Pultons Court co. Gloucester connected with Porter   X 69
—————————————————————————————   XIX 158
————— Oldisworth of Halifax in Yorkshire, Fairford, Bradley
    in the psh of Wotton under Edge co. Gloucester   XIX 125
————— Oldisworth of Halifax co. York Pultons Court Wotton
    under Edge co. Gloucester, London co. Middlesex, and of
    Taceford   VIII 379
————— Oldisworth of Wootton under Edge, Bradley, and of
    Coln Rogers co. Gloucester   XX 83
Oldfield of Rotherhithe connected with Newton   III 495
Oldham of Crumpsall co. Lancaster and of Jamaica connected with
    Heywood   III 457
Oldisworth see Oldesworth
Oliffe of Shipton Olive and of Bristol co.Gloucester   XIX 85
Olive connected with Cutler   XIX 118
Oliver connected with Bellingham   XXI 86
————————————— Hall   XXI 318
O'Neale Earl of Tirreon Baron of Dungannon connected with
    Fitzgerald   XIII 3
Onslow Onslowe of Knole, West Clandon co. Surrey, and of
    Plymouth   I 209
————— Onslowe of West Clandon co. Surrey, Warnham and
    Dnegwick co. Sussex   IV 246
————— Onslowe of Knoll West Clandon co. Surrey   VI 6
Onslowe see Onslow
Orbye co. Lincoln connected with Willoughby   XIV 19
Orchard connected with Cary   VIII 248
Ord connected with Dixon   X 144
————— of Sedgfield, Gateshead co. Durham, and of London
    co. Middlesex   I 313
————— of Weston New Biggin, Longridge, Hare Street
    Buntinford co. Herts, Staple Inn co. Middlesex, and of
    Madras   I 311
Orfeur lord of the Manor of Plumbland   V 326
—————————————————————— co. Cumberland co.

Wexford in Ireland connected with Howard and Palliser   VII 95

Orme connected with Walden   IV 128

———————————————————————————————   XVI 13

——————— of Peterborough   I 571

Ormerod of Foxtones co. Lancaster descended from Ormerod of
     Ormerod connected with Pilkington   IV 313

Ormond Butler Earl of – will –   IX 161

Orton of Orton on the Hill co. Leicester and of Holt Hall near
     Tamworth co. Warwick   III 54

Osbaldeston Bishop of Carlisle   XXI 234

Osbaldiston of Chadlington and Woodstock co. Oxon connected
     with Ockold   XIX 249

Osborn connected with Angell and Collin   I 75

——————— of London co. Middlesex   XI 55

Osborne connected with Byng   X 59

——————— Duke of Leeds Baron Conyers by descent   VIII 469

——————————————————— connected with Danvers   VI 208

——————— of Brenchley near Maidstone and of Horsemonden co.
     Kent   I 297

——————— of Carleton co. Suffolk connected with Shribb   V 300

——————— of Derby   VI 1

——————— of Purleigh, Tyld Hall co. Essex, Cricksand Abbey co.
     Bedford, and of Aldern Cross, Governor of New York, and
     of the Castles of Jersey and Guernsey   VII 299

——————— of Stoke Prior co. Hereford and of Carmarthen   VIII 29

——————— of Swiss Hole and August Holes, Horsemonden and of
     Littesden co. Kent   VIII 1

Ostrich als Austrye see Austry   XX 34

Oteby connected with Smyth   VI 94

Other or Othera, a Baron of England   XIII 4

Othera or Other ———————————   XIII 4

Otley of St Kitts and of London co. Middlesex   IV 263

Ottley of Antigua connected with Payne   IV 170

Ougan of Silveyn co. Somerset connected with Morgan   VIII 181

Oughton connected with Baber   I 27

Outlawe of Lawlshall and Little Wychingham co. Somerset
     connected with Gooch   XXI 253

Ovens of Bristol and of Binfield co. Berks, afterwards Elliott   II 466

Overbury of Cheltenham co. Gloucester   XX 177[a]

——————— of Gotherington in the psh of Bishops Close, Charlton
     Kings, Cheltenham, Westbury upon Severn co. Gloucester,
     connected with Withorne   II 334

Overend of Langdale connected with Thornborrow   XXI 89[b]

Overton connected with Warner   VIII 246

Owen ap Meredith ap Tuder called Owen Tuder   XIV 19

——————— connected with Lister   IV 101

——————— Glendour of Wales connected with Scudamore   XVIII 57

——————— M.I. at Morley co. Derby   VI 108

——————— of Cesn connected with Jones of Hendre   VII 255

——————— of Coalston near Croydon, afterwards of Reigate,
     Southwark co. Surrey, and of London co. Middlesex   III 310

Owen of Condover co. Salop connected with Kynaston — XVIII 115
————— of Glassallt co. Carmarthen Grays Inn co. Middlesex
and of Bath co. Somerset — VII 56
————— of Hurley and of Baxterley co. Warwick connected
with Orton — III 55
————— of Llanekyn in Merionethshire — II 355
————— of Llunillo co. Montgomery and of Woodhouse co.
Salop — VII 367
————— of Llunload co. Montgomery and of Woodhouse co.
Salop — XII 1–6
————— of Woodhouse co. Salop connected with Hatchet — II 280
————————————————————————— Hunt — XVIII 35
—————————————————————————————— V 74

Oxford connected with Fiott — III 180
————— de Vere Earl of connected with Scrope — XX 18
————— Earl of, connected with Trussel and Tyndale — X 124
————— Harley Earl of — XVI 30
————— Walpole Earl of connected with Rolle — IX 114
Oxley of Norwich co. Norfolk connected with Bell — III 314
Oynion connected with Baynham — XIII 100

P

Packe connected with Randulph — X 109, 112
Packer of Cheltenham co. Gloucester connected with Gibbes — VII 426
———————————————————————————— XIX 189
————— of Little Dean co. Gloucester — XX 68
————— of Shillingford Donnington Castle Co. Berks and of
Little Sodbury co. Gloucester connected with Stephens — VII 135
Packwood connected with Baylie and Norton — VIII 537
Padman of London co. Middlesex connected with Whitworth — III 452
Page M.I. Chester St Peter's Church — XIV 9
————— of Ramsgate connected with Matthews — IV 230
Pagenham connected with Clement — XIV 18
Paget or Pagett of Chipping Norton co. Oxon and of Bradon co.
Somerset — XVI 1
Pagett see Paget
Pain Paine connected with Healey — XIII 112
Paine of Stroud co. Gloucester — III 426
————— see Pain
Painsett of Castle Cary co. Somerset and of London co. Middx — IX 107
Pakenham of Lordington in Sussex connected with Sidney — XVI 95–6
Palgrave of Norwood, Barmingham, Lauringsete, and of Hackford
co. Norfolk — V 393

Palliser of Newby Super Wiske, North Deighton, Kirkby Wyske
    co. York, Porto Bello co. Wexford in Ireland, Vache co.
    Bucks, Askham co. Nottingham, and of Greenwich
    Hospital co. Kent   VII 96
Palmer connected with Hunt   IV 479
————————————————————————— XVIII 36
————————— Taylor and Whaley   VIII 529
————— le Palmer of Morton in the Marsh, Bourton on the Hill
    co. Gloucester, Compton, Scorphin Blockley co. Worcester,
    & of Kirk Hallom co. Derby   XIX 74
————————— M.I. in Bracon Ash Church co. Norfolk   VI 120
————————— in Worcester Cathedral   XIV 9
————————— of Dorney Court co. Bucks connected with Jennyns,
    see Palmer of Wingham   III 110
————————— of Great Chelsea co. Middlesex connected with
    Danvers   VI 206
————————— of Knowle co. Warwick and of Worcester   IV 320
————————— of London co. Middlesex   IV 374
————————————————————————— VII 404
————————— of Wanlip co. Leicester   IX 67
————————— of Wingham co. Kent, and Dorney Court co. Bucks –
    Earl of Castlemaine   XIII 60
————————— of Winthorpe and of Alvingham Abbey co. Lincoln
    connected with Halton & Rawlinson   XIII 11
Palmes of Nayborne   XXI 152
Palser connected with Sparks Brockenborough and Cox   VIII 398
Pansum of Forthampton co. Gloucester   III 68
Panton of Newmarket   IV 339
Pantulph Baron of Wem connected with Boteller   XIX 90
Papil connected with Jol   XVI 30
Papillion connected with Steere   IV 213
Papillon ———————————   III 327
Pardo connected with Dennis   XIX 157
Pardoe connected with Thon   IX 1
Pargiter of Lichfield extracts from will   VIII 314
Parham connected with Coel extract from Register   X 67
Park Parke connected with Ludwell   VII 333
————————————————————————— XXI 155
————————— of Wisbech in the Island of Ely connected with Sandis   XXI 16
Parke of Dibden co. Hants   I 283
————————— of Warton co. Northumberland connected with
    Thirlwall   III 489
————————— see Park
Parker connected with Fonnereau and Rogers   IX 61
————————— Gardner   V 222
————————— Mucklow   XIX 155
————————— Whinyates   I 153
————————— formerly Field of Moorhouse Hill in the psh of
    Hesketh in the Forest co. Cumberland   I 170
————————— of Coldbeck co. Cumberland connected with
    Smithson   VIII 464

Parker of Elkin Coates co. Lancaster, descended from Bron-
　　　sholme co. York, of London co. Middlesex, and of
　　　Waltham Holy Cross co. Essex   I 300
───────── of Gosport connected with Gazelee   II 290
───────── of Heaning in the psh of Staidburn & of Halifax   XVII 66
───────── of Heytesbury in Wilts and of Wadden in the psh of
Croyden co. Surrey   XXI 10
───────── of Honington co. Warwick and of Talton co. Worcester   XIII 28
───────── of Ipswich removed to Reigate co. Surrey of London
co. Middlesex, co. Cambridge and of Whaddon connected
with Hammond   III 196
───────── of Newtown co. Tipperary   XIII 15
───────── of North Molton Burrington Boringdon Saltram
Blagdon Sidmouth co. Devon Whiteway in the psh of
Chidleigh and Teale Monochorum   I 427
───────── of Notgrave Northleach and of Hasfield co. Gloucester   XIX 37
───────────────── co. Gloucester, Hasfield and of Montburye
co. Hereford   X 7
───────── of Park Hall co. Stafford connected with Roberts   V 213
───────── of Park Hall co. Stafford Earl of Macclesfield Viscount
Parker   XXI 170
───────── of Parkhill in the psh of Caverswell, Leche Almington
co. Stafford, Parwich, Norton Lees co. Derby, Viscount
Parker and Earl of Macclesfield   IX 102
───────── of Sheffield co. York   VI 170
───────── of Youghal co. Cork and of Sandbach co. Chester   VIII 224
───────── or Grimes – arms to be taken by Bourke   XIII 15
Parkes of Yoxall Tutbury co. Stafford & Sudbury co. Derby   III 4
Parmenter of Exeter connected with Vouler   III 360
Parnell of Penalt co. Monmouth, Thornbury, Bristol, Hampton in
　　　the psh of Almondsbury, Horseley and of Kingswood co.
　　　Gloucester   I 528
───────── of Winchelsea co. Sussex connected with Matthews   IV 230
Parr of Exeter and of Silverton co. Devon   VII 438
Parrett connected with Leach   IX 101
Parrott of Sandbach   X 165
Parry afterwards Hodges of Easton Gray, Salisbury Malmesbury
　　　co. Wilts, and of London co. Middesex   I 476
───────── afterwards Hodges of Salisbury, Easton Gray co.
Wilts, and of Monmouth   VI 228
───────── afterwards Hodges of Easton Gray co. Wilts   VI 383
───────── connected with Evans   VIII 457
───────────────── Webley   XX 237
───────── M.I. in Bracon Ash Church co. Norfolk   VI 120
───────── of Easton Gray co. Wilts, Baptisms   VI 289
───────── of Llandevaglogy co. Brecon connected with St John   I 25
───────── of London co. Middlesex, & of Town Malling Kent   III 173
───────── of Malmesbury co. Wilts   VI 234
───────── of Pwllaylog co. Flint, Llanrhaider co. Denbigh
Crichell co. Dorset, and of Calcutta   I 295

Parry of Shabery Edgeburton co. Salop, High Wycombe co.
    Bucks and of London co. Middlesex connected with Bibbee   IV 63
Parslow of Frocester co. Gloucester connected with Wilkins   XX 245
———— of Over, Dowle, Cowley, Cam, Morton in Thomb,
    and of Jamaica West Indies   XVI 14, 15
Parsons connected with Higford   VIII 427
————————————————————————   VIII 440
————————————————————————   XX 160[a]
———— of Kemerton co. Gloucester and of the City of
    Worcester   XX 180[a]
———— of Lymington, afterwards of Portsmouth co. Hants
    and of Chichester co. Sussex   III 431
———— of Northampton, Boveney and of Langley co. Bucks   VI 71
Parterich of the Isle of Ely   II 25
Partherick connected with Beale   IV 478
————————————————————————   XVIII 36
Partington of London co. Middlesex   XX 156
Pascale, de, Marquis, connected with Frampton   I 452
Paston came from France 3 years after the Conquest, of Paston,
    Berningham co. Norfolk, and Horton co. Gloucester, Earl
    of Yarmouth, Viscount Yarmouth   IX 113[b]
———— connected with le Groos   VII 503
———— of Appleton connected with Brough   XXI 285
———— of Barningham co. Norfolk and of St Omers   VI 370
———————————————————— connected with Compton
    and Townley   XIV 22
———— of Barningham co. Norfolk connected with Eyre   I 322
———————————————————————— Sheldon   III 331
Patrick of Burford co. Oxon and of London co. Middlesex   II 299
———— of Buriton co. Hants and of Lynch near Chichester co.
    Sussex   IV 211
Patten connected with Jackson   VIII 56
———————————— Peake and Weston   V 82
————————————————————————   XVIII 38
Paul connected with Hankey   II 162
———— of Ashton Keynes co. Wilts, and of Priory Place
    Wallingford co. Berks, formerly Tippetts, connected with
    Mathews   V 310
———— of Braywick connected with Fane Earl of Westmorland,
    and Dashwood   XXI 288
———— of Kings Stanley co. Gloucester connected with Peach   I 272
———— of Warnborough co. Wilts   XIII 120
Paulet connected with Popham   III 234
Paulett of Frefoulke co. Southampton connected with Andrews
    and Walshe   XVIII 12
Paull of North Petherton co. Somerset, Blackdown, Burnstock
    Grange co. Dorset, and of Exeter co. Devon   XX 178
Paulyn als Pollen descended from a family of that name in the
    County of Lincoln, of London co. Middlesex, Andover co.
    Hants, and of Little Bookham Surrey   V 154

Pauncefoot or Pauncefote of Hasesfield Preston co. Gloucester, Morton co. Wilts, London co. Middlesex, Wisham co. Lincoln, Early Court Reading, and of Bromyard co. Hereford   XIII 113

Pauncefort connected with Whitworth   XX 242[a]

Pauncefote of Hasfield, Pauntley, and of Newent Glosc.   XIX 99

———— see Pauncefoot

Pavey connected with Crane and Lovell   XIII 72

Pawlet connected with Jervoise   IX 112[b]

———— Marquis of Winchester   XIV 16

Payler formerly Turner of Heden co. Kent   VI 180

———— of Nun Monkton co. York, connected with Cressener and Tufnell   XI 3, 9

Payne connected with Angell   I 82, XI 55

———————— Willett   VII 1, 85

———————— Stodart   IV 518

———— of Antigua St Kitts Leeward Islands, and of London   IV 170

———— of Lagscheath, and Monks Hill, East Grinstead, and of Lewes Newick co. Sussex   IV 167–9

———— of Rodborough co. Gloucester   XIX 193

———— of the Island of St Christopher in the West Indies, Tempsford Hall in the psh of Tempsford Beds.   X 100

Peach connected with Cocks als Cox   II 98

———— co. Derby, Bristol Chalford, Woodchester, Minchin Hampton co. Gloucester, London co. Middlesex, and of Westbury co. Wilts   I 269

———— of Chalford, Woodchester, Bristol, Redborough co. Gloucester, and of Westbury co. Wilts   XIX 224

———— of Trysall and Seisdon co. Stafford, connected with Pudsey   IX 87

Peachey of Kirdford Petworth Rape near Arundel co. Sussex, Shipton Solers co. Gloucester, Shipton Olyffe, and of Gombroon   I 71

Peacock extract from Register   XVI 80

———— of Whitehall co. Durham and of London co. Middx   II 368

Peacocke connected with Dacre   III 177

Peak of Bowden co. Chester connected with Weston   V 82

———————————————————— XVIII 38

Peake connected with King   XVII 12

———— of Llyng Greene and of London co. Middlesex   IV 284

———— see Peak

Peal of Darlington co. Durham Rector of Ashley cum Silverley, Vicar of Kirtling co. Cambridge, Letters Patent conferring the Order of St Stanislaus   VIII 280

Pearce of Barbadoes connected with Hawley   VIII 452

———— of Barkeley co. Gloucester   XX 143[a]

———— of London co. Middlesex, and of Fort Limerick in Ireland   IV 475

———— of London co. Middlesex and of Ireland   XVIII 32

———— of Staverton co. Gloucester   VIII 429

Pearce of Tortworth co. Gloucester connected with Bell   XX 165[a]
————— of Wotten under Edge co. Gloucester   III 525
Pearch of Shoreham in Kent connected with Munn   III 23
Pearson connected with Hodgetts   IV 493
————— of Wakefield co. York   III 41
Peart of Grassington co. York   III 490
————— of London co. Middlesex afterwards Scrope   VII 498
Pease connected with Clifford   XI 40, 41
————————— Norton and Morgan   IX 6
————— of Leeds co. York and of London co. Middlesex   XXI 195
Peat letters as to the Order of St Stanislaus   XV 52
————— of Hull co. York, Darlington co. Durham Rector of
    Buxton and of Chelmerton co. Derby   VIII 167
Peche connected with Paston   IX 113[b]
Peckham of Little Green in the psh of Compton co. Sussex,
    connected with Phipps and Bettine   II 218
Pederton of Hardingham connected with Bamfield   XIX 96
Peers afterwards Symons of London and Hammersmith co.
    Middlesex   II 191
————— connected with Ellis   V 86
Pegg connected with Walker   III 143
Pegge connected with Strelley   XXI 323
————— of St Ives co. Huntingdon connected with Fortune   II 268
Peiarce of Calcutta in Bengal connected with Shiris   I 248
Peighan of Newcastle upon Tyne connected with Reed   X 137
Peirson of Grays Inn co. Middlesex and of Cheam co. Surrey
    connected with Grave   XIX 29
————— of Moulthorpe Grange co. York   VII 185
Pelham connected with Byne   IX 69
————— of Cottesford in Sussex connected with Woodward   XIX 241
————— of Crowhurst Sussex, and of Deptford co. Kent   IV 7
Pell of Gayton and Topham co. Lincoln   I 285
Pemberton of Darlington co. Durham connected with Killinghall   VII 275–7
Pembroke, Herbert Earl of, connected with Gam   XX 160
————— Mareshal Earl of, Lord Marshal, surnamed from his
    Office, connected with Poulton   XVI 18
Pembruge of Maunsel Gamage, Wellington co. Hereford,
    Maismore and Corse co. Gloucester   XIX 84
Pendarves connected with Trelawney   XVIII 7
————————————————— and Bassett   III 255
Pendrell of Walsall co. Stafford, Hubbold Grange in the psh of
    Tong co. Salop, and of London co. Middlesex   II 260–1
Penfold of Rodborough co. Gloucester   XX 187
Penn connected with Smyth   IV 264
Penneck of Gulwall co. Cornwall connected with Wroughton   II 8
Penning M.I. in Thurston Church co. Norfolk   VI 118
Pennington connected with Huddleston   XXI 23
————— Lord Moncaster of the Kingdom of Ireland   I 344
————— M.I.   XIV 9
————— of Kendal co. Westmorland   XXI 121

Penny connected with Dawbeny	III 329
	XVIII 67
——————————————— Urry	III 388
Pennyman of Ormesby co. York – took the name of Warton	VI 138
Penoyre of the Town of the Hay co. Brecon of the Moore in the psh of Clifford als Llandarne y Boyn co. Hereford connected with Garnons and Prosser	II 489
Penrhyn Lady	XVII 9
Penrose of Menacon Stonehouse Plymouth co. Devon, Hatfield co. Herts, Penrose co. Cornwall, Newbury co. Berks, Beckington cum Standerwick co. Somerset, and of the Island of Scilly	II 226
Penry of Brecon co. Brecon connected with St John	I 25
Penton of Winchester connected with Gulston & Simmons	XV 10
Percival of Huncenby near Penrith, Little Selkirk co. Cumberland, and of Appleby co. Westmorland	III 183
——————— of Northampton connected with Marriott	XVII 31
——————— of Royton Liverpool co. Palatine Lancaster	XIV 1
Percivall of London co. Middlesex and Hawarden co. Flint descended from the Percivalls of co. Somerset	IV 466
Percivel extract from register	XVI 80
Percy connected with Bedingfield	V 319
——————————— Throckmorton	VII 341
——————— Earl of Northumberland connected with Stafford	XVI 50
——————— origin of Name	XXI 118
Perfect of Pontefract	III 307
Perith connected with Dixon and Marley	X 143
	X 72
Perkins connected with Smith	VI 365
——————— of Caistor co. Lincoln and of London co. Middlesex	II 158
——————— of Monks Kirby co. Warwick, Bitchby, Orton on the Hill co. Leicester, Killingsbury co. Northampton, and of Blounts Hall near Uttoxeter co. Stafford	III 508
——————— of Monks Kirby co. Warwick, Orton co. Leicester, and of Bithby	XVIII 28
——————— of Pilston co. Monmouth	I 29
——————— of Richmond co. Surrey, Twickenham Staines co. Middlesex, connected with Aspeley	IV 422
——————— of Ufton Court co. Berks, Richmond co. Surrey, Staines Twickenham co. Middlesex, and of Sidmouth co. Devon	VII 83
——————— of Upton Court and of Richmond	VIII 311
	VIII 313
Perron als Credy connected with Mallet	VII 75
Perrot als Wickham	VIII 240
	XIX 94
——————— connected with Champneis	XIX 94
——————— of Amersham co. Bucks, Norleigh and Fawler co. Oxon, and of the Middle Temple co. Middlesex	XXI 7
Perry als Hunter of Wootton under Edge co. Gloucester	XIX 13
——————————————————— Winterbourne, Henbury co.	

Gloucester, and of London co. Middlesex   XX 150
―――――― als Hunter of Wotton under Edge co. Gloucester
connected with Fenn   XIV 23
―――――― connected with Barnesley   XXI 204
―――――― of Gloucester, Baynton and Warminster co. Wilts   XIX 234
―――――― of Turvil Heath co. Bucks connected with Barnesley   XIX 22
―――――― of Winterbourne co. Gloucester connected with Marsh   III 99
―――――― William   XIII 111
Persall als Peshall   XVI 19
Persey of Norton co. Suffolk connected with Fiske   IV 140
Pert of Arnolds co. Essex connected with Forster   XXI 250
Peshall als Persall of Horsley in the psh of Eccleshall, Canwell and
    Sugnal co. Stafford, also of Halne or Hawne in the psh of   XVI 16, 17,
    Hales Owen co. Salop   19.
Peters of Canterbury co. Kent, and of Bethnal Green co.
    Middlesex, connected with Barling   IV 77
―――――― see Petre
Petre Baron Petre of Writtle, West Hornden, Cranham Stanford
    Rivers and Margaretting co. Essex   XXI 141
―――――― Peters of London co. Middlesex, Boston New
    England, Andover co. Hants and of Hebron in Connecticut   III 322
Pettat connected with Hyde and Knight   XX 187
Pettigrew of Mount Malick in Ireland connected with Strangman   IV 68
Pettit of Bayn co. Salop connected with Kinardsley   XXI 308
―――――― of London co. Middlesex connected with Andrews   II 226
―――――― of York connected with Fleming   X 151
Pettiward of Bury St Edmunds co. Suffolk, London co. Middlesex,
    and of Putney co. Surrey   II 470
Petty connected with Baber and Keck   XVII 15
――――――――――――― Bray   XX 54
―――――― of Otford co. Kent, connected with Bell   XX 67
―――――― of Strickland near Kendall co. Westmorland, and of
    London co. Middlesex   I 390
―――――― Viscount Fitzmaurice   XIII 2
Peverell connected with Hungerford   V 49
―――――――――――――――――――――――――――――――――――――――   V 237
―――――――――――――――――――――――――――――――――――――――   XIX 204
―――――― Lord of Hatfield Peverell in Essex, Lord of Brun co.
    Cambridge   VIII 52
Peyton M.I. in Bracon Ash Church co. Norfolk   VI 118
―――――― of Knowlton co. Kent connected with Osborn   VII 302
Phaer of North Walton co. Norfolk and Kilgarron co. Pembroke
    connected with Jenkins   III 399
――――――――――――― and Vaughan   XVIII 16, 17
Phettiplace or Fhittyplace connected with Unton   XVI 51
Philip King of France connected with Edward I with Holland and
    Hookes   XVIII 105
―――――― III le Hardy connected with Stafford   XVI 50
Philipps of Picton Castle co. Pembroke, Baronet 1621, Governor
    of Nova Scotia   IX 105
Philips connected with Bowles   I 141

Philips connected with Jol and Thynne .... XVI 30
———————— of Bisley co. Gloucester .... XX 179
Philipson of Halling Hall Calgarth Thawterden Hall co. Westmor-
    land and of Cunnyshed co. Palatine Lancs. .... XXI 100
———————— of Swaterden co. Westmorland connected with Sandis .. XXI 15
Phillimore of London co. Middlesex .... VIII 382
Phillips of Astley co. Salop .... I 573
———————— of Brockton, Etherington, Bridgnorth co. Salop, and
    of London co. Middlesex .... III 92
———————— of Elsfield and of Headington co. Oxon .... IV 153
———————— of Lincolns Inn co. Middlesex, Putley co. Hereford,
    and of Gloucester .... I 273
———————— of Neston co. Chester connected with Walls .... I 49
———————— of Putley co. Hereford connected with Smith of
    Huntleys co. Hereford .... I 362
———————— of Riffhams Lodge in the psh of Danbury co. Essex .... XVII 1
———————— Robert – living 1797 .... VI 178
Philpot connected with Henry and Ashton .... IX 99
———————— of Vowchurch and Poston co. Hereford .... XIX 235
Phipps of Eton co. Bucks connected with Knott .... III 218
———————— of Evesham co. Worcester .... XX 230, 232
———————— Lord Chancellor of Ireland Lord Mulgrave .... II 146
———————— of Westbury co. Wilts connected with Peckham .... II 219
Pick of Ham in Berkeley Newnham and of Thornbury co.
    Gloucester .... XX 186ª
Pickering connected with Frederick .... IX 69
Pickersgill connected with Fothergill .... VII 239
Pierce of Canterbury connected with Halford .... III 73
———————— of the Devises Warminster co. Wilts, Bristol and
    Woodchester co. Gloucester .... XX 184
Pierrepont connected with Bayntun .... VIII 31
———————— Lord Pierrepont of Holm Pierrepont, Earl of Kingston
    upon Hull, Marquess of Dorchester .... XVIII 124–9
Pierson connected with Langdale .... I 396
———————— formerly Repinder .... I 396
Piester connected with Forterie .... XVIII 143
Pigot of Chetwynd co. Salop .... I 507
———————— of Lee Chapel and of Grays Throck co. Essex,
    connected with Button .... VII 307
Pike connected with Wiltshire and Greene .... IX 142
Pile of Winchester connected with Smith of Alton .... IV 173
Pilkington connected with Ayscough .... I 147
———————— lord of Pilkington, of Wigan, Rivington co. Lancs,
    Bradley, Nether Bradley co. York, Stanley Would Newton,
    Northcotes and Howerby co. Lincoln .... V 166–73
———————— of Bridgenorth co. Salop .... VI 183
———————— of Lever, Horwich, Manchester, Preston co. Lancaster,
    and of Derby .... IV 314
Pincerna afterwards Boteller .... XIX 90
Pinchback of Wisbich St Peter in the Isle of Ely .... VIII 461

Pincheon or Pinchon connected with Weston   XI 12–15
Pinchon see Pincheon
Pinckney of South Caroloina America   I 522
Pindar of Wellingborough co. Northampton, Southwell co. Nottingham, and of Edenshaw co. Chester, connected with Powell and Hurlestone   V 65
———————— of Wellingborough co. Northampton and of Southwell co. Notts connected with Powell and Steers   XVIII 120
Pinfold connected with Wild   IX 142
Pink of London co. Middlesex Kempshott, Ottenden and of Sharsted co Kent connected with Alured   I 498
———————— of Otterden Sharsted co. Kent and of Middlesex   I 184
Pinkerton connected with Burgess   XV 45
———————— of Markinch afterwards Drummond of Hawthornden   I 256
Pinnell Rector of Ducklington co. Oxford connected with Stonestreet   VIII 532
Pipard connected with de Lisle   VIII 255
Pipe of Bilton co. Stafford connected with Ducie   XX 106
Piper connected with Prowse   I 510
Pirke of Little Dean co. Gloucester connected with Colchester   XIX 153
Pirkes of Ledbury co. Hereford connected with Elton   XX 116[a]
Pitfield connected with Touchit   I 247
———————————— Walden   IV 129
Pitkin of Woolwich co. Kent connected with Thorowgood   IV 59
Pitman connected with Newte   I 320
———————— of Stow co. Gloucester connected with Alcock   VIII 432
Pitney of Shepton Mallet co. Somerset connected with Cooke   VI 168
———————— of Shepton Mallet co. Somerset connected with Martin   I 318
Pitot connected with Walker   III 353
    IV 98
Pitt lord of the Manor of Marden or Martherne co. Hereford and of Southwark co. Surrey   V 328
———————— of Bideford co. Devon and of London co. Middlesex   II 263
———————— Earls of Londonderry Earl of Chatham   X 160
———————— of Blandford co. Dorset Earls of Londonderry Earl of Chatham   X 62
———————— of Stratfieldsay co. Hants, London co. Middlesex and of Blandford co. Dorset   X 23, 159
Pitts of Kyre co. Worcester connected with Chamberlayne   XX 80[b,c]
Pix of Hawkhurst co. Kent Northeim co. Sussex and of London co. Middlesex   I 299
Plaister of Sotterley co. Suffolk connected with Tyrell   VIII 103
Plaistow see Plestow
Plantagenet of Woodstock Earl of Kent connected with Wake   VIII 252
———————— surnamed Woodstock Constable of England connected with Stafford   XVI 50
Playdell connected with Skerrett   I 161
———————— of Oxford and Swinbank co. Oxon   VII 359
Plestow or Plaistow, Watlington co. Norfolk, Banbury co. Oxon, and of London co. Middlesex   III 229

Pleydell als Wheler of Coleshill, Chipping Farringdon, Shrivenham
    Westcot co. Berks and of Chelworth in the psh of Crickdale,
    Hampton Turvill in the psh of Highworth, and of Mudghill
    co. Wilts   XIX 113, 114
————— connected with Bouverie and Stewart   XVIII 147
————————— Pratt   XXI 250
————— of Abingdon co. Berks   VII 357
————— of Estroud and Westbury co. Gloucester   XIX 112
————— of Holyrood and of Ampney co. Gloucester   XX 214
————— of Mughill co. Wilts connected with Bourchier   XIX 49
————— of Northmore co. Oxon and of the City of Gloucester   XIX 112
————— of Painswick co. Gloucester connected with Jones   XX 155[a]
Plomer connected with Elwes   III 248
————— of London co. Middlesex, Loucher in Garrington co.
    Oxon, and of Blakesware co. Herts   VI 28
Plowden of Lady Nelston near Ludlow   XXI 201
————— of Plowden co. Salop and of Shiplake co. Oxon   XXI 153
————————— connected with Stafford   IV 474
                                                                         XVIII 3

Plucknett connected with Dent   VII 479
Pluckwell M.I. St Nicholas Rochester   VI 125
Plumpton of Snaith, said to be descended from Plumpton of
    Plumpton, of Guiseley, Sproatley Everingham co. York,
    London co. Middlesex, North Witham co. Lincoln and of
    Jamaica West Indies   III 272
Plunket connected with Cusack   XIX 13
Plymley connected with Corbet and Flint   IV 515
————————— Flint   XVIII 135
                                                                         X 20

Pockley of Bradon co. York connected with Osbaldeston   XXI 234
Pocock Chaplin of Greenwich Hospital   XXI 132
————— connected with Barnesley   XXI 204
————— of Bright Waltham co. Berks, Danbury and Lash-
    ington co. Essex, Greenwich co. Kent, and of Long Ditton
    co. Surrey, also of Twickenham and of London co.
    Middlesex   VII 67
————— of Turvil Court co. Bucks connected with Barnesley   XIX 22
Poinz connected with Mallet   VII 397
Pole afterwards De la Pole of Shute, Colcombe in the psh of
    Culliton co. Devon, and of New England   I 234
————— of Radbourne co. Derby baptisms etc.   VI 264
————— of Shute, Colcombe in the psh of Colleton co. Devon   II 132
————————— co. Devon Baptisms etc.   VI 276
————— de la, connected with Handle and Rede   I 121
————————— see Pole
————— K.G. and Cardinal Pole connected with Stafford   XVI 50
————— Lord Montagu connected with Barrington   V 174
————— M.I. at Morley co. Derby   VI 109
————— of London co. Middlesex, Muggington and Bradbury
    co. Derby, co. Leicester, and co. Salop, connected with
    Clarke   I 5

Pole of Newborough, Radborne, and Dalbury Lees co.
    Derby   VIII 50
————— Sir William   VIII 115
Poley of Badley co. Suffolk connected with Croftes   IV 130
Poleyn of King's Weston co. Gloucester   XIX 102
Polhill connected with Cromwell and Ireton   XV 19
————————— Davys   I 149
————————— Frampton   VIII 426
————————— Ireton   IV 126
————— of London co. Middlesex and of Burwash co. Sussex   III 37
Poll connected with Thorold   X 76
Pollard of Newdigate co. Surrey connected with Dungate   IV 411
Pollen see Paulyn
Pollexsen of Mothecombe co. Devon connected with Hamlyn   II 286
————— of Wembury co. Devon connected with Davie   II 421
Pomfrey connected with Archdeacon   I 307
————————————————————————————————   XVI 69
————————————————————————————————   XXI 147
Ponsford of Stoke Canon co. Devon and of London co. Middlesex   II 367
Poole als Abraham of London co. Middlesex, Kingston in Jamaica,
    and of Poole   XVII 26
————— connected with Byne and Pelham   IX 69
————————— Lockey   II 294
————— de Pull, Pull of Poole in the County of Chester and of
    Paynswick   XIX 80
————— de St Poll connected with Stanton   X 69
————— of Chester South River co. Annandale in Maryland,
    Islington co. Middlesex and of co. Wilts   III 492
————— of Lynch's Estate in the Island of Antigua connected
    with Browne   VI 232
————— of Marley, Cholmondeley Chedle in Stockport co.
    Chester and of Woolden co. Lancaster   I 210
————— of Stretton Grantham co. Hereford   XVI 57
————— of Whitchurch near Edgeware co. Middlesex con-
    nected with Cuttel   IV 283
————— of Wirrall   I 351
Pooley of Hartest near Boxtead co. Suffolk connected with Butler   VI 204
Pope B. married to Winifred daughter of Barrington   IX 73
————— connected with Bell and Hayhurst   III 266
————————————— Creyghton   XIII 115
————————————— Keble   IV 258
————————————— Martin   VII 195
————— Roberts of Glastonbury   II 235
————— Earl of Downe M.I. in Shireborne Church co.
    Gloucester   VI 114
————— of Dodington, Wroxton co. Oxford, and of Little
    Compton co. Gloucester, Earl of Down in Ireland   XIX 21
Popham of Knebworth, Ragborough Wellington, Huntworth co.
    Somerset, Bernister, Church Stanton co. Devon, Littlecot,
    Mornington co. Wilts. Wincheser co. Hants and of Bourton
    on the Hill co. Gloucester   III 232

Popham of Huntworth Ragborough co. Somerset, Bernister co. Dorset, Littlecot co. Wilts, Winchester co. Hants, Bourton on the Hill co. Gloucester, and of the Temple co. Middlesex   XVIII 131
——————— of Huntworth co. Somerset Littlecot co. Wilts and of the City of Winchester   XIX 222
——————— of Wellington and Moncton co. Somerset   XX 113
Popkin of Forest in the psh of Llamsamlet and of Kettlehill co. Glamorgan connected with Lewes   I 404
——————— or Hopkin of the Forest   IX 91
Popley connected with Hollister   I 526
Porch connected with Ovens   II 466
Port formerly Newell   I 251
    I 241
——————— Sparrow   I 251
Port of Etwal co. Derby connected with Fitzherbert, and Gifford   XII 28–47
——————— of Ilam   IV 240
——————— of West Chester, Ilam in Epsdale co. Stafford, Canterbury co. Kent, and of Etwall co. Derby   I 249
Porter als Gloucester of Newark, Lanthony in the psh of Hempstead co. Gloucester, see Porter of Newark   XIX 158
——————— connected with Arnold and Denny   X 69
——————— Bennett and Cecil   XVII 34
——————— of Bolton in Aberdale and of Allerby co. Cumberland   XXI 34
——————— of Claynes co. Worcester connected with Scudamore   XVIII 60
——————— of Hoo, Horsemonnceaux co. Sussex and of Tunbridge co. Kent   I 289
——————— of London, Ham, and of Imber Court co. Surrey   I 301
——————— of Mickleton co. Gloucester connected with Keyt   XIX 57
——————— of Newark and Lantony co. Gloucester connected with Scudamore and Arthur, see Porter als Gloucester   XVIII 62
——————— of Scarborough connected with Cockerill   III 145
Portman connected with Popham   III 235
    XVIII 131
Portrey of Beverton co. Glamorgan connected with Aubrey   XX 1
——————— of Yniskedwyn co. Brecknock   XX 191
Portsmouth Earl of, connected with Fellowes   VIII 462
Pothan als Vlayd   V 443
Potter connected with Gardner and Venner   I 565
——————— Hudleston   V 349
——————— Yarde   III 506
——————— of Norton co. Suffolk, Thetford and Brettenham co. Norfolk connected with Gall and Fiske   IV 143
Pottinger of Mount Pottinger near Belfast in Ireland connected with Curwen or Culwen   II 461
Potts of Mottram Longdendale co. Chester, Stanwick co. Cumberland London co. Middlesex Saltwood near Hythe co. Kent Whitchurch co. Salop & of America   III 126
Poulton about the time of William the Conqueror, of Desborough co. Northampton   XVI 18
Powell als Symonds of Pengethley co. Hereford   VIII 373
——————— connected with Burrough   IV 176

Powell formerly Hinson   VI 29
———————————— Howell of St Albans co. Herts, Bocking
co. Essex, Egham Clapham Walworth co. Surrey, and of
London co. Middlesex   I 562
——————— Lord of Worthen connected with Higgons and Corbet
see Powell of Shrewsbury   V 64
——————— of Broadway co. Carmarthen connected with Pryce   II 221
——————— of Clapham co. Surrey Baptisms etc.   VI 275
——————— of Ednop co. Salop, Brampton Ralf co. Somerset,
Boughton Monchensy co. Kent and of London co. Middx   VI 4
——————— of Gloucester connected with Nourse   XIX 243
——————— of Hurdest co. Wilts connected with Priaulx   IV 482
————————————————————————————————————   XVIII 143
——————— of Llandiloe Grosenny co. Monmouth connected with
Smith of Huntleys co. Hereford   I 361
——————— of Penley co. Flint connected with Beddow   IV 357
——————— of Perthire co. Monmouth   IV 44
——————— of Priors Wood co. Hereford, Bristol co. Gloucester
Cadiz in Spain, and of Charles Town South Carolina   III 101
——————— of Shrewsbury and All Stretton co. Salop connected
with Higgons   V 64
——————— of Shrewsbury All Stretton co. Salop, Lord of
Worthen connected with Kynaston   XVIII 119
——————— of Tiddenham co. Gloucester connected with Warren   XX 252ᵃ
Power of Derbyshire or Bucks connected with Owen   III 54
——————— of Glashy in the Barony of Glencheragh co. Waterford
and of London co. Middlesex   IV 366
——————— of Kenelworth co. Warwick   III 22
——————— of the Island of Teneriffe connected with de Strickland   VII 296
——————— of Thackham in Sussex connected with Clothall and
Wiltshire   XXI 86
——————— of Teneriffe – list of his children   VIII 340
Powers of Coventry co. Warwick connected with Davis   II 375
Powis connected with Spence   IX 69
——————— Grey Lord connected with Vernon and Curson   III 276
——————— Lord connected with Brandon   XX 56ᵇ
Powle of Leominster, came from Quennington co. Gloucester,
connected with Wall   VIII 28
Powles of Redbroke in Newland co. Gloucester   XX 188
——————— of Ross Hereford connected with Elton   XX 116ᵃ
Powlet Lord Nassau   XVI 58
——————— M.I. in Hamildon Church co. Bucks   VI 124
——————— Marquess of Winchester of Artford co. Wilts   XIII 95
Powlett Marquess of Winchester connected with Ingoldesby and
Limbrey   VIII 12
Pownall connected with Majendie   I 347
Pownoll of Chatham connected with Roberts   II 235
Powys connected with Steyt   XX 209
Poyner connected with Kynaston and Powell   XVIII 120
Poynings connected with Paston   IX 113ᵇ
Poyntz Baron, of Corye Mallet connected with Mallet   VII 74

——————— of Iron Acton and Alderley co. Gloucester connected with Hale II 89

Poyser of Worthenbury co. Flint Lockwood in Staffordshire and Calver Hall co. Salop XXI 111

Prankard connected with Masters XVII 30

Pratt connected with Forster XXI 250

Pratt Sir Henry III 386

Precedence, question of. IX 15

Prescot connected with Blencow II 65

Prester connected with Forterie IV 481

Preston of Cricket Thomas co. Somerset connected with Hippisley II 419

——————— of Holker co. Lancaster connected with Benson XXI 78

——————————————————— M.I. XIV 4, 5, 7

——————— of Preston Patrick co. Westmorland XIV 23

——————————————— and Levens co. Westmorland connected with Carus VIII 319

——————— Viscount see Grahme III 511

——————————— Gormanston of Gormanston I 303

Prestwich went to Ireland with Oliver Cromwell I 298

Prettiman see Prettyman I 557

Prettyman of Lodington co. Leicester XXI 164

——————— or Prettiman connected with Bourchier I 557

Prewett connected with James XX 160

Priaulx of London co. Middlesex, Salisbury co. Wilts, Buckland co. Surrey, and of Southampton co. Hants IV 481

——————— of Southampton co. Hants and of London co. Middlesex, Archdeacon of Salisbury connected with Forterie XVIII 143

Price afterwards Price-Clarke of Scilly co. Cork in Ireland and of Chesterfield co. Derby, see Price of Chesterfield VIII 53

——————— connected with Cambell VI 76

——————— of Castle Frome co. Hereford and of Lewisham Kent IV 47

——————— of Chesterfield Sutton co Derby Scilly co. Cork connected with Clarke see Price afterwards Price Clarke I 6

——————— of Glen IV 215

——————— of Kanon y blane in psh of Clerow co. Radnor XXI 191

——————— of Maesyrom in Llangammarch co. Brecknock XX 189

Price of Rhiwlas, Towyn co. Merionethshire IV 254

——————— of the City of Gloucester XVII 42, 43

——————— Vicar of Llewgellen and of Cunnington X 58

——————— Viscount Hereford connected with Sandys I 434

Price-Clarke formerly Price VIII 53

Prichard connected with Watts IX 21

Pricket of Aldborough in Holderness co. York & of London II 327

Pride connected with Bladen I 67

Prideaux of Netherton co. Devon connected with Bayntun and Rolt VIII 31

——————— of Orcharton Adeston, Thewborrow, Salden Netherton co. Devon, London co. Middlesex, and of Ford V 439

Prilley connected with Sir Guy de Mancester & Waver IX 93

Primrose of Carrington, Viscount Primrose, connected with
    Montgomery   II 37
Prince of Swillington co. York and of London co. Middlesex
    connected with Allen   X 77
———— of Swillington co. York connected with Tetlow   X 92
Pringle of Richmond co. York connected with Thornborough   XXI 90
Prior see Pryor   XXI 242
Pritchard connected with Elton and Hall   I 109
———— of Stoke connected with Bonnor and Vaughan   VIII 431
Prius connected with Sutton   XVIII 27
Probyn formerly Hopkins of London co. Middlesex   XX 151
———— of Newland and of Great Dean co. Gloucester   XIX 40
Procter M.I.   VIII 44
———— of Ripon in Yorkshire connected with Turner of
    Totenhill   VIII 43
———— of Ripon co. York connected with Turner & Calver or
    Calvert   VIII 41
———— connected with Gascoign   VIII 538
———— of London co. Middlesex connected with Bibbee   IV 62
Proddy M.I.   XIV 8
Prosser connected with Bond   XX 51
———————————— Penoyre   II 489
Prout of Wickwar co. Gloucester   XX 145ᵃ
Prowse of Exeter Harford and of Dawlish co. Devon   I 510
Pruen of Cheltenham co. Gloucester   XX 185ᵃ
Prujean of Sutton Gate Essex   XXI 137
Prust als Hamlyn   XV 23
———— of Wolfardisworthy co. Devon and of the City of
    Winchester   XV 23
Pryce of Buckland co. Brecon & New Town Hall co. Montgomery   II 221
Prynce of Charlton Kings co. Gloucester connected with Stephens   VII 11, 5
Pryor connected with Gray and Walker   III 267
———— Prior of Anglesea   XXI 242
Pudsey connected with Dawson and Marsden see Pudsey of
    Weybridge   VIII 133
———— of Pudsey, Bolton in Craven, Bolton in Bolland,
    Lawfield, St Johns co. York, Tursell, Berford and Arnforth
    in Craven   II 430–435
———— of Seisdon in the psh of Trysal co. Stafford   IX 87
———— of Weybride co. Surrey came from Bolton Hall co.
    York, see Pudsey connected with Dawson & Marsden   VIII 131
Pugh connected with Evance   VIII 479
———————————— Scudamore   IX 22ᵇ
————————————————————————   XVIII 61
———————————————— Wright and Ware   II 240
———— formerly Coytmer   V 162
———— of Llangadvan co. Montgomery & London co.
    Middlesex   II 208
———— of Montgomery   XVI 83
Pujolas connected with Molloy   X 8

Pujolas connected with Williams   IX 41
Puleston connected with Edwards of Wales   XVIII 15
———————— of Emrall co. Flint   IV 72
Puliston of Cheshire, Emrall co. Flint, Havolywern and Berse co.
    Denbigh   XVIII 104
Pull de Pull see Poole   XIX 80
Pulleine connected with Babington   XVI 26, 37
———————— of Yorkshire connected with Collingwood   XIII 114
———————————————————————————————— and Biggs   X 136
Pullen of Lechlade co. Gloucester   XX 190
Pulley of Mamble co. Worcester, Bridgnorth co. Salop,
    Titherington, Wotton co. Gloucester, & of Leigh in Essex   XIX 213
———————— of Tumby connected with Everingham   IV 377
Pulleyne of Burley co. York connected with Hammond   III 355
Pulteney question of precedence   IX 15
Pulton of Eldersfield co. Worcester Hartpury and Newent co.
    Gloucester   XIX 44
Purchas of Whitton co. Hunts, London co. Middlesex, and of
    Fown-hope co. Hereford   III 418
Purefoy connected with Lewis   IX 93
———————— formerly Jervoise   I 175
Purnell of Kingshill co. Surrey connected with Small   II 95
———————————————— in the psh of Dursley, Wick in the psh of
    Berkeley, North Nibley, and of Stinchcombe co. Gloucester   XX 181–3
Purser of Northampton   XVII 31
Pury connected with Danvers   XIX 10
———————— of the City of Gloucester and of Taynton co.
    Gloucester   XIX 161
Pybas M.I. at Thirsk   VI 126
———————————————— of Thirsk co. York Dover co Kent Cheam co. Surrey
    and of Greenhill Grove co. Herts   VII 97
Pycroft of Queenhithe connected with London   III 107
Pye connected with Stephens   VII 136
———————— M.I.   X 65
———————— of Boyce in the psh of Dymock   IX 22
———————— of Farringdon and of Fismarsh co. Bedford   II 103
———————————————————— and Wadley co. Berks connected with
    Mainwaring   IV 329
———————— of Farringdon co. Berks connected with Walker   IX 20
Pyke connected with Wiltshire   XXI 321
Pym of London co. Middlesex, Linslade co. Bucks, Hasle Hall,
    Leighton Buzzard co. Bedford, Norton Bury, Baldock,
    Winmondley House, Hitchen co. Herts, and of Radwell co.
    Berks   II 464
Pyne connected with Marchant   VII 75
Pyrke formerly Watts   XX 255
———————— of Little Dean and of Bristol co. Gloucester   XX 255
———————————————— co. Gloucester connected with Walker   VIII 419
Pytot connected with Walker   I 435
Pywell of Alexton Hall co. Leicester connected with Hartop   XV 25

Q

Quarles lived in Essex, of Haverhill, Neyland co. Suffolk and of Foulsham co. Norfolk	III 38
Quarrington of Gloucester and of London co. Middlesex	II 332
Quayle of Castle Town and of Douglas in the Isle of Man	II 128
Quil of Whitechapel, Plaistow co. Middlesex, connected with Burnell	IV 56
Quin Richard Valentine Baronet	II 68

R

Radcliffe Radclyffe Ratcliffe Earls of Derwentwater	VIII 511
———————————————————————	XVI 32
———————————————————————	XXI 1
————— of Derwentwater co. Cumberland	XXI 13
————— of Dilston co. Northumberland connected with Tunstall	II 409
Radclyffe of Dilston co. Northumberland, Baron Tyndale, Viscount Radcliffe and Langley, Earl Derwentwater afterwards Earl of Newborough	XVI 32
Radford of Sheffield co. York connected with Gunning	IV 54
————— of Somerset and of Exeter co. Devon	III 25
————— of Whitchurch and of Tavistock co. Devon	VII 29
Rae of Edinburgh	XXI 206
Raikes of Kingston-upon Hull, Hessle co. York, Peterborough co. Northampton, Headon co. Nottingham, London and Neason co. Middlesex	I 163
————— Raykes extracts from Register	VII 225–37
Raincock connected with Fleming	X 151
Raine M.I.	XIV 8
Raines of London co. Middlesex and of Lewes co. Sussex connected with Stonestreet	VIII 531
Rainsford of Steverton co. Northampton	II 90
Rake of Penn and of Holcomb co. Somerset conneted with St Lo	IV 440
————— of Penn co. Somerset connected with St Lo	XVIII 10
Raleigh of Downton co. Wilts	VII 410
————— of West Horsley Tenchley Meer co. Surrey, and of London co. Middlesex, Sir Walter Raleigh	I 263
Ramsay formerly Burnett	XV 55

Ramsay of Balmain in the psh of Fellercaim in the County of
    Kincardine, Montrose and of East Harlsey co. York   XV 55
Ramsey connected with Clarke   IV 491
————————————— Dent   VII 478
——————— of Eden Bridge co. Kent and of London co. Middx   XIX 167
Randall connected with Arthur   XX 196
————————————— Colyard   VIII 426
————————————— French   V 209
Randolph of Tilehurst co. Sussex, Beddenden and Canterbury co.
    Kent   X 109–12
Ranelagh, Jones Earl of   XIII 7
Raper connected with Soame   I 495
——————— of Bodersby, Wendover Dean co. Bucks, Thorley Hall
    co. Hertford, London co. Middlesex and of Langthorn co.
    York   I 393
Rashleigh connected with Bennet   XIII 23
————————————————————— and Morden   XVII 44
Ratcliffe of Dilston, Earls of Derwentwater, see Radcliffe   XXI 1
——————— of Rotherhithe co. Surrey connected with Cousins   X 126^a
Ravensworth, Baron, of Ravensworth Castle co. Durham   XVI 21
Rawdon afterwards Hastings   V 261
——————— Baronet connected with Popham   III 235
——————— connected with Popham   XVIII 131
——————— of Broxbourne co. Herts   II 404
Rawe M.I. St Nicholas Church Newcastle upon Tyne   VII 376
Rawlins of Dorsington co. Gloucester   XX 33
————————————————————— connected with Astry   XIII 101
——————— of St Christopher's   V 226
——————— of Saperton co. Gloucester connected with Mills   XX 164
Rawlinson connected with Ray   XXI 307
——————— of Cark   XIV 8, 9
————————————— Hall in Cartmell, in Lancashire and of
    Grays Inn co. Middlesex   XIV 5, 9
——————— of Carkhall co Lancaster connected with Wilson   II 164
——————— of Fairigg M.I.   XIV 8
——————— of Garthwaite co. Palatine Lancaster connected with
    Palmer   XIII 11
——————— of Greenhead Cark Hall in Cartmell co. Lancaster
    connected with Crackenthrope and Askew   XVI 82
——————— of Greenhead in Furness Fells, The Ridding, Carke in
    Cartmell co. Lancs. Bucknall co. Oxon, and of Springfield
    co. Essex   I 474
——————— of Griesdale or Greysdale co. Lancaster, Charlwood
    co. Surrey, Chichester co. Sussex, Calcutta, Little Leigh co.
    Chester, and of Hendon   I 471
——————— of London co. Middlesex, and of Stow Longtoft co.
    Suffolk, Rector of Charlwood   XXI 112
Ray of Alton Carlbrick near Strabolgie Aberdeen and of London
    co. Middlesex   I 151
——————— of Denston and of Wickham Brook co. Suffolk   XXI 112

Ray of Hawleigh Rockells Shelland hall co. Suffolk and of Colnworth co. Bedford – alteration as to arms –   XVI 22
———— of Wickham Brook, Denham and of Hawleigh co. Suffolk   XXI 307
Raykes Raikes, baptisms, marriages, burials, & extracts from wills   VII 225
Raymond connected with Tyndale   X 123
———— Lord, connected with Northey and Jol   XVI 30
———— of Badgley Anfield co. Southampton and of Lyme co. Dorset   II 174
———— of Ilchester Old Sock co. Somerset, Thornbury co. Gloucester, and of Bosley in the Forest of Dean   XVI 88
———— of Ilchester Northous & Chard co. Somerset Marpole in Withicombe Raleigh co. Devon, Barking co. Essex and of Beckenham co. Kent   I 430
Raymond of Sibland by Thornbury and of Yate co. Glousc.   XIII 103
———— of Tibland in the psh of Thornbury co. Glousc.   XVI 65
———— of Thornbury co. Gloucester   XVI 22
Rayner of Leeds co. York connected with Milnes   XV 16
Raynsford of Thackham and of Little Compton connected with Astry   XIII 101
Read connected with Eaton and Pell   I 285
———— of Castle Roche and Castle Moyle, Maynorgayng co. Carmarthen, Maes Mawr, Freshelyg Cutland and of Taurisge   IX 76
———— of Chester and Coed Oun Parish of Flint connected with Williams   VII 110
———— of Maes Mawr co. Montgomery   I 31
———— of Seddlescomb co. Sussex   IX 118
———— of Wrangle co. York connected with Croftes   IV 134
Reade of Barton, Shipton co. Oxon & of Apleford co. Berks   VI 50
———— of Shipton co. Oxon and of London co. Middlesex   II 189
Ready connected with Edwards   XVI 52
Rebello of Hackney connected with Alvarez & de Mendoza   III 317
Reddall of Eversholt, Ampthill co. Bedford, and of Stonehouse co. Gloucester   XX 201
Rede connected with James   I 121
Rederick of Shrewsbury co. Salop and of Chipping Norton co. Oxford   IX 43
Reed M.I. St Nicholas Church Newcastle upon Tyne   VII 379
———— of Gateshead co. Durham and of Stratford co. Essex   X 137
———— of Hartlepool co. Northumberland connected with Collingwood   X 155
———— of Roch Castle co. Pembroke, Castle Moyle, Bodington co. Gloucester, Mitton co. Worcester, and of Bromshill Castle co. Hereford   XIX 254
———— of Trevales in the psh of Stythians & of Perran co. Cornwall   I 369
Reedman of Bishopstone co. Wilts, London co. Middlesex and of Newcastle upon Tyne   I 496
Rees Lord or King of South Wales   XIV 20

Rees Prince of Wales connected with Hookes   XVIII 104
──────── see Rhys
Reeve connected with Lysons   I 45
───   XIII 97
───   XIX 139
──────── of Rushton in Norfolk connected with Hookes   XVIII 108
Reeves of Tubberboo in Queens County in Ireland   II 128
─────────────────────────── connected with Nevill   I 418
Render of London co. Middlesex connected with Beresford   XXI 168
Repinder afterwards Pierson, of Alexandria de la Paille in Piedmont I 396
Revell connected with Egerton and Saunders   XXI 171ᵃ
Rey of Grindon Ridge co. Durham connected with Ord   I 312
Reynolds afterwards Baron Ducie of Tortworth   XX 100ᵃ
──────── connected with Harmer   XX 144
──────── of Kelsall co. Suffolk connected with Shrubb   V 300
──────── of Ombersley co. Worcester, London co. Middlesex,
    Folkestone co. Kent, and of Bengal   I 255
──────── of Strangewayes in the psh of Manchester   XX 197
──────── of Winchcomb co. Gloucester connected with
    Durham   XX 108ᵃ
Reynst of Haarlem connected with Clifford   XI 40
Rhys Rees of Llandisilio co. Carmarthen, co. Herts, and of London
    co. Middlesex, connected with Griffiths, Davis, and Bull   IV 346
Riach Highland spelling of Ray till 1746   I 151
Rial of Shad Thames, Peckham and Horsleydown co. Surrey   III 451
Ricardes of Welch extraction (by tradition of the family) als
    Fermour of Whitney co. Oxford   VIII 497
──────── als Fermour   V 7
Riccard came from Province in France, of York & London   III 333
Rice connected with Hoby   VII 65
─────────────────── Newland   II 79
Rich afterwards Milnes   XV 16
──────── of Bullhouse in the psh of Pennistone in the West
    Riding of York connected with Milnes   XV 16
──────── of Lexden co. Essex, North Cerney, Withington,
    Stratton co. Gloucester, London co. Middlesex, Lambeth
    co. Surrey and of Barbadoes   XIX 106
──────── of Minty co. Wilts, Sonning in the County of Berks,
    and of the City of Gloucester   XIX 171
──────── Sir Edwin M.I.   XVI 40
Richard Duke of York   XVI 9
──────── Earl of Cambridge   XVI 9
──────── King of England   XVI 9
──────── II   XVI 9
Richards connected with Lacey   II 149
─────────────────── Martin and Tristram of Dillington   XXI 224
Richardson connected with Potts   III 126
──────── M.I.   XIV 8
──────── Bracon Ash Church co. Norfolk   VI 118
──────── of Lambeth co. Surrey connected with Johnson   XXI 163ᵃ

Richardson of co. Lancaster, Marlborough co. Wilts, Leeds co. York, and of Derbyshire III 21
——————— of London V 230
——————— of Wick near Worcester connected with Higford XX 160
Richeir connected with Bigland VIII 323
——————— of Lincoln extract from will XVI 84
Richmond als Webb XIX 156
——————— connected with Legh III 309
——————— Edmond of Haddame Earl of, XIV 18
——————— of Highett Castle co. Cumberland XXI 35
XXI 91
——————— of Weston sub Edge XX 197[a]
Rickards of Launceston co. Cornwall and of the City of Bristol VIII 218
Ricketts' of London co. Middlesex connected with Butler III 86
Riddell M.I. St Nicholas Church Newcastle upon Tyne VII 378
VII 379
——————— of Enfield and of London co. Middlesex V 214
——————— of Fenham, Swinburne Castle, and of Chesham Grange co. Northumberland X 71
——————— of Tenham co. Kent, Swinburne Castle, and of Newcastle upon Tyne co. Northumberland X 24
Ridge als Boulder of Hope Boulder co. Salop, and of Marple co. Chester VIII 477–85
——————— formerly Bowdler of Ridge co. Salop VIII 201
——————— M.I. Chester St Peters Church XIV 9
Ridgeway see Ridgway
Ridgway Ridgeway of Hiptonstall and Harleywood co. Lancaster connected with Whip III 120
Ridler connected with Kingscote XVI 29
——————— of Edgeworth co. Gloucester connected with Stephens VII 146
Ridley connected with Browne VI 223
——————— M.I. XVI 54
——————— of Haltwisle co. Northumberland & of Baltimore Town Maryland XXI 12
——————— of Micklebank in Haltwistle co. Northumberland and of London III 238
——————— of Newcastle upon Tyne and of Heaton co. Northumberland connected with White II 210
Rigby Rector of Ickford co. Bucks, and of Ringmore Vicar of Ipplepen both in the County of Devon; of London co. Middlesex, and of Risborough co. Bucks IX 83
Rigg connected with Seccombe II 115
——————— of Church Town M.I XIV 9
Riggs of Hollis House III 211
Rimes connected with Ayliffe I 543
X 34
Ringrose of Miniple co. Clare connected with Prestwich I 298
Ripley of London co. Middlesex connected with Thornber IV 89
Risden connected with Webb and Berrington I 59
XIII 118

Rittenham connected with Windsor   XIII 1
River de la, of Thormorton   XX 200
Rivers de la connected with Russell   XX 49ª
———————— Woodvile Earl, connected with Stafford   XVI 50
Rivett connected with Thurbane and Russell   VIII 244
Rixton of Rixton, Ditton co. Lancs and of Bewmorris co.
     Carnarvon, connected with Hookes   XVIII 104
Roach of Castle Cary co. Somerset, connected with Lucy   I 293
———————— of London co. Middlesex connected with Coxwell   XIX 116
———————— of West Pennard co. Somerset connected with Harris   IV 523
Robartes Baron   VII 86
Robert II King of Scotland connected with Stewart of Ascog   XVIII 146
Roberts of . . . .   III 526
———————— Baron Robartes   VII 86
———————— connected with Coke   XVI 89
———————————————— Constable   IX 152
———————————————— Parker   IX 102
———————— of Bredon co. Worcester connected with Webb   XX 240
———————— of Britfieldstoun   IX 148
———————————————— Ballyfoyle Bridgetown co. Cork and of
     Dublin   XXI 317
———————— of Bristol Lord of Westerleigh   XIII 104
———————— of Enfield co. Middlesex connected with Kilham   II 76
———————— of Fyddington in Ashechurch co. Gloucester connected
     with Coote   XVI 24
———————— of Glastonbury co. Somerset, Boursell co. Sussex and
     of Thorpe co. Surrey   II 233
———————— of Holkam co. Norfolk afterwards Coke   I 485
———————— of Light Pill   XX 187
———————— of Narquis co. Flint   V 213
———————— of St Athen near Cardiff co. Glamorgan Exeter co.
     Devon Bridgewater co. Somerset, Malaga Spain and of
     Kingston Jamaica   II 11
———————— of Standon in the psh of Arreton connected with
     Holmes   VI 235
———————— of Wilsdon co. Middlesex connected with Barne   II 383
———————— of Worcester connected with Turner   IV 274
Robin connected with Dumaresq   III 462
Robins came out of Gloucester into Oxon of Bucknell near
     Bycester co. Oxon   IX 149
———————— of Matsdon and of Bristol co. Gloucester   XIX 85
Robinson connected with Bourchier   I 560
———————————————— Clifford   XI 40
———————————————— Repinder afterwards Pierson   I 395
———————————————— Stebbing   VII 320
———————————————— Yates   VIII 23
———————— M.I. in Kirkby Ravensworth Church   VI 122
———————————————— in Winkburn Church co. Nottingham   VI 117
———————————————— of Fellfoot in Staveley   XIV 8
———————————————— of Newby Bridge in Cartmel co. Lancs   XIV 6

Robinson of Denston Hall in Suffolk connected with Alleyn   XXI 157
———————— of Farmley in the psh of Otley co. York & of London   III 414
———————— of Grindon co. Stafford connected with Lister   I 18
———————— of Lincoln and of Holbeach co. Lincoln   II 7
———————— of Litchfield co. Stafford connected with Boulton and Babington   IV 389
———————— of London co. Middlesex and of Kentwell Hall co. Suffolk   VI 90
———————— of Neston co. Chester connected with Phillips   I 49
Robson of Hurst Court co. York and of Walkingham co. Nottingham   XIX 37
Roche connected with Wombwell   I 470
———————— de la, lord of Roche Castle   IX 76
———————— Sir Boyle   VIII 229[b]
Rochester Lord connected with Mallet   VII 397
Rock of the City of Bristol connected with Grosset   III 207
Rockingham Earl of, connected with Tufton   XVI 58
———————— Earls of, connected with Tufton, and Sondes Earl of Feversham   XIII 68
———————— Marquis of, connected with Sturgeon   XV 44
Ro-cliffe connected with Palmer   XIX 74
Rodbard change of name from Ellis   IX 17
Rodborne of Maysey Hampton co. Gloucester   XX 198[a]
Roddam of Rodham connected with Collingwood   XV 6
Roddom connected with Collingwood and Reed   X 156
Roderick the Great King of all Wales   III 394
———————————————————— connected with Davies   XVIII 89
———————— the Great King of Wales connected with Evance   VIII 473
Rodes of Barlbrough Sturton co. Nottingham, connected with Wintringham   IV 371
———————— of Long Houghton co. York connected with Rich   XV 16
Rodney of Stanlinch in psh of Dounton co. Wilts, Alton co. Hants, and of London co. Middlesex   IX 139
———————— of Stoke Rodney co. Somerset   XX 32
Rodway connected with Phillips and Smith   I 273
———————————————————— Smith   I 362
Roc of Clapham co. Bedford connected with Seckford   I 197
Rogers connected with Coles   X 35
———————————————————— Creigh and Isaacson   XXI 147
———————————————————— Furney   III 446
———————————————————— Hawley   VIII 453
———————————————————— Lewis and Gwyn   II 447
———————————————————— Montagu Earl of Sandwich   XVI 69
———————————————————————— and Creigh   I 308
———————————————————— Pendrell   II 261
———————— de la Home, Myndton, Ydsall als Shiffnall, Stirch, Kington co. Hereford, Forten, Moor, and of London co. Middlesex   I 442
———————— left co. Bucks and settled at Fishguard, of Goodwick co. Pembroke, and of the Island of Antigua   VIII 429

Rogers of Blandford co. Dorset, Heddington, Wrainscomb co.
    Wilts, London, Islington, Bushey, Eastcott co. Middlesex,
    and of Guildford co. Surrey   I 99
——————— of Bradford co. Wilts & of Sutton Valence co. Kent   XIX 101

    and of Evesham co. Hereford   XIX 232
——————— of Bristol   XIII 103
——————— of Canington co. Somerset connected with Hele or
    Heale   V 397
——————— of Catswood and of Bisley   VIII 425
——————— of Lancashire Todesmore and of London co.
    Middlesex   IV 248
——————— of Llandinabo Broomy Close co. Hereford connected
    with Hoskins   II 311
——————— of Rainscombe co. Wilts connected with Johnson and
    Tipping   III 470
——————— of Stamford co. Lincoln connected with Gawdy   VI 80
Rohan Viscount de   VIII 249
————————————— connected with Tate   VII 259
————————————————— Poulton   XVI 18
Rokeby of Hotham, Sandall Skyres & Ackworth Park co. York   VI 34
Rolle afterwards Walter   VI 389
——————— connected with Clinton   IX 114
——————— of Stevenstone Petrickstowe, Heanton, Parkgate in
    Tavistock, Torrington co. Devon, Tuderly, Shapwick co.
    Southampton, also of Beam & Horwood   VI 391
Rolleston of Aston co. Derby connected with Chambers   VI 99
Rolt of Sacomb co. Herts, Spy Park, Rector of Bromham and
    Yatesbury co. Wilts, connected with Bayntun   VIII 30
Romans connected with Clarke   IV 109
Romilly connected with Garnault   VIII 168
Romney connected with Taylor Wild and Kynaston   XVIII 115
——————— of Tetbury co. Gloucester   XIX 132
Ronals of Kings Stanley co. Gloucester connected with Wilkins   XX 244
Rooke connected with Dawson and Pudsey   II 434
——————— of Biggesware   VI 363
——————— of Bigswear co. Gloucester   XVI 32
    XX 47
——————— connected with Catchmay   XIII 37
    XX 10
——————— of Broadwell co. Gloucester and of Stanmore co.
    Middlesex   XX 203
Rookwood connected with Pearce   IV 476
    XVIII 32
Roope of Little Dartmouth co. Devon   III 118
Roos Baron of Kendal of Woderslake and Dent Westmorland   XXI 15
——————— notes on the Barony of   XIII 8
Roper connected with Dawson   I 406
——————————————— Knee   XX 230
——————————————— Tattershall   X 46
Rose of Cornwall and of Southampton   VII 22

Rose of Poolmire Mickleham Betchworth Buckland and of Walton on the Hill co. Surrey — II 118

———— of the Island of Jamaica descended from the Roses of Mickleton near Camden in the County of Gloucester connected with Sloane of Chelsea — XIX 16

Roskel M.I. — XIV 9

———— of Cartmel — XIV 7

Ross formerly Gray — VII 221

Rosse of Yate co. Gloucester — XX 194

Rotherford of Rochester, Beaufront co. Northumberland connected with Errington — XVI 36

Rotherham of Somerset House and of Kensington co. Middlesex connected with Creed — III 61

Rothery of co. York and of London co. Middlesex — XIII 24

Rothes Earl of, connected with Anstruther — VII 130

Rothwell of Stapleford co. Lincoln connected with Longe — IV 397

Rotsey of Kings Norton co. Worcester connected with Walshe — XVIII 13

Rous connected with Huntercombe — XIII 1

Rouse of Barbadoes connected with Estwick — II 302

———— of Exeter co. Devon – a Cornish family originally – connected with Haine — IV 73

Rousselet of London co. Middlesex – took the name of Whitefoord of Egham Lodge co. Surrey — VI 136

Rowe connected with Codrington — X43

———————————————————— — XVIII 62

———————————————————— — XIX 158

———— Draper and Harper — I 251

———— Senior — II 477

Rowell of Nedingworth connected with Purchas — III 418

Rowles of Cockshoot in the psh of Newnham — VIII 385

———— of the Cockshut and of Newnham connected with Walter — VIII 419

Rowley of Mancester connected with Lewes — IX 93

Rowlls connected with Sandford — XVI 89

Rowney connected with Noel — I 518

Rudde of Manchester co. Palatine Lancaster — XXI 296

Rudder formerly Rutter — XV 50

Rudge of Cirencester co. Gloucester and of London co. Middlesex descended out of Worcestershire — XIX 66

Rudhall connected with Whittington — XIX 35

———— of Gloucester and Bristol — XX 202ª

Rudston of Newcastle upon Tyne connected with Reed — X 137

Rudyard of Rudyard connected with Ley & Gibbons — III 448

Ruffin of Eynsham co. Oxford connected with Woodward — XIX 241

Ruffle of Norton co. Suffolk connected with Fiske — IV 137

Rugeley of Dunton Hall — II 384

———— of Hakesyard co. Stafford connected with de la Zouche — I 445

———— of Tubington co. Stafford connected with Lawley — V 116

Rugge of Norwich and of Felmingham co. Norfolk — III 163

Rule of Dumfries — XXI 12

———————————————————— — XXI 320

Rumsey of Chubb Hall in Ross co. Hereford	II 298
Rundell of Bath Norton St Philips co. Somerset and of Calcutta connected with Ketelby	I 41
Rush of Bishop Stortford and of Bonile Lodge co. Suffolk	XIII 72[a]
Rushburgh of Baldock co. Herts, and of Ailesham co. Norfolk, connected with Calver	V 27
———— of Baldock co. Hertford and of Ailsham co. Norfolk connected with Carver	VIII 41
connected with Calver	VIII 43
Rushout Lord Northwick connected with Bowles	VII 90
Rushworth of Newport Isle of Wight connected with Holmes and Troughear	VI 238
Russel connected with Corbett	X 20
———— of Dirham	XX 200
Russell connected with Beazley	VIII 348
———————————— and Hopkins	VIII 407
———————————— Cromwell	XV 21
———————————— Stonestreet	VIII 530
———————————— Unton	XVI 51
———— held the Manor of Kingston Horsington and Russell	XX 49[a]
———— of Chippenham co. Cambridge, and Checkers co. Bucks, Governor of Fort William in Bengal, connected with Cary	VIII 244
———— of Herefordshire Charles Town near Boston in New England and of Antigua	III 156
———— of Newcastle under Lyne co. Stafford, London co. Middlesex and of Walthamstow co. Essex	I 16
———— of Osmotherly co. Yorkshire Ingleby and Hanslop co. Bucks	IV 4
———— of Peckham co. Surrey connected with Harrison	IV 405
———— of Wolverhampton co. Stafford and the Island of Dominica connected with Lewis and Wrottesley	IV 344
———— Quarterings of Sir George	IX 85
Rutland, Manners Earl of, connected with Montagu	X 46
——————————————— Pierrepont	XVIII 129
Rutter afterwards Rudder – from Cheshire – of Cirencester co. Gloucester, and of Birmingham co. Warwick	XV 50
———— descended from the family of Kingsley Hall co. Chester and settled at Hitcot co. Gloucester of Queinton, Bourton on the Hill, Chipping Campden co. Gloucester, and Stratford upon Avon co. Warwick	XIX 68
Ryan connected with Frith	III 208
Rycaut of Heston near Hounslow co. Middlesex connected with Shoreditch	I 324
Ryder connected with Wilmot	IX 123
———— of London co. Middlesex	XXI 322
———— of Wisbech, and of London, Rector of Bedworth Baron Harrowby of Harrowby in the County of Lincoln	X 18, 19
Rye of Culworth co. Northampton connected with Newell	XX 66

Ryland connected with Ashby   IV 458
Ryley connected with Thorold   X 76
Rymer connected with Crayle   I 157
Ryred ap David Lord of Penlyn in the County of Merioneth,
    afterwards Middleton   VIII 485

S

Sabine connected with Taunton   VIII 117
———————————— Williams   VI 233
Saccome connected with Fluck   XX 124
Sacheveral of Kibworth in Leicester connected with Ayliffe   X 35, 36, 40
Sacheverell M.I. at Barton co. Nottingham   VI 111
———————————— Morley co. Derby   VI 106–10
———————— of Barton co. Nottingham and of Morley co. Derby.
    Baptisms etc.   VI 292
Sacheverille connected with Wilmot   IX 125
Sachiverell of Morley co. Derby   VI 1
Sackville Baron Buckhurst Earl of Dorset connected with Curzon   XVI 53
———————— Earl of Dorset connected with Tufton   XIII 68
Sadler of Cranham co. Gloucester connected with Stock   I 400[b]
Sadlier of Birmingham Fillingly co. Warwick and of Cleobury co.
    Salop   I 348
———————— of Temple Disney, Basingbourne, Southampton and
    of Pennington near Lymington co. Hants   I 350
St Barbe M.I. at Black Burton co. Oxon   VI 132
St Benets' Paul's Wharf, Register of   VI 307
St Clair formerly Erskine connected with Wedderburn   VII 167
St Clare, de, seized of lands in Sussex, of Aston Clinton co. Bucks
    connected with Gage   XIX 64
———————— of Aston Clinton co. Bucks connected with Gage   XX 126
St George connected with Lloyd   III 230
———————— Garter Principal King of Arms   VII 407
———————————————————— connected with Cooke   XX 161
———————— of Athlone in the County of Roscommon   X 2–5
Sainthill of Wandsworth co. Surrey   XIII 86
St John connected with Cromwell   XV 21
———————————— Gould   IX 4
———————— formerly Mews of Odiam co. Hants   I 25
———————— of Battersea co. Surrey Baptisms etc.   VI 272
———————— of Bletsoe connected with Reed   XIX 254
———————— of Farley co. Hants   I 25
———————— of Lydiard Tregoze co. Wilts & of Battersea Surrey   V 38

St John connected with Toppe and Hungerford   V 247
——————— of Mottesfant co. Hants connected with Pollen als
    Paulyn   V 154
——————— of Westcourt near Hertford Bridge connected with
    Paulyn als Pollen   V 154
——————— of Woodford co. Northampton   X 55
St Leger connected with Hoo   VIII 245
St Lo of Little Fontmill, Rector of Pulham and Stoke Gailard, Vicar
    of Sturminster & Newton Castle co. Dorset   XVIII 10, 11
——————— of Little Fontmill, Pulham, Stoke Gailard, Sturminster,
    Newton Castle, Maiden Newton co. Dorset, and of
    Holcomb Burnell co. Devon   IV 440
St Maur Baron of Castle Cory connected with de la Zouch and
    Bamfield   XIX 97
——————— Lord of Poulton co. Wilts connected with Tate and
    Zouche   VII 260
St Omer connected with Hoo and Malmaines   VIII 245
St Paul of Carleton, Snarford co. Lincoln, Byrom co. York,
    Copland Ewart, Coventry co. Warwick Earl of St Paul and
    Lord Fines   XIII 32–5
St Peters Paul's Wharf extracts from Register   VI 302
St Poll de, or Poole connected with Stanton   X 69
——————— see St Poole
St Poole came into England with Isabel wife to Edward II,
    connected with Stanton   XIX 158
Sale or Sayle of Wentbridge co. York connected with Sunderland   VII 284
Salford connected with Welbeck   XXI 286
Salisbury connected with Conway Donne and Hookes   XVIII 107
——————— Earl of   X 52
—————————————— connected with Tufton   XVI 58
——————— Earls of   VIII 252
Salkeld of Fulladon in the psh of Embledon co. Northumberland,
    of Fifehead Nevil co. Dorset, & of London   III 387
——————— of Whitehall, Trepland co. Cumberland, and of
    Brayton co. Yorks   XI 63
Salmon of Itchington co. Warwick connected with Seale   III 66
——————— of Middle Temple co. Middlesex connected with
    Sprignell   V 406
Salter of London co. Middlesex Rector of Stratfield Say, and
    Stratfield Turgis co. Hants   VIII 444
Saltonstall M.I. Minster Church Isle of Sheppey and Chatham
    Church   VI 125
——————— of London co. Middlesex connected with Sunderland   VII 280
                                                             VIII 501
Salusbury formerly Lloyd connected with Thelwall   XIII 41
——————— of Llewenny co. Denbigh and of Erbystock co. Flint   V 334
Salvador of Tooting co. Surrey   VIII 116
Salven of Sunderbriggs   XXI 270
Salvetti connected with Colbrond   VII 12
Salvin of Croxdale Sunderland Bridge co. Pal. Durham   X 49
Salvine of Eastingwold   III 308

Sambourne of Southcote and of Sonning co. Berks   XX 212[a]

Sampson of Dover co. Kent   XVII 12

————— of Ninfield co. Sussex connected with King   XVII 12

Sanders or Saunders of Egham in Surrey and of the City of Bristol   VIII 222

Sanderson connected with Hieron   II 182

————— of Bishop Wilton co. York   XII 48

Sandes Lord Sandes of the Vine   III 401

————— of the Vine and of Motsfont co. Hants also of Islehampsted co. Bucks.   II 442

Sandford connected with Neale   XVI 89

————— of Howgill Castle co. Westmorland   V 401

————— of Sandford co. Salop   I 37

Sandiford of Speights Town in the psh of St Peter in the Island of Barbadoes, and of Martinique   VI 92

Sandis of St Bees co. Cumberland, Ombersley co. Worcester, Gratwayte, Furness Fell, East Thayte co. Lancs London co. Middlesex, Northborne co. Kent, Hardwick co. Essex, Latimer co. Bucks, Miserden, Brimsfield co. Gloucester, and of South Petherton co. Somerset   XXI 15–22

Sandon connected with Huxley   XV 9

Sandwich Earl of   XXI 147

Sandy connected with Smyth   XX 47[a]

Sandys of Ombersley co. Worcester, Lord Sandys, connected with William of Wickham   VIII 240

————— of Woodham Ferrers co. Essex and of Ombersley co. Worcester Lord Sandys   I 434

————— of Worcester   XXI 139

Sanford of Exeter co. Devon   XIX 215

————— of Ninehead co. Somerset connected with Anstruther   VII 130

Sanson of Colchester co. Essex & of London co. Middlesex   VII 103

Sargent of Cockermouth connected with Bell   III 268

————— of Southampton, Plymouth co. Devon, Halsted Place co. Kent, and of London co. Middlesex   I 455

Saunders connected with Miller   I 14

————————— Monck   XXI 208

————— of Bromsgrove co. Worcester, London co. Middlesex, Ledbury co. Hereford, and of the City of Gloucester   V 268

————— of co. Bucks, London co. Middlesex, and of Bengal in the East Indies   IV 351

————— of Oxon connected with Spencer   VI 55

————— or Sanders of Egham in Surrey and of the City of Bristol   VIII 222

————— Rear Admiral   I 226

————————— of the Red, Knight of the Bath, Vice Admiral of the White   XXI 171[a]

Saunderson of Barton upon Humber connected with Bentley and Bennett   II 157

————— of Barton upon Humber connnected with Bentley   IV 301

————— of Owlton and Dockray near Wigton in Cumberland and of London co. Middlesex   VIII 119

Sauresmarez see Sausmarez   III 384

Sausmarez or Sauresmarez of the Island of Guernsey and of
    Newington co. Surrey   III 384
Savage of Meone co. Gloucester, Egiock, Tidmington and of
    Calloway Hill co. Worcester   XIX 102
———————— came out of Cheshire with Savage of Elmley; of Meone
    co. Gloucester, Egiock Tidminton and Callayhill co. Wor-
    cester   XIX 129
———————— Lord, of London co. Middlesex   I 371
———————— of Coaly and Cam co. Gloucester   VIII 384

———————— of Elmley Castle, Broadway co. Worcester, Tetbury
    co. Gloucester, see Savage of Meone   XIX 103
———————— of Middlehill co. Worcester   XX 93ᵃ
———————— of Tachbroke co. Warwick connected with Burslem   V 197
Savile connected with Dacre   II 122
———————————————— Dawson and Shepherd   VII 189
———————— of Elland, Thornhill, Tankersley Lupset near
    Wakefield, and of Midgeley als Stanley Hall all in the
    County of York   IX 129
———————— of Lupset co. York connected with Hatfield   IX 128
Saville connected with Dacre   III 175
Sawrey of Plompton co. Palatine Lancs. connected with Carus   XXI 63
Sawyer of Abingdon co. Bucks, and of London co. Middx   II 305
Saxby of Penthurst Lawton Place, Rodmill near Lewes co. Sussex,
    Chiddington, and of Tunbridge co. Kent   I 520
Say and Sele, Lord, see Fienes and Fiennes
Sayer connected with Evelyn   XV 2
———————— M.I.   XIV 4
———————— of Great Worsall   XXI 183
———————— of Harwell co. Berks   IV 214
Sayle see Sale of Wentbridge
Scaresbrick took the name of Euleston   XXI 152
———————— of London co. Middlesex afterwards of Scaresbrick co.
    Lancs.   XXI 152
Scarlett of London co. Middlesex, and of Great Massingham near
    Lynn co. Norfolk   II 362
Schamburgh or Schomburgh   IX 60
Schaw of Trelawney in the Island of Jamaica connected with Jarrett VII 194
Schoen of Mulhaussen in Switzerland London co. Middx and of
    Brittons in the psh of Horn Church co. Essex   VII 251
Schofield connected with Brathwaite   IV 85
Schomburgh or Schamburgh   IX 60
Schrieber of Enfield and of London co. Middlesex connected with
    Lateward   I 392
Sclater connected with Pollard and Dungate   IV 411
———————— of Leighton Buzzard co. Bedford, Pitminster co.
    Somerset, London co. Middlesex, Loughton Chingford co.
    Essex, and of Tangier Park co. Hants   II 151
Scorie connected with Walshe   XVIII 12
Scotland David King of,   VIII 251

Scotland Malcolm Canmore King of	VIII 251
Scott connected with Dobyns Yate	I 12
———————————— Harrison and Dickson	I 88
———————————— Jocelin	II 125
———————————————— and Dacre	III 177
———————————— Watts	XX 230
———————————— formerly Gibb letter as to change of name	XVII 35
———————— of Ledstone co. York connected with Fenton	I 480
———————— of Longage in Kent connected with Graves	XIX 30
———————— of Wensley co. York connected with Wilson	III 16
———————— of Wootton under Edge co. Gloucester and of London	
co. Middlesex	II 363
Scrimgeour of Birkhill connected with and afterwards Wedderburn	VII 161
Scrivenor of London co. Middlesex connected with Akerman	IX 135
Scroop M.I.	XIV 29[b], 32
———————— or Scroope connected with Newton	V 138
Scroope case of the Barony of	VIII 9
———————— connected with Clarke	III 409
———————— see Scroop	
———————— or Scrope	III 198
Scrope connected with Hungerford	V 51
————————————————————————————	V 235
———————— formerly Peart	VII 498
———————— Lord Scrope, of Masham, Upsal, and of Bolton co.	
York	XII 28–47
———————— Lord of Bolton	XX 5, 8, 18
———————— M.I. of Hamildon Church co. Bucks	VI 124
———————————— in South Cockerington	VI 123
———————————— in Trinity Church Coventry	VI 124
———————— of Cockerington co. Lincoln and of Eastcott co.	
Middlesex	XVI 76
———————— of Cockerington co. Lincoln connected with Newton	XX 175
———————— of Spenithorne, Danby co. York, Walmesley co.	
Oxon, Colby co. Norfolk, Hambledon co. Bucks, Cock-	
erington co. Lincoln, London and Eastcott Park co.	
Middlesex	II 496
———————— of Spenithorne Danby upon Yore co. York, Hamble-	
don co. Buckingham, Colby, Cockerington co. Lincoln,	
Eastcott Park and Inner Temple co. Middlesex	VII 498
———————— or Scroope	III 198
Scudamore connected with Hoskins	II 9
———————————— Somerset	I 259
———————— formerly Fitzroy	XVII 33
———————— of Holme Lacy co. Hereford, Viscount Scudamore	XVII 33
———————— Baron Scudamore of Dromore, and Viscount Sligo	IX 22[b]
———————— Skydmore, Skeydemore, Escudamore, of Ewyas,	
Homelacy, Ballingham, Kenchurch, Roleston co. Hereford,	
Burnham Hintercomb co. Bucks, Baron Scudamore of	
Dromore, and Viscount Scudamore of Sligo in Ireland	XVIII 56–61
———————— of Herefordshire in the City of Gloucester	XIX 43

Seaborne of Sutton co. Hereford   XIX 18
Seacole of Southley co. Oxford connected with Woodward   XIX 241
Seacroft of London co. Middlesex, and of the psh of St Andrews
    Hertford   XVII 60
Seagrave, Lord, connected with Stafford   XVI 50
Seale of London co. Middlesex, and Mount Boon in the psh of
    Townstall Dartmouth co. Devon   II 144
———————— of Morton Pinkney co. Northampton   III 66
Searancke of Newmarket co. Suffolk, Stamford Hill and Hackney
    co. Middlesex   XVII 7
Sears connected with Peachey   I 70
Seatle M.I.   XIV 9
Seccombe als Thorne, of Widworthy Bideford co. Devon, London
    co. Middlesex, Launceston co. Cornwall, Swansea co.
    Glamorgan, and of Cameley co. Somerset   II 114
———————— als Thorne of Wiworthy in the psh of North Petherin
    co. Devon, Launceston co. Cornwall, Swansea co. Glamor-
    gan, London co. Middlesex, and Rector of Cameley co.
    Somerset   VIII 17
———————— als Thorne of Widworthy in the psh of North Petherin
    co. Devon, St Stephens near Launceston co. Cornwall
    Swansea co. Glamorgan, Cameley co. Somerset, and of
    London co. Middlesex   VIII 294
Seckford connected with Brewster   V 115
———————— of Clerkenwell co. Middlesex and of Woodbridge co.
    Suffolk   I 197
———————— of Seckford co. Suffolk connected with Wingfield   IV 292
Sedgwick of Colebroke co. Berks and of London co. Middlesex   II 359
Selbe M.I. St Nicholas Church Newcastle upon Tyne   VII 375
Selby connected with Brandling   II 59
———————————————— Ferry   XXI 133
———————————————— Hodshon   IX 132
———————— formerly Browne   VI 224
———————— M.I. St Nicholas Church Newcastle upon Tyne   VII 376
———————— of Biddleston – notes as to the family   VIII 265
———————— of Bitelsdon co. Northumberland   XVIII 90
———————— of March in the Isle of Ely, and of Colmworth co.
    Bedford connected with Hele   I 416
———————— of Navern co. Pembroke   III 320
———————— of Twisel co. Northumberland connected with Forster   II 61
———————— Serjeant at law   XXI 206
Selfe of Benacre co. Wilts connected with Ash   II 352
Selkeld of Cawbarrow and of Bolnerock connected with
    Huddleston   XXI 26
———————— of Denton in the Dale co. York, Dent co. Westmorland   XXI 14, 18,
    and of Woodbridge co. Suffolk   19
Sells of Amersham co. Bucks and of London co. Middlesex   I 539
Selvens of Gravesend connected with Angell   I 76
Selwine Vicar of Blockley co. Worcester   XXI 175
Selwyn of Frampton, Cam, Wheatenhurst Matson and of
    Stonehouse co. Gloucester   XX 217–18[a]

Senhouse of Alnbrough and of Netherhall co. Cumberland   VII 361
———————— of Seascale co. Cumberland connected with Eglesfield   XXI 200
Senior of Shaftesbury co. Dorset and of Jamaica   II 477
Sergeaunt of Michel Dean, Longhope, Taynton co. Gloucester,
    and of London co. Middlesex   XIX 130
Serjeaunt formerly Baynham – de Baynham   XIX 44
Serle connected with Witherill and Roe   I 197
Seton of Garleton and of Newcastle upon Tyne co. Northum-
    berland, and of London co. Middlesex   I 500
Seward connected with Hake   VII 131
———————— of Downlands co. Devon London co. Middlesex and
    of London co. Middlesex   X 126^d
———————— of Downlands co. Devon connected with Drake   IV 419
——————————————————————————————————————   XVIII 44
———————— of Leominster co. Hereford, Ross Hall co. Lancs and of
    Farringdon co. Berks   X 127
Sewell of Ottershaw in the psh of Chobham co. Surrey and of
    London co. Middlesex   VII 127
———————— of Queenwood Hall co. Chertsey   VII 101
Seyborne of Sutton co. Hereford connected with Elton   XX 116
Seymour connected with Hungerford   I 44
——————————————————————————————————————   V 51
——————————————————————————————————————   V 235
———————————————— Popham   III 233
——————————————————————————————————————   III 235
——————————————————————————————————————   XVIII 130–1
———————————————— Zouch   IX 45
———————————— Duke of Somerset   XV 54
———————————————— Earl of Hertford   XVI 30
——————————————————————————————————————   X 113
———————————————— connected with Bruce Earl of Aylesbury   VI 391
———————— Duke of Somerset connected with Unton   XVI 51
———————— Earl of Hereford   XIV 17
———————— of Bookham or Leatherhead connected with Marter   IV 537
———————— of Hache Beauchamp co. Somerset, Wolfhall, and of
    Bury Pomeroy, connected with Mallet   VII 76
Seyndolk M.I. at Morley co. Derby   VI 106
Shackleton of Harden in the psh of Bingley Bolton near Bradford
    co. York, Heptonstal and of Stone Edge near Colne co.
    Lancaster   I 1
Shafesbury Astley Cooper Earl of   X 46
Shafto M.I. St Nicholas Church Newcastle upon Tyne   VII 378–9
Shaftoe   XXI 1
———————— connected with Riddell   X 24
———————— of Benwell co. Northumberland connected with
    Jenison   X 147
———————— of Kerricoats and of Babington   X 75
———————— of Whitworth co. Durham   XXI 124
Shalcross of Shalcross co. Derby connected with Joudrel   III 362
Shales connected with Barrington and Lowndes   V 175
———————— of Hatfield Broad Oak co. Essex connected with Shales

and Barrington	II 44
———— of Stony Dean House in the psh of Bishops Waltham co. Hants connected with Atkins	XVII 51
Shanacan, Walsh Baron	VIII 458
Sharp of Baydon co. Cumberland and of Winge co. Rutland	XXI 73
———— of Grafton Park co. Northampton connected with Hosier	VIII 418
———— of Northumberland, Durham, Hartburn near Morpeth, and of London co. Middlesex	I 541
Sharpe connected with Rial	III 451
Shaw ———— Grimston	XVI 95
———— formerly Macfie	XV 53
———— of Eltham co. Kent and Basthorpe co. Norfolk	IV 286
———— of Mosshead in the psh of Riccarton, Irvine, and of the City of London	XV 53
———— Sir James, of the City of London, and of Kilmarnock, arms of	VIII 475
———— Sir John	XXI 145
Shawcross connected with Hurleston	XVIII 121
Shebbeare of Oakhampton Abbotsham co. Devon and of Acton co. Middlesex	II 292
Sheene of Little Dunham co. Norfolk	III 485
Sheffield connected with de la Zouche	I 445
———— of Butterwick co. Stafford connected with Ducy	XX 106
———— of London co. Middlesex and Naverstock co. Essex, enquiry as to,	XVII 29
Sheldon afterwards Constable	VII 46
————————————————————————————	XIV 21
———— connected with Paston	VI 369
———— of Besley co. Worcester connected with Brayne	XV 79
———— of Ditchfield co. Warwick and of Winchester	I 321
———— of Little Ditchford co. Warwick, and of Winchester co. Hants	III 330
———— of Rowley Regis co. Stafford, Winchester co. Hants, Burton Constable Wycliffe co. York, Balford Hall in the psh of Besley, Pershore; Spechley, Aberton Broadway co. Worcester, Bath co. Somerset, Grays Inn co. Middlesex, Lord of Stratton co. Gloucester, Enns in Upper Austria Ditchford Weston, Temple Grafton co. Warwick, Steeple Barton co. Oxon, and of the Dungeon als Dan John near Canterbury co. Kent	VII 45
———— of Stanton in the psh of Elleston co. Stafford Archbishop of Canterbury	XXI 252
Shellard of Tithering Sodbury	XX 207[a]
Shelley connected with Gage	V 430
Shelton of co. Leicester connected with Harrison	IV 181
Shene see Sheene formerly Brooks	III 485
Shepherd connected with Lescaleet	II 238
———————————— Wight	V 332
———— of Hampton and of Hackney co. Middlesex	XX 214

Shepherd of Maidstone Weavering co. Kent & Walworth co.
Surrey   V 462
——————— of Thorne co. York connected with Wilkin   IV 201
——————— of Tillbrook co. Huntingdon, Bocking, Braintree co.
Essex, Cockside in the psh of Charles near Plymouth, and of
Bideford co. Devon   VII 190
Sheppard connected with Cotton and Tyrell   VIII 98
——————————————— Whorwood   XX 248
——————— of Horsley, Minching Hampton, Hempstead, Tetbury
co. Gloucester, and of London co. Middlesex   XX 205
——————— of Kintbury Holt in the psh of Hempstead Marshal,
Speenhamland, Benham co. Berks, Barton near Winchester
co. Hants, and Farnham Surrey   II 484
Sherard connected with Methuen   II 285
——————— of Great Staughton co. Huntingdon   XIII 43
Sherborne of Leominster co. Hereford connected with Ridley XXI 12
——————— of Stoneyhurst co. Lancaster, and of Carthington co.
Northumberland, connected with Charlton   XI 63
Sheridan of the County of Cavan in Ireland who assumed the title
of Baronet of Ireland to which he had no pretensions   VII 492
——————— to Westby   XI 46–54
Sheriden, Sir Henry, Bart   VIII 227
Sheriff of the Thorne near Leomister connected with Elton   XX 116
Shermur of Charlton Kings co. Gloucester connected with
Withorne   II 335
Sherson of Lancaster and London co. Middlesex   III 440
Shewen connected with Bate   XVI 55
Shields of Newcastle upon Tyne connected with Stodart   IV 516
Shien of Slyfield House in the psh of Great Bookham co. Surrey
connected with Blomberg   XIII 81
Shipley connected with Miller   I 14
——————— of London co. Middlesex, Canon of Christ Church
Oxford, connected with Jackson   VIII 60
Shipman of Scarrington and Mansfield co. Nottingham   VII 355
Shiris connected with Cotton and Simmonds   I 248
Shirley Earl Ferrers, connected with Bathurst   XX 42ª
——————— Governor of New England and the Bahama Islands
connected with Western   XXI 284
——————— of Westneeton connected with Lord Delawar and with
Kempe   IV 102
——————— of Wisneston co. Sussex connected with Kempe and
Onslow   I 209
Shorditch of Ickenham, Stanmore, London co. Middlesex, and of
Jamaica   I 323
Shorples connected with Newell   IV 15
Shorswell of Shorswell co. Bucks connected with Roe   I 197
Short connected with Smith   I 321
——————— formerly Hassard   IX 74
——————— Lord of the Manor of Sutton Hall and Bradford co.
Suffolk connected with Smith   III 330

Short of Bawtry Doncaster in the West Riding co. York London co. Middlesex, East Keale, Claythorpe Bellew and of Edlington co. Lincoln   IV 393

———————— of Bawtry, Doncaster co. York, London co. Middlesex East Keale, Edlington co. Lincoln, connected with Carr and Lange   IX 74

———————— of Bury St Edmunds co. Suffolk   IX 59

———————————————— Sutton Hall by Bradfield co. Suffolk and of London co. Middlesex   VI 366–7

———————————————————————————— connected with Smith and Sheldon   VII 48

———————— of Tenterden co. Kent connected with Blunt and Burrell   II 27

———————— of Witresham and of Tenterden co. Kent connected with Burrell   II 194

Shortall of Ballylareen, Clara, Killaterclough co. Kilkenny, Kilbline and of Spain   I 414

Shorter connected with Philipp   IX 105

Shovell Sir Cloudsley – connected with Narborough and Mansell   V 448

———————— Sir Cloudsley connected with Narborough   VII 399

Shrewsbury Earl of connected with Hastings   XII 28–47

    XIV 24

———————— Talbot Earl of, connected with Eyton and Dodd   XXI 301–13

Shribb of Kelsall co. Suffolk connected with Osborne   V 300

Shuckburgh connected with Evelyn   XV 2

Shurmur of Woodchester co. Gloucester connected with King   XX 102[c]

Shuttlewood of Ashby Folville co. Leicester connected with Smith and Dormer   XXI 324

Sibley connected with Huxley   XV 9

Sibthorpe of the County of Louth and of Dublin   III 524

Sicklemore of Wetheringsett co. Suffolk and of London co. Middlesex   VI 190

Siddal of Bingley connected with Ferrand   I 54

Siddons connected with Kemble   VII 183

Sidney connected with Brandon   XX 56[a]

———————————————— Dormer   XVI 95

———————————————— Jullion   II 308

———————————————— Marlowe   IX 88

———————————————— Earls of Leicester   III 185

    X 52

———————— Lord   XIV 17

———————— of Herefordshire, Boreham co. Essex, and of London co. Middlesex   VII 126

———————— of Worcester   VIII 390

———————————————— connected with Marlowe   XXI 322

Sighstone connected with Leigh and Sommersall   V 285

Sikes of Hackney co. Middlesex   II 250

Silk of London co. Middlesex   II 321

Silvertopp of Stella co. Durham Minster Acres and of Benwell co. Northumberland   II 202

Silvester connected with Carteret   VIII 437

Silvester of London co. Middlesex   IV 415
———— to whom the Earl of Chester gave the Lordship of
    Stourton   XXI 289
Simeon of Bucklebury   XX 213[a]
———— of Lower Liddington co. Wilts, Bucklebury and
    Reading co. Berks   II 371
Simkinson connected with Clifford   XI 40
Simmons connected with Gulston and Penton   XV 10
———— of Sheffield co. York and of London co. Middlesex
    connected with Smith   II 20
———— of Wolvey co. Warwick   III 52
Simpson connected with Clutterbuck   I 514
———————— Methuen   II 285
———— of Babworth co. Nottingham and Stokes co. Derby
    connected with Stringer and Newton see Simpson of . . . .
    near Maidstone   V 138
———— of Bath   XIII 92
———— of Chelmsford connected with Chalmers   II 342
———— of Derby connected with Blythe   III 361
———— of Mile End co. Middlesex connected with Pinchback   VIII 461
———— of . . . . near Maidstone co. Kent, Sheffeild co. York,
    Blythe, Babworth co. Nottingham, and of Stoke co. Derby,
    see also Simpson of Babworth   V 124
———— of Wapping co. Middlesex connected with Anderson
    and Griffith   III 136
Singleton connected with Grose   IX 57
———— connected with Thon and Daws   IX 1
Sinnott of Ballabrenan co. Wexford and of Kelkenny   III 493
Sissmore of Portsmouth, Wickham co. Hants, and of London co.
    Middlesex   V 383
Sitsilt connected with Winston   XIX 32
Sitwell M.I. at Barton co. Nottingham   VI 111
———————— at Morley co. Derby   VI 109–10
Six connected with Clifford   XI 40
Skay of Queinton co. Gloucester connected with Rutter   XIX 68
Skeffington of Fisherweek co. Stafford connected with Danvers   VI 205
Skeirne als Bennet   XVIII 83
———— als Steward als Bennet als Castle Lion Lord of Skeirne
    and Norththroppe connected with Hotham   XVIII 82
Skelton M.D. Fellow of Jesus College   VII 474
———— of Armethwayte co. Cumberland   XXI 34
———— of Braithwait in ————   XXI 76
———— of Yorkshire connected with Sells   I 539
Skerrett of Galway, St Kitts, Jamaica, Montserrat, Carrownacow,
    Funchunmore   I 89
———— of London co. Middlesex   I 161
Skey of Falfield – notes as to family of   XIII 105
Skeydemore Skydmore Escudamore see Scudamore   XVIII 56–61
Skinn of Colford Newland co. Gloucester, Middle Temple co.
    Middlesex, and of Okehampton co Devon   XX 31
———— of St Briavels, Colford Painswick co. Gloucester

Oakhampton Germanswick co. Devon and of London co Middlesex   III 147

Skinner connected with Dobyns   I 11

———————————————————   XX 263[a]

———————— Elton and Jauncey   XX 116

Skinner connected with Harvey   X 58

———————— of Bickerton co. Hereford connected with Smith of Huntleys in the same County   I 362

———————— of London co. Middlesex and Charlwood near Reigate co. Surrey   III 226

———————— of Lyd co. Kent   II 23

———————— of Southampton co. Hants   II 1

Skip of Theobalds Park co. Herts, and of Doddington co. Hereford, connected with Bucknall   II 141

Skipp of Ledbury connected with Symonds   VIII 373

Skottowe of Great Ayton co. York, Chesham co. Bucks, Little Melton co. Norfolk, Waterford, Stradbally, Queens County, Kinsale, London co. Middlesex, South Carolina, and of Bombay   XV 11, 12

Skydmore Escudamore Skeydemore see Scudamore   XVIII 56–61

Skynner of Lyd co. Kent connected with Clare and Taylor   I 22

Slade of Bromley co. Kent connected with Matthews   IV 230

———————— of Colyton co. Devon connected with Haine   IV 74

———————— of Rushton connected with Sheldon and Leweston   XX 159

Slater connected with Giles and Curtis   I 332

———————— of London co. Middlesex   I 257

Slaughter connected with Knight   IX 41

———————— of Slaughter co. Gloucester   XX 208[a]

Slegg of co. Cambridge and of Sleggs Castle   XVII 61, 62

Sleigh of London co. Middlesex connected with Skinner and Jauncey   XX 116

Slicer connected with Cecill   XIX 82

Slingsby of Connock co. Galway Usher Keys co. Dublin Richmond co. Surrey and of London co. Middlesex   III 77

Sloane of Chelsea co. Middlesex connected with Rose   XIX 16

Slocombe of Buckland Monachoram Tavistock Topsham co. Devon Taunton co. Som. & of Rhode Island America   I 215

Sloper of Tetbury co. Gloucester   XX 226

Small came out of Gloucestershire of Otford co. Kent   IV 465

———————— connected with Shorples and Newell   IV 15

———————— extracts from the Register of Ulley co. Gloucester   VI 350

———————— M.I. at Cheam   VI 128

———————— of Cirencester, Uley co. Gloucester, and of Lewisham co. Kent, extracts from Registers   VI 331

———————— of Cirencester, Minching Hampton, Naylsworth in the psh of Avening, Painswick and of Uley co. Gloucester   XIX 162

———————— of Nailsworth, Rooksmore in the psh of Rodborough Ulley co. Gloucester, and of London co. Middlesex   II 93

———————— of Nailsworth connected with Peach   I 269

———————————————————   XIX 224

———————— of Portsmouth connected with Gazelee and Sweeting   II 291

Small of Uley, Bristol, Whaddon, Cirencester co. Gloucester, and
of London co. Middlesex   II 96, 97

Smallpage of Chichester co. Sussex, connected with Wheatley and
Devenish   VIII 244

Smallpeece of Norwich co. Norfolk and of Warlingham co.
Surrey, connected with Fox   I 166

Smalwood of Chelford and Chorley in Cheshire   X 54

Smart connected with St Lo   IV 440

——————————————————————————— XVIII 10

——————— of Chetenham connected with Freeman Hughs of
Caslip   X 58

——————— of Wollaston Culverhouse and Bishton in Tidenham
psh co. Gloucester   XX 215

Smith connected with Binfield   X 97

————————————————— Carter   XVII 44

————————————————— Castleman   XIX 105

————————————————— Crowe   VIII 383

————————————————— Dore   VII 462

————————————————— Eburne   XVIII 139

————————————————— Feake   XVI 33

————————————————— Hollester   I 525

————————————————— Kettleby   VIII 439

————————————————— Mosley   VIII 336

————————————————— Rial and Sharpe   III 451

——————— formerly Smyth of Dymock co. Gloucester   IV 264

——————— Smyth of London co. Middlesex   VI 94

——————— of Alnwick co. Northumberland & of Shields co.
Durham   VI 163

——————— of Alton, Compton co. Wilts, connected with
Burrough   IV 173

——————— of Bath connected with Webb   XIX 156

——————— of Belsadock co. Meath   VII 249

——————— of Boseley Park near Alvachurch co. Worcester,
London co. Middlesex, Birmingham co. Warwick, Charles
Town, South Carolina, Calcutta and of Bengal   I 274

——————— of Boseworth Edmundsthorp co. Leicester   VI 66

——————— of Botesdale co. Suffolk and of London co. Middlesex
also of Oxford   XVI 67

——————— of Botesdale co. Suffolk   II 209

——————— of Braco, Warkland, Methvin and of Orkney   I 481

——————— of Bulcot, Stoke East Bridgeford co. Nottingham and
of Gaddesby co. Leicester   XVI 43

——————— of Buscott co. Berks connected with Kiblewhite   I 532

——————— of Cookham, Bray co. Berks, Hammersmith,
Isleworth, London co. Middlesex   VIII 129

——————— of Cottishall co. Norfolk connected with Athill   IV 50

——————— of Coventry connected with Ingram and Hansom   III 65

——————————————————————————— IV 267

————————————————— Norton and Holbeck   VIII 537

——————— of Deeping co. Northampton & of Stepney co.
Middlesex   I 214

Smith of Desbro co. Nottingham connected with Cole   VIII 438
————— of Drogheda connected with Brett and Feattus   IV 532
————— of Earthcott connected with Hollister   I 525
————— of Edwardsthorpe co. Leicester   XX 178ᵃ
————— of Elberton connected with Hollister   I 525
————— of Ely and Downham co. Norfolk   VI 91
————— of Hackney co. Middlesex connected with Monoux   XIX 93
————— of Hendon connected with Nicoll   III 137
————— of Holbech near Leeds connected with Berry &   IX 104
Whalley
————— of Huntleys co. Hereford and of Gloucester   I 362
————— of Kidlington co. Oxon   II 153
————— of Long Ashton co. Somerset and of the City of Bristol
connected with Gwinnett   XX 128
————— of Mackley in the psh of Sudbury co. Derby, the
Borough of Southwark, Wolverhampton co. Stafford
London co. Middlesex and of the East Indies   III 88
————— of Middle Temple co. Middlesex, Whitchurch co.
Oxon, Burnham, of the City of Winchester, and of Stoke
Charity co. Southampton, connected with Sheldon and
Short   VII 48
————— of the Middle Temple co. Middlesex, Whitchurch co.
Oxon, and of Stoke Charity co. Southampton connected
with Short   VI 365
————— of Moolham co. Somerset Honiton co. Devon and of
London co. Middlesex   I 394
————— of New Cross co. Wexford in Ireland, Bideford,
Southcott in the psh of West Leigh co. Devon, and of
London co. Middlesex   IV 450
————— of Nottingham connected with Lister   I 18
————— of Oatleys in the psh of Much Marcle co. Hereford,
and of Gloucester   I 273
————— of Quineborough co. Leciester connected with
Dormer and Shuttlewood   XXI 324
————— of Radcliffe co. Berks   VI 84
————— of Sheldon co. Durham connected with Hutton   II 48
————— of Staining   III 191
————— of Stoke Charity co. Southampton   I 321
——————————————————— connected with Sheldon   III 330
————— of Stony Stanton co. Leicester connected with Callis
and Browne   XXI 284
————— of Thornbury co. Gloucester connected with Heynes   XIX 242
————— of Wapping co. Middlesex from Sussex connected
with Mellish   VII 102
————— of Whitechapel co. Middlesex and of Madeira   I 378
————— of Withcock co. Leicester connected with Dalison   XXI 295
——————————————————————————— Dalyson   XVIII 4
————— Rectors of Castle Eaton co. Wilts Arcot co. Oxford
and of Farmington co. Gloucester   XIX 168
————— see Smyth

Smithson of Coldbeck co. Cumberland, London co. Middlesex,
    and of Croydon co. Surrey   VIII 464
Smiton of . . . . near Dunbar in Scotland and of London   II 416
Smyth afterwards Smith of Dymock co. Gloucester   IV 264
———————— als Neville   XVI 66
———————— connected with Feake   XVI 93
———————————————— Whitchurch   VIII 419
———————— of Ayldbarton near Lydney and of Bristol co. Gloucester Lord of Long Ashton co. Somerset   XX 199
———————— of Crow Hall, Stutton, co. Suffolk, Dedham, & of
Great Bromley co. Essex   I 276
———————— of Dufferin co. Hereford connected with Seward   X 127
———————— of Humberston co. Lincoln Hooley co. Leicester
North Nibley, Stonehouse Smithfield in the psh of Kingswood see also Smyth of Humberton   XIX 142
Smyth Smith of London co. Middlesex   VI 94
———————— of Long Aston and Bristol co. Somerset   XXI 237
———————— of North Nibley, Condova Hall co. Salop see also
Smythe of Humberston   XX 48
———————— Smith of Pillerton Hersey co. Warwick, and of
Battersea co. Surrey   II 20
———————— of Ravenhall, Blackmore, Laynham co. Essex Holt co.
Leicestershire, Yalford co. Oxford, and of London co.
Middlesex   XVI 66
———————— of Samelsbury – came out of Yorkshire – of Liverpool co.
Palatine Lancaster, and of Stoke Newington co. Middlesex   II 278
———————— of Staining and of Tottenham co. Middlesex   VI 377
Smythe connected with Holford   IX 159
———————— of Humberstone co. Lincoln, Hoby co. Leicester and
of North Nibley co. Gloucester, connected with Browning
see also Smyth   XIX 83
———————— of Ostenhanger, Leeds Castle, Bidborough co. Kent,
and of Corsham co. Wilts   IX 51
Snaith of Bedall co. York, connected with Becket and Marshall   II 273
Snelling of Portsmouth connected with Gazelee   II 291
Snow of Bisley co. Gloucester connected with Taylor   XIX 166
Snowden of London co. Middlesex and of Jamaica   IV 398
Snowdon of Stokesley Kirkby Moorside co. York, and of
Philadelphia connected with Ward   IV 238
Soame of Little Thurlow co. Suffolk, Hampstead and London co.
Middlesex   I 495
Soley connected with Kettleby   VIII 439
Solicitor and Attorney General Order as to place and audience of   XVII 28
Sollers connected with Capel   XX 81
Solley of Lickhill and of Sandborne co. Worcester   XX 207
Solomon connected with Canning   XII 65
Somers see Sommers   II 425
Somersall connected with Sighstone and Leigh   V 285
Somerset, Beaufort Duke of   VIII 249
    XXI 229

———————————————— connected with Stafford   XVI 50

———————— Earl, and afterwards Duke of, connected with Hookes   XVIII 105

———————— connected with the Earl of Worcester and with Brayne   XV 79

———————— Earl and Marquess of Worcester   XXI 229

———————————— of Worcester   I 259

———————— of Lambeth co. Surrey   XVI 61

———————— of Pauntley Court co. Gloucester, Canon Pexon co. Hereford, London Acton co. Middlesex, Cambray in Flanders and of Rome   I 259

———————— Seymour Duke of   XV 54

———————————————— connected with Bruce   VI 391

Somerton connected with Paston   IX 113[b]

Somervile of Wichnore co. Stafford connected with Stafford   XIV 19

Somerville connected with Vernon   II 168

———————————— Bainton   IV 338

———————————— Rolt and Bayntun   VIII 30

Sommers Somers of Whiteladies and of Clifton upon Severn co. Worcester   II 425

Sondes Watson Viscount   XIII 68

Soulegre of the Island of Antigua connected with Mills   VI 249

Souter als Johnstoun of Perth, Forfar, and of London co. Middlesex – change of name –   VII 23

Southcot connected with Cole   XX 82[a]

Southcote connected with Mansergh   XXI 46

———————— of Mestham co. Surrey and of Witham co. Essex   XVIII 3

———————— Chertsey co. Surrey and ————————   IV 473

Southcott of Southcott, Chudleigh, Bovey Tracey, Calwoody, Listleigh, Mohuns Autrie, Hedgend, Dartmouth Shillingford, Chilton Killmyngton, Blyborough co. Lincoln   VI 44

Southgate of Tylney in Marshland co. Norfolk connected with Turner   V 28

———————— of Tylney in Marshland co. Norfolk connected with Turner of Pentney   VIII 43

Southley connected with Stanhope   II 119

Southwell als Darcey   II 130

———————— of Felix Hall in the psh of Kelvedon co. Essex Norwich, Woodrising co. Norfolk, Ipswich Barham co. Suffolk, and Mereworth co. Kent   II 131

———————— of Felix Hall in Essex, Ipswich, Banham co. Suffolk, Morton, Wood Rysing co. Norfolk, Kingsale Polylong co. Cork, and of London co. Middlesex   XIX 176

———————— of Kings Weston and of Frampton Cotterel co. Gloucester   XX 48[a]

———————— of Kings Weston co. Gloucester – Principal Secretary of State in Ireland   XVI 58

———————— of Kings Weston and of Frampton Cotterell co. Gloucester   XIII 68

———————— of Walpole co. Norfolk, Wisbech in the Island of Ely, and of London co. Middlesex   II 106

Sowerby of Whitehaven connected with Young   I 71

Sowle of Blandford co. Dorset connected with Holmes   VI 235

Sowles connected with Bradford   V 90

_____   IX 110

Spalding of Clare co. Suffolk and of London connected with Parry   III 172

Sparke of Exeter connected with Luccombe   III 212

——————— of Wellingborough Knuston Hall Wollaston cum Archester co. Northampton connected with Hodson   III 479

Sparrow afterwards Port of Ilem co. Stafford   I 251

——————— of Hapworth Hall near Halstead co. Essex connected with Owen   III 313

——————— of Red Hill co. Anglesea connected with Lloyd   II 315

——————— of Stonehenge, Walthamstow co. Essex, connected with Beard   II 180

——————— of Wolverhampton connected with Newell   IV 241

Speed of Westminster   I 314

Speke see Le Espek   II 163

——————— of White Lackington co. Somerset   II 378

Spelman of Narborough co. Leicester connected with Harman   VII 505

Spence of Nyland in Balcomb co. Sussex   IX 69

Spenceley of Norton connected with Fiske   IV 137

Spencer als de la Spencer Lord of the Manor of Marchley Defford Wormleighton co. Worcester, Lord Spencer, Earls of Winchester and Gloucester, of Badley co. Northampton, Althorp co. Lincoln, Yarnton co. Oxon, and of Clarendon co. Warwick   VI 52

——————— connected with Beaufort and Cary   VIII 248

——————— de la, see Spencer   VI 52

——————— M.I. at Barton co. Nottingham   VI 111

——————— of Ashton co. Lancs. Lord Spencer and Earl of Sunderland   XX 178[a]

Sperring of Bath co. Somerset, London co. Middlesex, and of Philadelphia   XIII 91

Spert of Stepenhithe co. Middlesex Kingswood co. Wilts, Tetbury co. Gloucester, Founder and Master of Trinity House   XIX 183

Spicer of Ware co. Devon connected with Williams and Baring   III 358

Spiller of London connected with Thorowgood   IV 59

Spilman connected with Payne of Rodborough co. Gloucester   XIX 193

Spitta of London co. Middlesex connected with Cobb   XIII 65

Spriggs of Gosport, Plymouth Dock co. Hants, connected with Lloyd   IV 189

Sprignell of Bedford, London, and of Coppenthorpe in Lincolnshire or Yorkshire   V 405

Springett of Goving co. Oxon connected with Brownrigg   VII 441

Spurrell of Norfolk, Stepney co. Middlesex, and of Barking co. Essex   IV 1

Spurstow of London co. Middlesex   XXI 168

——————— of Spurstow connected with Legh   II 170

Squier connected with Lynch   IV 509

Squire Bishop of St Davids connected with Ardsoif   IX 135

——————— notes as to date of births   XIII 13

——————— of Peterborough connected with Bigland   XIII 12, 13

——————— and of Stilton co. Huntingdon   XXI 272

Stables of Northampton connected with Williamson   XVII 31
Stackpole connected with Turbevile and Rees Griffith   XIV 18
Stackpoole of Pembrokeshire knighted by William the Conqueror   XXI 4
Stafford connected with Eyre   II 395
——————————— Forster   III 130
——————————— Lovell   VIII 248
——————————— Somervile   XIV 18
——————————— Strickland   VIII 347
————————————————————————   XIV 10, 27
——————————— Vernon   XIV 2
———————— Earl connected with Southcote   XVIII 3
———————— Duke of Buckingham   XVI 50
———————— Earls of connected with Southcote   IV 474
———————————————————————— Strickland   VII 295
———————— of Blatherwick connected with Tame   XIX 154
———————— of Grafton co. Northampton and of co. Norfolk   XX 215ᵃ
———————— of Thornbury co. Gloucester   VII 510
Staker connected with Woodyer and Ayliffe   X 36–9
Stalker of Whitehaven connected with Young   I 71
Stallwood connected with Fisher and Jeddere   X 165
Stamford of Stamford co. Lincoln connected with Ashby   IV 459
Standerf connected with Master   II 111
Standish of Standish co. Lancs   XIX 13
———————————————————— connected with Byndlosse   XXI 49
——————————————————————— Howard and Mollineux   XIV 22–3
——————— of Standish co. Palatine Lancaster connected with
     Townley and Strickland   VII 298
Stanford connected with Cocks   II 426
———————— M.I.   XIV 29ᵇ
Stanhop M.I. at Morley co. Derby   VI 106
Stanhope connected with Aspinwell Dutton & Bridges   II 205
——————————————— Bridges   XVII 33
——————————————— Southley and Berriman   II 119
——————— Earl connected with Pitt   X 62
————————————————————————   X 160
——————— of Mansfield Woodhouse co. Notts Earl of
     Chesterfield   V 249
——————— of Mansfield Woodhouse co. Nottingham, from whom
     descends Philip Stanhope Earl of Chesterfield, connected
     with Toppe   V 66
Stanier of St James near Bridgewater Pepperell co. Salop and of
     London co. Middlesex   IV 16
Stanifarth of Darnall co. York and of Liverpool co. Pal. Lancs.   XIII 42
Stanleigh als Audeleigh see Stanley   XXI 12ᵃ-12ᵇ
                                                                         XXI 289–95
Stanley als Stanleigh als Audeleigh Lord of Stanleigh co. Stafford,
     Stourton, and of Hooton in Wirral, of Elford co. Stafford,
     Weever co. Chester, Greys Withen, Awsthwaite in Cum-
     berland, Crosshall, Dalgarth, and Arnaby, Earl of Derby,
     Lord Stanley & Strange   XXI 289–95

Stanley als Stanleigh lord of Stanleigh and Stuton of Grey
    Swethin, Austwaite or Dalgarth, Arnaby, Halthweytes co.
    Cumberland, and of Eaton co. Derby   XXI 12[ab]
———————— connected with Hoby   VII 65
———————— Earl of Derby   XIV 18
———————— Lord of Stourton co. Wilts and of Hooton co. Chester,
    Wilmington & West Peckham co. Kent connected with
    Dalyson   XVIII 5
———————— Lord Strange and Earl of Derby connected with
    Spencer   VI 55
———————— of Bickerstagh and of Crosshall co. Lancs   I 327
———————— of Hooton and of Flint connected with Hookes   XVIII 107
———————— of Ponsonby co. Cumberland connected with Appleby   X 140
———————— of Tatton co. Chester connected with Tiptoft   XIII 122
———————— of Workington co. Cumberland   VIII 35
———————————————————————— connected with Christian
    Curwen or Culwen   II 462
Stannow of Norfolk connected with Bickerton   XIV 24
Stansall of Chesterfield co. Derby connected with Armiger & Ash   I 124
Stanton connected with Bingley   III 115
———————————— Cheseldon   XIX 158
———————————— St Pool   X 69
———————————— Sells   I 540
———————— of Berwick upon Tweed, Baptisms etc   VI 274
———————— of Burgem in the Shire of Berwick upon Tweed, of
    Bristol, Senegal and of Dominica   II 109
———————— of London co. Middlesex and of Galway   IX 2
Stapleton connected with Chamberlaine and Fane   II 254
Stapleton formerly Errington see also Stapylton   I 94
———————— of Bedell, Carleton, and Ingham connected with
    Hudleston   XXI 38
———————— of Bedell and of Ingham co. Norfolk connected with
    Hudleston   I 107
Stapylton formerly Errington   X 16, 17
———————— of Carleton and Drax co. York   X 16, 17
———————————————————————— connected with Errington   X 16, 17
Starck Patent of Nobility granted by the King of Sweden to the
    family of,   VIII 277
Starr of Dover & Folkestone co. Kent   I 359
Statham M.I. at Morley co. Derby   VI 106
———————— of Tidswell connected with Wigley   XV 25
———————— of Wigwall co. Derby   XXI 226
Staughton of Staughton in the psh of Stoke near Guildford co.
    Surrey   VI 31
Staunton M.I. at Barton co. Nottingham   VI 111
———————— Morley co. Derby   VI 109
———————— of Ferland co. Somerset, and of Wickham co. Essex
    connected with Latham and Cole   XIX 174
Stawell Lord, connected with Pert   XXI 250
Stebbing of Monewden, Framsden, Brandeston, Earlsoham,

Wisset, Kettleborough, Bottesdale, Wickham Market co. Suffolk, Norwich co. Norfolk, and of London co. Middlesex	VII 318
Stede of Stede Hill co. Kent connected with Stanhope	II 205
Stedman of the Abbey Estate or Strait of Florida	XVII 48
Steel connected with Barnesley	XIX 23
——————— Steele of the Manors of Orton and Moor Barns co. Leicester connected with Perkins	III 509
	XVIII 28
——————— connected with Barnesley	XXI 204
——————— of Trelawney in the Island of Jamaica connected with Jarrett	VII 194
Steele of Belchamp co. Essex connected with Hinson	II 179
——————— see Steel	
Steere formerly Witts of Jayes in the psh of Wootton co. Surrey	VIII 341
——————— of Jays in the psh of Wootton	III 327
——————————————— and of Ockley	IV 212
	VIII 341
——————— of Ockley and of Wootton co. Surrey extracts from Registers	VI 345
——————— of Surrey and of Hedingham Castle co. Essex	V 287
Steers of Farley co. Northampton connected with Kynaston and Pindar	XVIII 121
Stephens connected with Harries and Berrington	VII 58
——————— of Burderop, Chisledon, Froxfield, Hodson and Swindon co. Wilts, connected with Kibblewhite	IX 8
——————— of Cherrington and Alderley co. Gloucester connected with Rainsford	II 90
——————— of Colchester co. Essex	XVI 62
——————————————————— and of Clerwell co. Gloucester connected with Bourchier	XIX 49
——————— of Eastington, Horton, Frocester, Horsley, Beverstone Stroud co. Gloucester, and of Leicester, extracts from Registers	VI 352
——————— of Frocester, Eastington, Stonehouse, Over Lipiate in the psh of Stroud, Little Sodbury, Horton, Cheriton, Alderley, Painswick, Bexwell, Horsley, Alveston, Chevenage, Bisley co. Gloucester, Middle Temple, Fulham co. Middlesex, Alphamstone co. Essex. Horsford, St Faith's co. Norfolk, Illsington co. Devon, The Castle near the Borough of Leicester, and of Shillingford co. Berks	VII 140
——————— of Frocester, Eastington, Lupyeat, Little Sodbury, Cherington co. Gloucester, and of the Middle Temple co. Middlesex	XIX 262
——————— of Lancant co. Gloucester	VIII 417
——————— of Radnorshire connected with Harris & Bowen	IV 192
——————— of St Ives and of Lincolns Inn co. Middlesex	XXI 221
——————————————— co. Cornwall	XXI 232
——————— of Upper Lippiat in the psh of Stroud co. Gloucester	X 43
Stephenson of Croftlands in the psh of Adston co. Cumberland	XXI 204

Stepney of St Albans co. Herts, Eastham co. Essex, and of
    Prendergast co. Pembroke   V 423
Steuart of Dublin and of London co. Middlesex   III 427
Stevens   XXI 103
——————— a deed   XVI 81, 85
————————————————————————————   XVI 90
——————— connected with Bigland   VIII 328
——————— of Bisley co. Gloucester connected with Sperring   XIII 91
——————— of Jamaica connected with Jackson   VIII 57
——————— of North Aston co. Oxon – will –   XX 210
——————— will etc.   X 153-4
Stevenson M.I. St Nicholas Church Newcastle upon Tyne   VII 377
Stevenson of Baladoole Isle of Man, connected with Heywood and
    Cannell   II 128
——————— of Boston and of Garthorp co. Lincoln connected with
    Grenfeld and Newcomen   VIII 232
——————— of Tealby and Boston co. Lincoln connected with
    Beverley   III 139
Steventon of London co. Middlesex   II 14
Steward als Skeirne als Castle Lion, Lord of Skeirne and
    Norththroppe connected with Hotham   XVIII 82
——————— of Cottestock co. Northampton connected with Creed   IX 64
Stewart connected with Andrew and Wolrich   V 204
——————————— Browne   XV 13
——————— of Ballymorran co. Down in the Kingdom of Ireland   IX 18
——————— of Blairhall connected with Rae   XXI 206
——————— of Ely co. Cambridge connected with Poole   XIX 80
——————— of Fymock heritable Sheriff of the Islands of Bute and
    Arran, of Kilcattan Bellingboy in Ireland, and of Ascog   XVIII 146
Steyt of Bledington co. Gloucester   XX 209
Stibbs Edward   XIII 92
Stickland connected with Bowles   I 145
Stiff connected with Burland   VIII 420
———————————————————————————————   XX 30ª
Stiles connected with Clifford   XI 40
——————— of Deerhurst co. Gloucester connected with Fluck   XX 124
Stillingfleet M.I. Worcester Cathedral   XIV 9
Stirkland see Strickland   XIV 29
Stirling of Keir connected with Watson and Christie   III 96
Stock connected with Rodney and Smith   I 362
——————— of Chaseley co. Worcester, Chiseldon co. Wilts,
    Glasbury co. Radnor, London co. Middlesex, Postling co.
    Kent, and of the City of Gloucester   I 399
Stockdale of Worcester connected with Hayward   XIX 255
Stockdalle of Kirkby Lonsdale, Barbonne co. Westmorland Hull
    co. York, and of Dalston psh co. Carlisle   XXI 92
Stocker of Chilcompton co. Somerset connected with Preston   II 419
Stocks connected with Hoyle   III 415
Stodard of Conway connected with Rixton and Hookes   XVIII 106
Stodart connected with White of Branspeth   II 175

Stodart of Gateshead and Newcastle upon Tyne | II 147
─────── of London co. Middlesex, Sunderland co. Durham, Newcastle upon Tyne co. Northumberland, and of Epsom co. Surrey | IV 517
─────── of Newcastle upon Tyne connected with Babington | XVI 37
─────── of Newcastle upon Tyne connected with Errington | XVI 26
| XVI 36
Stoddard of London settled in New England, of Boston | XXI 193
Stoke of Estoke connected with Chantmarle and Trenchard | VIII 179
Stokes connected with Ash | VI 195
─────── of Lucas Stawtenford co. Wilts, Stanshawe, Horton, Westerley, Wickwarr and of Sodbury co. Gloucester | XIX 190
Stone connected with Stephens | XIX 263
─────── of Basildon and of Englefield co. Berks | XVII 13
─────── of Bedminster co. Gloucester connected with Gregory | XX 127ª
─────── of Clanger, Tiverton co. Devon, and Lond. co. Middx | III 75
─────── of Thornbury co. Gloucester connected with Heynes | XIX 242
─────── of Upcott whose descendents were called by the name of Upcott, of Tiverton co. Devon, co. Somerset, and of London co. Middlesex | III 178
─────── of Witheridge, Crewes Morehard co. Devon, came out of Somerset | III 423
Stonehewer of the Hurst co. Stafford and of Houghton le spring co. Durham | II 356
Stonehouse connected with Cole | XX 82ª
Stonestreet connected with Kemp | XXI 276
─────── of Conningbrook near Ashford, Kennington co. Kent, Lewes, Steyning co. Sussex, Haver de Grace and Honfleur in France | VIII 533
─────── of Halesham, Kinemer Lewes co. Sussex, Eaton Bray and Tattenhoe co. Bedford, London and Islington co. Middlesex, and of Southwark co. Surrey connected with Thomason | VIII 517
─────── see Griffin connected with Jepson | I 95
Stoney afterwards Bowes | X 131
Stote connected with Bewick | I 103
─────── of Newcastle Jesmond co. Northumbeland, and of Tollerton co. Nottingham | I 576
Stothart of Dumfries, Cargin in the Shire of Kirkcudbright, and of Montego Bay Jamaica | VIII 157
Stott connected with Howard | III 87
Stourton of Taleby, Little London co. Lincoln, and of London co. Middlesex | VII 84
─────── of Tealby co. Lincoln connected with Beverley | III 140
Stout connected with Webley | XX 237
Stowe of Berwick upon Tweed connected with Blake | III 256
| XXI 148ª
Stowell of Cotherston connected with Astyn | V 388
Stowmarket co. Suffolk extracts from Registers – | VIII 107
Stradling of St Donnats connected with Hookes | XVIII 107
Strange Master of the Rolls connected with Strong and Gould | XXI 127

Strange Stanley, Lord, and Earl of Derby — VI 55
Strangeways Strangways of Charlton Adam, Taunton, Shapwick
    co. Somerset, Newington and of Sharford co. Surrey — II 258
————— of Charlton Adam, Mare Court, & of Shapwick co.
    Som. — III 296
————— of Melbury co. Dorset connected with Trenchard — VIII 187
Strangman of Hadley Castle co. Essex connected with Bigland — VIII 318
————— left Essex and went into Ireland, of Moat co. West-
    meath, Mount Malick Queens County, Waterford, Leake
    co. Stafford, and of London co. Middlesex — IV 68
Strangways see Strangeways — II 258
Stratford connected with Banaster — XXI 214
————— of Temple Guiting, Farmecot, and of Sudeley co.
    Gloucester — XIX 260
Strathmore, Earl of, connected with Bowes — X 131
Stratton connected with Lotterell — XIII 1
————— of Bramble and of Brinkworth co. Wilts connected
    with English — XIX 255
Streatfield of Chiddingstone in Kent connected with the Earls of
    Leicester — X 52
Street M.I. Worcester Cathedral — XIV 9
Strelley connected with Pegge and Burnell — XXI 323
Strelly M.I. in Winkburn Church co. Notts. — VI 116
Strettell of Philadelphia, London co. Middlesex, and of Croydon
    co. Surrey connected with Owen — III 310
Strickland certificate of birth — IX 15
————— connected with Goodchild Griffin and Stonestreet — VIII 514
————— of Sisergh co. Westmorland, Thornton Bridge and of
    Catherick near Richmond co. York — VIII 339
————— of Sizerg co. Westmorland, Thornton Bridge,
    Catterick near Richmond & of Boynton of the Wold co. — XIV 10–12
    York
Strickland of Sizergh co. Westmorland, Thornton Bridge Catterick
    near Richmond & of Boynton of the Wold co. Yorks — XIV 27–9[b]
    ————————————————————————————— — XIV 31, 32
————— of Sisergh M.I. — XIV 4
Stringer connected with Barnesley — XIX 23
————— of Eaton als Idleton co. Gloucester, Sutton upon
    Lound co. Nottingham Stoke co. Derby connected with
    Eyre — V 139
————— of Oxroad co. Chester — XXI 204
————— of Sutton upon Lound connected with Newton and
    Fitzwilliam — XX 175
Strode connected with Fitz James — XX 159
————————— Gonning — XVIII 102
————— of Barrington co. Somerset connected with Ellys — XVII 35
————— of Downside co. Somerset connected with Gonning — IV 52
————— of Westerham co. Kent connected with Windham — II 84
Strong of . . . . . near Bridport co. Dorset Rector of Marchwiel
    near Wrexham co. Denbigh — II 293
————— of Rickmansworth co. Herts connected with Burdett — V 181

Strother of Alnwick co. Northumberland	XXI 145
———————————————	XXI 161
———————— and of London co. Middlesex	XXI 148
Stroud or Strode connected with Greville	XVI 20
Strudwick of London	II 345
Stuart Duke of Lenox	XIV 24
———————— Lady Elizabeth, descent from Duffus	XXI 154
———————— of Dowman, Towiebeg Strathdon & Glenlivet, arms	XVIII 149
Stubbins of Bramcote and Holme Pierpont co. Notts.	V 464
Stubbs of Blandford co. Dorset, from Middleham co. York, connected with Smiton	II 416
Studley Lord of the Manor of Studley and Cadenham co. Wilts	XX 212ᵃ
Stupart of Elphingston in the Shire of Stirling	XXI 241
Sturgeon of Wicklow in Ireland	XV 44
Sturges connected with Lowth	X 53
———————————————	X 62
Stuteville Estuteville Lord of Burton Agnes co. York connected with Colville	VIII 52
———————— of St Katherines near the Tower connected with Angell	XI 55
———————— of London co. Middlesex and of co. Suffolk connected with Angell and Payne	I 82
Stydolfe of Micklam co. Surrey and of Norbury	VI 19
Suckley of Tamworth connected with Luddington	XIX 152
Sudeley Baron of	XIX 90
Sudgrave Sudgrove	
Sudgrove connected with Gage	XIX 12
———————— Sudgrave connected with Gage	XIX 64
———————— of Sudgrove ———————————	XX 126
Suffield M.I. in Bracon Ash Church co. Norfolk	VI 119
Sufolk Charles Brandon, Duke of,	XIV 18
———————— Grey Duke of	XIV 18
Sulyard of Eye co. Suffolk and of Flemyngs in the psh of Runwells co. Essex	VII 16
Sumner of Hamstal co. Stafford and of Spital Fields co. Middlesex	IX 150
Sumpter of Histon co. Cambride connected with Whish	IX 136
Sunderland of Aykton, Badsworth, Featherstone, Doncaster co. York, Newcastle upon Tyne co. Northumberland, and of Bigland co. Lancs.	XIV 25
———————— of Emley & Wakefield co. York	X 145
———————— of High Sunderland near Halifax, Doncaster, Billingly, Badsworth co. York, Newcastle upon Tyne co. Northumberland and of London co. Middlesex	XIII 109–10
Sunderland of High Sunderland near Halifax, Coley Fairweather Green near Bradford, Marsden, Doncaster, Aikton, Bradley near Skipton co. York, and of Bigland Hall co. Palatine Lancaster	VIII 501
———————— of High Sunderland near Halifax, Fairweather Green near Bradford, Harden, Aykton, Nostall Featherstone Bradley in the psh of Kildwick near Skipton in Craven co. York, Bigland Hall in the psh of Cartmel and of Whittinghall co. Palatine Lancaster	VII 279

Surman of Tredington and of Natton Ashchurch co. Gloucester
    M.I.   IX 47–9
Surrey Howard Earl of, and Duke of Norfolk, connected with
    Orfeur and Palliser   VII 94
Sussex Yelverton, Viscount Longville Earl of   XVI 59, 60
Sutherland of London connected with Hardwick and Moore   III 142
Sutton born in London educated at Ch. Ch. Oxon   IV 504
———— connected with Mansergh   XXI 47
———— descended from the family of Sutton, of Aram co.
    Nottingham; Rectors of Bredon co. Worcester, and of
    Abingdon co. Berks   XIX 69
———— Lord and Baron of Dudley connected with Blount   XIII 1
———— of Gwersilte connected with Hookes   XVIII 108
———— of London co. Middlesex   XVIII 27
Swaile see Swale   XII 7–16
Swaine Tristam of co. Devon and of London co. Middx   XXI 219[a]
Swale connected with Pell   I 285
———— of Gargrave co. York connected with Peart   III 491
———— Swaile of South Stanley, Green Hamerton Swale Hall
    Copmanthorpe co. York Malaga in Spain and of London co.
    Middlesex   XII 7–16
Swan of London co. Middlesex connected with Danvers and Boyse   XIX 14
Swanton connected with Paston   IX 113[b]
———— of Grimstone co. Norfolk connected with Tooke   IV 46
Swayne of Norwich co. Norfolk; Rector of the Worthys near
    Winchester, Vicar of Pucclechurch   XVI 86–7
Sweet connected with Smith   IV 265
Sweeting of Gosport connected with Small   II 291
Sweetland connected with Withale   XVII 39
Swinburne connected with Bedingfield   V 316
———— of Capheaton   X 18
Swindel of Boroughs Ash co. Derby connected with Dalby   IV 280
Swinnock connected with de la Barre   I 19
Swymmer connected with Champneys   VII 113
Sykes from York, of Twickenham and Lincolns Inn Fileds co.
    Middlesex   I 56
———— of Brookwood co. Southampton connected with
    Henniker   XI 67
———— of Hull and Leeds co. York connected with Lodge   VII 473
Symeon of Baldwins and of Brightwell co. Oxford   IX 70
Symes connected with Andrews   VIII 268
———— of Chard Poundesford co. Somerset and of Frampton
    Cotterell co. Gloucester, connected with Berkeley   XIX 251
Symonds als Powell of Pengethley co. Hereford   VIII 373
———— of the City of Westminster and of Hampstead co.
    Middlesex   XIII 27–[a]
———— of Dorchester co. Dorset London and Hampstead co.
    Middlesex Kendal co. Westmorland and of co. Cardigan   I 329
Symons connected with Haynes and Clifford   IX 160
———— formerly Peers   II 191
———— of Clowerwall in Newland co. Gloucester and of

London co. Middlesex   XVI 65
——————— of the Meend co. Hereford   II 191
Sympson connected with Markham   VII 483
Syndercombe connected with Lenthall   III 373
Synge of Cloyne in Ireland, Bridgenorth co. Salop and of Bristol
    co. Gloucester   I 364

T

Tahourden of Clapham connected with Wright and Small   II 94
Talboise came into England with William the Conqueror and was
    Baron of Kendal, connected with Curwen or Culwen   II 455
Talbot connected with de la Barre   I 20
———————————— Mortimer   XVIII 95
——————— Earl of Shrewsbury connected with Eyton & Dod   XXI 301
————————————————————————————————   XXI 313
———————————————————————————— Hastings   XII 28–47
———————————————————————————— Howard of Norfolk   XIV 24
——————— of Witham Place Essex connected with Sheldon   VII 43
Talboyes of the County of York   XIII 123
——————— see Talboys
Talboys of Whiston co. York and Tetbury co. Gloucester   XIX 233
Talmache connected with Wilbraham   V 131
Tame of Fairford co. Gloucester   XIX 154
Tancred of London co. Middlesex   I 554
Tanfield of Gayton and of Everton co. Huntingdon connected with
    Cary   VIII 256
Tarleton of Liverpool Walton Childwell co. Lancs. Baptisms   VI 279
——————— of West Derby co. Lancs. connected with
    Collingwood   XV 4
————————————————————————————————   IV 424
Tarleton see Tarlton
Tarlton Tarleton of Liverpool, Aigburth in the psh of Childwall
    co. Lancs, and of Dublin   I 383
Tate of Delapré co. Northampton   I 204
————————————————————————————————   III 201, 202
————————————————————————————————   VII 71
——————— and of the Middle Temple co. Middlesex   VII 259
——————— of Hardingstone co. Northampton, Baptisms etc   VI 271
——————— of London co. Middlesex and of Mitcham co. Surrey,
    connected with Wynne   IV 146
———————————————— of Mitcham in Surrey and of the City of
    London   XVIII 52
Tatem connected with Huxley   XV 9

Tatem of London co. Middlesex   XV 15
Tattershall als Tigerchal   X 46
Tatton of Withering connected with Pool   I 210
Taubman connected with Curwen   VIII 36
———————————— Christian and Curwen or Culwen   II 462
———————— see Tubman   III 525
Tauke connected with Devenish   VIII 246
Taunton connected with Sabine and Williams   VI 233
———————— of Wrackleford co. Dorset connected with Sabine   VIII 117
Tawyer of Raundes co. Northampton connected with Gage   XIX 64
Taylard connected with Leweston   XX 159
Taylor als Forshew   XX 198ᵃ
————————— connected with Chamberlaine   II 255
—————————————— Cotton and Whithall   XVIII 119
—————————————— Evans   VIII 528
—————————————— Owen   III 313
—————————————— Perfect   III 307
—————————————— Poole   III 492
—————————————— Romney Wild and Kynaston   XVIII 116
—————————————— Sunderland   XIV 25
————————— M.I.   XIV 8
————————— of Beaconsfield co. Bucks connected with Tilly and
Ash   I 125
————————— of Blockley co. Worcester   III 4
————————— of Calverton connected with Crayle   I 157
————————— of Carnwal co. Northumberland, and of Chillingham
Castle connected with Hume   I 225
————————— of Cherrington co. Gloucester connected with
Edwards   III 51
————————— of Islington co. Middlesex connected with Duke   III 104
————————— of Lynne Beecham Well co. Norfolk connected with
Barrow   III 319
————————— of Nimpsfield came from Lincolnshire, of Cam
Hastleton Grange   XIX 167
————————— of Norfolk County connected with Tucker   IV 221
————————— of Sandford near Great Tew in Oxford, Chancellor of
Salisbury   XXI 197
————————— of Totnes co. Devon connected with Clare   I 22
————————— of Walthamstow, Islington, Bombay, East Indies,
London co. Middlesex and of Jamaica West Indies   III 224
Teerling connected with Seacole and Woodward   XIX 241
Tempest of Broughton connected with Scrope   VII 495
————————— of Sherborne, Wynyard and of Durham   I 260
————————— of Studley co. Yorks connected with Mallory   VIII 259
Temple connected with Knollys   XVII 30
Tench connected with Tarlton   I 382
————————— of St Oves co. Huntingdon connected with Browne   V 468
Terrick of Penkley, Bearson co. Salop, Bishop of London con-
nected with Ryder   X 18
Terry connected with Winter and Langton   XIII 122
Test connected with Codrington   X 43

Tetlow of Knottingley Pontefract co. York, and of Werneth als
    Chamber in the psh of Oldham co. Lancs   X 78–96
——————— of Liverpool co. Lancaster   III 205
——————— of Manchester co. Lancaster, Pot Shrigley co. Chester
    & of Knottingly co. York connected with Allen   X 77
Thackeray of Harrow connected with Whish   IX 136
Thackwell of Rye Court in the psh of Berrow co. Worcester
    connected with Cam   XX 94ª–95ª
Thanet Tufton Earl of   XIII 68
———————————————————————————   XVI 58
——————— Earls of   V 354
Thatcher of London co. Middlesex and of Blewberry Mills near
    Wallingford co. Berks   XVII 27
Thayer connected with Hinde   III 337
Theed of Ledburne connected with Cleaver   VIII 493
——————— of Linslade co. Bucks Edmonton and London co.
    Middlesex   IV 323
Thelwall of Blaenyall co. Denbigh   XIII 41
——————————————— connected with Miles   XIII 17
Theobald connected with Hale and Bourchier   I 559
Thicknesse connected with Audley   I 150
——————— of Farthingoe co. Northampton, London co.
    Middlesex, and of Bath co. Somerset   I 148
Thirkeld connected with Williamson   XXI 14
Thirlwall of Thirlwall co. Northumberland connected with Parke   III 489
Thisllethwayte connected with Keck   XVII 15
Thomas ap Howell connected with Davies   XVIII 88
——————— came from Wales   III 410
——————— connected with Earl of Salisbury   X 52
——————————————— Woodhouse   III 473
——————— from Freeman – Petition.   VI 382
——————— M.I. Worcester Cathedral   XIV 9
——————— of Alberbury, Criggen co. Salop, and of London   IV 66
——————— of Buckingham connected with Andrews   VII 93
———————————————————————————   VIII 270
——————— of Dublin list of Baptisms – Newington Butts.   XII 71
——————— of Lantwit vardre co. Glamorgan connected with Dere   II 10
——————— of Llelly-mawn in the psh of Llannon in co.
    Carmarthen   III 98
——————— of Tyglyn co. Cardigan afterwards Jones and also
    Gwynne   XV 26, 32
——————— of Wellington co. Somerset connected with Gunston   II 252
——————— of West Titherley and of Lockerley co. Hants   I 142
Thomasman connected with Wildman   I 392
Thomason or Thompson of London co. Middlesex and of Trowse
    co. Norfolk, Rector of Halston co. Lincoln   VIII 515
Thomond, Earl of, connected with Cockaine   I 97
Thompson connected with Barron   XIII 112
——————————————— Osborn   VIII 2
——————————————— Plowden   XXI 153

Thompson formerly Twisleton	XIII 11
———— of Baildon	IV 529
———— of Bishop Auckland co. Durham and of Newcastle upon Tyne co. Northumberland	VIII 377
———— of Carlisle co. Cumberland, Southwark co. Surrey Walbrook and London co. Middlesex	II 410
———— of Chiswick co. Middlesex connected with Alye	XX 39[a]
———— of Edinburgh connected with Hamilton	II 36
———— of Humbleton co. York	XXI 157
———— of Huncenby co. Cumberland	III 182
———— of Kilham co. York	IV 528
———— of London – certificate of arms –	IX 162
———— of Marston and Escrick	IV 527
———— of Mireside	XIV 8, 9
———— of Sheriff Hutton co. York	IV 531
———— of Wadhingham co. Lincoln and of London co. Middx	XIII 74
———— see Thomason	
Thon connected with Singleton and Daws	IX 1
Thorald of Blankney co. Lincoln	XIV 21
———— of Thoresby Cuxwold co. Lincoln, and of the Middle Temple co. Middlesex	XXI 177
Thorl connected with Harmer	XX 144
Thorley connected with West	XII 51
Thornber or Thornburgh of Settle, Little Bradford in Bolland, Greenbank, Bentham co. York Blackburn co. Lancaster, London co. Middlesex, and of Hayles Wharf co. Surrey	IV 90
Thornborough of Hampsfield connected with Bigland	VIII 319
———— of Salisbury	XX 222[a]
———— of Thornborough co. York, Hampsfield co. Palatine Lancaster, Whitwell and of Methap co. Westmorland	XXI 82, 88–90
Thornborrow of Ellergill co. Westmorland and of Southwark	XXI 89[b]
Thornburgh M.I.	XIV 6
———— of Celside co. Northumberland connected with Hawley	VIII 451
———— see Thornber	
Thornbury of Thornbury Hall co. Stafford connected with Wooldridge	VIII 301
Thorne als Seccombe see Seccombe	
———— of Marshbrook, Bristol and of Huelsfield co. Gloucester	XIX 133
Thornhill connected with Smith	II 21
———— of Stanton, Pleasley co. Derby descended from a younger branch of Thornhill of Fixby co. York	III 300
———— of Stanton co. Derby connected with Eyre	V 136
———— of Thornhill co. Derby ————	II 390
Thornton afterwards Astell	IV 349
———— connected with Cam	XX 94[b]
———— of East Newton descended from Thornton of Thornton and of Birkin co. York	XV 24
———— of London co. Middlesex, Albury Park, Kingston	

upon Hull, Clapham co. Surrey, Rectors of Birkin co. York   XII 91
——————— of Netherwitton   II 314
   III 411
——————— of Risebrough   IV 387
Thornycroft connected with Pink and Alured   I 497
——————————— De Laune   I 184
Thorold of Marston co. Lincoln   VI 1
——————————— and Cranwell co. Lincoln   X 76
Thorowgood of Tharfield co. Herts   IV 336
——————— of Ware co. Herts and of London co. Middlesex   IV 58
   IV 334
Thorp Thorpe Throp left Lancashire and settled in Dublin 1694.
   Judje of Sierra Leone   XVII 6
Thorpe connected with Penrose   II 226
——————— of Nottingham, Blidworth co. Nottingham, and of
   Buxton co. Derby   III 46
——————— of Salisbury; and Embley in Hants   XXI 214
——————— Throp see Thorp
Thring formerly Dring of Hatchbury co. Wilts – supposed to be
   from Yorkshire   I 268
Throckmorton connected with Berkeley   VIII 322
——————————————— and Vaux   XI 16
——————————————— Romney   XIX 132
——————— Throkmorton of Throckmorton in the psh of Fladbury
   co. Worcester, Coughton co. Warwick, and of Tortworth
   co. Gloucester   XIX 63
——————— Throkmorton de Throkemerton de Throkemertona of
   Throckmorton in the psh of Fladbury co. Worcester, Lone
   co. Gloucester, Allhallows in Southalmham in Suffolk,
   Higham Ferras co. Northampton, Coughton co. Warwick,
   Rowlwright co. Oxford, and of Weston co. Bucks   XVI 34
——————— of Ellington co. Huntingdon and of Ware co.
   Gloucester   VII 341
——————— of Tortworth co. Gloucester   XX 219[b]–221
Throgmorton assumed the names and arms of Carew   XIII 6
Throkmorton see Throckmorton
Throp Thorpe see Thorp
Thurbane of Checkers co. Bucks connected with Cutts and Russell   VIII 247
Thurgood of Danbury co. Essex and of Hoxton co. Middx   II 318
Thurloe Rector of Abbotts Roding in Essex, Lord of the Manors of
   Whittlesey St Mary and Whittlesey St Andrew, Governor of
   St James' Island in the River Gambia   VIII 152
Thurlow of Burnham co. Norfolk, Master of the Temple, Bishop
   of Lincoln and Durham, Baron Thurlow of Ashfield co.
   Suffolk, Baron Thurlow of Thurlow co. Suffolk   VIII 134
Thursby connected with Pigot   I 507
Thurston of Kington connected with Grove   XX 132[a]
Thynn connected with Strode and Grevil   XVI 20
Thynne connected with Fitz James   XX 159
——————————— Jol   XVI 30
——————— of Long Leats co. Wilts and of Richmond co. Surrey   IV 338

Tichborne of Sherfield co. Hants   XXI 215[b]
Tigerchal als Tattershall   X 46
Tilby connected with Ash   I 125
Tildesley of Hewcroft and Molies, also of Ollerton co. Chester I 386
Tilner Child Earl   XIII 61
Timbrel of Cirencester co. Gloucester connected with Willet   XX 247
Timbrell of Bradfield   VIII 435
——————— of Cirencester   III 50
——————— of Notgrove co. Gloucester and of London co.
  Middlesex   VIII 6
Tindale or Tyndale   XVI 2
Tinker Governor of Providence connected with Bladen   XVII 55
——————— of Providence ———————   I 67
Tippetts afterwards Paul of Tetbury co. Gloucester   V 310
——————— connected with Cam   II 295
——————— of Dursley, Painswick co. Gloucester, and of London   II 213
Tipping connected with Cosyn   XIX 203
——————— of Dracot co. Oxon   III 470
Tiptoft of Castlecombe co. Wilts, Baron of Langer, Earl of
  Worcester, Lord Tiptoft and Powis   XIII 121–2
——————— Earl of Worcester connected with Grendor   XIX 45
Tirrey connected with Wollaston   III 381
Toban of Kimshenin co. Munster, Court Canon co. Wexford,
  connected with Frith   III 209
Todd connected with Shackleton   I 2
Toll connected with Limbrey   VIII 12
Tolson connected with Healey and Bathurst   XIII 112
——————— of Tilbury Fort co. Essex   IX 151
Tombes connected with Hickes   VIII 437
Tomkins of Morecourt co. Worcester connected with Machen   XX 167
Tomlinson connected with Harrison   XV 85
——————— of Ongar, Rector of High Ongar   IX 164
Tooke of Grimstone co. Norfolk connected with Bunting   IV 46
——————— of Norwich co. Norfolk and of London co. Middx   VIII 226
Top of Stockton co. Wilts connected with Everard and Balch see
  also Topp and Toppe   VIII 25
Topp connected with Bold and Wigley   XV 25
——————————— Fisher   I 182
——————— of Hamborough Tormanton and Survills Acton co.
  Gloucester see also Top   I 537
——————— of Stockton co. Wilts and of Leicester see Top   I 536
——————— of Tormarton co. Gloucester connected with St John   V 89
Toppe of Bridmore Combe Bisset co. Wilts, and of Broxton co.
  Nottingham   V 66
——————— of Bridmore, Comb Basset co. Wilts, Broxstowe co.
  Nottingham, Tormarton and Turville Acton co. Gloucester   V 248
——————— of Stockton, Fisherton, Salisbury co. Wilts, Witton
  Shrewsbury co. Salop, Lincolns Inn co. Middlesex, see also
  Top   V 67
Torin connected with Bevan   XXI 179
Torriano connected with Master   II 111

Torrington Byng Viscount   X 59
                                                                           XXI 256
———————— Viscount – precedence   IX 15
Torshill connected with Hawley   VIII 450
Tothill of Peamore co. Devon connected with Northleigh   II 420
Totman of Castle Hedingham co. Essex connected with Winter   III 347
Touchet connected with Walden   IV 129
———————— Lord of Audeleigh see also Touchett   XXI 289–95
Touchett Lord Audley of Highley connected with Hookes and
    Holland   XVIII 105
Touchit connected with Walden and Pitfield   I 247
Tove of Baing Farm psh of Frockfield co. Hants   XVIII 50
Tovie connected with Hollister   I 525
Towgood connected with Hickes   XIX 239
Towneley of Towneley in the County Palatine of Lancaster
    connected with Strickland   VII 298
———————— of Towneley in co. Palatine Lancaster connected with
    Widdrington & Bernard   XIV 20–3
Townley connected with Western   VII 506
———————— of Lower Darwen near Blackburn in co. Palatine
    Lancaster and of London co. Middlesex   IX 149
Townshend connected with Selwyn   XX 218ª
———————— of Elmley Lovat co. Worcester connected with Dobyns   XX 263ª
———————— of Rainham co. Norfolk, Baron Townshend and
    Viscount Townshend of Rainham   V 40
———————— Viscount of Rainham co. Norfolk   XVIII 23
Tracey see Tracy
Tracy connected with de Brian   VIII 249
———————— of Stanway connected with Keck   XVII 15
                                                                           XIX 173
———————— or Tracey   IX 155
Trafford change of name from Leigh   VI 383
———————— of Dunton Hall co. Lincoln connected with Southwell   II 106
———————— of Liverpool, Over Darwin co. Lancaster, connected
    with Leigh   II 222
Trape of Westerleigh co. Gloucester connected with Hollester   I 526
Trapps, connected with Walton and Bridges   XVIII 92
———————— of Waltham Holy Cross connected with Walton   V 46
Travell connected with Chute   XVII 15
Trebeck of Hutton and Queenhithe connected with Davies   III 397
                                                                           XVIII 88
Tredington co. Gloucester M.I.   IX 47
Treeke connected with Colchester   X 69
Trefusis of Trefusis, Millor co. Cornwall connected with Rolle   VI 395
Trelawney formerly Darell   XVIII 7
———————— of Trelawne Bishop of Winchester Governor of
    Jamaica   XVIII 6
———————— of Trelawney Coldrinick co. Cornwall, and of Poole
    co. Dorset   III 252
Trelawny of Exeter co. Devon, and of Coldrinick co. Cornwall   II 293

Trench of Gresinhall co. Norfolk, Westham and of London co.
    Middlesex   XIII 62
Trenchard formerly Gordon – petition as to change of name   IX 13
——————— of Herdeheilan Schaldiling Hordhull Wolverton near
    Dorchester, Litchett Matravers Warmwell co. Dorset,
    Cuttredge and Normington co. Wilts   VIII 177
Tresillian als Kerne – notes as to wills –   IX 166
Trevor connected with Clark   XVI 30
——————————— Hedges and Nicoll   III 138
Trewren of the psh of Constantine co. Cornwall connected with
    Sandes and Davis   II 442
Trigge connected with Broderick and Raikes   I 164
Trimmer of London connected with Griffith and Crayle   I 159
Trinder of Barrington co. Gloucester   I 360
Trippet connected with Sheppard and Clifford   IX 160
Tristram connected with Bathurst   XIX 1, 2
Trollope connected with Annesley   X 124
——————— of Bourne co. Lincoln   XXI 258
Trotman of Cam co. Gloucester and of London co. Middx   XIX 164
——————— of Nibley connected with connected with Holbrow   I 172
Trott of Petney   VIII 44
Trotter connected with Pudsey   II 433
Troughear of Northwood Freshwater Carisbrooke Westover
    Lodge in the psh of Calborne Isle of Wight – took the name
    of Holmes – created Baron Holmes   VI 237
Trussel connected with Kene and Tyndale   X 124
Try connected with Berkeley and Mornington   XX 138[a]
——————— of Hardwick near Gloucester connected with Jones see
    also Trye   XIX 155
Trye connected with Mee   I 46
——————— of Alkerton in the psh of Berkeley and Hardwick co.
    Gloucester see also Try   XIII 97
——————— of Hardwick, Clinger in the psh of Cam, and of
    Sudgrove co. Gloucester   XIX 135
——————— of Sutgrove co. Gloucester connected with Mills   XX 164
Tryon of Bulwik co. Northampton connected with Stydolfe   VI 19
——————— of London, Edmonton co. Middlesex, and of Har-
    ringworth co. Northampton   XV 15
Tubman or Taubman of the Isle of Man formerly of Cumberland   III 525
Tucker connected with Gulston   XV 10
——————————— White   XVII 20
——————— of Crediton co. Devon and of London co. Middlesex
    connected with Bidlake   XIII 54–5
——————— of Gwyiner co. Cornwall   VII 332
——————— of Norfolk Bridge Town, Barbadoes and of Middlesex
    County in Virginia   IV 220
——————— of Norfolk Town connected with Walker   XXI 111
——————— of St Anne in the Island of Jamaica   V 179
——————— of Thornley co. Devon, Milton and Gravesend co.
    Kent, connected with Machan   XIX 234

Tuckwell of East Leach co. Gloucester connected with Yarneton   XX 164
Tuddenham of Tuddenham connected with le Groos   VII 502
Tuder Owen   XIV 19
Tudman connected with Perkins   I 29
Tudor ap Grono Lord of Henmynyd   XIV 19
———— connected with Seward   X 127
———— Earl of Richmond   XVI 9
———— of Welchpool co. Montgomery and of Sheffield   X 66
Tuffnel of Nun Monkton co. York, Langleys co. Essex, and of
    Chichester co. Sussex   V 141
Tufnell of Monken Hadley co. Middlesex, Langleys in the psh of
    Much Waltham co. Essex, Southwark co. Surrey, Middle
    Temple co. Middlesex, and of Chichester co. Sussex   XI 3–11
Tufton Earl of Thanet   XVI 58
————————————— connected with Southwell   XIII 68
——————— Earls of Thanet   V 354
Tugwell of Brimble, Bradford co. Wilts, Beverstone and of
    Tetbury co. Gloucester   XX 224
Tuit connected with Cusack   XIV 13
Tuite connected with Skerrett   I 90
Tull of Hungerford, Streatley co. Berks, Elvetham near Hertford
    Bridge co. Hants   I 374
Tunno of Kelso in the Shire of Roxburgh, London co. Middlesex,
    Bermondsey co. Surrey, and of South Carolina   VI 188
Tunstall of Scargill Castle and Wycliffe co. Ebor   II 409
——————— of Thurland Castle co. Lancaster, Scargill, Hutton, and
    Wycliffe co. York   X 106
Tupper connected with Eure   III 416
Turbevile Lord of Coyte connected with Stackpole   XIV 19
Turgis connected with Urry   III 388
Turner connected with Dymond   III 161
————————————— Pettiwood   II 471
————————————— Robinson   III 415
——————— Lord of the Manor of Wichenford: Stourbridge, Little
    Comberton Elmly Castle co. Worcester, Berrow co. Salop
    and of Loughborough House co. Surrey   IV 274
Turner of Ambrosden co. Oxon   XX 162
——————— of Chapel Houses, Casterton, Barban near Kirkby
    Lonsdale co. Westmorland   IV 88
——————— of Ebley, King Stanley co. Gloucester, and Vicar of
    Sherston co. Wilts   XX 219
——————— of Hedon co. Kent afterwards Payler   VI 180
——————— of Kirkleatham co. York   III 302
———————————————————————————   IV 109
——————— of London co. Middlesex   VIII 306
——————— of Malmsbury Abbey co. Hants, Farnham co. Surrey
    and of Begner co. Sussex   XXI 324
——————— of Nether Newton M.I.   XIV 9
——————— of Swanwick co. Southampton   VIII 482
——————— of Tortenhill or Totenhill and Pentney co. Norfolk
    Wratting co. Suffolk connected with Calver   V 28

Turner of Totenhill and Pentney co. Norfolk connected with
Calver or Calvert   VIII 41
———————— of Tottenhill M.I.   VIII 44
———————— of Wadham co. Norfolk connected with Neale   I 267
———————— of Wratting and Little Wratting co. Suffolk, Tottenhill
and Pentney co. Norfolk connected with Carver and Calver   VIII 43
Turnor Baron of the Exchequer   X 59
———————— Sir Edward, Kt   XXI 255
———————— of Llangoedmore co. Cardigan – descended from
Somersetshire – and of Wervil Brook   VII 60
Turton of Orgrave co. Stafford connected with Beckford   XII 91–100
———————— of Stafford; Olveston, Tockington co. Gloucester, and
of Jamaica   I 379
Turvile of Newhall Park Thurleston, Aston Flamville, Sowerby
co. Leicester, Tenby co. Pembroke and of Holborn co.
Middlesex   V 94
Tutt of Idmiston co. Wilts connected with Bowles and Daungers I 143
Tutte of Chichester co. Sussex, Sheering co. Essex, and of Hart-
land co. Devon   VII 200
Tutton of Twickenham and of Bladon co. Somerset connected
with Bergum   XX 68–8ª
Tweed of Bocking co. Essex   II 377
Twenge als Dodingselles of Kendal co. Westmorland   XXI 263
Twinihoe of Shipton Solers co. Gloucester connected with Heydon I 72
Twisleton afterwards Thompson   XIII 11
———————— of Bailey: Dartford co. Kent Gray's Inn co. Middlesex
Rawcliff co. York and of Broughton   XIII 11
———————— of Broughton Castle co. Oxon connected with Turner
and Leigh   XX 162
———————— of Drax co. Ebor, Dartford co. Kent, Grays Inn co.
Middlesex, Widdington co. Essex, and of Llyer co.
Carnarvon   I 424
Twyford connected with Chandos   VIII 49
Tyes connected with de Lisle   VIII 255
Tyler connected with Rosse   XX 194
———————— of Alverston and the City of Bristol co. Gloucs.   XIX 27
———————— of Boston in New England connected with Heard   XIX 166ᶜ
———————— of Gloucester connected with Rudhall   XX 202ª
Tyndale connected with Raymond   XVI 88
———————— of Bristol and Bathford co. Somerset   X 123–4
———————— or Tindale   XVI 2
———————— Rector of Charfield co. Gloucester   XIII 37
Tyndall connected with Trotman co. Gloucester   XIX 165
Tyndall of Stinchcombe co. Gloucester connected with Elliott II 466
Tyrell connected with Trye   XIX 134
———————— extracts from account book, Wever's Funeral
Monuments etc.   VIII 105
———————— of Gipping & Stowmarket co. Suffolk   VIII 104
———————— of Great Thorndon, South Okendon, Buttesbury,
Warley co. Essex, Oakley Thornton co. Buckingham, and
of Thotover   VIII 96

Tyrell of Heron co. Essex, Thornton co. Buckingham, Gippinge
　　co. Suffolk, and of Becher　　　　　　　　　　　　　　　VIII 90
————— of Heron, Warleye co. Essex, Gyppinge co. Suffolk,
　　and of Wokendon　　　　　　　　　　　　　　　　　　VIII 87
————— of Heron co. Bedford, Gipping co. Suffolk, London
　　co. Middlesex, Battle Abbey co. Sussex, and of Cotton　　IX 89
————— of Langham Heron, Herne in East Horndon, Great
　　Sandford, Ramsells Tyrell, South Kerton or Wokingdon,
　　Springfield Buttlesbury, Billericay, Hatfield Peveril, Great
　　and Little Wakering, Warley Ashdon Place, Bolebrook, and
　　Beches, all in the County of Essex, Thornton, Okeley,
　　Waddon Chase co. Bucks, Gipping, Columbine Hall co.
　　Suffolk, London co. Middlesex, Carisbrooke Isle of Wight,
　　Shotover co. Oxon, & of Jamaica　　　　　　　　　　　VI 397
————— of Langham, Heron, Beches, Warley, Ramseys Tyrell,
　　Springfield, Buttesbury, Billericay, Boreham House, Hat-
　　field Peveril, Great and Little Wakering co. Essex, Caris-
　　brooke Isle of Wight, South Kirton, Columbine Hall,
　　Gipping co. Suffolk, Thornton co. Bucks, and of London
　　co. Middlesex　　　　　　　　　　　　　　　　　　　VII 14
————— of Thornton co. Bucks　　　　　　　　　　　　　XIII 97
Tyringham Lord of Tyringham co. Bucks, Stanton, Barkby co.
　　Leicester, & of Weston Favell co. Northampton　　　　　VII 153
Tyrrell of . . . . co. Essex & of Maidstone co. Kent　　　　　IV 288
Tyrwhitt of Kettleby co. Lincoln　　　　　　　　　　　　　XIII 7
Tyson connected with Nevill　　　　　　　　　　　　　　　II 492
Tyssen of Ghent in Flanders, afterwards of Ulyssing in Zealand,
　　London, Shacklewell in the psh of Hackney co. Middlesex,
　　Cheshunt co. Herts, and of Narborough Hall co. Norfolk　VII 18
Tyton of London Ealing co. Middlesex, and of Barnwall co.
　　Northampton　　　　　　　　　　　　　　　　　　　IV 290

U

Umfreville of Isleworth London co. Middlesex, Earl of Angus in
　　Scotland, of Miserdine, Farnham Royal co. Bucks, Langham
　　co. Essex, and of Stoke co. Suffolk　　　　　　　　　　III 518
Umpton see Unton　　　　　　　　　　　　　　　　　　　XVI 51
Uniake of Cottage co. Cork, and of Carincham co. Chester,
　　connected with Manwaring　　　　　　　　　　　　　　VIII 223
Unton als Umpton of Wadley co. Berks　　　　　　　　　　XVI 51
Unwyn of Horton co. Wilts connected with Cooper　　　　　X 29
Upcott formerly Stone　　　　　　　　　　　　　　　　　III 178

Upham connected with Huxley   XV 9
————— of Cadbury Broad Clyst, and of Topsham co. Devon   XV 15
Upjohn connected with Smith   IV 450
Upton connected with Newton   XIX 216
Urquhart of Byth   VIII 150
————— of Craigston in the Shire of Aberdeen   VIII 149
————— of Cromarthy, Dunlugo, Craigfintray, Crombie, Old
   Craig, Lathers, Meldrum, and of Bethelne   VIII 144
————— of London co. Middlesex   VIII 151
Urry of Sheet or Street, of Gatcombe, Yarmouth, Mill Place,
   Colborne Isle of Wight, Lymington co. Hants, and of
   London co. Middlesex   III 514–16
————— of Thorley, Freshwater, Gatcombe, Whitecross Aston
   Isle of Wight, Mashwood, Lymington co. Hants,
   Tingewick co. Bucks, Luke psh of Great Canford co.
   Dorset, and of London co. Middlesex   III 388
Uthwatt formerly Andrewes   VIII 269
————— of Linford co. Bucks connected with Andrews   VII 92
————— of Rickmansworth co. Herts, and of Great Linford co.
   Bucks, connected with Andrewes   VIII 268

V

Valdesotto Count Nugent Marquis de   XVIII 39
Valetort connected with Cliff of Coripole and Mallet   VII 75
Van Dam connected with Reynst and Clifford   XI 40
Vander Esch of the Hague in Holland and of London   XVI 22
Vander Lyn connected with Clifford   XI 40
Vanderplank of Georgia and of London co. Middlesex, connected
   with Koostray   IV 318
————— of London co. Middlesex   III 109
Vandiest of London co. Middlesex and of Lambeth co. Surrey   VIII 456
Vane afterwards Fletcher   VII 171
————— Lord connected with Joll   XVI 30
————— of Longnewton co. Durham and of Hutton co. Cum-
   berland   VII 171
Van Lennep connected with Clifford   XI 40
Vann of Llanwaine co. Monmouth connected with Morgan   IV 271
Vasey extract from the will of   XV 52
————————————————————————————————————   VIII 283
Vaughan connected with King and Cheston   XX 85
————————————— Kynaston   XVIII 115
————— of Abergavenny co. Monmouth afterwards Lloyd   XIX 236

Vaughan of Abinghell co. Gloucester connected with Cheston   VIII 431
———— of Bedworth co. Warwick connected with Jenkins   III 398
———— of Clyro co. Radnor, Salisbury co. Wilts, Upper Rase
co. Hereford, and of Ruardean co. Gloucester   XIX 21
———— of Gosport connected with Morse   I 513
———— of London co. Middlesex connected with Moulson   III 91
———— of Milton co. Kent connected with Moulson   IV 414
———— or Vychan of Bedwarden, Gadlys in the psh of
Llangynwyd co. Glamorgan, and of Kilgarran co. Pembroke   XVIII 17
———— see Vychan
———— who came out of the house of Hargest, of London co.
Middlesex, and of Anst co. Gloucester   XIX 121
Vaulx of Caterlyn co. Cumberland & of co. York   XXI 28
Vaux Lord connected with Throckmorton   XI 16
———— of Claphill co. Bedford, Spital Fields co. Middlesex,
and of Greenwich co. Kent   I 375
———— of London co. Middlesex, Birmingham co. Warwick,
Philadelphia and of Pensilvania, connected with Owen   III 312
Vavazor of Wisbich co. Cambridge   XXI 238
Veele of Longford   XIX 101
Venables connected with Wilbraham   V 127–9
Vere Earl of Oxford connected with Trussel & Tyndale   X 124
———— of Addington magna co. Northampton connected with
Poulton   XVI 18
Verney connected with Tame   XIX 154
———— of Compton Verney co. Warwick Lord of
Titherington   XIII 103
———— of Fletmerston; Penley co. Herts, and of Middle
Claydon co. Bucks   VI 62
Vernon connected with Malbanc and Wilbraham   V 127
———————— Nicoll   III 137
———————— Stafford Rees Griffiths   XIV 17
———— of Antigua connected with Pym   II 465
———— of Hanbury connected with Keck   XVII 15
———— of Hilton co. Stafford   I 377
———— of Hodnet co. Salop connected with Cholmondeley
and Atherton   III 279
———— of Hodnet, Stokesey co. Salop, claimed the Barony of
Powis connected with Curson   III 276
———— of Holgrave, Wheatcroft, Sudbury, The Peak co.
Derby, Napton co. Warwick, Lostock co. Lancaster,
Hodnet co. Salop, Hilton and Essington co. Stafford, Great
Thurlow co. Suffolk, Baron Orwell in the Kingdom of
Ireland   XIV 2, 3
———— Rector of Hanbury of Mareley and of Areley co.
Worcester connected with Wylde   XIX 153
Vieux le, see le Vieux   IV 74
Vincent of Yate Minster near Sherborne co. Dorset connected with
Cozens   I 335
Virgo of Belmont Estate in the psh of Trelawney in the Island of
Jamaica   XII 86–90

Vivian connected with Scrope	II 497
————————————————————	VII 498
————————————————————	XVI 76
————————————————————	XX 175
Vlayd als Pothan	V 443
Vowler of Exeter connected with Baring and Parmenter	III 359
Voyl of Mechin connected with Evance	VIII 473
Voysey of Crediton co. Devon, Lymington co. Hants, and of Salisbury co. Wilts	III 441
Vychan of Glyndwrddye connected with Puliston & Hookes	XVIII 106
————— of Kilgerran co. Pembroke connected with Phaer	III 399
————— of Wrexham co. Denbigh connected with Jeffreys	V 151
————— see Vaughan	
Vyner of Coopers Hall Essex, & of Church Downe co. Gloucester	IX 163
————— of North Cerney co. Gloucester, London co. Middlesex, and of Warwick	VIII 124
————— of Swakely in the psh of Ickenham co. Middlesex	VIII 142

W

Wachscel of East Friesland	VII 364
————————— connected with Beckman	VII 116
Wacke Lord of the Manor and Castle of Burne co. Lincoln	XVIII 82
Waddington afterwards Ferrand of North Byerley in the psh of Bradford, Fishlake, Wakefield, Patrington co. York, Harworth, Walkerham, Mattersey co. Nottingham, London, and of New York	I 55
Wade connected with Smith	X 97
————— Field Marshal, Governor of Fort William Fort Augustus and Fort George, of Fetcham Grove and Leatherhead co. Surrey	VIII 445
Wadham connected with Lyte	IV 523
Waine of Fairford co. Gloucester	XX 241
Wainhouse afterwards Emmott of Halifax co. York and of London co. Middlesex	VII 221
Wainwright connected with Jackson	IX 149
————— of Barnsley connected with Glover	VI 215
Wake Hereward de connected with Jones of Hendre	VII 253
————— of Benwell co. Northumberland connected with Stodart	IV 517
————— of Newcastle and of Benwell co. Northumberland	X 133
Wakebridge connected with Pole	VIII 50
Wakefield connected with Bell	III 264
————— of Harwich co. Essex and of Chatham co. Kent	II 414

Wakelin connected with Degge   XXI 112
——— XXI 306
Wakeman of Ashton under Hill and of Beckford co. Gloucs.   X 57
————————— of Beckford co. Gloucs. connected with Griffith   VIII 427
Walcot of Oundle co. Northampton connected with Creed   XV 35
Waldegrave of Binham co. Norfolk   X 25
Walden connected with Orme   IV 129
Waldo connected with Leigh   XX 162
————————— of London co. Middlesex   I 325
Waldron connected with Creyghton   XIII 115
Wale als Wales see Wales
————————— of Bardfield, Shelford, Halston, and of Radwinter co.
Cambridge   I 493
————————— of London connected with Thorowgood   IV 336
————————— see Wales
Wales als Wale of Thorpe Abbots and of Brockdish Green co.
Norfolk   V 27
————————— als Wale of Thorp Abbots and Brockdish co. Norfolk
in connection with Carver   VIII 43
Walford of Birdbrooke and Finchingfield co. Essex   II 309
————————— of Wem co. Salop, Wingfield Abbey co. Suffolk and of
London co. Middlesex   IV 310
Walkeden connected with Mansergh   XXI 47
Walker afterwards Heneage   XX 64
————————— connected with Bagster   IV 97
——— III 353
————————————————————— Button and Heneage   XX 64
————————————————————— Byne and Spence   IX 69
————————————————————— Jepson   I 96
————————————————————— Knowles   VIII 155
————————————————————— Mitford and Hatsell   XXI 188
————————————————————— West   IV 150
——— XVIII 46
————————————————————— Westley Lovell and Raines   XIII 72
————————— formerly Walklegar Walkfar etc. of Wotton, Langdon,
Cundover co. Salop, Danby, Kighley, Morley in the Lord-
ship of Wakefield co. York, Estbridgeford co. Derby,
Bringwood co. Herts, Borham, Wiston, and Normanton   VII 328
————————— of Bushey Hall co. Hertford   III 164
————————— of Cockermouth Castle co. Cumberland, London and
Stoke Newington co. Middlesex, and of co. Warwick
connected with Bell   III 267
————————— of East Dereham, Walsingham co. Norfolk,
Woodstock co. Oxon, Apley in the Isle of Wight, and of
Abbots Worthy co. Hants   VIII 75
————————— of Exeter co. Devon   III 56
————————— of Hampton in Elizabeth Virginia, connected with
Tucker, see also Walker of Virginia   IV 220
————————— of Horton connected with Gregory   XX 127[a]
————————— of Limpsfield co. Surry, Norwich co. Norfolk, & of

the City of Oxford, connected with Zouch, see also Walker
of Quarne   III 344
————— of Lincoln, Aber near Lincoln, and of Kensington   III 143
————— of Liverpool co. Palatine Lancaster connected with
Leigh   VIII 404
————— of London, and of Charles Town South Carolina   I 436
————— of Newland in the psh of Norton, Whittington,
Yarington, and of Shraley co. Worcester   XIX 20
————— of Putney connected with Cam   XX 94[b]
————— of Quarne co. Derby and Castle Dunnington co.
Leicester, connected with Zouche, see also Walker of
Limpsfield   III 346
————— of Virginia connected with Tucker   XXI 111
————— of Wetherby in the psh of Spofforth, Beckwith, Shaw
Lodge, Knaresborough Forest, Skipton co. York, Haileybury
co. Herts, London co. Middx, & the East Indies   IX 20
————— of Yearon in the psh of Lindridge connected with
James   IV 403
Walkfare Walklegar etc. see Walker   VII 328
Walkir of the Island of Barbadoes connected with Keate and
Hungerford   I 43
Walklate of London co. Middlesex   XXI 305
———————————————— connected with Deggé   XXI 112
Walklegar Walkfare etc. see Walker   VII 328
Wall M.I. Chester – St Peters Church –   XIV 9
————— of Cambridge; Chatham co. Kent, Rector or Vicar of
Chedworth co. Gloucester   XX 256[a]
————— of Hayes in the psh of Newent co. Gloucester,
descended out of Somerset, of Lintridge in the psh of
Dimock co. Cornwall   XIX 247
————— of Luxton in the psh of Eye, Leominster Lady Meadow
and Luston, Vicar of Kington co. Hereford   VIII 28
————— of Stratford S. Mary co. Suffolk, and of Colchester co.
Essex   III 217
————— of Worcester connected with Martin   IX 37
Wallbanke of London co. Middlesex, Candle Green, and of
Chalford co. Gloucester   XX 257[a]
Wallensis Lord of Hooton in Wirrall connected with Stanley   XXI 289
Waller of Beaconsfield co. Bucks connected with Hampton, see
also Waller of Billsington   XX 153[a]
————— of Billsington, Spelhurst, Groombridge co. Kent,
Beaconsfield co. Bucks, Old Stoke co. Hants, & of   XVIII
Abingdon co. Berks   94–100
————— of Demara connected with Matthews   VIII 84
————— of Gregories co. Bucks connected with Adye   XXI 211
————— of York, Kensington and Grays Inn co. Middlesex,
connected with Burrow   I 567
Wallington of Dursley and Frampton on Severn co. Gloucester   XX 181
———————————————— connected with Heart   XVI 89
Wallis of Copland connected with Ogle   I 281

Wallis of Lashborough connected with Holbrow   I 173
———————— of Whitchurch co. Oxon and of London   I 372
Wallop Earl of Portsmouth afterwards Fellowes   VIII 462
Walls of Burton co. Chester, and of London co. Middlesex,
    connected with Phillips   I 49
———————— of Spilsby co. Lincoln connected with Booth   II 49
Walmsley of Dunkenhalgh co. Lancaster connected with Danvers   VI 208
Walpole connected with Rolle   VI 393
———————— Earl of Oxford connected with Rolle   IX 114
Walrond connected with Crekelade   XX 212ᵃ
———————— of Bradfield, Wood, Upham, Ottery S. Mary, Bovey,
    Sydbury, and of Exeter co. Devon   VIII 115
Walsh Baron Shanacan, of Castle Heale and of Lestrolan   VIII 458
———————— M.I. Worcester Cathedral   XIV 9
———————— of Dollardstone co. Kildare, and Queens County,
    connected with Clarke and Pole   I 5
———————— of Sheldesley Walsh co. Worcester connected with
    Porter – see Walshe   X 69
———————— of Sheldesley Walsh co. Worcester connected with
    Porter   XIX 159
Walshe of Sheldisley Walshe co. Worcester, London co. Middlesex,
    and of Wresbury co. Bucks see Walsh   XVIII 12, 13
Walsingham connected with Williams   XIII 7
Walter ap Dermaner of Carmarthen connected with Lloyd   XVIII 16
———————— connected with Webb   XX 240
———————— formerly Rolle   VI 389
———————— of Lopley co. Stafford connected with Jackson   VIII 59
———————— of Stapleton co. Gloucester   VIII 418
Walters connected with Orfeur   V 327
———————— of Barnyforth co. Wexford connected with Palliser   VII 95
———————— of Cunall M.I. in Winkburn Church co. Notts.   VI 117
———————— of Portsmouth, Bishops Waltham co. Hants, and of
    Shadwell co. Middlesex   I 7
Waltheof Earl of Northumberland   VIII 254
Walton connected with Jarman and Trapps   V 47
———————— of London co. Middlesex   XVIII 92
———————— of Marsden co. Palatine Lancaster, and of Skipwith co.
    York, connected with Emmott   VII 222
Walwin connected with Baynham see Walwyn   XIII 100
Walwyn of Bykerton connected with Baynham and Grendour see
    also Walwin   XIX 45
Wandesford connected with Lowther   XVI 73
Wanley of Basil in Switzerland London co. Middlesex and of
    Eyford co. Gloucester   XIX 248
Wansey connected with Greene   IX 142
Warburton als Dutton of Arley Hefferston co. Chester and of
    Newark upon Trent co. Nottingham   XIX 181–2
———————— connected with Egerton   XIII 14
———————————————— Leycester of Toft   XVII 9
———————————————— Windsor   XIII 5

Warburton from Morgan – change of name –   VI 384
──────── of Bank and Walshall in the psh of Bury co. Palatine
Lancaster, Bradford co. York, Dublin, London, Fulham co.
Middlesex, Upleadon co. Gloucester, and of Worcester,
Somerset Herald   VII 288
──────── of Bank Walsall in the psh of Bury co. Lancaster,
Bradford co. York, London Fulham co. Middlesex, and of
Dublin, Somerset Herald   I 450
──────── of Dublin and of London co. Middlesex   I 200
Warcup of Smerdale co. Westmorland   XXI 60
Ward afterwards Errington of co. Surrey, Whitby co. York,
Bebside, Newcastle upon Tyne co. Northumberland,
Nether Stowey co. Somerset, and of London   I 94
──────── connected with Brickdale   I 506
──────────────── Danvers   VIII 416
──────────────── Grey and Wolrich   V 198
──────────────── Hunt of Boreaton   XVIII 35
──────────────── Wilkinson   X 165
──────── Lord Chief Baron of the Exchequer connected with
Hunt   V 73
──────── of Boreham co. Essex connected with Fauntleroy
extract from will etc.   XV 63, 65
──────── of Bristol connected with Brickdale   VII 394
──────── of Danby co. York   VIII 312
──────── of Hellam co. York and of London co. Middlesex
connected with Miles and Snowden   IV 239
──────── of Morpeth connected with Biggs   X 136
──────── of Pontefract co. York, London co. Middlesex, and of
Hutton Pagnel near Doncaster   IX 134
──────── of Postwick, Bixley, & Norwich co. Norfolk   VI 15
────────of Preston co. Rutland and of Chipping Norton co.
Oxon   VII 89
──────── Rector of Strensham co. Warwick connected with
Hayward   XIX 255
Warde connected with Blackburn   IX 146
Wardeboys als Lawrence the last Lord Abbot of Ramsey   XVII 47
Wardlow of Drogheda in Ireland connected with St George   VII 407
Ware of Shoreditch and Stepney co. Middlesex, Baptisms etc. VI 284
──────── of Shoreditch co. Middlesex connected with Lescaleet II 240
Warham connected with Stonestreet   VIII 535
Warne of Radcliff Somerset connected with Yate   XX 262
Warner connected with Tauke and Overton   VIII 246
──────────────── Topp   I 536
──────── of Chiswick and London co. Middlesex & of Upwood
co. Huntingdon   III 124
Warneford of Warneford Place in Sevenhampton connected with
Calverley and Nutt   XXI 173
Warre La Warre of Hestercombe, Chipleigh, Swill Court, South
Petherton, Shepton Beauchamp, Gotton, Tytherton co.
Somerset, London co. Middlesex, Madras East Indies,

Oporto, and of Dublin in the Kingdom of Ireland   I 465

———————— of Cheddon Fitz Paine co. Somerset, and of Lincoln's Inn co. Middlesex   VII 64

———————— of Hestercombe, Chaddon Fitz Pain, and of Taunton co. Somerset   IX 109

———————— of Hestercombe Swill Court, South Petherton, Shapton Beauchamp, Bradford, Saltmore co. Somerset, Soundall co. Hants, Peterborough, Dublin in the Kingdom of Ireland, Oporto, and of Madras East Indies   II 4

———————— of Madras East Indies, Oporto, Dublin in the Kingdom of Ireland, Bradford and Saltmore near Taunton co. Somerset   III 155

Warren connected with Cockaine   I 97

————————————— Williams   XIX 192

———————— of Bristol co. Gloucester   XX 253ª

————————————— connected with Cocks   II 98

———————— of Cheddington Lyme co. Dorset, and of London   III 26

————————————————————————————   I 487

————————————— Clerkenwell and of Marylebone   IV 304

———————— of Etlowe in the psh of Aure, Fretherne co. Gloucester, and of Sheperton co. Middlesex   XX 252ª–3

———————— of Ferring co. Essex connected with Cromwell   XV 18, 22

———————— of St Brivals co. Gloucester connected with Gough   XIX 187

————————————————————————————   XX 2ª, 11

———————— of Wantage co. Berks and of Priors or Friars Court near Bourton co. Oxon   I 302

Warriner of Wakefield connected with Pearson   III 41

Warton formerly Pennyman of Ormesby co. York   VI 138

Warwick and Holland, Earl of, connected with Middleton   XV 10

———————— Beauchamp Earl of, connected with Hookes   XVIII 105

———————— Earl of, concerning the titles of   IX 72

————————————— connected with Peachey   I 69

———————————————————————— Pole & Barrington   V 174

———————— Earls of   VIII 254

———————— Maudit Earl of   XVI 82

———————— Nevill connected with Spencer   VI 53

Wase of Holton Castle co. York   II 372

Washer of Lincolns Inn co. Middlesex, & Sundridge House co. Kent   IX 152

Washington connected with Tempest   VIII 259

Waster of the Island of Barbadoes connected with Mawson   VII 411

Wastneys of Hedon co. Nottingham and of Todwick co. York   V 399

Waters of Whitehaven co. Cumberland connected with Bigland   VIII 327

Waterton connected with Welles and Fleming   VIII 246

———————— of Walton co. York connected with More   V 10

Wathen connected with Small and Baghot   II 93

———————————————————— Shurmur and Whithorne   II 335

Watkins connected with Wilson   III 15

———————— of Daventry co. Northampton connected with Lord   IV 233

Watkinson of Leeds co. York connected with Lodge   VII 474

Watlington connected with Dillingham   IX 101

Watson connected with Christie   III 96
———————————— Clarke   VIII 460
—————— Dethick   VIII 452
—————— Earls of Rockingham connected with Southwell   XIII 68
—————— of Appleton in Bolton in Percy co. York and of
Cawood   IV 84
—————— of Bengworth co. Worcester, and of Stratton co.
Gloucester   XIX 211
—————— of Brookhill co. Antrim from Lancashire   XXI 128
—————— of Goswick and Swinhoe co. Northumberland   II 143
—————— of Madam's Court co. Kent   XXI 324
—————— of North Seaton co. Northumberland connected with
Milford   X 132
Watters of Whitehaven co. Cumberland   XXI 45
Watts afterwards Steere of Jayes in the psh of Wootton co. Surrey   VIII 341
—————— Canon of Hereford   IX 21
—————— connected with Steere   III 327
—————— of Bromsgrove and Evesham Inkberrow Bengworth,
and of Alcester co. Warwick   XX 230–232
—————— of Grossmount co. Monmouth afterwards Pyrke   XX 255
—————— of Guildford co. Surrey   XVIII 1
——————————————— & London co. Middlesex   IV 490
—————— of North Carolina, Lovington, Westcombe near
Bruton co. Somerset   II 361
—————— of Old Walls in the psh of Polmont Carse, Falkirk in
Stirlingshire, & of Northam Place Herts   V 87
—————— of Sidling St Nicholas co. Dorset, Wells Chard co.
Somerset and of London co. Middlesex   II 301
Watts of Stroud co. Gloucester connected with Taylor   XIX 166
—————— of co. Wilts connected with Lister   I 306
Waver connected with Prilley   IX 93
Weale of Dymock, Weales Place Ockington, Grove House
Broomsberrow co. Gloucester, and of London co. Middx   XX 228
Weare connected with Evans Peek and Coxe   XX 136
Webb als Richmond of Rodburne co. Wilts and of Ashwick in the
psh of Marshfield   XIX 156
—————— connected with Marten   VII 99
——————————————— Potter   IV 144
—————— of Bagpath, after of Woodchester co. Gloucester, and
of Guiddinap   IX 28
—————— of Berrow and Ledbury co. Worcester connected with
Cam   XX 95[a]
—————— of Bishops Cleeve co. Gloucester   XX 240
—————— of Minty co. Gloucester connected with Nott   XIX 88
—————— of Nailsworth Bristol co. Gloucester, London co.
Middlesex, and of the Mill in the psh of Hampton   XX 258–9
—————— of Sherborne co. Dorset   VI 221
—————— of Wotten under Edge co. Gloucester connected with
Draper   II 336
—————— see Webbe   XIII 117–8
Webbe connected with Monington   V 195

Webbe connected with Tancred   I 553
———————————————— Wolff and Weston   XI 14
——————— of Brookgreen and of Sarnsfield Court co. Hereford   I 50
——————— of Dolmansham in the psh of Stroud, the Hill in the
    psh of Painswick and of Wallbridge in the psh of Rodberow
    co. Gloucester   XIX 8
——————— of London co. Middlesex Odstock co. Wilts and of
    Hatherop co. Gloucester   XIII 117–18
——————— Weston   XI 14
Webley of Anwards Tiddenham, Lidney, Hanham co. Gloucester,
    and of London co. Middlesex   XX 237
——————— of Anwards in the psh of Tidenham co. Gloucester
    connected with James   XX 158
Webly of Wrighton in Dymock co. Gloucester connected with
    Clarke   IV 266
Webster formerly Wedderburn of Shenley Hill co. Berks   VII 162
Wedderburn afterwards Halket   VII 165
———————————————— Webster   VII 162
——————— formerly Scrimgeour   VII 161
——————— of Tofts in the Barony of Tulloch, Hiltoun of Craigie,
    Blackness co. Forfar, Baron of Kingennie, Baron Lough-
    borough, of Pitfirran Piersie in Angus, Inverness, Dundee,
    Gosford, Chesterhill in co. Haddington, Inverisk in East
    Lothian, Ballindean co. Perth, Cantra in Scotland, Clapham
    co. Surrey, Shenley Hill co. Berks, and of Jamaica West
    Indies   VII 154
Weeks of North Weekes in South Tawton, and of Hatherleigh co.
    Devon, connected with Parker   I 428[b]
Weight of Clinger in the psh of Cam co. Gloucester   I 356
Weir connected with Stewart   XVIII 147
——————— of Belliburrough in the County of Tyrone and of
    London co. Middlesex   XXI 249
——————— of Craig Hall in the psh of Devenish co. Fermanagh   VIII 83
Welbeck of Reading, Aldermaston co. Berks, and of London co.
    Middlesex   III 316
——————— of Ashborne co. Derby London co. Middlesex Putton
    Heath co. Surrey Cartington co. Oxon and of Reading co.
    Berks   XXI 286
Welby of Denton and of Allington co. Lincoln   II 331
——————— of the Middle Temple co. Middlesex   XVI 52
——————— of South Rawsby co. Lincoln   II 330
——————— Wilbie of Moulton and Friskney co. Lincoln Baptisms
    etc. see also Wilbie   VI 322
Welch connected with Carnes   IX 97
Weld connected with Corbet   V 65
————————————————— Corbett Powell and Kynaston see also Wild   XVIII 120
——————— of Eaton in Cheshire connected with North   XIX 16
——————— of Lulworth Castle co. Dorset, connected with
    Widdrington   X 71
——————— see Wild   XVIII 115
Weldon of Beverley co. York   XVII 7

Welford of Wistanton co. Hereford connected with Andrews and
    Walshe   XVIII 12
Well or Welles of Bucksted   XXI 190
Welles of Ashton under Hill co. Gloucester and of Holme co.
    Derby   XIX 58
——————— or Well of Bucksted   XXI 190
Wellington Duke of – titles   XVII 23
Wells connected with Bigland   VIII 325
———————————————— and Huddleston   XVI 45
——————— of Callington co. Cornwall connected with Kerswell   XXI 318
——————— of Cuddesdon connected with Ford   XI 39
——————— of Riseley co. Bedford connected with Bayley   IX 137
——————— of Sandbach M.I.   XIV 9
——————— of Wigan M.I.   XIV 9
Wendy of Cambridge connected with Martyn and Whish   IX 136
Wenlock K.G. connected with Wyvill   V 116
——————— see Wyvill   V 117
Wentworth Baron Wentworth connected with Pope   XIX 21
——————— connected with Adye   XXI 211
Wescomb of Langford Green co. Essex afterwards Emmerton   XVII 66
Wesenham of Wesenham co. Norfolk connected with Turner of
    Tottenhill   VIII 43
West Baron de la Warre afterwards Earl de la Warre connected with
    Mallet   VII 76
——————— connected with Killigrew   VI 150
——————————— Thompson   IV 530
——————— Lord Delawar   IV 102
————————————————————————————   XII 51
————————————————————————————   XIV 23
——————— of Banbury co. Oxon London co. Middlesex and of
    Alscot co. Warwick   IV 150
——————— of Banbury co. Oxon, Favesley co. Northampton, and
    of Alscot co. Warwick   XVIII 46
——————— of Chichester co. Sussex & Petersfield co. Hants   IV 206
——————— of Lincoln connected with Drewry   III 148
——————— of Ripponden near Halifax co. York, connected with
    Baynes   III 171
Westby from Sheridan – change of name –   XI 46–54
——————— of Elmton Hall, Whalley, Highwood in the psh of
    Whitwell, Norton co. Derby, Gilthwaite Overwhiston,
    Ravenfield, & Carhouse in the psh of Rotherham co. York   VII 511
Westenholme connected with Andrew   III 243
Western of Abington and of Magna co. Cambridge connected with
    Harman   VII 505
——————— of Ravenhall Place near Witham co. Essex connected
    with Callis and Shirley   XXI 284
Westley connected with Churchey and Walker   XIII 72
——————————— Hall   VIII 109
Westley connected with Pope   XIII 115
Westmorland Earl of, connected with Barrington   V 174
——————— Nevil Earl of, connected with Stafford   XVI 50

Westmorland Neville Earl of, connected with Eyre   II 390
———————— Vere Fane Earl of, connected with Dashwood   XXI 288
Weston connected with Jones   XX 155ᵃ
———————— of Christleton co. Chester connected with Gamull   V 81
——   XVIII 38
———————— of Christow co. Devon and of London co. Middlesex   IV 152
———————— of Weston and Blumenhull, Beterton and of Rugeley
co. Stafford   VIII 414
———————— settled in Essex of Skrynes Prested Hall and of
Colchester co. Essex Earl of Portland   XI 12–16
Westrop connected with Steele   II 179
Wethampstedus als Whethampstedus   IX 167
Wetmore connected with Nurse   XX 243ᵃ
Whaley of Blackburn and of Liverpool co. Lancaster   IV 237
———————— Rectors of Ecton co. Northampton connected with
Palmer and Hood see also Whalley   VIII 529
Whalley of Ecton, Cogenho-c co. Northampton, Birmingham co.
Warwick, Sherston co. Stafford, London co. Middlesex,
Hinckley co. Leicester – see also Whaley   IX 104
Wharton connected with Sheridan   VII 492
———————— Marquess of, and Duke of, connected with Holmes   VI 240
———————— of Gillingwood near Richmond co. York   XVI 43
———————— of Hertford connected with Clutterbuck   I 514
———————— of Kirkby Thomer, Winston, Old Park in the psh of
Whitworth co. Durham, and of London co. Middlesex   XXI 178
———————— of St Christophers connected with Rawlins   V 229
———————— of Wharton co. York or Westmorland a Lieut- Major
in Elliotts Dragoons fled to Halifax and assumed the name
of Collins   VIII 221
———————— of Wharton Lord Wharton   XXI 56
Wheat of Walsall co. Stafford, Coventry co. Warwick, and of
Glympton co. Oxford   XX 235
Wheate of Glympton co. Oxon and of Lechlade co. Gloucester   I 355
Wheatley of Pevensey, Catesfield co. Sussex, connected with
Russell   VIII 244
Wheeler als Fowke of Laverton in the psh of Buckland co.
Gloucester – descended from Garvirds Court – and of
London co. Midddlesex   VIII 263
———————— connected with Peach   IX 87
———————— of London co. Middlesex   VIII 373
Wheelwright of Rishworth Mill in the psh of Halifax and County
of York extract from will   XVII 10
Wheler als Pleydell   XIX 113
Whelyn connected with Ewyas and Scudamore   XVIII 57
Whethampstedus als Wethampstedus   IX 167
Whichcote of Stoke co. Salop, Aswarby co. Lincoln, London co.
Middlesex, and of Virginia   III 332
Whinyates of Chellaston co. Derby, Baptisms etc.   VI 296
————————————————————————————————— Peterborough   co.
Northampton Charleton co. Devon, Downpatrick in
Ireland and of Calcutta   I 153

Whinyeates of Peterborough co. Northampton connected with
Bigland .... VIII 323
Whip of Townley Hall co. Lancaster .... III 119
Whish of Cambridge .... IX 136
Whitaker connected with Greene .... IX 142
.... XXI 320
Whitbread connected with Hinde .... III 336
Whitchurch of Bristol co. Gloucester connected with Walter .... VIII 419
Whitcomb of co. Lincoln connected with Jones and Chinn .... I 112
Whitcombe of Morrey co. Salop Rectors of Eastham co. Worcester ..... XV 57
White connected with Fletcher .... II 56
——————————————— Johnson .... X 99
——————————————— Kiblewhite .... I 531
.... IX 8
———————————————————————— and Packer .... VII 426
——————————————— Ludlow .... X 125
——————————————— Martin .... XXI 224
——————————————— St Lo. .... IV 441
.... XVIII 10
——————————————— Stapylton .... X 16
——————————————— Strickland .... VIII 347
——————— M.I. St Nicholas Church Newcastle upon Tyne .... VII 376
——————— of Blagdon co. Northumberland .... II 210
——————— of Branspeth co. Durham and of London co.
Middlesex .... II 175
——————— of Britwell co. Oxon, London co. Middlesex, and of
Brasted co. Kent .... II 3
——————— of Cotgrave, Tuxford co. Nottingham, London co.
Middlesex, St Ives co. Hunts, and of Woodhead co. Rutland ...... XIII 75–8
——————— of Enlingham co. Gloucester .... XVII 20
——————— of Langley Burrell and of Grittleton co. Wilts .... IX 7
——————— of Penzance in Cornwall connected with Mathew ...... XVIII 80
.... IV 437
——————— of Wolvey connected with Arnold .... III 52
Whitefoord formerly Rousselet of Egham Lodge co. Surrey .... VI 136
Whitehead of Oporto connected with Warre .... III 155
——————— of Tockington connected with Cassamajor & Turton ... I 379
Whitfield connected with Robinson and Niblett .... X 58
——————— of Biddenden & of Cranbrook co. Kent .... I 373
——————— of Houton near Barnstaple Cheriton and of Plymouth
co. Devon .... I 241
——————— of Newsbury co. Cumberland, Worth, Cliff, West-
field, Wadehurst, Rousant co. Sussex, Mortlake Okely co.
Surrey, Tenterden, Biddenden, Bethersden co. Kent,
London co. Middlesex, and of Whiteswall co. Kilkenny .... I 546
Whithall of Whitchurch co. Salop connected with Hill .... V 68
——————— of Whithall and Whitchurch connected with Hill and
Kynaston .... XVIII 119
Whitehead of Southampton connected with St John .... I 25
Whithorne of Charlton Kings, Dursley co. Gloucester and of
Jamaica .... II 333

Withorne of Charlton Kings, Tewkesbury co. Gloucester, and of
    London co. Middlesex   XIX 179
Whitley of Allisty co. Flint connected with Lewes   IX 94
——————— of Dublin   I 286
Whitmore of Frocester co. Gloucester connected with Wilkins   XX 245
——————— of Leighton in Wirrel connected with Hough and
    Beeston   XXI 242
——————— of London co. Middlesex, and Apley co. Salop,
    connected with Lawley – see also Whitmore of Madeley –   VII 196
——————— of Madeley co. Stafford, Aston in the psh of Claverley,
    Apley co. Salop, London co. Middlesex, and of Lougher
    Slaughter co. Gloucester   XIX 257
Whitney of Whitney connected with Puliston & Hookes   XVIII 106
Whitter Rector of Tiverton co. Devon and of London   I 444
Whittingham connected with Bucknall   II 139
——————— M.I. at North Weald Basset co. Essex   VI 130
Whittington Lord of Panntley, of Cold Ashton co. Gloucester, and
    of London co. Middlesex   XIX 35–6
——————— of Lippiat co. Gloucester connected with Wye   XIX 185
Whitwell afterwards Griffin – took the name by Act of Parliament   XXI 262
——————— connected with Milnes   XV 16
Whitwick als Knightley of Offchurch co. Warwick   XXI 109
——————— als Knightly of Oschurchbury co. Warwick connected
    with Marow see also Whitworth   VII 27
Whitworth als Knightley of Oschurchbury co. Warwick connected
    with Marow, see also Whitwick   VII 370
——————— connected with Pauncefote   XIII 113
——————— of Adbaston co. Stafford Lord Galway of Guildford   XX 242[a]
——————— of Horsleydown co. Surrey, and of Boston in New
    England connected with Rial & Meade   III 452
Whorewood see Whorwood   XX 249[a]
Whorwood connected with Gravenor   IV 535
——————— of Holton co. Oxon and of Heddington   XX 248[a]–9
Whytell of Gilmonby in the psh of Bowes co. Yorks and of
    Liverpool   XXI 164
Wickens of Woolhampton, Wallingford, Ashamsted, Salhamsted
    co. Berks, and of Mapperton co. Dorset   III 49
Wicks Wykes of Tetbury co. Gloucester   XX 226[a]
Wickham als Perrot   VIII 240
—————————————————————————— XIX 94
——————— of Cottingley near Bradford co. York connected with
    Lamplugh   IX 3
——————— of Horsleyton co. Somerset connected with Martin   XXI 224
——————— of Swalcliff co. Oxon, and of Sulgrave co.
    Northampton, connected with Viscount Say and Sele   IX 113
——————— William of, Bishop of Winchester, Founder of New
    College   VIII 240
Wickins of Petworth co. Sussex, Rector of Kirkby Thore co.
    Westmorland, connected with Mitford and Osbaldeston   XXI 234
Widderington see Witherinton   IX 157

Widdrington, Baron Widdrington of Blankney co. Lincoln,
    connected with Fairfax and Thorald   XIV 21
——————— Lord, connected with Eyre   III 287
——————— of Cartington co. Northumberland connected with
    Charlton of Heselside   XI 63
——————— of Coal Park connected with Errington see also
    Widrington   XIII 88
——————— of Widdrington Castle co. Northumberland   X 71
Widrington of Coal Park connected with Errington and Blacket –
    see also Widdrington –   X 135
Wiggin of Bramford co. Warwick and of Bayswater co. Middlesex   VI 244
Wight and Martin of London and of Barking co. Essex – extracts
    from Registers   VI 351
——————— of Greshams Hall in the psh of Barking, Little Ilford als
    Berengers co. Essex, Chertsey co. Surrey, and of Blakesley
    Hall co. Northampton   V 332
——————— of Kingscote, The Rudge Wootton under Edge, and
    Tetbury co. Gloucester   XX 192[a]
Wightman of co. Warwick and of Harrow on the Hill connected
    with Strensham and Master   VII 69
Wighton of Garforth, Witherly co. York, Wrexham co. Denbigh,
    connected with Winn   III 503
Wightwick of Tunstall   V 77
——————————— baptism certificate and M.I.   XVI 7, 8
——————— of Wightwick co. Stafford   XVIII 36
Wigley connected with Makepeace   IV 470
———————————————————————————   XVIII 139
——————— formerly Hartop   XV 25
——————— of Pensham co. Worcester and of the Middle Temple
    co. Middlesex   I 101
——————— of Warmingham co. Chester, Ulstrop & Scraptoft co.
    Leicester   XXI 226
——————— of Wirksworth, Middleton Cromford, Matley,
    Winsley Middleton Wigwall co Derby, and of Sheen co.
    Staff   XV 25
Wikes co. Somerset connected with Lowle   XIX 265
Wilbie Welby of Moulton and Friskney co. Lincoln Baptisms etc.   VI 322
——————— Wilby Wilbye of Friskney Wrangle Gedney Denton
    Moulton, Boston co. Lincoln, co. Suffolk, London co.
    Middlesex, Stratford, Halsted co. Essex, and of Golsell   II 448–54
Wilby Wilbye see Wilbie
Wilbye Wilby see Wilbie   II 448
Wilcocks Bishop of Rochester and Dean of Westminster   IV 413
——————— connected with Thorold   X 76
——————— of Newnham co. Gloucester and of Bristol connected
    with Pitt   V 329
——————— of New Romney co. Kent connected with Edolphe and
    Andrews   VIII 267
Wilcox connected with Stephens   VII 140
——————————— Webb   VI 221

Wild connected with Buck and Greene　　　　　　　　　　　IX 142
————————————————— and Penfold　　　　　　XXI 320
————————————— Kynaston　　　　　　　　　XVIII 115
Wildbore of Nottingham connected with Milnes　　　　　　　XV 16
———————— of Peterborough connected with Southwell　　II 107
Wildman connected with Schrieber　　　　　　　　　　　　I 392
——————————————— Wingfield and Fleming　　I 198
Wilkes of Clerkenwell　　　　　　　　　　　　　　　　　I 501
Wilkes of Wendon Lofts co. Essex connected with Fiske　　　IV 139
Wilkie connected with Collingwood　　　　　　　　　　　X 156
———————— of Ratho Midlothian and Gilchristian in East Lothian　X 128
———————— of Ratho Midlothian, London co. Middlesex, and of St
Vincents West Indies　　　　　　　　　　　　　　　　　I 381
Wilkin of Patrington, Headon, Thorne co. York, Norwich co.
Norfolk, and of London co. Middlesex connected with
Atkinson　　　　　　　　　　　　　　　　　　　　　IV 200
Wilkins connected with Sanford　　　　　　　　　　　　　XVI 89
———————— of Frocaster co. Gloucester connected with Bigland　VIII 328
———————————————— Eastington and Whitminster co. Gloucs.　XX 30
———————————————— and Coaly co. Gloucester　XX 243–5
———————— of Maeslough co. Radnor connected with Hayward　XIX 115
———————— of Oxford　　　　　　　　　　　　　　　II 340
———————————————— connected with Hall and Browne　XX 235[a]
Wilkinson connected with Stephens　　　　　　　　　　　VII 151
————————————— Ward　　　　　　　　　　X 165
———————— of Ollerton or Allerton Hall in Kipake co. York, and of
Hilcote　　　　　　　　　　　　　　　　　　　　　VIII 481
Willaby als Willarby connected with Smyth　　　　　　　　VI 94
Willarby als Willaby ————————————————　VI 94
Willaume of Tingrith co. Bedford connected with Dymock　　VII 354
Willes of Compton and Newbold co. Warwick　　　　　　　XXI 325
———————— of Newbold　　　　　　　　　　　　　IX 127
———————— of Norfolk, Chelsham Court co. Surrey, Fillingham
co. Essex, and of London co. Middlesex　　　　　　　　XVII 41
Willet of Barbadoes and of the Isle of Wight co. Hants connected
with Hill　　　　　　　　　　　　　　　　　　　　III 59
———————— Rector of Stratton co. Gloucester　　　　　XX 247
Willett formerly Adye　　　　　　　　　　　　　　　　VII 485
———————— of Broadwell co. Gloucester, Marley in the psh of
Great Canford co. Dorset, London co. Middlesex, Little
Horseley near Colchester, St Kitts West Indies, and of New
York, Rector of Jecomb co. Worcester　　　　　　　　　VII 488
Willey connected with Nutting　　　　　　　　　　　　　III 375
Willeys see Willes
Wilbraham connected with Vernon　　　　　　　　　　　XIV 2
———————— of Woodhay co. Chester　　　　　　　　V 421
———————————————— and of Weston co. Stafford connected with
Newport　　　　　　　　　　　　　　　　　　　　I 315
———————— of Woodhay co. Chester and of London co. Middlesex　V 421
———————— Wilburgham Wilburham of Woodhey, Namptwich,

Leftwich co. Chester, London co. Middlesex, and of Darfold   V 127–35

———— Sir Thomas   V 122

Wilburgham Wilburham see Wilbraham   V 127

Wilburham Wilburgham Wilbraham   V 127

William I connected with Clifford and Bedingfield   V 319

———————— Stafford   XVI 50

Williams afterwards Bacon of Camden Place Bath   VIII 160

———— als Cromwell   XXI 242–3

———————————— took the name of Cromwell being heir to his uncle   XV 18–22

———— ap Yeuan ap Morgan connected with Pryor   XXI 242

———— connected with Allen   XVII 31

———————— Bacon   VIII 160

———————— Coningsby   XIII 7

———————— Cornwall   III 439

———————— Edwards   XVII 45

———————— Hopkins   IX 38

    XX 151

———————— Pope   IV 259

———————— Sabine and Taunton   VI 233

———————— with Yeo and Callis   XXI 284

———— of Brondannu co. Merioneth & Harlington co. Middx   I 176

———— of Charter House and of co. Dorset   IX 41

———— of Exeter connected with Spicer and Baring   III 358

———— of Grays Inn co. Middlesex, and of Cadhay co. Devon, Prebendary of Peterborough, see also Williams, W. Peer   XXI 219

———— of Guernevet co. Brecon, Corneden, and Charlton Abbots co. Gloucester   XIX 192

———— of Heringstone connected with Trenchard   VIII 183

———— of Ponty Gwyddel in the psh of Lanufydd co. Denbigh, and of Nerquais co. Flint   VII 119

———— of Shadwell co. Middlesex and Chatham co. Kent   V 186

———— of Stoke Neyland co. Suffolk   III 34

———— of Westmoreland   VIII 20

———————— connected with Blake   III 379

———— Rector of Chepstow co. Monmouth   IX 2

———— W. Peer, see Williams of Grays Inn co. Middlesex   XXI 144

Williamson connected with Hudleston   V 350

    XXI 42

———— of Canterbury connected with Port   I 250

———— of Durham   II 268

———— of Milbeck co. Cumberland   XXI 50

———————— Newhall co. Cumberland, Minster Lovell co. Oxon, and of Denford co. Northampton   XXI 14

———— of Northampton connected with Purser   XVII 31

———— of Woolwich connected with Pelham   IV 6

Willis afterwards Fleming of Water Hall and Stoneham Park – see Willis of Whaddonhall   XIX 143

———— connected with Bourchier   IV 406

Willis connected with Browne   VII 346

—————————————————————————   XVI 23

————————————————— of Frampton   X 162

         Elliot   XXI 218

————————— of Hasledon co. Lancaster and of Ealing co. Middlesex   I 284

————————— of Virginia and of Iron Acton co. Gloucester connected
with Hans Packer and Stephens   VII 133

————————— of Waddon Hall connected with Smyth   XX 48

————————————————— Water Hall co. Bucks and of Stoneham
Park co. Southampton connected with Smyth   XIX 142

Willoughby connected with Huncks   XIX 149

————————— Lord Brooke   XVI 82

————————— of Dublin; co. Lancaster, Teddington, and of London
co. Middlesex   III 167

————————— of Eresby, of Pareham   XIV 16–18

————————————————— Earl of Lindsay connected with Harvey or
Hardeby of Evedon   XIV 21

————————— of Eresby connected with Montagu and Geffry   I 545

————————— of Parham   V 193

—————————————————————————   XIII 7, 9

————————— of Risely co. Derby connected with Knollys   XXI 309

Wills connected with Hudleston   XXI 43

Wilmot connected with Beconshaw   IX 113[b]

————————————— Sainthill   XIII 86

————————————— Yardley   XXI 192

————————— of Lamborne co. Berks   IX 115

————————— of Osmaston and Duffield co. Derby connected with
Bigland   VIII 323

————————— of Osmaston co. Derby connected with Marow   XXI 109

—————————————————————————   VII 370

—————————————————————————   VII 27

————————— Wylimot or Wylymot of Sutton upon Soar,
Bonyngton, Sutton Bonyngton co. Nottingham, Chaddes-
den, Spondon, Osmaston co. Derby, and of London co.
Middlesex   IX 121–6

Wilson afterwards Fountayne-Wilson   XVII 14

————————— als Wolston of Overflaneley and of Strickland in
Kendal co. Westmoreland   XXI 97–9

————————————————— connected with Abrahall and Brayne   XV 78

————————————————————— Ash   VI 198

————————————————————— Ashe and Bonyer   V 42

————————————————————— Cropley   XVIII 22

————————————————————— Crossfield   XXI 156

————————————————————— Sells   I 540

————————— M.I.   XIV 5

————————— of Attercliffe and Tinsley near Sheffield, Ripon,
Haworth Hall near Rotherham, Wensley near Middleham
co. York, London co. Middlesex, and of Jamaica West
Indies   III 13

————————— of Barton co. Norfolk and of Eyam co. Derby   XV 16

Wilson of Haversham Hall, Dalham Tower, Casterton co.
Westmorland, see Wilson of Kendal   II 165
———— of Kelso, Coldstream in Scotland, London co.
Middlesex, and of Snaresbrooke co. Essex   VIII 456
———— of Kendal and Dalham Tower co. Westmorland
connected with Wilson of Haversham   VIII 326
———— of Leeds co. York connected with Sykes and Lodge   VII 473
———— of Leyburn co. York, Rector of Dissington co.
Cumberland, afterwards Morley   VIII 3
———— of Liverpool and Barnacre co. Lancaster connected
with Kilham and Bradley   II 75
———— of London co. Middlesex and of Northleigh   II 153
———— of Manchester co. Lancs and of London co. Middlesex
connected with Hesketh   V 2
———— of Middleham, Wensley co. York, connected with
Fothergill   VII 239
———— of Pontefract, the Manor of Crofton and Birkwood co.
York, Newcastle co. Northumberland and of Dantzie in
Polish Pomerania   XVII 14
———— of Sheffield in Fletching psh and of Eastbourne co.
Sussex   VI 48
———— of Thirsk co. York connected with Pybus & Palliser   VII 97
———— of Wheatley co. Nottingham, Martin co. Surrey, and
of Keythorpe co. Leicester   I 261
Wilton connected with Appelby   X 140
———— of Snaresbrooke in the psh of Wanstead co. Essex and
of Newcastle upon Tyne   IX 98
Wiltshire connected with Bellingham   XXI 86
—————————————— Greene   IX 142
—————————————— Pyke   XXI 321
———————— Walter   XIII 99
Winch of Everton Hanner co. Bedford, and of Tewin co. Herts   V 452
Winchcomb of Cholgrave see Winchcombe   XIX 208
Winchcombe afterwards Clifford of Frampton Stroud co.
Gloucester, and of Brownhams in the psh of Roborough   I 30
———— connected with Bradshaw and Hall   XX 153
—————————————— Hungerford   V 239
———— of Chalgrove Nokes co. Oxon, connected with Hall,
see Winchombe   IV 365
Winchester connected with Playdell   VII 360
———— Pawlet Marquess of   XIV 16
Winckley of Preston co. Lancaster descended from the family of
Winckley of Winckley in that County   XIII 94
Windham of Dunraven Cowbridge co. Glamorgan Clowerwell,
Clearwell co. Gloucester, Silton co. Dorset, Ufford Hall
Cromer co. Norfolk – took the surname of Edwin.   II 85
———— of Felbrigge co. Norfolk connected with Ashe   V 41
———— of Orchard co. Somerset Felbrigg and Earsham co.
Norfolk   V 43

and of London co. Middlesex   XVIII 22

———— of Yately co. Hants   II 283

Window of the City of Gloucester & of London co. Middlesex   XV 50

Windowe of Church Downe   XVI 89

Windsor connected with Newport   I 317

———— formerly Fitz Other or Fitz Walter   XIII 4

———— of London co. Middlesex and of the Island of St Vincent in the West Indies, Lord Windsor of Brandenham   XIII 5

———— of West Horsley co. Surrey, and of Stanwell co. Middlesex – Baron Windsor   XIII 1

Winford of Glacehampton co. Worcester   V 450

Wingfield of Letheringham and Goodwins co. Suffolk   I 556

———— Wantisden & Crowfield co. Suffolk   IV 292

———— of Limehouse co. Middlesex Letheringham Bucklesham co. Suffolk, Southwark co. Surrey, Henton Hampton co. Hants, Wakefield co. York, Norton and of Hasleborough   I 198

———— of Shrewsbury co. Salop connected with Hunt   XVIII 36

————————————————————————   V 72

———— of Stanley near Wakefield co. Ebor connected with Clarke   I 508

Winn connected with Meade   III 453

———— of Nostill Bramham, Biggin Pontefract co. York and of Warley co. Essex   III 503

Winnington connected with Wilbraham   V 127

———— of Stanford Court co. Worcester   XXI 271

———— said to be a younger branch of the Winningtons of Cheshire, settled at Ponrick near Worcester   IV 124

Winstanley died at Chorley co. Lancaster   III 521

Winston of Stanton co. Gloucester and of Barbadoes   I 178

————————————————————————   I 405

———— de Wynston Lord of the Manors of Trewyn Wynston and Langaron, of Standish and Painswick co. Gloucs.   XIX 32

———— Lord of Winston, of Standish co. Gloucester, and of Hereford, connected with Knee and Watts   XX 230, 232

————————————————————————   XX 234

———— of Standish connected with Fitz James   XX 159

Winter connected with Langton   XIII 122

———— of Dirham   XX 200

———— of Hoober near Rotherham co. York, Southwark co. Surrey, London and Bedfont co. Middlesex   III 347

———— of Maynorgayng co. Carmarthen connected with Read   IX 76

———— Wintour, of the Castle of Mayett in France, Dyrham, Lidney in the Forest of Dean co. Gloucester, and of Clopton   II 197

———— Wynter connected with Blathwayt   XX 49[b,c]

———————————— of Fort St George & of Jamaica   II 199

Winthrop of London co. Middlesex   XXI 261

Wintle connected with Haynes and Clifford   IX 160

———— of Gloucester connected with Vyner   IX 163

———— of Minsterworth co. Gloucester   VI 186

—————————— and of Southwark	XVI 74
Winton Earl of	I 500
Wintour of Lidney co. Gloucester	XX 239
—————— see Winter	II 197
Wintringham of East Redford co. Nottingham and of York	IV 370
Wise of Newnham co. Oxon connected with Ford	V 297
	XI 39
Wiseman M.I. in St Paul's Cathedral	VI 125
Wish of Offwell and Farway co. Devon	I 494
Wisham connected with Daston	XX 109ᵃ
Witchall of Kingswood in Wilts and of Charfield co. Gloucester	XX 238ᵃ
Witham of Cliffe connected with Stapylton	X 16
—————— of Ledstone co. York and of Darnston	X 148
—————— of Long Melford co. Suffolk connected with Dean and Bulley	IV 381
Witherill connected with Roe	I 197
Witherinton or Widderington of Swinburne Castle co. Northumberland	IX 157
Witherley connected with Bromfield	XVIII 48
Witsen connected with Clifford and Marselis	XI 40
Witter of London and of Danes Valley	III 128
—————— of Medhurst co. Sussex connected with Greenfield	IV 210
—————— of St Elizabeth in the Island of Jamaica and of co. Westmorland connected with Blake	III 379
Wittey of Cockermouth connected with Bell	III 265
Witts connected with Steere	IV 212
—————— of Alborne co. Wilts Witney and Chipping Norton co. Oxon	V 290
—————— of Chipping Norton co. Oxon and London co. Middlesex, connected with London	III 108
Wodehouse or Woodhouse of Makney co. Derby, Norwich co. Norfolk, and of Dunkirk in France	IX 29
Wodvile Earl Rivers connected with Stafford	XVI 50
Wogen of Pembrokeshire connected with Savage	XX 93ᵃ
Woldridge connected with Mogg	VIII 423
Wolfe connected with Gardner	V 222
Wolff connected with Weston	XI 14
Wollaston connected with Holbrow	I 173
—————— of Perton Hall Trescot Green, Trescot Grange, Walsall, Oncott co. Stafford; London co. Middlesex, Waltham Holy Cross co. Essex, Abbots Langley co. Herts, Shenton co. Leicester, and of Finborough Magna co. Suffolk	III 380
Wollet connected with Wilmot	IX 126
Wolley of Woodhall near Shrewsbury co. Salop connected with Hunt	V 73
	XVIII 34
Wolrich of Dudmaston in the psh of Quatt and sometime of Bislow both co. Salop, Dinmere, Kippernowle Webley co. Hereford, London co. Middlesex, and of Devellington	V 198

Wolson als Wylson of Overstaveley co. Westmorland, Hewgill, Stykeland in Kendal, Hertford co. Herts, co. Wilts, & of co. Somerset II 167

Wolston als Wilson of Overflaneley, Strickland in Kendal co. Westmorland XXI 97–99

Wombell M.I. in Winkburn Church co. Nottingham VI 116

Wombwell connected with Rawlinson and Ray XXI 307

———— of Wombwell and of Leeds co. York III 293

———————————— Blacker Wath, Leeds & Wakefield co. York, East Indies, Norton co. Derby, & of London co. Middlesex I 470

Wood afterwards Davis of Pedlestone connected with Dale and Duppa II 339

———— als Cranmer XIII 90

———— connected with Hayward and Thompson XXI 156^c

———— of Aylesham co. Norfolk M.I. at Thurston Church VI 118

———— of Bracon Ash co. Norfolk M.I. there 1680 VI 118

———— of Brokthorp, Harescomb co. Gloucester, and of London co. Middlesex XIX 41

———— of Deptford connected with Woolstone III 368

———— of Ford House Newent co. Gloucester, connected with Cam XX 95^a

Wood of Guernsey connected with La Serre VIII 402

———— of Hackney co. Middlesex XIII 90

———— of Hallenhall by Halifax, Shinewood House, White Abbey; Chancellor of St Asaph and Rochester – descent from Chichele – X 61

———— of Leonard Stanley connected with Wilkins XX 245

———— of Rotherham, Eckington co. York, Hockerwood in the psh of Southwell co. Nottingham, and of Newark upon Trent III 111

———— of Willsell in Netherdale in the psh of Ripon co. York IV 110

———— of Woodford Bridge co. Dublin, Putney and Richmond Hill co. Surrey – supposed to be of the family of Wood of Colpny in Scotland – connected with Skottowe XV 11, 12

Woodcock of Keame, Barkby, Kilby co. Leicester VI 192

———— of Keyham co. Leicester, Lincolns Inn and of Limehouse co. Middlesex XXI 138

Wooddeson connected with Fane V 205

Woode of Bracon Ash co. Norfolk, M.I. in Bracon Ash Church VI 118

Woodfield of Gloucester connected with Lysons I 45

Woodhouse of Elleston, Leominster co. Hereford and of Kingston in Jamaica West Indies III 472

———— see Wodehouse of Mackney co. Derby, Norwich co. Norfolk, and of Dunkirk in France IX 29

Woodier see Woodyer X 34, 36, 39

Woodifield connected with Lysons XIII 97

———————————————————————————— XIX 139

Woodman connected with Hastings II 24

———— Lord of the Manor of Clapton VIII 434

Woodroff of Woolaston co. Gloucester XX 17

Woods of Barnsley co. York connected with Mawhood   IX 53
Woodstock see Plantagenet   XVI 50
Woodthorp connected with Blount   XVI 64
Woodthorpe ————————————   XIX 219
Woodward came from Butler's Marston co. Warwick of the Mote,
    Cudley in the psh of Newent co. Gloucester, and of the City
    of Worcester   XIX 150
———————— connected with Chinn   I 112
————————————————————————————————————   XX 77ᵃ
———————— of Bristol   XXI 146
———————— of Cam co. Gloucester   XIX 166
———————— of Great Deane co. Gloucester and of Lincolns Inn co.
    Middlesex   XIX 241
———————— of Reading co. Berks connected with Knollys   XVII 30
———————— of Worcester connected with Rudhall   XX 202ᵃ
Woodyer of Cleave Waters and Oving co. Hants   X 34, 36, 39
———————— of Runkton co. Essex connected with Peachey   I 71
Woolball connected with Nutt   XX 49ᶜ
Wooldridge of Draycot co. Stafford   VIII 301
Woolfe of Haseley connected with Webbe   I 50
Woollam of Northleigh from Saxony, of Wells co. Somerset,
    sometime of Witney co. Oxford   III 521
Woolldredge of Ogborne St George co. Wilts, connected with
    Blackman   VII 405
Woolley of Tong, Oaken Gates, co. Salop, and of Spital Fields co.
    Middlesex   IV 362
Woolmer Edw.   XIII 92
———————— M.I. in Bracon Ash Church co. Norfolk   VI 118
Woolstone connected with Barnham   III 368
Worcester Earl of   I 259
————————————————————————————————————   XXI 229
Worgan of the Roads in St Briavels & of Bristol co. Gloucester   VIII 436
Workington, Gospatrick Lord of, connected with Curwen   II 457
Wormald of Hope co. Derby and of Leeds co. York   V 336
———————— of York connected with Bigland   XVI 100
Worsley formerly de Workedsly Lord of Worsley co. Palatine
    Lancaster   XXI 296
———————— of Gatcombe   VI 185
———————————————————— in the Isle of Wight, Kingston, Wolverton
    co. Hants, and of Appledorecomb Park   VI 182
———————— of Gatcombe, Pidford Isle of Wight, and of Dunmer
    co. Hants, connected with Troughear and Holmes   VI 236
———————— of Ware co. Herts connected with Darby   XVII 36
———————— of Widcombe, Ford in the psh of Whitwell and of
    Billingham Isle of Wight   XV 72
Worsop formerly Arthur   V 301
Worth connected with Sanford   XIX 215
Worthington of Manchester co. Lancaster connected with Rial and
    Bromley   III 449
Wragg connected with Owen, Bell, and Chorley   III 314
Wragge connected with Ashby   IV 457

Wragge of Ongar co. Essex and of London co. Middlesex — IV 276

Wraxall of Wraxall or Portbury co. Somerset, Mayse Hill and Frenchay near Bristol co. Gloucester — III 216

Wray connected with Thomas and Lisle — I 141

Wren of Windsor; Durham; Newbald Revel & Monks Kirby co. Warwick, East Knoyle co. Wilts, and of London co. Middlesex – Sir Christopher Wren. — I 156

———— of Monks Kirby co. Warwick and of London co. Middlesex — XXI 166

Wrey Sir Bourchier, Bart, connected with Rolle — VI 387

Wright als Calver als Carver als Calvert — V 26

———————————————————————————— VIII 40

———— from Greetham – change of name. — XVII 65

———— connected with Bache and Stanier — IV 16

———— connected with Ware — II 240

———— of Cronton in the psh of Prescot co. Lancaster, London and Islington co. Middlesex, and of Sandbach co. Chester — I 486

———— of Feniton co. Devon — XV 56

———— of Kelvedon Hall co. Essex — IX 159

———————————————— and of Ness co. York — II 483

———————————————— Wealside and of London co. Middlesex — XXI 129

———— of Ormsby Hall Yarmouth co. Norfolk, and of Moseley co. Worcester — IV 277

———— of Walton upon Thames — VIII 131

———— of Warwick and of Doles Lodge co. Hants connected with Huband — IX 144

Wrighte of Englefield House co. Berks — XV 58

Wrightson connected with Fenwick — X 75

———— M.I. St Nicholas Church Newcastle upon Tyne — VII 376

———— of Ireland — I 223

———— of Naryholme Dinsdale, Yorkshire, Springhouse and Cockerton co. Durham — IV 38

Wroth of Durance; London co. Middlesex, Petherton Park co. Somerset, and of Blendenhall in Bexley co. Kent — VI 12

Wrottesley of Wrottesley — IX 41

———————————— Hall co. Stafford, connected with Lewis and Russell — IV 345

Wroughton of Ludgvan Penzance co. Cornwall — II 8

Wyatt connected with Anderson — III 102

———— of Bisley and Stroud co. Gloucester — XVII 56, 58

———— of Thickbroom in the psh of Weeford, Seany Park Burton upon Trent co. Stafford, & of London co. Middx — X 44

Wybergh of Clifton Hall — X 157[b]

Wycliffe Family, M.I. in psh Church of Wycliff — X 108

———— of Wycliffe Hall near Richmond co. York — X 104

Wye of Tewkesbury, Lippiat, South Cerney, and of Awre co. Gloucester — XIX 185

Wyke of Priors Lee co. Salop connected with Hunt — XVIII 36

———————————— and Harrow on the Hill co. Middlesex connected with Hunt — V 72

Wykeham Bishop of Winchester, Founder of New Coll. in Oxford, and of Winchester School	XIX 94
Wykes see Wickes	XX 226[a]
Wylde Bart. note as to his property	XVII 52
———— connected with Throckmorton	XX 219[b]–221
———— of the Commanders, Droitwich, Kemsey co. Worcester, and of London co. Middlesex	XIX 152
Wyles of Amptill co. Bedford connected with James	III 460
Wylimot Wylymot see Wilmot	IX 121
Wylson als Wolson	II 167
Wylymot Wylimot see Wilmot	IX 121
Wyndham connected with Elyott	X 55
———— Earl of Egremont	I 544
Wynn Lord Newborough of Ireland, of Carnaervon, and of London co. Middlesex	V 160
Wynne of Capel Forthen and Dollabanna in psh of Kelwich or Kelwith near Welch Poole co. Montgomery, London co. Middlesex, of the Castle of Falkingham co. Lincoln, and of Virginia	IV 145
———— of Capel Frothen near Welshpool co. Montgomery, London co. Middlesex, Ealkingham and Bedwell Park co. Lincoln	XVIII 50
———— of Eyarth connected with Thelwall	XIII 41
———————————— House in the psh of Llanfair in the County of Denbigh	XIII 17
Wynniatt of Dymock and of Stanton co. Gloucester	IX 35
————————————————————————————	XX 250–1[a]
Wynter see Winter	
Wyrall of English Bicknor	X 43
———— or Wyrhale of English Bicknor co. Gloucester	XX 256[a]
Wyrhale see Wyrall	
Wyrley formerly Birch	X 88
Wyrrall of English Bicknor co. Gloucester, and of Malthraval co. Montgomery	XIX 178
Wyse came out of Kent and settled in the City of Gloucester, of Stone in the psh of Berkeley co. Gloucester	XIX 245
Wytherley connected with Bromfield	IV 162
Wyvell connected with Stokes and Gunman	XXI 167
Wyvill called Wenlock from his habitation, connected with Lawley	V 117
———— connected with Gunman	IV 269

X

nil,

Y

Yalden of Lugershall co. Wilts and Blackdown co. Sussex, connected with Brickendon — I 176

————— of West Deare; and of Newton Valance co. Hants, connected with Fort — II 101

Yapp of Middleton super Montem co. Hereford connected with Seward — X 127

Yard connected with Warre — II 4

————— Yarde of Churston Ferrers, Bradley, Chittleniton co. Devon, and of Stapleton Fitzpaine co. Somerset — XVIII 112

————— of Christon Ferrers connected with Northleigh — II 420

————— see Yarde

Yarde of co. Devon, connected with Champernowne — IV 33

————— of Stapleford Fitzpain co. Somerset, St Mary Ottery, Treasurer's Beare in the psh of Honiton, Bradley, and Churston Ferres co. Devon — III 504–6

————— see Yard

Yarde-Buller formerly Buller of Shillingham Morvall, Keverell co. Cornwall, Ospring co. Kent, and of Downes co. Devon — XVIII 53

Yardley of Killingworth co. Warwick and of Yardley co. Stafford — XXI 192

Yarmouth, Paston Viscount — IX 113[b]

Yarneton of Saperton co. Gloucester, and of London co. Middlesex, connected with Rawlins and Mills — XX 164

Yarranton of Grimley co. Worcester & of London co. Middx — IV 48

Yate formerly Dobyns — XX 263[a]

————— of Arlingham, Coldthorp in psh of Standish, Bromsberrow co. Gloucester, and of the Inner Temple co. Middlesex — XX 260–2, 3, 5

————— of Buckland co. Berks connected with Throckmorton — XVI 34

————— of Charney Lyford and Buckland co. Berks — V 441

————— of Coldthorpe, Longhope, Arlingham, Langerdwine co. Carmarthen, and Bromsberrow co. Gloucester — I 12

Yates connected with Robinson — VIII 23

————— of Boscobell co. Salop, and of London co. Middlesex connected with Pendrell — II 260

Yeamans or Yeomans of Bristol, Redlands co. Gloucester, and of Barbadoes — II 348

————— of Bristol, and Westbury on Trim co. Gloucester — IV 122

Yeates a founder of Brazen Nose College connected with Hoper — II 137

————— connected with Beale — IV 478, XVIII 36

Yeeles of St Elizabeth Jamaica connected with Keith and Senior — II 477

Yelverton of Eastern Mauduit co. Northampton; Viscount de Longueville, Earl of Sussex Lord Grey of Ruthin — XVI 59, 60

————— of Rackeith connected with le Groos — VII 502

Yeo of Mountgold co. Devon connected with Williams and Callis — XXI 284

Yeoman connected with Bristol — XX 196

Yeomans see Yeamans   II 348
Yereford see Hereford   XX 139
Yerworth of Cowley co. Gloucester   V 20
Yollen ap Dycus afterwards Humphrey   II 81
Yonge connected with Dormer and Newdigate   XVI 96
York de Langley, Duke of   XVI 9
————— of Dover in Kent connected with Billingsley   X 73
————— Richard Duke of,   XVI 9
Yorke from Wiltshire and of London co. Middlesex   XVII 27
————— of Edington co. Wilts and London co. Middlesex   IX 150
Young connected with Merrricks   I 71
————————— Turner   VIII 306
————— of Otterton co. Devon   XX 93ª
————— of Purslinch and Plymouth co. Devon connected with
  Duke   III 105
————— Patent of Arms granted by King of Sweden   XVIII 132
Younghusband of Bendle co. Northumberland connected with
  Hilton of Hilton   X 131
Youngson of Lorgan and of Clanbrozil co. Ardmagh arms and
  crest confirmed   IX 11
Yvery Earl of   VIII 250
Yyon a Nobleman of Normandy, came into England 1066 and had
  lands in the County of Chester by gift of Hugh Lupus his
  Kinsman   XIX 181

Z

Zeagle of Exeter co. Devon connected with Colserat   IV 10
Zouch de la, of Codnor   I 445
————— of Harringworth and of Ashby co. Leicester connected
  with Bamfield   XIX 97
————— le, le Zusche, Earl of Brittany, Viscount Roan of
  Northampton, of Harringworth, Bulwick, Benefield co.
  Northampton, Codnor co. Derby, Pitton co. Wilts, and of
  Ashby, connected with Tate   VII 259
————— Lord of Harringworth – connected with Tate   VII 71
                                                               I 204
————— of Ashby co. Leicester and of Harringworth co.
  Northampton   IX 44, 45
————— of Harringworth co. Northampton, Pitton co. Wilts
  London co. Middlesex, Codnor co. Derby, Benefield and
  Bulwick co. Northampton   III 342
————— of Harringworth, Lord Zouch of Ashby, connected
  with Poulton   XVI 18
Zusch le, see Zouch

Appendix
Index to Pedigrees
Vols XLIII–XLIX

Adelmare or Dalmarius XLVIII 34[b]
Adlam XLIII 4 (s), 6 (s)
Adye XLIII 19 (s)
Albouy XLV 25–27
Alexander (letter relating to family property) XLV 69
Anderson XLVII 78 (s)
Angell XLV 56
Arden or Arderne XLVII 103–115, 119–124; XLIX 215, 219[b]
Ashe XLIX 1–20, 57, 58
Ashley XLV 176[b], 177[b], 182, 187; XLVII 125–127
Atkins XLIV 122[b]
Atkinson XLVIII 93
Aylesbury, Earl of XLIII 77, 82

B

Baber XLVII 72–73
Baguly XLIX 215 (s)
Baker XLVI 62–71
Banger XLVIII 21[b]
Barham XLVIII 3–6
Barnard XLIII 117 (s)
Basing XLIX 216
Baugh XLVIII 29[b]
Beach XLIII 1–11
Beauvoir XLVIII 82, 83
Beckford XLV 188; XLVII 125[b] (s), 126 (s), 127 (s)
Bedford XLVI 5 (s)
Bell XLV 130, 141, 150, 157
Benefold (will) XLV 80
Benyon XLVIII 83
Berridge XLV 169 (s)
Betton XLV 2–20
Biddulph XLVIII 27 (s)
Bilke XLIII 172–190
Blick XLIV 117
Block XLIV 39
Blount XLIV 107 (s)
Blundell XLV 66

Boate XLVI 87 (s)
Booreman XLIV 25
Booth XLIV 109 (s); XLV 23 (s); XLVIII 85
Boscawen XLIII 38 (s)
Bowden XLIV 111 (s)
Bowdidge XLIX 214 (s)
Bowyer Bart XLIV 120[b], 122[b], 123, 125
Braine or Brayne XLVII 62–65
Breton XLVI 30; XLVIII 24[b], 25, 70–74; XLIX 60–60[h]
Bridgeman XLV 64[b]; XLVI 21 (s)
Bright XLV 2–20
Brown XLIII 190 (s)
Browne XLIII 16, 17
Bruce (Earl of Aylesbury) XLIII 77, 82
Brudenell (Earl of Cardigan) XLIII 77 (s), 82(s)
Buccleugh, Duke of XLIII 77 (s), 82 (s)
Buchanan XLVI 66 (s)
Bunbury XLVII 17–38
Butler XLVI 72–76
Byrnand XLVIII 93 (s)
Bythesea XLIII 19 (s)

C

Caesar XLVIII 34[b]
Calvert XLVI 54, 55
Campden, Viscount XLIII 3 (s)
Cardigan, Earl of XLIII 77, 82 (s)
Carpenter XLVI 11, 15, 18[b], 19
Champ XLIII 172
Chetham XLIII 124, 136, 143, 152
Chichele XLV 171[b] (s)
Child XLVI 86 (s), 87 (s)
Churchill XLIII 172 (s), 186 (s)
Clarke XLIII 85–92; XLV 122 (s)
Clarke-Jervoise XLIII 90
Claryton XLVI 94–101
Cleaver XLIV 111
Clifford XLV 130–157
Clinton, (Earl of Lincoln) XLIII 38, 39, 62

Clutterbuck XLV 130 (s), 141 (s), 150 (s), 157 (s)
Collingwood XLV 159–165
Collins and Rigby XLVII 130, 139
Cook XLVII 129 (s)
Cooper XLVI 53 (s)
Corona XLIX 219[b] (s)
Courronell, Marquis de XLVI 2 (s), 3 (s)
Courtenay XLIV 107 (s)
Cracroft or Craycroft XLIX 182–190
Cradock XLV 64[b] (s)
Craycroft or Cracroft XLIX 182–190
Cresswell XLVI 62–71

D

Dalmarius or Adelmare XLVIII 34[b]
Damervall XLVI 2 (s), 3 (s)
Darcy XLVI 107 (s)
Davis XLVII 12
Debrett XLV 72–96
De la Beche XLIII 1–11
De la Bere XLV 44
De Lanoy ⎫
Delany ⎬ XLVI 51 (s), 52 (s)
Demailly XLVI 2 (s), 3 (s)
Denison XLVI 72–76
Dennis XLIII 77 (s), 82 (s)
Denys XLVI 56–59 (letters)
De Vere XLVI 107 (s)
D'ewes XLV 44 (s)
Dillon XLVI 4 (s)
Dinham XLVI 11 (s)
Dodd XLIV 27 (s)
Dodwell XLV 128
Done XLVII 105
Douglas (certif.) XLVIII 15
Dove XLIX 57[b] (s)
Duke XLIII 6 (s)
Dulany XLVI 51 (s), 52 (s)
Duncan XLV 166[b]
Dunford XLV 169 (s)
Dyson XLVI 60, 61

E

Earle XLIII 4 (s); XLV 21 (s)
Eastabrooke, XLV 46, 48 (certif)
Eaton XLVII 142–152; XLVIII 1, 2
Elliot XLIV 59
Elliott-Murray-Kynynmound, (Baron Minto) XLIX 21–26
Ellis XLIV 31 (s); XLVII 127 (s); XLVIII 84, 86–88
Elmore XLIX 96 (will), 194–196 (extracts of registers)

Elton XLVIII 27
Evans XLIII 12 (s)
Everard XLVIII 85 (s)
Every Bart. XLIX 62–179, 202–206[b], 209–214, 218–222

F

Farquhar XLV 123, 127
Featherstone XLIII 12
Fenton XLIV 111 (s)
Fenwick XLVIII 21[b]–23
Fielder XLIV 112
Fiennes XLIII 38, 39
Fines XLIII 38, 39
Fisher XLV 129 (s)
Fitzwalter XLVI 107 (s)
Folliott XLVIII 29[b]
Forster XLVIII 3
Fortescue XLIII 38 (s)
Foster XLVIII 3–6
Foster-Barham XLVIII 36, 90–92

G

Gabb, XLIX 57 (s)
Gaitskell XLVII 125, 125[b]
Gane XLVII 129 (s)
Gibson XLV 78 (will), 96 (s); XLVII 92, 100, 89 (m)
Giffard XLV 161 (s)
Gifford XLIII 60 (extracts of registers)
Gilbert-Elliot,-Murray-Kynynmound, (Baron Minto) XLIV 59
Gillman XLVI 85 (s)
Gowland XLIII 6, 9 (s)
Grainge XLVI 62–71
Grainger XLV 72, 74, 82–94
Green XLIV 106 (s)
Griffin XLIII 12
Griffith XLVIII 85 (s)
Gumpel XLIII 93–114
Guthrie XLIII 6 (s)
Guy XLVI 15 (s), 18[b] (s), 19 (s); XLVII 78

H

Hall XLVIII 27 (s)
Hamilton XLVIII 75–81
Harewell XLV 155
Hatley XLVIII 83 (s)
Herbert XLIV 111 (s)
Hervey XLV 177[b]; XLVII 72 (s)
Heys XLVII 144 (s)
Hicks Bart. XLIII 3

Hicks-Beach XLIII 3
Hildyard (will) XLVIII 8
Hill XLIII 7 (s)
Hirst XLVII 140, 141
Hoadly XLIX 57, 58
Hoadly-Ash XLIX 1–20, 57–58
Hodges XLVI 32–35
Hodgkin XLIII 18 (s)
Holloway XLV 49
Holme (extracts of registers) XLVII 117
Holmes XLVI 21, 27, 28
Holt XLVI 86 (s), 87 (s)
Hope XLIV 106 (s)
Hopkins XLVI 53 (s)
Horsford (extracts of registers etc.) XLIII 154–157
Horton XLIII 4 (s), 6 (s)
Howard XLV 171ᵇ (s)
Howland XLVI 86 (s), 87 (s)
Humphry XLIII 7 (s)
Hungerford XLIV 107, 108ᵇ; XLV 171ᵇ (s)
Hutton XLIII 12 (s)
Hynes XLIII 6 (s)

I

I'ans XLIII 81
Israel XLIV 29

J

James-Woodhouse (see Woodhouse)
Janssen Bart. XLIV 56 (s)
Jervoise XLIII 90

K

Keate, XLIV 107 (s)
Kelk XLVIII 21ᵇ (s)
Kelso XLVIII 75–81
Kemp XLIII 19, 20, 24–26
Kerby XLIII 148 (s)
Kerr XLV 97–122
Keylway XLIX 57ᵇ (s)
Killingworth XLVII 68
King XLIII 6 (s)
Kirsopp XLVII 91, 92, 96–102
Kynaston XLV 64ᵇ (s)

L

Lambert XLIV 47
Lathbury XLIX 219ᵇ (s)
Lawson Bart. XLVII 7
Leadbiter XLVII 89 (m)

Lee XLV 51 (s), 64 (s)
Lefevre XLVIII 17
Leigh XLIX 198–200, 208, 215, 216, 219ᵇ
Le Neve XLV 56ᵇ
Levy (Change of Name) XLVI 36–50
Lincoln, Earl of XLIII 38, 39
Lindley XLV 62 (s)
Littlehales XLVI 32 (s), 35 (s)
Lloyd XLVIII 84, 86–88
Locke and Stratton (papers) XLV 30–40
Loftus XLVII 54, 55
Loulegre XLIV 56 (s)

M

Mac Connell XLIII 152 (s)
Mc Dowell XLVIII 83 (s)
Martyn XLIII 7 (s), 9ᵇ (s)
Matthews XLV 64ᵇ (s)
Maurice XLIV 42
Maynard XLVII 66, 140 (s), 141 (s)
Mence XLVII 12
Micham Church (M.I.) XLIX 61–61ᶻ
Middleton Bart. XLIV 47 (s)
Mills XLIV 56
Minto, Baron XLIV 59; XLIX 21–56
Monck (letter) XLIV 48
Montague, Duke of XLIII 77 (s), 82 (s)
Morson XLIII 18
Mosley XLIV 108, 109; XLV 23

N

Neave XLVI 81
Nelson XLV 97–122
Newport XLV 64ᵇ (s)
Newton (extracts of registers) 116–118ᵇ
Nicholas XLVIII 83 (s)
Noel (Viscount Campden) XLIII 3 (s)
Norton XLVIII 93 (s)

O

Oreby XLIX 219ᵇ (s)
Orford, Earl of XLIII 77 (s)
Owen XLIV 43 (s)
Oxford, Earl of XLVI 107 (s)

P

Parry XLVI 31–35
Paulet XLIII 77 (s), 82 (s)
Pearce XLVI 22–24
Peard XLVI 5 (s), 6 (s), 9 (s), 15 (s), 19 (s)

Pensam XLIV 34
Perrott (letters) XLVIII 10–14
Pettat XLIII 3 (s)
Peverell XLIV 107 (s)
Phelp XLIV 118 (s)
Phillips XLVI 7–19
Pitfield XLV 172, 176[b], 180, 181, 182, 192; XLVII 125 (s), 125[b] (s)
Pomeroy XLIII 18 (s)
Potticary XLIII 7 (s), 9[b] (s)
Poulet XLIII 77 (s)
Prescot XLVII 58–60
Protheroe XLVII 61
Prust XLIV 49–53
Pugh XLVII 69 (s)
Punshon XLVII 75
Purefoy-Jervoise XLIII 89

R

Radcliffe XLVIII 93 (s)
Raynton XLVIII 70, 74; XLIX 60–60[h]
Read XLIII 19 (s); XLVI 53; XLVIII 39[b] (s), 41 (s)
Reed XLVI 62–71
Revell XLVI 53; XLVIII 38[b]–69
Reynolds XLVI 15 (s), 19 (s), 53 (s); XLVIII 40
Richardson XLVII 17–38
Riddell XLVII 93
Rigby XLVI 1
Rigby and Collins XLVII 130–139
Rivers (will) XLIV 121
Roberts XLIV 106, 110, 111
Rolle XLIII 39–82
Rowlls XLIV 114; XLV 48 (Certif)
Roxby XLV 129 (s)
Russell XLVI 86 (s), 87 (s)
Rutter XLVI 62–71

S

St. John, Lord XLIV 108[b] (s)
Salkeld XLVII 75–78
Salway or Salwey XLVIII 27–37
Sandbach XLIV 27 (s)
Sanders XLV 24 (s)
Sanderson XLV 129 (s)
Savile XLVII 14
Saxye XLVIII 93 (s)
Say XLIII 38, 39
Say and Sele XLIII 39
Scott XLIV 113; XLVII 49–53
Scrope XLVI 80
Scrope Lord XLVII 10, 11
Scudamore XLVII 57

Secretan (change of name) XLVII 39–47
Seymour (Duke of Somerset) XLIII 77 (s), 82 (s)
Shaw-Lefevre XLVIII 16–20
Sheldon XLVI 102–110; XLVII 1–5
Shirt XLVII 140, 141
Simpson XLV 62; XLVI 21 (s); XLVII 70 (s)
Skinner XLVIII 27 (s)
Slade XLVII 9
Sloper XLIII 5 (s)
Smart XLIII 172 (s)
Somerset, Duke of XLIII 77, 82
Spenceley XLV 96
Steere XLV 50–64
Stewart XLVI 20
Stileman XLIII 5 (s)
Stodart XLV 169
Stokes XLIX 58 (s)
Stonehouse XLIV 122[b] (s)
Stonestreet XLIII 12–15, 20–33
Stovin XLVIII 21[b] (s)
Stratton XLV 43
Stratton and Lock (papers) XLV 30–40
Strode XLIII 115–153
Sturt XLV 171, 176[b], 180
Swettenham XLVIII 1, 2; XLVII 142–152
Swift (letter re change of name) XLVI 60

T

Talbot XLIII 4 (s)
Tarleton XLV 164
Tawke XLVI 82–93
Theed XLIV 111 (s)
Thomason XLIII 12 (s)
Thompson XLIII 12 (s)
Thornhagh XLV 21 (s)
Thornton XLV 1
Throckmorton XLVII 79–88
Tolson XLVII 7, 15 (s)
Tonmain XLIV 106 (s)
Tourney XLIV 45
Tracy XLV 128 (s)
Trappes XLVIII 93
Trefusis XLIII 39, 49–51, 53, 56, 59, 81
Treves (change of name) XLVI 36–50
Troughear XLVI 21 (s), 28 (s)
Tuck XLVI 79 (s), 82, 85
Tunstall XLVIII 93 (s)
Turney XLIV 45
Turton XLVI 89 (s)
Tydd XLVII 17–38
Tyssen XLVIII 83 (s)

V

Vaughan XLVIII 7
Venables XLIX 215 (s), 216 (s)
Verney XLVI 54, 55
Vere XLVI 107 (s)
Vivian XLVII 11 (s)

W

Walden XLV 180, 185, 190, 191, 192[b]
Walpole (Earl of Oxford) XLIII 77 (s)
Walrond XLIII 80 (s)
Walter XLV 101, 108, 114, 122
Ward XLIV 35 (s)
Webb XLIX 57[b]
Webb and Wise (papers) XLIV 60–104
Wedloke XLVIII 22 (s)
Westby XLVII 140 (s)
Weston XLVI 61 (s)
White XLIII 3 (s)
Wilbraham XLV 62 (s)
Williams XLIV 37 (s)
Williamson XLIII 192, 194
Wilson XLIX 58 (s)
Winchcombe XLV 130–157

Windham XLV 174 (M.I.), 192[b]
Winfield XLIV 106 (s)
Wingfield XLVI 2–4
Winn Bart. XLIII 192, 194; XLIV 1–20
Winsloe XLVI 7–19
Wise and Webb (papers) XLIV 60–104
Witham XLVIII 93 (s)
Wither XLIII 4 (s)
Witts XLV 50 (s), 51 (s), 53 (s), 64 (s)
Wolstenholme XLVIII 24[b], 25, 70–74; XLIX 60–60[h], 61[aa]–61[hh]
Wolstenholme Bart. XLVI 30
Wood XLIII 83 (M.I.); XLIV 37 (s)
Woodhouse (change of name) XLVII 39–47
Woodward XLVI 79, 82, 85
Worsley Bart. XLVI 21, 25[b]–29
Wrey XLIII 81 (s)
Wrighte XLVIII 82, 83
Wyndham XLV 174 (M.I.), 192[b]
Wynne Bart. XLIV 1–21; XLVI 78

Y

Yeo XLIII 81 (s)

The Harleian Society.

FOUNDED 1869.   INCORPORATED 1902.

INSTITUTED FOR THE

Publication of Inedited Manuscripts

RELATING TO

GENEALOGY, FAMILY HISTORY, AND HERALDRY

Registered Office

Ardon House, Mill Lane, Godalming, Surrey.

Report for the Year 1989

The Harleian Society

COUNCIL FOR THE YEAR 1989

Report for the Year 1989

The rate of increase in the number of subscribers was maintained with a further seventeen new subscribers enrolled during 1989. Eight subscriptions were cancelled. The number of paid-up subscribers at the end of 1989 stood at 361. Income from subscriptions during the year was approximately £6,600 Direct sales of publications brought in just over £800 and a credit was received for a further £170 for sales on commission by our agents in 1988. Cash and covenanted donations worth £130 was received and £228 was reclaimed from the Inland Revenue on covenanted subscriptions and

donations and there were other receipts of £350, for an estimated total of about £8,300.

The Council wishes to express its thanks on behalf of the Society for cash donations to the General Fund from Rodney Armstrong, Esq. and A.H. Ayers, Esq.

During the year two publications were issued. The 1988 Catalogue of Welsh Manuscripts in the College of Arms was distributed at the end of January, and the 1989 title – The Visitation of Derbyshire 1662–1664 – during June.

The accounts for the year ending 31 December 1988 have been audited by the Society's Honorary Auditors, Messrs Deloitte Haskins & Sells. They are available for inspection on application to the Honorary Secretary, College of Arms, Queen Victoria Street, London EC4.

By Order of the Council
J.P. BROOKE-LITTLE, Norroy and Ulster,
Chairman

The Society is a Company limited by guarantee, incorporated in England in 1902. Registered No. 72647. It is also a Registered Charity, No. 253659, National Code, 590.

The Members of the Council are the Directors of the Company. The Company was instituted for transcribing, printing and publishing the heraldic Visitations of the Counties, Parish Registers or any Manuscripts relating to Genealogy, Family History and Heraldry. The Company is a non-profit making Society. No dividend is payable, and no remuneration is payable to the Directors. The income is applied solely towards the promotion of the objects of the Society.